WAR IN THE ST. LAWRENCE

ALSO IN THE
History *of* Canada Series

WAR IN THE ST. LAWRENCE
The Forgotten
U-Boat Battles
on Canada's Shores

ROGER SARTY

General Editors:
MARGARET MacMILLAN
and ROBERT BOTHWELL

ALLEN LANE

ALLEN LANE
an imprint of Penguin Canada

Published by the Penguin Group
Penguin Group (Canada), 90 Eglinton Avenue East, Suite 700,
Toronto, Ontario, Canada M4P 2Y3 (a division of Pearson Canada Inc.)

Penguin Group (USA) Inc., 375 Hudson Street, New York, New York 10014, U.S.A.
Penguin Books Ltd, 80 Strand, London WC2R 0RL, England
Penguin Ireland, 25 St Stephen's Green, Dublin 2, Ireland (a division of Penguin Books Ltd)
Penguin Group (Australia), 250 Camberwell Road, Camberwell, Victoria 3124, Australia
(a division of Pearson Australia Group Pty Ltd)
Penguin Books India Pvt Ltd, 11 Community Centre, Panchsheel Park,
New Delhi – 110 017, India
Penguin Group (NZ), 67 Apollo Drive, Rosedale, Auckland 0632, New Zealand
(a division of Pearson New Zealand Ltd)
Penguin Books (South Africa) (Pty) Ltd, 24 Sturdee Avenue, Rosebank,
Johannesburg 2196, South Africa

Penguin Books Ltd, Registered Offices: 80 Strand, London WC2R 0RL, England

First published 2012

1 2 3 4 5 6 7 8 9 10 (RRD)

LIBRARY AND ARCHIVES CANADA CATALOGUING IN PUBLICATION

Sarty, Roger, 1952–
War in the St. Lawrence : the forgotten U-boat battles on Canada's shores / Roger Sarty.

Includes bibliographical references and index.
ISBN 978-0-670-06787-9

1. World War, 1939–1945—Campaigns—Saint Lawrence, Gulf of.
2. World War, 1939–1945—Naval operations, Canadian. 3. World War, 1939–1945—Naval
operations, German. 4. World War, 1939–1945—Canada. I. Title.

D779.C2S265 2012   940.54'5971   C2012-900316-6

Visit the Penguin Canada website at **www.penguin.ca**

Special and corporate bulk purchase rates available; please see
www.penguin.ca/corporatesales or call 1-800-810-3104, ext. 2477.

ALWAYS LEARNING   **PEARSON**

In loving memory of my parents,
Glenn Sarty (1930–2007) and
Joan (Bartlett) Sarty (1932–2007)

CONTENTS

INTRODUCTION TO THE HISTORY OF CANADA SERIES

Canada, the world agrees, is a success story. We should never make the mistake, though, of thinking that it was easy or foreordained. At crucial moments during Canada's history, challenges had to be faced and choices made. Certain roads were taken and others were not. Imagine a Canada, indeed imagine a North America, where the French and not the British had won the Battle of the Plains of Abraham. Or imagine a world in which Canadians had decided to throw in their lot with the revolutionaries in the thirteen colonies.

This series looks at the making of Canada as an independent, self-governing nation. It includes works on key stages in the laying of the foundations as well as the crucial turning points between 1867 and the present that made the Canada we know today. It is about those defining moments when the course of Canadian history and the nature of Canada itself were oscillating. And it is about the human beings—heroic, flawed, wise, foolish, complex—who had to make decisions without knowing what the consequences might be.

We begin the series with the European presence in the eighteenth century—a presence that continues to shape our society today—and conclude it with an exploration of the strategic importance of the Canadian Arctic. We look at how the mass movements of peoples, whether Loyalists in the eighteenth century or Asians at the start of the twentieth, have profoundly influenced the nature of Canada. We also look at battles and their aftermaths: the Plains of Abraham, the 1866 Fenian raids, the German submarines in the St. Lawrence River during World War II. Political crises—the 1891 election that saw Sir John A. Macdonald battling Wilfrid Laurier; Pierre Trudeau's triumphant patriation of the Canadian Constitution—provide rich moments of storytelling. So, too, do the Expo 67 celebrations, which marked a time of soaring optimism and gave Canadians new confidence in themselves.

We have chosen these critical turning points partly because they are good stories in themselves but also because they show what Canada was like at particularly important junctures in its history. And to tell them we have chosen Canada's best historians. Our authors are great storytellers who shine a spotlight on a different Canada, a Canada of the past, and illustrate links from then to now. We need to remember the roads that were taken—and the ones that were not. Our goal is to help our readers understand how we got from that past to this present.

Margaret MacMillan
Warden at St. Antony's College, Oxford

Robert Bothwell
May Gluskin Chair of Canadian History
University of Toronto

LIST OF MAPS

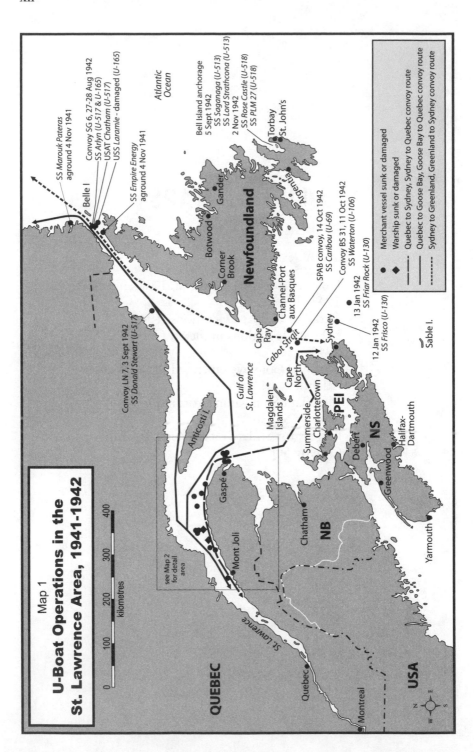

Map 1
U-Boat Operations in the St. Lawrence Area, 1941-1942

kilometres
0 100 200 300 400

see Map 2 for detail area

QUEBEC

Montreal
Quebec

St. Lawrence

Mont Joli
Gaspé

Anticosti I.

Gulf of St. Lawrence

Magdalen Islands

Convoy LN 7, 3 Sept 1942
SS Donald Stewart (U-517)

Chatham

NB

Yarmouth

Greenwood

Summerside
Charlottetown

PEI

Cape North

NS

Debert

Halifax-Dartmouth

USA

Sable I.

Cape Ray

Channel-Port aux Basques

Cabot Strait

Sydney

12 Jan 1942
SS Frisco (U-130)

13 Jan 1942
SS Friar Rock (U-130)

Convoy BS 31, 11 Oct 1942
SS Waterton (U-106)

SPAB convoy, 14 Oct 1942
SS Caribou (U-69)

Newfoundland

Corner Brook

Botwood

Gander

Argentia

Bell Island anchorage
5 Sept 1942
SS Saganaga (U-513)
SS Lord Strathcona (U-513)
2 Nov 1942
SS Rose Castle (U-518)
SS PLM 27 (U-518)

Torbay
St. John's

Atlantic Ocean

Belle I.

SS Marouk Pateras
aground 4 Nov 1941

Convoy SG 6, 27-28 Aug 1942
SS Arlyn (U-517 & U-165)
USAT Chatham (U-517)
USS Laramie – damaged (U-165)

SS Empire Energy
aground 4 Nov 1941

Merchant vessel sunk or damaged
Warship sunk or damaged
Quebec to Sydney, Sydney to Quebec convoy route
Quebec to Goose Bay, Goose Bay to Quebec convoy route
Sydney to Greenland, Greenland to Sydney convoy route

N E S W

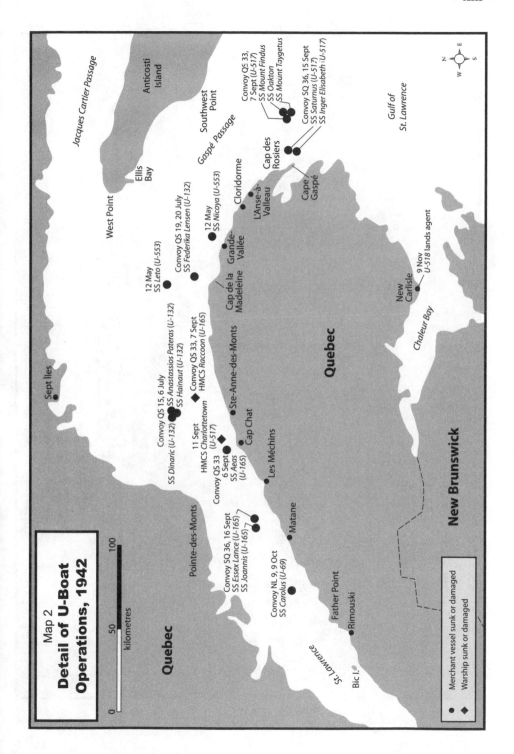

Map 2
Detail of U-Boat Operations, 1942

0   50   100
kilometres

Quebec

Jacques Cartier Passage

Anticosti Island

West Point

Southwest Point

Ellis Bay

Gaspé Passage

Convoy QS 33, 7 Sept (U-517)
SS Mount Findus
SS Oakton
SS Mount Taygetus

Convoy SQ 36, 15 Sept
SS Saturnus (U-517)
SS Inger Elisabeth (U-517)

Cap des Rosiers

Cap Gaspé

Cloridorme

L'Anse-à-Valleau

12 May
SS Nicoya (U-553)

Grande-Vallée

Cap de la Madeleine

12 May
SS Leto (U-553)

Convoy QS 19, 20 July
SS Federika Lensen (U-132)

Gulf of St. Lawrence

New Carlisle

9 Nov
U-518 lands agent

Chaleur Bay

Quebec

New Brunswick

Ste-Anne-des-Monts

Convoy QS 15, 6 July
SS Anastassios Pateras (U-132)
SS Hainaut (U-132)

Convoy QS 33, 7 Sept
HMCS Raccoon (U-165)

Convoy QS 33
SS Dinaric (U-132)

11 Sept
HMCS Charlottetown (U-517)

Convoy QS 33
6 Sept
SS Aeas (U-165)

Cap Chat

Les Méchins

Pointe-des-Monts

Sept Îles

Convoy SQ 36, 16 Sept
SS Essex Lance (U-165)
SS Joannis (U-165)

Matane

Convoy NL 9, 9 Oct
SS Carolus (U-69)

Father Point

Rimouski

Bic I.

St. Lawrence

N
W   E
S

Merchant vessel sunk or damaged
Warship sunk or damaged

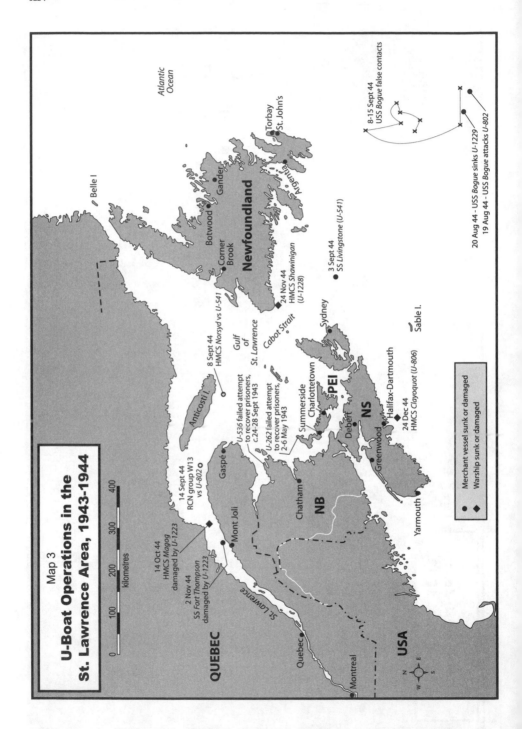

Map 3

U-Boat Operations in the St. Lawrence Area, 1943-1944

Kilometres

0   100   200   300   400

14 Oct 44
HMCS *Magog*
damaged by *U-1223*

2 Nov 44
SS *Fort Thompson*
damaged by *U-1223*

QUEBEC

Montreal

Quebec

St. Lawrence

Mont Joli

Gaspé

14 Sept 44
RCN group W13
vs *U-802*

8 Sept 44
HMCS *Norsyd* vs *U-541*

Anticosti I.

Belle I.

U-536 failed attempt
to recover prisoners,
c.24-28 Sept 1943

U-262 failed attempt
to recover prisoners,
2-6 May 1943

Gulf
of
St. Lawrence

Cabot Strait

24 Nov 44
HMCS *Shawinigan*
(*U-1228*)

Botwood

Gander

Corner
Brook

Newfoundland

Torbay
St. John's

Argentia

Atlantic
Ocean

8-15 Sept 44
USS *Bogue* false contacts

20 Aug 44 - USS *Bogue* sinks *U-1229*
19 Aug 44 - USS *Bogue* attacks *U-802*

Sydney

3 Sept 44
SS *Livingstone* (*U-541*)

Summerside
Charlottetown

PEI

Halifax-Dartmouth

Sable I.

24 Dec 44
HMCS *Clayoquot* (*U-806*)

Debert

Greenwood

NS

Chatham

NB

Yarmouth

USA

N
W   E
S

Merchant vessel sunk or damaged

Warship sunk or damaged

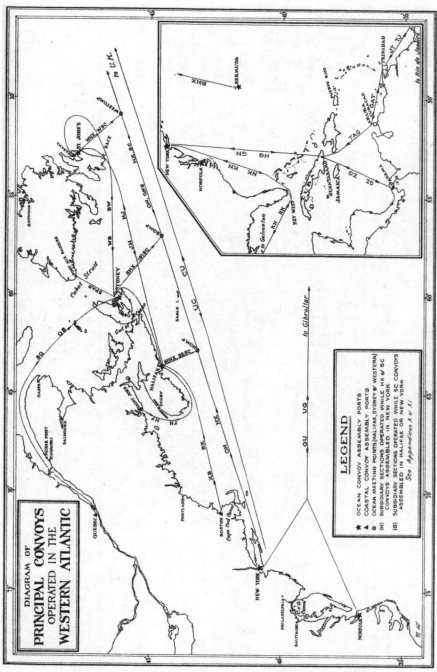

This map shows the changes in the convoy system introduced in August–September 1942. Source: Tucker, *Naval Service of Canada, vol. II*, plate XIII, courtesy of the Department of National Defence.

MERCHANT SHIP SAILING FORMATION FOR CONVOY SQ 36

COLUMN NUMBER	1	2 VICE COMMODORE[1]	3	4 COMMODORE[1]	5	6	7
Pendants	U.S. 11	British 21[4]	British 31	British 41	British 51	British 61[3]	British 71
Ship	Panyork	Essex Lance	Cragpool	Llangollen	Peterston	Inger Elisabeth	Northbrook
Destination	Montreal	Montreal	Montreal	Montreal	Three Rivers	Port Alfred	Port Alfred
Cargo	Ballast	Ballast	Ballast	Ballast	Coal	Coal	Newsprint
Speed	14 knots[2]	9 knots	7.5 knots	10 knots	9 knots	8 knots	7.5 knots
Pendants	Norwegian 12	Greek 22[4]	British 32	Dutch 42[3]	Greek 52	British 62	British 72
Ship	Rolf Jarl	Joannis	Picotee	Saturnus	Anna	Janetta	Trenora
Destination	Montreal	Montreal	Montreal	Montreal	Montreal	Quebec	Buffalo
Cargo	Ballast	Ballast	Coal	Ballast	Coal	Ballast	Newsprint/Sulphite
Speed	8 knots	8.5 knots	7.5 knots	8.5 knots	9 knots	9.5 knots	8 knots
Pendants	Norwegian 13	Greek 23	Greek 33	British 43	British 53	Norwegian 63	British 73
Ship	Solhavn	Aglos Georgios	Katinga Hadjapatera	Transriver	Royalite	Askot	Winna
Destination	St. Anne de Mont Sorel		Montreal	Montreal	Montreal	Quebec	Clarke City
Cargo	Ballast		Ballast	Ballast	Ballast	Paper	Ballast
Speed	8 knots		8 knots	7.5 knots	8 knots	10.5 knots	9 knots
Pendants				British 44			
Ship				Yildum			
Destination				Chicoutimi			
Cargo				Coal			
Speed				7 knots			

Before the sailing of Second World War merchant ship convoys the naval control of shipping staff at the port of departure filled in a standard sailing diagram form, like the one shown here. In it each ship was assigned to a particular position in one of the columns of ships. Each ship thus received a two-digit pendant number. The first digit was the number of the column, and the second digit the position within the column. The merchant ships sailed in the positions indicated in the diagram, each ship following about two cables (366 metres) behind the other, with each column five cables (971 metres) from the column(s) next to it. This example is the sailing diagram for convoy SQ 36, one of the larger convoys that sailed from Sydney, Nova Scotia, to Quebec City in 1942. (Adapted from the original in NSS 8280 SQ 36, RG 24, reel C-5535, LAC.)

1. The Commodore and Vice Commodore of the convoy, who in this case were the masters of SS *Llangollan* and SS *Essex Lance*, were responsible for keeping the merchant ships in their correct sailing positions, and in ordering manoeuvres under the instructions of the senior officer of the naval escort, in this case, the commanding officer of the British destroyer HMS *Salisbury*.

2. 1 knot = 1.85 kilometrres per hour.

3. SS *Inger Elisabeth* (pendant 61) and SS *Saturnus* (pendant 42) both sunk after hits by torpedoes from *U-517* at about 1:38 PM local time on 15 September 1942.

4. SS *Essex Lance* (pendant 21) damaged and SS *Joannis* (pendant 22) sunk after hits by torpedoes from *U-165* at approximately 7:10 and 7:15 AM respectively on 16 September 1942. At the time of the attack, the first column of ships, pendants 11, 12, and 13, had fallen in behind the second column, so *Essex Lance* and *Joannis* were leading the left-hand (shoreward) side of the convoy.

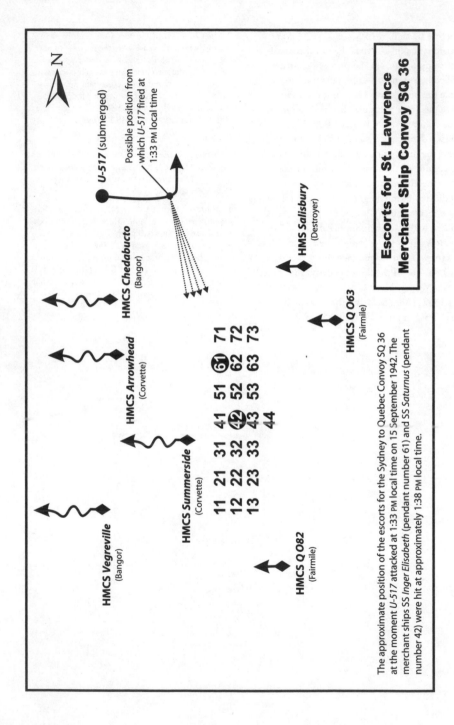

N

U-517 (submerged)

Possible position from which *U-517* fired at 1:33 PM local time

HMCS *Chedabucto*
(Bangor)

HMCS *Arrowhead*
(Corvette)

HMCS *Summerside*
(Corvette)

11 21 31 41 51 ⑥1 71
12 22 32 ④2 52 62 72
13 23 33 43 53 63 73
        44

HMCS *Vegreville*
(Bangor)

HMCS Q 082
(Fairmile)

HMS *Salisbury*
(Destroyer)

HMCS Q 063
(Fairmile)

Escorts for St. Lawrence Merchant Ship Convoy SQ 36

The approximate position of the escorts for the Sydney to Quebec Convoy SQ 36 at the moment *U-517* attacked at 1:33 PM local time on 15 September 1942. The merchant ships SS *Inger Elisabeth* (pendant number 61) and SS *Saturnus* (pendant number 42) were hit at approximately 1:38 PM local time.

INTRODUCTION

DISCOVERING
UNWRITTEN HISTORY

After darkness fell on the early evening of 13 October 1942, the German submarine *U-69* rose from its hiding place in the depths of the Cabot Strait off North Cape, the northern tip of Cape Breton. The submarine repeatedly probed out into the strait and back. At 9:30 PM, about two-and-a-half hours after *U-69* began its patrol, the Newfoundland Railway ferry SS *Caribou* sailed out past the headlands of Sydney harbour, beginning a night crossing to its home port, Port aux Basques, Newfoundland, 180 kilometres away on the far side of the strait. The Royal Canadian Navy Bangor-class minesweeper HMCS *Grandmere* provided protection, zigzagging about 1370 metres[1] off the right-hand stern of the ferry. On that moonless night, *Grandmere*'s people could barely make out *Caribou*'s high superstructure when the defensive sweeps took the warship out to a distance of 2300 metres from the big ship.[2]

The navy sailors had no chance of spotting the low hull and narrow conning tower of *U-69* which at 12:30 AM on 14 October sighted the two ships. That was the big advantage a submarine running on the surface had at night: the submariners could clearly see the tall silhouettes of merchant ships and warships highlighted against the sky, but the submarine, amidst the shadows and swell of the ocean surface, was invisible to crews looking down from the decks of the ships.

For nearly three hours the submarine tracked the vessels, pulling ahead of the warship to get a clear shot into the broadside of the ferry. At 3:21 AM, *U-69* fired a torpedo into *Caribou* from a range of 650 metres. "High dark explosive plume," the U-boat's log reported, and, minutes after, two more explosions as the ferry's own boilers blew up, dooming the vessel. "The steamer immediately sinks down to her railings and lists to port. I had fired from the more advantageous side but it was here that the destroyer [*Grandmere*] was screening and she is now into 900–1000 m[etres] ... At first, she turns towards the steamer but then apparently sights me and alters towards and comes foaming towards me." The submarine crash-dived, turning towards the rapidly sinking ship, expecting that the Canadian captain would not dare attack there.

Grandmere had indeed sighted *U-69*, at a distance of only 320 metres. Even then the Canadian sailors could make out the submarine, mainly because it was rushing off at high speed and throwing up "a distinct white wake." Despite the submarine's attempt to hide under the wreck, *Grandmere* was able to drop twelve depth charges on the swirl left by the plunging U-boat, clear of the shattered ferry that was already slipping below the surface. All the charges were wide of the mark. In the disturbed waters, the warship's asdic (the term used by British Commonwealth navies for the underwater sound detection equipment now known as sonar) was unable to make a contact that would have helped aim the charges. *Grandmere* swept back and forth over the area for an hour and forty minutes, but the asdic set never was able to pick up the submarine, which had gone deep, 140 metres. *Grandmere*'s captain, Lieutenant James Cuthbert, Royal Canadian Naval Reserve, had no choice but to hunt for the submarine: that was the first duty of an escort warship, and it was also a question of survival. A vessel that stopped for rescue work in the wake of a submarine attack without confirming that the enemy was not in a position to attack again risked being a sitting duck. The absence of any contact after a thorough search was actually a blessing: the warship was finally free to look for survivors.

The situation was a nightmare. The ferry had gone down so quickly that, despite heroic efforts on the part of the crew, most of whom were lost, only one lifeboat with twenty people aboard was launched. The rest of the people were in the frigid water, clinging to overturned lifeboats and bits of wreckage. They were so scattered by the wind and currents that it was 6:30 AM, nearly three hours after the people had gone into the water, that *Grandmere* was able to find the first survivors in the still inky darkness. Two Royal Canadian Air Force aircraft soon arrived from Sydney and dropped flares to illuminate the surface, directing the minesweeper to the groups of survivors spotted by the aircrew. Of the 237 passengers and crew aboard *Caribou, Grandmere* recovered only 103 survivors, two of whom died of exposure in the vessel. There were eleven children under the age of ten among the passengers; only one survived. Of the twenty-six women aboard, only eight survived. The ferry's crew suffered particularly heavy losses, thirty-one of forty-six, including six pairs of brothers, a heavy blow to the small Newfoundland twin communities of Channel and Port aux Basques from which they hailed. Some of those killed were personnel in the engine room, near where the torpedo hit, but accounts from survivors show that other crew stayed too long in the ship in heroic efforts to help passengers get away.[3]

Caribou was the twenty-third ship to be sunk or severely damaged by enemy action in the Gulf of St. Lawrence since a U-boat had first struck there in mid-May 1942. The heavy loss of life in *Caribou* brought the total number of deaths resulting from the U-boat attacks to some 272 people. *U-69*, although operating on the doorstep of Sydney, the second largest naval and air base in Canada, got clean away. So too did the four submarines that had preceded her into the gulf. *Caribou*'s dreadful demise, moreover, took place in the glare of full publicity. News spread like wildfire in Cape Breton and Newfoundland. To spare the families of victims and survivors from rumours and misinformation, the navy allowed detailed reports to be published in the press as early as 17 October. Normal practice was to wait at least a week in order to deprive the U-boat command in occupied France of prompt confirmation of success that might allow time to rush additional submarines to exploit a vulnerable area. More than any other event, the destruction of *Caribou* convinced the public, the government, and the armed forces that Canada faced utter defeat in the gulf. Quebec's premier warned the prime minister that the inadequate response of the Canadian forces to the U-boats was causing well-justified panic in the coastal districts of his province. At that very moment, the federal government's own experts concluded that the public information campaign in the region had completely failed either to reassure the public or win support for the war effort. The senior commander on the east coast, Rear Admiral L.W. Murray, convinced that the Germans had achieved signal success in 1942, was certain they would renew the campaign in 1943. He worked closely with the Ottawa headquarters of all three armed services to improve the defences greatly, which the Cabinet made clear must be a top priority.

In the bleak fall months of 1942, bad news—appalling news—was the order of the day. The heaviest losses in the gulf followed close on the heels of the Canadian Army's bloody repulse at Dieppe and the bitter political crisis over conscription that opened a wide division between French and English Canadians. In the First World War, the Conservative government of Sir Robert Borden had introduced compulsory overseas military service due to the heavy casualties suffered by the Canadian Corps that fought as part of the British armies in France, thereby alienating French Canadians who had always rejected the idea that they should be compelled to fight for the British Empire. William Lyon Mackenzie King had won leadership of the Liberal party in 1919 and then led it to a series of election victories by recalling the Conservatives' decision for conscription and solidifying the Liberal power base in Quebec. In the Second World War, his government's fundamental policy was a pledge against overseas conscription to ensure national unity. In 1941 and 1942, the discouraging course of the war for the Allied powers brought largely English Canadian demands for compulsory overseas military service that threatened the survival of the government and aroused intense opposition in Quebec. The prime minister spoke darkly of violence in the streets.

The news from the St. Lawrence was all the more disturbing for military authorities because the attacks occurred in the midst of a long blackout of high-grade intelligence about the German U-boat force. The Canadian military had no definite information about how many submarines were present, when they might leave, if others were on their way, or if the defence forces had done anything to contain the enemy. In these circumstances, the most difficult time of the war for Canada, the loss of *Caribou* was especially compelling evidence of failure. Still more followed. Early in November 1942, less than three weeks after the destruction of *Caribou,* convoy SC 107, sailing for Britain under the protection of a Canadian naval escort, came under attack by a large group of U-boats off Newfoundland. In the space of forty-eight hours, the enemy sank fifteen of the forty-two merchant ships, a loss rate so disastrous that the British high command would demand that a major part of the Canadian navy's Atlantic fleet be transferred to British waters for retraining by the British navy. Something, it seemed, was badly wrong with Canada's maritime forces.

The pessimistic view of the St. Lawrence battle from that terrifying time went untested until the mid-1980s. Indeed, the few accounts that appeared tended to confirm the worst. Yet those accounts of the battle were incomplete, based on little more information than had been available at the time of the events. Fuller accounts, based on once-classified government records and German records that fell into Allied hands at the end of the war, began to appear only in 1985–86, and the first account based on a comprehensive search of these records only in 2002.

The long delay in probing what actually happened might seem remarkable. After all, this was the only battle of the twentieth century fought within Canada's boundaries and the only battle of the two world wars fought under Canadian high command, by Canadian forces operating independently and not as part of larger Allied formations. The Canadian government exercised overall direction, which was not true of any of its other major combat operations.

These operations, moreover, took place in a region of special significance to the country that goes far beyond its importance for maritime transport, and for fish, timber, and mineral resources. This is the great water route by which French explorers and traders first penetrated North America in the sixteenth and early seventeenth centuries, and it was on the shores of the St. Lawrence that French settlers created the first European communities in what is now Canada. The destiny of the country was changed for all time in an earlier St. Lawrence campaign. In 1759 Britain's navy was able to transport General Wolfe's army up the river to Quebec City to defeat the French forces under General Montcalm in the battle that is perhaps the most intensely commemorated in the nation's history.

Yet tales from the country's heroic age had greater appeal than a recent battle in which Canadian forces were, it seemed, utterly defeated for apparently obvious reasons. That is why, in part, the considerable resources needed for research into the massive and diffuse records of the Second World War were a long time in coming.

The belated research into the records of the St. Lawrence battle of 1942–44 has raised questions about the common view of Canada as an unprepared, hapless victim. Was the arrival of the U-boats a surprise? Were the defences as weak and poorly directed as the most dramatic and widely publicized ship losses suggest? *Caribou*, the last victim of the U-boats in the 1942 campaign, came under attack because *U-69* was lurking on the very edge of the gulf, within easy reach of safety in the broad waters of the Atlantic. Why was the submarine so far removed from the main traffic routes within the gulf? Might *Caribou*'s destruction have been the terrible and unintended result of Canadian success in protecting the St. Lawrence? Yet, if *U-69* really was on the run, how had the Canadian forces achieved this result in the midst of the blackest time of the war for the navy? Why was the government so candid with the public about the losses, to the point where the effect of the detailed reports was to exaggerate the gravity of the setbacks? The 1942 campaign, moreover, was not the end of the U-boat assault. They returned in strength with new technology designed to defeat the Canadian defences in the late summer and fall of 1944, but that second phase of the battle of the St. Lawrence is almost unknown. Why?

This book is an attempt to answer these questions. It is a detective story, for some of the most important records of the campaign were always widely scattered, and although forty years later they were declassified and opened for research, they had become still more scattered and difficult to assemble. The book also has elements of a memoir. For one reason and another I was drawn, in various capacities and at various times, into different projects about the U-boats in the St. Lawrence. Some of these projects re-examined the wartime events in light of newly accessible Canadian, British, American, and German records. Others helped bring the battle back into prominence in the national media.

I first learned about the battle early in 1972 when *The Canadian Magazine* ran a two-part front-page story, "The Second World War Battle We Lost at Home"[4] by the journalist Peter Moon. The articles were based on interviews with Paul Hartwig, commander of *U-517*, the most successful of the eight submarines that entered the gulf in 1942. The boat sank nine ships during its six-week mission in August–October 1942, and its feats in the face of massive increases in the defences largely account for the Canadian forces' sense of frustration and defeat when *U-69* then destroyed *Caribou* only one week later.

Hartwig was a vigorous 56 years of age when Moon met him, and, having entered the new West German navy in the 1950s, had risen to become deputy commander of the service. His precise, professional account of his submarine's exploits even when relentlessly pursued by bombers and warships scarcely painted a flattering picture of the Canadian forces.

In 1978 or early 1979, Brian McKenna, the Montreal-based producer for the CBC national current affairs program *the fifth estate*, made a proposal for a feature on the St. Lawrence battle. He too had become aware of it through Peter Moon's articles and saw the opportunity for a film item in a reunion for veterans of the St. Lawrence operations that was to be held at Gaspé, the main Canadian military base during the battle, in the summer of 1979. The main reason why the veterans organized the reunion was that the battle had been so completely forgotten, despite the significant losses of naval and merchant marine personnel *"in Canada."*[5]

My father was the executive producer of *the fifth estate*. He had come up through the ranks from CBC Halifax, and east coast history and culture was a leitmotif in his filmmaking career. Still, he had never heard of the St. Lawrence battle. I was then a graduate student, specializing in east coast military history, and he asked me to verify the basic facts in the proposal. I had by that time discovered Joseph Schull's *The Far Distant Ships: An Official Account of Canadian Naval Operations in the Second World War,* which the navy had first published in 1950. Schull's brief account of the St. Lawrence battle also featured Paul Hartwig and *U-517* in near heroic relief and underscored the key point that Canada lost the battle. This was a persuasive confirmation of Peter Moon's account and of Brian McKenna's proposal. The government's wilful amnesia about an embarrassing defeat became a theme in the feature, "To lose a battle," that was broadcast later in 1979. Indeed, as the veterans gathered at Gaspé to remember their comrades who had died as a result of U-boat torpedo attacks in the river and gulf complained, there was not even a Canadian naval battle honour for the St. Lawrence. I do not recall whether I twigged to an anomaly. If the Canadian government had sought to cloak events in the gulf, why did the navy's own official history reveal the essentials in a cold critical light?

Yet the charge of amnesia was not entirely off the mark. In 1948, the Department of National Defence, strapped by post-war budget cuts, shut down its wartime "official history" program for the navy and the air force, the armed services that carried out the major operations in the St. Lawrence. The leader of the navy historical team, Dr. Gilbert N. Tucker, was able to complete a volume on naval administration and activities on shore. He would not, however, rush ahead with the planned volume on operations because his team had not yet been able to examine enemy records or highly classified Allied intelligence records, both essential to interpret the day-to-day operational reports his team had gathered during the war. The naval staff therefore assigned Schull, a well-known writer then serving as a public relations officer in the navy, to quickly produce a volume based on only the materials the team had been able to assemble; this was the genesis of *The Far Distant Ships*.

The 1948 cuts had a more serious impact on the air force, which cancelled work on the large home defence air commands and their important role in supporting the navy. The poor state of air force history was finally addressed in the late 1960s. At that time, the historical offices of the three armed forces were combined into a single Directorate of History; this was part of the combination of the three armed services into the present unified Canadian Armed Forces. The new directorate's first big project was to produce a full history of the air force.

WHEN I JOINED THE DIRECTORATE in 1981 as a junior civilian historian, Dr. W.A.B. (Alec) Douglas, the director, asked me to find out what the air force had done in the St. Lawrence battle. There was no reason to suspect there was much to find, which made it a good training exercise for a neophyte researcher. My instructions were to bang out a thirty-page paper that would require only part-time work for a couple of months. It was the beginning of a career-long adventure in research.

It turned out that the air force had in fact played a very large—often predominant—role in the St. Lawrence. This was truly hidden history, not because of any conspiracy, but because little had been done to gather or organize the diffuse records as a result of the cuts to the historical program in 1948.

The St. Lawrence became the central focus of my work until 1986. In that year, Alec Douglas published *The Creation of a National Air Force: The Official History of the Royal Canadian Air Force, Volume II,* which filled the yawning gap on the history of the air force in Canada, 1919–1945. There was a full chapter on the battle of 1942 and a substantial part of another chapter on the large-scale operations in 1943 and 1944.

The air force volume was only the beginning of new research. Douglas, a former naval officer, had long been urging the defence department to support a fresh operational history of the Royal Canadian Navy in the Second World War to build on the preliminary account in *The Far Distant Ships*. The work on the air force's support of the navy for *The Creation of a National Air Force* drew on precisely the kinds of high-level intelligence material, Allied and Canadian policy files, and, of course, enemy records that had not been available to Schull and to Tucker. The air force research not only highlighted the need to expand upon and amplify the accounts by Tucker and Schull, but also became one of the foundations for the new naval history started in 1987. Somewhat ironically, history then repeated itself. Government budget cuts in the early 1990s, as severe for the defence historical program as those in 1948, delayed the completion of the new naval history volumes until 2007.

ONE

No Surprise: Canadian Defence Planning and the St. Lawrence

The attack on the St. Lawrence in 1942 was no surprise. Far from it. As early as the 1870s, Canadians had worried about raids in these waters. The threat at that time was newly developed, fast, steam-driven cruisers, the beginnings of the industrial-age technological revolution in warships that would culminate during the twentieth century in the submarine, the supremely stealthy surprise attack weapon. Since the British conquest in 1759, the world dominance of the Royal Navy had always been the northern colonies' shield, but how effective was that shield in the age of steam? Warships free of the vagaries of wind propulsion could more easily evade British squadrons and strike like a "bolt from the blue," using powerful new types of artillery and explosives to wreak havoc on coastal towns and shipping before defending forces could reach the scene.[1]

Britain encouraged the confederation of the northern colonies into the new Dominion of Canada in 1867 to stimulate them to use their collective resources to do more for their own defence, including forming local naval organizations. There were occasional initiatives, notably after a war scare in 1878 which brought convincing intelligence that Russia was preparing to operate cruisers in the St. Lawrence. Still, Canadian efforts came to little, even after 1904 when the Royal Navy closed its dockyards in Canada and removed the last warships permanently stationed in North American waters in order to allow Britain to meet the accelerating naval armaments race in Europe. In 1909, when there was a panic throughout the Empire over news that Britain might be losing the naval race with Germany, now the most likely enemy in a future war, the Liberal government of Sir Wilfrid Laurier responded by creating Canada's own navy in 1910 for the defence of the coasts and offshore shipping.

The new armed service was a political disaster. French-Canadian nationalists, who believed that any Canadian service would be nothing more than a branch of Britain's Royal Navy and therefore embroil Canada in every distant British war, wanted no navy at all. Pro-British English-speaking Canadians, by contrast, wanted to do much more, in direct support of the Royal Navy. This helped to defeat Laurier's Liberals in 1911 and bring Robert Borden's Conservatives to power. His attempt in 1912–13 to give funding directly to the Royal Navy foundered in the face of political discord that erupted into a parliamentary crisis. That was on the eve of the First World War. During that conflict, the threat of attack by fast cruisers demanded substantial British support. But Britain was then able to give little help in the face of a new weapon: long-range submarines that struck close to Nova Scotia and Newfoundland. The experience profoundly influenced Canada's response to the outbreak of the Second World War in 1939, with worries about the vulnerability of the St. Lawrence in the forefront.

When the First World War broke out in 1914, Canada's only naval force was the neglected remnants of Laurier's initiative, about 300 personnel and two obsolescent cruisers, HMCS *Niobe* on the east coast and HMCS *Rainbow* on the west coast, both purchased from Britain to serve as training ships. The tiny naval staff had warned Borden not to disband this cadre because even the single cruiser could help to cover the St. Lawrence. So it proved. One of *Niobe's* first missions was to patrol the Cabot Strait approaches in response to warnings that fast German cruisers were in the area.

These reports were false, but threats of maritime raiders in the St. Lawrence ultimately breathed new life into the Canadian navy against heavy political odds. Determined not to get burned again by the naval issue, Borden's government focused on land forces. The Royal Navy, or so it seemed at first, could look after the defence of Canadian waters. It was in the Royal Navy's interests to do so, because the heavy transatlantic shipping that sustained the British economy passed close by Nova Scotia and Newfoundland on the north Atlantic route that is the shortest and most efficient one between the Americas and the British Isles. In August 1914, British trade defence cruisers rushed to Halifax, part of the global deployments by the Royal Navy's powerful surface fleet that soon swept German raiding cruisers from the high seas and bottled up the main German battle fleet in the North Sea.

The Germans responded by using a new weapon, the submarine (or "U-boat" from the German *untersee boot*), to attack merchant ships in the northeastern Atlantic as they approached the British Isles. The British surface fleet, especially the type of cruisers that protected trade off Canada's east coast, proved helpless in the face of this assault. The destruction of the giant ocean liner *Lusitania* by torpedoes from the U-boat *U-20* in May 1915 caused a chill among Canadian authorities. The attack, which resulted in the loss of 1098 lives, two-thirds of those aboard, took place in heavily patrolled waters close to the large British naval base at Queenstown, Ireland. It was only too easy to visualize a similar disaster in the St. Lawrence. Liners loaded with troops at Quebec City and sailed the whole breadth of the gulf, where there was no protection at all except occasional patrols by the British cruisers that had proved little better than targets in contests with U-boats. Worse, the islands and shallows in the gulf forced large ships to follow constricted routes where submarines could easily locate them, while the broad waters and isolated, sinuous shores of the gulf and lower river offered nearly limitless possibilities for escape by the submariners. Soon, reports of U-boats were flowing into Halifax and Ottawa—the waters in the gulf and around Newfoundland were cluttered with flotsam and, in the frequently foggy conditions, drifting logs, barrels, and other detritus took on the shape of periscopes or even fully surfaced submarines to observers on shore and the crews of fishing vessels and other civilian craft.

Canada immediately called on the Admiralty to dispatch anti-submarine vessels. The best types were destroyers. These craft, which in the First World War were about eighty metres in length and displaced about a thousand tonnes, were a fraction of the size of cruisers, but were just as speedy (in the order of fifty kilometres an hour), and, most important, much more manoeuvrable. Unlike a big cruiser, the destroyers could rapidly zigzag to avoid torpedoes fired by a submarine or match the rapid course changes of a submarine attempting to escape, whether at high speed on the surface or at slower speed when submerged. Destroyers were also big enough that they carried a strong gun and torpedo armament to attack submarines manoeuvring at high speed on the surface and ample numbers of a new underwater weapon, depth charges. The latter were barrel-like canisters of high explosives that detonated at depths set on triggers that were activated by water pressure.

The Royal Navy was desperately short of destroyers and similar warships for the defence of British waters. Help would be sent to Canada and Newfoundland only when it was clear the Germans were going to strike, and thus far there was no intelligence that showed that German submarines could or would cross the Atlantic. Finding this advice anything but reassuring, the Borden government directed the Canadian navy to set up its own anti-submarine force specifically to cover the St. Lawrence. Initially, in 1915, the "St. Lawrence Patrol" comprised seven civilian steamers—including large, fast yachts surreptitiously purchased in the neutral United States. They were armed with light guns, utterly unequal to a U-boat's armament, in the hope that a submarine would easily be deterred when it was so far from its home base and would not want to risk even minor damage. In fact, the expectation was that the Canadian vessels would not have to engage in combat. Their main role was to keep a close watch on the remote shores of the gulf to ensure that German agents, who were known to be operating in the neutral United States within easy reach of the Maritime provinces, would not set up the refuelling caches that the Admiralty advised would be needed for the existing short-ranged German submarines to cross the Atlantic and make the return voyage. Still, this was the beginning of the anti-submarine role that became the Canadian navy's specialty for the rest of the twentieth century. *Niobe* was now worn out, but Canada refused a replacement cruiser offered by the British so that her crew could be used to operate the anti-submarine patrols.

The battle with the submarines in British waters did nothing to encourage Canadian confidence. The Royal Navy deployed hundreds of patrol vessels in the approaches to British ports and still failed to reduce merchant shipping losses. Submarines were indeed the supremely elusive weapon. The patrol vessels could not be everywhere at once, and the submarines easily avoided them to attack merchant ships in unpatrolled areas, using their surface speed or ability to submerge to disappear within minutes of an attack, long before defending forces could reach the scene even if the merchant ship managed to radio for help.

In the spring of 1917, when a fresh all-out U-boat offensive was sinking one in four ocean-going ships sailing from British ports, the Admiralty turned to the ancient method of convoy, sailing forty and more merchant ships together under the protection of naval escorts.

It was an immediate success. Individual merchant ships scattered the sea with numerous targets for the submarines; a convoy, however, is nearly as difficult to locate at sea as one ship, and many convoys slipped through without ever being detected by the submarines. Even when the U-boats found a convoy, they had limited opportunity to attack because of the presence of the escorts. The first shot revealed the submarine's location to warships that were only a few hundred metres away, leaving the submarine commander little choice but to flee the scene as quickly and quietly as possible. The large port of Sydney, Cape Breton, at the mouth of the gulf, became the assembly port for slow ships sailing from Canada and the northeastern United States to Britain. Halifax became the assembly point for faster ships.

Submarine tactics and the tactics for defence against submarines changed little in the years between the world wars and, in important respects, the new war at sea in 1939 picked up where the first war had left off. With benefit of hindsight, the British quickly introduced convoy in 1939, and Halifax and then Sydney resumed their role as assembly ports. From the first, the Canadian navy focused its efforts on convoy defence, including plans to extend the convoy system into the Gulf of St. Lawrence should, as seemed likely, the U-boats once more come to Canadian waters and, as seemed still more likely, senior Allies be unable to help, an equally important lesson from the First World War.

The United States had entered the First World War on 6 April 1917, but Canada's hope that the large U.S. Navy could augment Canada's defences was quickly dashed. Britain, urgently needing reinforcements, arranged for all available U.S. destroyers and smaller types useful for anti-submarine work to be sent to British and French ports for convoy escort and patrol duty. Indeed, Britain turned to Canada's modest shipbuilding industry and placed orders for 160 small anti-submarine vessels: forty-metre steel trawlers and eighteen-metre wooden "drifters" that were both modelled on commercial fishing craft whose manoeuvrability made them useful for anti-submarine patrols near the mouths of harbours and along the coasts, where the U-boats could most readily find ships to attack.

When early in 1918 good intelligence indicated that new, large U-boats with ample fuel for transatlantic missions would come to Canadian and U.S. waters, the only help the British could offer was to turn over to the RCN thirty-six of the trawlers and thirty-six of the drifters being built on British account in Canadian yards. As the new trawlers and drifters arrived on the east coast close on the heels of the spring breakup of ice on the St. Lawrence, they were assigned in about equal numbers to three groups: new convoy escort forces at Halifax and at Sydney, and the existing St. Lawrence patrol, which was still based at Sydney. Each of these three forces reached a strength of about thirty vessels during the summer of 1918. The St. Lawrence patrol was reorganized into divisions, each comprising three or four warships that patrolled together in the hopes that a group of small, lightly armed craft might have some chance in combat against the big submarines.

None of the ships in the Canadian patrol were big, or fast, or heavily armed enough to pursue the submarines. The Admiralty advised a striking force of at least six destroyers, but the Royal and U.S. navies could spare none. On the Admiralty's advice, the Canadian navy turned to a new technology, aviation. The navy built seaplane stations at Halifax and at North Sydney, and a U.S. Navy squadron of six big Curtiss HS2L flying boats operated at each place, while Canadian aviation recruits received training at air bases in central Canada and the United States.

On 5 August 1918, before the air patrols began to operate, U-156 appeared off Halifax and sank the tanker Luz Blanca just beyond the sight of the headlands. The anti-submarine flotilla was further out at sea, escorting a valuable troopship convoy, and thus there was nothing available to pursue the submarine. Because of Halifax's vulnerability to surprise attack from the sea, the Admiralty transferred the troopship convoys to Quebec City. Canadian and local British staff, with their longstanding worries about the ability of an enemy to hide and strike in the gulf and river, persuaded the Admiralty to release additional trawlers and drifters built in Canadian yards to the RCN. The additional vessels went to Gaspé in September to patrol the channel between the Gaspé Peninsula and the south shore of Anticosti Island and also in the Strait of Belle Isle. Had the war continued into 1919, plans were to establish another aviation station, possibly on the Magdalen Islands to cover the central gulf, and another at Red Bay, Labrador, to cover the Strait of Belle Isle. These efforts to control the "choke points" in the gulf antici-pated the defence arrangements of the Second World War.

The Admiralty was likely influenced in its decision to move the troopships onto the St. Lawrence route by decryption of German radio signals which showed that the U-boats were assigned to the heavily travelled waters between Halifax and St. John's, Newfoundland. Still, the submarines came close. On 20 August 1918, *U-156* appeared off the Canso Strait and captured the Canadian commercial trawler *Triumph*. The Germans put a light gun and a supply of demolition charges in the little fishing vessel, and both she and the submarine proceeded to destroy fishing schooners along the Atlantic coast of Cape Breton. The Germans evidently scuttled the trawler when she ran out of coal after a few days, but *U-156* continued north to the fishing banks off the French islands of Saint-Pierre and Miquelon and on 25 August destroyed five schooners there, "just a 100 miles [185 kilometres] from this port," as the *Sydney Daily Post* reported.[2] On 26–27 August, *U-117* passed further out at sea and sank the Norwegian freighter *Bergsdalen* less than 300 kilometres east of Sydney.

The navy's achievement in the last two years of the war was consid-erable. With almost no resources, the service had built up the east coast flotillas to a strength of 130 small warships by the fall of 1918, crewed by a total of some 5000 personnel, most of whom had entered as untrained volunteers. The organization was crucial to the effective operation of the convoy system for merchant ships, and convoy was a brilliant success. Only two substantial merchant vessels were sunk in Canadian waters, the tanker off Halifax and the freighter off Sydney; both sailed without escorts. The U-boats could find no other such large, undefended targets, and it was for this reason that they concentrated on the destruction of small fishing craft. In every case, the submarine captains ensured that the fishermen got away in their lifeboats, and this strict adherence to international law helped spread terror as the fishing crews streamed ashore and retailed the stories of the German "pirates" to the press. Rather than celebrate the navy's achievement in protecting the large ocean ships that were crucial to the Allied war effort, the press and politicians vilified the navy for its failure to protect the far-flung fishing fleets, an impossible task.

Although the wartime experience convinced Robert Borden and some of his Cabinet ministers that they had been wrong to reject the Laurier navy project (which had included plans to build destroyers in Canada, the type that had been needed for anti-submarine defence), there was no support in either party for the necessary expenditures in the wake of the "war to end all wars." When the new Liberal leader, William Lyon Mackenzie King, came to power in the federal election of 1921, he slashed the naval budget. The service could retain only a single destroyer on each coast—these had been gifts from the Royal Navy's surplus of wartime construction—and had to become largely a reserve organization. In 1923, the navy established the Royal Canadian Naval Reserve, for professional seamen who took naval courses every year or two, and the Royal Canadian Naval Volunteer Reserve, for interested citizens with no professional experience who trained an evening or two each week at drill halls in the major cities across the country and attended courses at the Halifax and Esquimalt dockyards in the summers. The new Royal Canadian Naval Air Service had been quickly disbanded after the war, but the U.S. Navy left the flying boats it had operated in Nova Scotia, and these became an important asset of the small Canadian Air Force established in 1920, which in 1924 received the King's permission to use the prefix *royal*. The air station at North Sydney was dismantled, but the one on the Dartmouth shore of Halifax harbour remained in service (as it does in much expanded form today, now known as Canadian Forces Base Shearwater, the support facility for the navy's ship-borne helicopters).

Despite the dismal lack of resources, the navy succeeded in enhancing its role in the control of shipping. During the First World War, Canada's senior naval officers had been continually frustrated by the commanders of British warships operating from Halifax and Esquimalt who had so ignored Ottawa that the Canadian staff often had no clear idea of shipping developments in the country's own waters and ports. Information had flowed to the British North American headquarters in Bermuda and thence to London. In 1919–21 the Canadian staff worked out new arrangements that made Ottawa the British Admiralty's centre for control of all British Empire merchant shipping in the North American area north of Florida. It made sense. Ottawa, unlike Bermuda, was a hub of telegraph, telephone, and radio communications. Because the tiny RCN—whose regular officer corps was only about sixty in strength—had no one qualified for specialist intelligence duties, the Admiralty seconded such an expert for duty as the "director of naval intelligence" in Ottawa.[3]

It would be difficult to overstate the importance this development would acquire in the Second World War. Shipping control involved the gathering of information on the movements of all British Empire and Allied merchant ships and the collation of this information in close consultation with the Admiralty. On that basis, the director of naval intelligence in Ottawa issued instructions to the merchant ships departing from North American ports about the routes they should follow to avoid areas where enemy forces were known to be operating, or direction of the merchant ships to ports like Halifax and Sydney to assemble for convoy. Shipping control was thus at the heart of merchant shipping defence and especially the convoy system that became one of

Canada's foremost commitments and the principal reason for the rapid, vast expansion of the naval service and the maritime commands of the Royal Canadian Air Force.

Only in the mid-1930s, in the face of aggression by military dictatorships in Japan and Germany, did the Canadian government endeavour to rebuild the country's coastal defences. The military applied the lessons of the First World War. The navy wanted, as a bare minimum for the defence of one coast, the striking force of six destroyers that had been glaringly absent in 1918; the air force wanted long-range reconnaissance aircraft to keep a watch over the vast coastal area, and aircraft armed with bombs and torpedoes to strike at hostile intruders; the militia wanted modern long-range coast guns for port defence.[4]

The coastal defence program was the centrepiece of the limited rearmament effort launched by Mackenzie King's Liberal government, which returned to power in the general election of October 1935. Defence was a minefield for the prime minister. Increased expenditure suggested a commitment to support Britain in a future general war and raised the spectre of conscription. Yet many Canadians, like Americans and Britons, worried more than ever about coastal raids as Japan and Germany built up their navies and air forces in the late 1930s. Dramatic developments in technology, such as trans-oceanic flight and the operation of high-performance aircraft from ships, were a particular source of fear. Mackenzie King had no doubts about the need to prepare for the possibility of a general war, but he intended that Canada's part should be mainly naval and air forces. These services were essential for home defence against maritime attack. Naval and air forces, moreover, required much less manpower than land forces and thus posed no danger of requiring conscription. (For this reason, the nationalist Mackenzie King, who was wary of professional links between the Canadian and British armed forces, actually encouraged the liaison work with the British navy carried out by the director of naval intelligence in Ottawa.)

Mackenzie King presented the limited rearmament program in the House of Commons in January and February 1937. There were no specific measures, he explained, for the preparation of forces for service overseas, only for home defence, the most basic security requirement. He highlighted the priority given to the air force and the navy, the front-line coastal defence forces, over the army and underscored that the army's increased funding was intended largely for coastal defence measures in support of the other two services. He renewed his pledge, first made as early as 1922, that Canada would never again go to war automatically when Britain did, as had happened in 1914. He would allow "Parliament to decide" the country's course of action. He also promised that, in the event of war, his government would never introduce conscription for overseas service.

Although the greatest fears in 1936–37 were of a Pacific war with Japan, Mackenzie King nevertheless emphasized the vulnerability of the St. Lawrence. Quebec might object to an overseas war, but it could hardly protest expenditures designed to protect its own shores. On 18 December 1936, the Cabinet agreed to carry out the coastal defence program. At that meeting, Mackenzie King emphasized the danger to the St. Lawrence, as he would time and again in public and private, in a bid to win consensus. "I said that our country was like a house with open door at the front and open door at the back, and without any real means of dealing from within with a marauder or invader; that we needed at least something that appeared like a protection of the gateway of Canada at the mouth of the St. Lawrence and something which might serve emergency purposes at harbours on the Pacific." As Mackenzie King had anticipated, the strongest resistance came from his Quebec lieutenant, Ernest Lapointe, minister of justice. Lapointe was Mackenzie King's bellwether of Quebec opinion, and Mackenzie King relied on him to interpret the government's policy for that province. What was unusual at this meeting was the pressure Mackenzie King put on his minister: "Lapointe seemed greatly concerned about Quebec, fearing the nationalistic part will soon become a solid block in Parliament against any expenditures for defense [sic] purposes. I have no fears of that if the matter is presented in its true light. With conditions what they are in Canada today without the help of British or American Navy, a single ship could sail up the St. Lawrence and close both the ports of Quebec and Montreal, and return and close the ports of Halifax and St. John [New Brunswick] as well. We are living in a fool's paradise in this mad age to think that because we are so completely unprotected, we should not even have the appearance of the least protection on either coast."[5]

Mackenzie King's emphasis on the danger to Canada's shores, particularly the St. Lawrence, the heart of the province of Quebec, was a political success. The important French-Canadian caucus of the Liberal party did not defect as Lapointe had feared. Events, however, quickly overtook the program when Hitler's Germany became more aggressive in 1938. There was immediate danger to both the Pacific and the Atlantic coasts, the chiefs of the armed forces warned. The navy, which had got its six destroyers thanks to the provision by the Royal Navy of a few modern ships at a fraction of the cost of new construction, now needed at least a dozen more, as well as a very large number of smaller patrol vessels to protect the heavy shipping in the St. Lawrence and off the coast of Nova Scotia and southern Newfoundland.

Worst of all, Germany was openly rebuilding its submarine force. Rear Admiral Percy Nelles, the chief of the naval staff, had been a junior staff officer at naval headquarters in Ottawa during the U-boat crisis of 1918, so he knew well the threat the country faced and what would be needed to meet that threat. In the late 1930s, he assembled information on the very large coastal patrol forces that had had to be improvised under nearly impossible conditions because of the lack of British—or American—help and repeatedly urged the government to fund the construction of Canadian warships to avoid the kind of panic situation that had occurred in the First World War. Still, the government was unwilling to make the substantial investment that would have been necessary to tool up the Depression-wracked shipbuilding industry and prepare it for the large technical challenges of naval construction. Although the government did place orders for British-designed coastal patrol aircraft, the infant Canadian aviation industry could not expand rapidly, and there would be long delays before production became available. Even so, the government rejected a generous offer by the U.S. Army to provide aircraft immediately from its own production because the American designs were expensive and Mackenzie King did not want to be seen spending such large amounts of the Canadian taxpayers' money outside the country.

The Canadian military did the best it could, making plans to develop defences in the gulf similar to those of 1918. As in 1917–18, Sydney would be the main operating base, although there were no military facilities there. Limited budgets allowed for only one initiative—to start construction of an air landing strip. Thus, Second World War plans for the defence of the gulf were built on the experience of 1918: there might well be a shortage of naval forces, and air forces would have to fill the gap.

TWO

How an Un-naval Country Became a Key Combatant in the Battle of the Atlantic

Seldom has the bitter disappointment of being "passed over for promotion" led to such a life-changing adventure, or at least so quickly. On the other hand, Eric Brand was no ordinary disappointed hopeful. Like several members of an earlier generation of British officers whose bleak prospects in the Royal Navy led them to come to help build Canada's new navy, Brand possessed uncommon energy and determination, and a wealth of professional experience. Unlike the earlier officers, he arrived in Ottawa on the eve of a whirlwind—July 1939—just weeks before the world descended into war and Ottawa, overnight and for the first time ever, became a centre for international maritime operations. Eric Brand was the ringmaster. The organization he built, for the protective control of British, Canadian, and international merchant shipping, and the decisions in which he had a leading voice were at the heart of Canada's maritime war effort. His organization and decisions would fundamentally shape the battle of the St. Lawrence.

In photographs, Brand looks serious, with a long face and intense eyes that give a sense of deep thought. That, his widow Margaret told me, was what his reserved manner also communicated. He would listen and, when he had the full story, say "I'll think about it." Some hastily concluded that he had either failed to grasp the issue or was unwilling to help. They were mistaken. He was already forming a plan about what to do and setting in place the precise steps needed to make it happen. Margaret told me of his fury at the minister of a church in Ottawa who asked Brand's help in organizing a Remembrance Day service. "I'll think about it," Brand responded, and in a couple of days he called back with arrangements in place. The minister, an impatient man, told him not to bother; he had made other plans in view of Brand's evident lack of interest. It might seem difficult to reconcile "fury" with the reserved countenance in the photographs. However, the 1942 log of a belea-guered censorship official, responding to Brand's complaint about the publication in the press of sensitive naval information, provides a rare unvarnished glimpse: "Captain Brand opened the day's hostilities with the usual irate phone call ... [He] immediately flew off the handle ..."[1]

It must be said that Margaret Brand's beauty and vivaciousness, still radiant in 1993 when she was in her eighties, also suggest another side to Brand, as did the warmth of her every word about him. She was very much "in the navy" too, for the whole of her life. She was the daughter of Engineer Rear Admiral W.S. Mann, RN, and by her late teens, with the death of her mother, helped organize the household and manage social events for her father. She was carrying out these duties during her father's posting to Malta in the late 1920s when she met Brand, who was serving in the Mediterranean fleet. She recalled that Brand always said "his bell had rung immediately" from the moment he first laid eyes on her; he always remembered the blue dress she was wearing.

Brand launched a campaign to spend time alone with Margaret, but at least once was rebuffed by Admiral Mann. Always determined, the young officer then hit the winning strategy. Margaret had a difficult time managing the household because she had to rely on the public trolley for transport. Brand would teach her how to drive—and he did. In fact Brand's "very patient" teaching helped to win her heart.

Born in Ipswich, England, in 1896, Brand's boyhood dream had been to serve in the Royal Navy. According to his obituary, he failed in his first application and therefore joined *Conway*, the training ship for merchant marine officers at Liverpool, in January 1909. With this marine experience, he succeeded in entering the Royal Naval College Dartmouth in January 1911. Brand spent the First World War in the battleships of the Grand Fleet. At the battle of Jutland in May 1916, he was senior sub-lieutenant and assistant to the gunnery officer on HMS *Valiant*. Brand was awarded a "mention in dispatches" for his conduct during the battle and received early promotion to acting lieutenant. During the interwar years, he qualified as a specialist in gunnery, then in navigation, and in 1931 qualified as a staff officer. He did well in a wide range of sea-going appointments in most of the major classes of warships, including the aircraft carrier HMS *Courageous*. Nevertheless, promotion from commander, the rank he had achieved in 1929, eluded him. The step from commander to captain was and still is one of the most competitive. Brand suspected that his early promotion after the battle of Jutland had actually hurt his later career by giving him a reputation as having a leg up on the promotion ladder, with the result that senior officers for whom he had worked did not sufficiently lobby on his behalf.

He again missed promotion in December 1937, the last time he was eligible for consideration. He had married Margaret in 1934, and, as she later told me, neither of them had any interest in retiring to a housing estate in England and being pegged for the rest of their lives as "Commander and Mrs. Commander" in the highly stratified

English class system. "So," in Brand's words, "we took the Navy List," the fat volume that listed all officer appointments in the Royal Navy. "We turned it over, we said 'This DNI [Director of Naval Intelligence] Ottawa looks a damned good place and we have always wanted to see North America.'"[2] Brand decided for the first and only time in his career to lobby for an appointment, his last; the Ottawa job would be available in 1939 in the normal course of postings.

In January 1938, Brand was appointed chief of staff to the admiral commanding the coast of Scotland. His job, which took on greater urgency with the escalating confrontation with Germany, was planning for war mobilization at ports in Scotland, including local defence measures and staffs for the control of shipping, precisely the challenge that he would face in Canada.

Brand did not become the leading candidate for the Canadian job until the spring of 1939. Admiral Nelles had requested another officer. When that officer demurred, the Admiralty put forward Brand's name, but Nelles was not happy about the change. In Brand's words, "Well it so happened by a good piece of luck that a very old friend of mine was on his way back to England from Singapore where he had been Director of Intelligence ... [H]e passed through Ottawa and called on the CNS and the CNS said to him 'Look, I am sick of these passed over commanders coming. They are going to try and give me another one.' So my friend [E.G.N.] Rushbrooke said 'Well, who are they going to give you?' and he said 'Oh, I don't know, a fellow called Brand.' So good old Rushy said 'By God, if you get him you'll be lucky.'"[3]

Brand arrived in Ottawa on 17 July 1939 and was met by his predecessor, Commander H.A.C. Lane, who took him to Naval Service Headquarters (NSHQ). Two things immediately struck the new arrival. The first was the tiny scale of the operation. The headquarters occupied two floors in the Robinson Building, whose main floor was a delicatessen: "eleven men [the grand total of officers and civil service officials] over a grocer's shop"[4] was how he described it. In the oppressive heat of the Ottawa summer, Brand was also a bit surprised at the incongruity of the first order of business. Lane turned over to him the fur coat that was passed from each of the seconded British officers to his successor, a necessity to endure the Ottawa winters.

With the possibility of war looming close on the horizon, Brand was anxious to lay the groundwork for local defence measures and control of merchant shipping at Canada's main ports. Ideally these efforts should be integrated with those of the British commander-in-chief, America and West Indies at Bermuda, whose warships would help defend trade in Canadian waters.[5] On 18–19 August when Vice-Admiral Sir Sidney Meyrick, the commander-in-chief in Bermuda, visited Halifax, Brand travelled from Ottawa to review his plans with Meyrick's staff and Commander H.E. Reid, the RCN's commander-in-charge at Halifax.

Brand was just back from Halifax when on 21 August the first messages arrived from Britain warning that war was a possibility. Admiral Nelles was in Colorado visiting his son who was there for treatment of tuberculosis, and Captain L.W. Murray was acting as chief of the naval staff. When on 22 August Brand asked Murray if it was possible to follow the British lead by warning retired officers designated for service in control of shipping that they might soon be called out, Murray took Brand to see the minister of national defence, Ian Mackenzie. Mackenzie agreed, so long as any measures taken were purely defensive. Brand, who had said and done nothing in the meeting, asked Murray why he had had to be there. Murray gave Brand some insight into the tensions in civil–military relations in Ottawa: "You never must get anything from that man without a witness present."[6] From this cautious and modest beginning—typical of the Mackenzie King administration's approach to defence matters in the 1930s—Brand built the large, effective North American shipping control organization that was to engage in the deadly struggle against German submarines and their threat to Canada, the United States, and the lifelines to Great Britain. Without this organization, the "brain" that coordinated the defence of shipping, Canada would not have been able to achieve anything like the leading role it was to assume in the Atlantic war.

In fact, by August 1939 the Mackenzie King government was more ready to support shipping defence measures than Mackenzie's and Murray's caution suggested. The prime minister had concluded at the time of the Munich crisis in the fall of 1938 that he would have no choice but to lead Canada into war in the event of a conflict between Britain and Germany. On 23 August, Mackenzie King issued a press release that sanctioned military preparations by stating that the government was taking measures to meet any emergency. He was enormously relieved when Cabinet met on 24 August that all the ministers agreed that Canada must participate should war break out.

The armed forces and other government departments took action promptly in response to "precautionary" telegrams from Britain. On 26 August, Brand was able to place Canada's small merchant marine—only about thirty-five ocean-going ships—under naval control at the same moment the Admiralty took control of the vast British merchant marine. In the following days, naval headquarters called out the retired officers needed to establish local harbour defences and naval control of shipping offices at Canada's principal ports, while the commander-in-chief at Bermuda called out those who had been assigned to carry out naval control of shipping duties at American ports.

In the case of the United States, such obviously war-related activity by foreign military personnel could not openly take place on the soil of a sovereign nation that was not a party to the confrontation in Europe. The British officers therefore worked in civilian clothes under the guise of Consular Shipping Advisors (CSAs), attached to the British consular offices at the major ports. One of the chief responsibilities of Brand and his staff all through the war was to maintain close contact with the CSAs in the United States through correspondence and personal visits. Aside from the basic requirement for daily shipping report signals to

Ottawa that were accurate and timely, the naval control service took on an increasing role in ensuring ships were operated on the most efficient schedules and were promptly loaded or unloaded, refuelled, and serviced in North American ports.

German forces invaded Poland on 1 September 1939. Britain and France, honouring their guarantee to Poland, demanded a German withdrawal within forty-eight hours. When, on 3 September, Germany ignored the deadline, Britain and France entered the war. By this time, the Canadian armed services had mobilized their meagre coastal defence forces, and the government authorized them to open fire on German warships or aircraft that showed themselves to be hostile.

The same day, Mackenzie King summoned Parliament back from summer recess as he had promised, and the House of Commons met on 7 September. The government recommended entry into the war. Only four members, three Quebec nationalists and a convinced pacifist, spoke against the measure. On 10 September, Canada declared war on Germany.

The key question for the British Admiralty, like the Canadian navy, was whether Germany would once again risk American intervention, as in 1917, by allowing submarines to attack unarmed merchant ships without warning. The shape of Allied maritime operations hung on the answer to that question. British policy was not to attempt a general convoy system for merchant shipping, as had existed in 1917–18, unless and until an "unrestricted" submarine campaign began. Otherwise, precious resources would be squandered. The efficiency of the merchant ships would be greatly reduced by the delays in port for convoy assembly and passages that could be no faster than the speed of the slowest ship in the convoy. As well, convoy protection required the commitment of vast numbers of warships and aircraft urgently needed for other purposes.

Only hours after Britain's entry into the war, *U-30*, one of the submarines positioned to the northwest of Ireland in the Atlantic shipping approaches to the British Isles, torpedoed and sank without warning the unarmed liner *Athenia*. The U-boat commanders were under orders not to attack unarmed ships, and *U-30* had mistaken *Athenia* for an armed merchant cruiser. The Germans, however, did not admit responsibility or to having made an error. Judging that Germany was bent on unlimited warfare on British commerce, the new first lord of the Admiralty, Winston Churchill, ordered the introduction of convoys for merchant ships. Convoyed merchant vessels were liable to attack without warning under international convention, but it made little practical difference. In the following weeks, Hitler loosened restrictions on the U-boat force to the point where they were free in most circumstances to attack unconvoyed ships without warning in the northeastern Atlantic.[7]

Halifax became the convoy assembly port for ships bound for Britain. Senior British officers had supervised convoy operations at Halifax in the First World War, and Britain now offered help, which the RCN refused with thanks. Commander Richard Oland, a retired RCN officer (and a member of the well-known beer-brewing family), returned to active service and, under Brand's supervision, had matters well in hand. HX 1, the same "homeward from Halifax" designator used for Halifax convoys in 1917–18, sailed on 16 September, and the series continued, initially at intervals of three to five days, until the end of the war. Convoy, more than any other measure, ensured Britain's survival and Allied victory in the Battle of the Atlantic, a struggle that, having begun on the opening day of the war, continued to the very end in May 1945. Brand's organization ensured that, from the beginning of the new conflict, the RCN had a leading part in the convoy system.

The greatest danger of submarine attack was in coastal waters where the concentration of shipping in approaches to ports enabled the enemy most readily to find targets. For the first forty-eight hours (about 740 kilometres) out of Halifax, the convoys were escorted by two of the RCN's destroyers. There was support for the first twenty-four hours by Supermarine Stranraer twin-wing flying boats operated by 5 Squadron

RCAF at the Dartmouth air station. There were only five Stranraers in the squadron, and these were the only modern maritime patrol aircraft in the RCAF's inventory.

The whole convoy schedule was driven by the necessity for the merchant ships to rendezvous with British escorts and aircraft off the British coast where U-boats were active. There was immense pressure on Brand's organization to ensure that ships proceeding to Halifax from the St. Lawrence, U.S. ports, and ports to the south were properly reported, scheduled, and serviced to join the right convoy and that all that information reached the Admiralty promptly and in a clear, standardized format.

Halifax, now the major Allied convoy port as well as naval base in the western part of the vital north Atlantic theatre, had to have priority for the meagre resources available. The story of the naval organizations at the other principal east coast ports (Saint John, New Brunswick; Sydney, Nova Scotia; and Quebec City) was one of improvisation, making do, and doing without. Brand called out retired officers: Commander J.E.W. Oland, of the RCN, for Saint John, Commander Massy Goolden of the Royal Navy for Sydney, and Commander R.L. Jermaine, also of the RN, for Quebec City. They were double-hatted as the naval officers-in-charge and as the naval control service officers at each of the three ports. All lived in British Columbia, and, at the end of August, they flew to Ottawa together in a two-engine Trans-Canada Airlines aircraft. After more than a day of travel, they turned up at Brand's office at lunchtime still half deafened by the roar of the engines. Brand sent them off for lunch and then told them, "I want you to listen carefully to me for an hour and take notes while I try to tell you how to rig up a defended port." As he wrote in his diary, "They did—and then off they went and ... did it without any other guidance."[8] Assisted in each port by staffs of no more than four or five other officers called up from the retired list or the reserves, they rented office space, arranged with the local telephone company for communications, and negotiated access to wharfs on the waterfront. They immediately took over merchant ship reporting duties from the customs officials and began to undertake the important routing function. Ships were required to put into the ports to receive route instructions designed on the basis of the latest intelligence to keep them clear of the suspected enemy activity or hazards to navigation. All the routes given by the Canadian naval control of shipping officers and by the CSAs at U.S. ports were reported to Brand's office in Ottawa, which plotted them on charts to provide a clear picture of Allied shipping movements in the whole Canada–U.S. area.

Defences at the ports were exceedingly limited. At Sydney, the army installed four pairs of coast guns, mostly old and short-ranged, on temporary quick-set concrete pads near the entrance to the harbour. The RCAF's 8 Squadron, a permanent force unit from Ottawa, had flown in five Northrup Delta float planes, a type designed for civil work and without any armament, and set up a temporary base on the Sydney River. The only naval force was a half-dozen RCMP motor craft, the largest thirty-five metres in length and unarmed other than the hand-held weapons of the crews. Virtually the whole of the RCMP marine service had enrolled in the RCNR in the 1930s, and the crews together with their boats were now on active service with the navy. One of them served as the examination vessel, which stopped every incoming merchant ship just outside the entrance of the port to establish its identity and ensure it was not a disguised enemy raider packed with explosives as a floating bomb or with hidden mines and torpedoes with which to destroy ships and piers.

Even with these meagre facilities, Sydney was the only principal naval base other than Halifax on Canada's Atlantic coast. The Cape Breton port was the bastion for the defence of not only the Gulf of St. Lawrence, but also Newfoundland. Feeble as the Canadian resources were, they were more substantial than the British or bankrupt Newfoundland (still a colony separate from Canada) could provide. One of the first missions of the newly arrived 8 Squadron was, on 4 September 1939, to dispatch two of its still-unarmed Northrup Delta float planes on a week-long circumnavigation of the vast island. Admiral Meyrick in Bermuda requested the reconnaissance to ensure that the Germans had not, in anticipation of the outbreak of war with Britain, pre-positioned submarines or surface warships, or vessels to refuel and supply them, in any of Newfoundland's numerous isolated bays. This, of course, was the threat that had so worried the Canadian government during the First World War and again since the mid-1930s.

Vital as the marine industries in the Quebec City area were for the construction and servicing of ships, the danger of naval attack was much less than at Sydney. The local militia units brought the big 7.5-inch coastal gun battery on the south shore of the St. Lawrence into action. It had been installed before the First World War for defence against major warships and was retained largely to reassure the local population, despite the fact it was extremely unlikely that an enemy would risk large surface warships in an attack that would be suicidal in the age of coastal air surveillance. As at Sydney, RCMP motor craft taken up for naval service formed the local force, and one of these served as the examination vessel.

Within weeks of merchant shipping coming under naval control, captains complained about the difficulty of putting into Quebec against the strong river current in order to receive routing instructions. Most shipping originated from Montreal or ports further west, so Brand established a routing office at Montreal. Initially, the office was a sub-unit of the Quebec City organization, but soon it became a full-fledged naval control of shipping unit. Montreal, as the economic hub of eastern Canada, was the location of the head offices of key transportation firms, and the close relations the naval control of shipping staff established with those firms proved critical to efficient shipping operations.

The speed and efficiency with which Canada deployed its paltry resources to implement basic shipping defence measures in lockstep with the British showed the full extent to which the Dominion in 1939 was still a central part of Britain's maritime empire—and crucial to the British war effort. Britain's imports on the eve of the war accounted for nearly 23 percent of all world trade. In the early months of the war, 36 percent of these imports came from North America in ships that sailed from Canadian ports, or came from U.S. ports to join the Halifax convoy, or proceeded independently on the short north Atlantic passage close by Nova Scotia and Newfoundland.[9] This trade, it should be added, was vital to Canada's economy. Britain in 1939 purchased 35 percent of Canadian exports, not much less than the proportion, 41 percent, that went to the United States.[10]

The big challenge for Canada's tiny maritime armed forces in 1939 was to get the resources—bases, warships, aircraft, and tens of thousands of trained people—needed to flesh out the good organization.

In some respects, the air force was in the best position. This was partly the result of that service's top priority in the Mackenzie King government's limited rearmament program and partly the product of the emerging defence partnership with the United States. One of the government's first big initiatives was to dispatch a new aircraft purchasing mission to Washington, which arrived in the American capital on 25 August. So strong was isolationist opinion in the United States that President Franklin Roosevelt had had to accept stringent neutrality legislation passed by Congress. Roosevelt, who had been assistant secretary of the navy in Woodrow Wilson's administration during the First World War, personally believed that the United States could not avoid participation in a new European conflict and was looking for means to support the democratic powers. An indication of the administration's attitude was the U.S. Army's renewed offer to give Canada access to its own production. The sole suitable type under manufacture at the time was Douglas Aircraft's B-18 "Digby" twin-engine bomber. The RCAF ordered twenty, which, with equipment and spare parts, cost nearly $4 million.[11] With a wingspan of 27.3 metres and a loaded weight of 9979 kilograms, the Digby was about the same size as the Supermarine Stranraer flying boat, but the single-wing land plane had better performance. The Digby could make maritime patrols to a distance of about 650 kilometres as compared to 460 kilometres or less for the Stranraer, at a higher cruising speed (275 kilometres per hour in contrast to the Stranraer's 145 kilometres per hour) that allowed it to cover more ocean.

The RCAF mission also inquired about another, newer, twin-engine bomber, Lockheed Aircraft's "Hudson." The American manufacturer had developed the type from its successful fourteen-passenger "Super Electra" airliner for the British Air Ministry, which in 1938 turned to U.S. firms to supplement Britain's overburdened aircraft industry.[12] The Hudson, with a 19.8-metre wingspan and loaded weight of 6500 kilograms, was smaller than the Digby, but, with a cruising speed of 350 kilometres per hour, considerably faster. It could also patrol to a distance of about 650 kilometres, although because of its higher speed it had less endurance, about six hours compared to ten hours or more for the Digby.[13] All Hudson production was tied up by British and Australian orders, but the British agreed to release ten of their Hudsons to Canada.

The Digbys equipped 10 (Bomber Reconnaissance) Squadron, and the Hudsons went to 11 (BR) Squadron, both based at the newly completed airfield at RCAF Station Dartmouth. These, together with 5 Squadron's Stranraers, were Eastern Air Command's main strength until the latter part of 1940, when Canadian-produced Bristol Bolingbroke twin-engine bombers became available. The aircraft re-equipped 8 Squadron, which began to operate from Sydney's recently finished landing field, and 119 Squadron, a new unit at Yarmouth, the third east coast aerodrome included in pre-war planning. The Bolingbroke, however, was inferior to the Hudson. Procurement of additional Hudsons as replacements for the Bolingbrokes became a pressing priority, but could not be achieved until 1942 because of competing Allied demands for U.S. production.

Right from the outbreak of war the RCAF wanted a larger and more capable flying boat than the Stranraer. In the mid-1930s, the U.S. Navy had worked with Consolidated Aircraft to develop the twin-engine PBY, which would become the most successful and widely used flying

boat of the Second World War.[14] It had an enormous single wing, 31.7
metres in length, mounted on a parasol above the fuselage; the top of
the wing was 5.5 metres off the ground when the aircraft was hauled
up on land. With a loaded weight of some 15,000 kilograms, it was
60 percent heavier than the Stranraer and nearly double the weight of
the Hudson. Like the Stranraer, it had a slow cruising speed, about 185
kilometres per hour, but a remarkable endurance of twenty-four hours
and the ability to patrol out to distances of 900 kilometres and more.[15]
The RCAF mission to Washington in August 1939 discovered that the
big flying boats cost nearly twice as much as the Digby and the Hudson,
which may be why Canada did not place orders until the summer of
1940, when the increased danger of major German transatlantic attack
trumped financial concerns.[16] As it turned out, the big flying boats began
to arrive in quantity in late 1941 and 1942, at the same time as the
additional Hudsons; these new aircraft would play a critical role in
supporting the thinly stretched naval forces in the St. Lawrence.

The severe constraints faced by Eastern Air Command, despite its
high priority in 1938–39, were the outcome of unexpected turns in the
course of the war and the Canadian government's adjustment of its
own policies in response to those events. British requests for Canadian
support in the recruitment and training of aircrew, which resulted in the
British Commonwealth Air Training Plan agreement of December 1939,
were on a much vaster scale than the Canadian government had anticipated. Canada's share of the training scheme became greater still when,
with the fall of France in June 1940, Britain's survival depended on air
forces even as she was much less able to meet her obligations under the
air training agreement. Expansion of the training plan and the dispatch
of aircrew overseas became the RCAF's foremost commitment, with the
home coastal commands a distant second in line for resources.

That was the case despite great expansion of Eastern Air Command's
mission. In April–May 1940, German airborne and ship-carried forces
had seized Norway, raising the danger of similar long-range force

projections across the northern Atlantic. Since the British had nothing to spare for the defence of Newfoundland, Canada accepted that responsibility. The most urgent need was for air defence, and 10 Squadron moved from Dartmouth into Newfoundland Airport at Gander. This was only the first element in a new air formation, No. 1 Group with headquarters at St. John's, organized as an integral part of Eastern Air Command. Work began on a new RCAF aerodrome at Torbay just outside St. John's (now St. John's International Airport) to complement the facilities at Gander, and 1 Group had priority for the few new squadrons it was possible to organize in 1941.

For the Royal Canadian Navy, the shift of commitments in 1940–41 away from coastal defence, and particularly the St. Lawrence, was still greater. Expansion of the navy, moreover, posed greater difficulties. Warships take much longer to build than aircraft, and there was no source of supply like that provided by U.S. aircraft manufacturers. It also takes much longer to train ships' crews—a closely integrated team of some seventy personnel in many specializations for the smallest ocean-going vessels—compared to the four to nine men that crewed a multi-engine bomber.

Canada had to build her own naval vessels. Yet Canadian shipbuilding firms, reeling under the effects of the Depression, had never been large or sophisticated and, in contrast to aircraft manufacturers, had not received substantial orders in the rearmament program. The Mackenzie King government had been careful to avoid defence industry co-operation with Britain on the large scale that would have been necessary to kick-start warship construction in Canada, so careful that the naval staff in Ottawa only learned of important new British warship designs for defence against submarines as war broke out.

Events at that same moment—*U-30*'s attack without warning on *Athenia* and the Admiralty's initiation of transatlantic convoys— convinced Admiral Nelles that he must have a large flotilla of coastal patrol vessels, and soon. These had to have anti-submarine armament and be fitted for minesweeping. The main component of minesweeping gear at that time was a large winch with which to tow buoy-mounted cables that cut the mooring lines of mines anchored below the surface of the water; soon the minesweepers would also be fitted with towed devices that harmlessly exploded new German non-contact mines whose triggers were designed to be activated by the magnetic field of steel-hulled ships passing nearby. During the First World War, the Germans had inflicted heavy losses with their excellent sea mines, dropped from disguised merchant vessels and from specially equipped submarines. The big U-boats in 1918 planted minefields in U.S. waters that sank the large cruiser USS *San Diego* and deposited six mines in the southern approaches to Halifax harbour, which fortunately were poorly located and did no damage. In the fall of 1939, the Germans were again mounting a submarine and mining offensive, but much more quickly than in the First World War. Nelles was sure that the St. Lawrence, where the Germans had seemed certain to strike had the First World War continued into 1919, would be an early target. He warned his fellow chiefs of staff and the minister on 17 September that the Admiralty's prompt introduction of convoys to protect merchant shipping in British waters would force the enemy, as in 1918, "to work further afield if he is to cut off the flow of munitions and foodstuffs from Canada and Eastern United States ports to Great Britain."

> We must, therefore, be prepared, in addition to the patrol and mine-sweeping services, to escort all shipping with properly equipped A/S vessels, not only from the Convoy Assembly Ports on our Eastern seaboard to the open sea, but also (1) in the St. Lawrence River below Isle of Orleans to and from the Convoy Assembly Ports, and (2) along our coasts to and from the Eastern United States Ports.
>
>   If this is not done we must expect heavy losses of important shipping and cargoes within sight of our own shores.[17]

One immediate question was this: What kinds of suitable warships could be produced by Canada's underdeveloped shipbuilding industry?

Information about two new British designs, which would become the mainstay of Canada's anti-submarine fleet, reached the naval staff only on 12 September 1939.[18] These were a new minesweeper, later known as the Bangor type, which was also outfitted with anti-submarine armament, and an anti-submarine patrol vessel, later known as the "corvette," which also carried minesweeping gear. The Admiralty had recently adopted both designs in light of experience in the First World War when thousands of auxiliary armed vessels had proven essential, particularly to protect coastal waters against submarine and mine attack. The Bangor, although designed to exacting naval specifications, was simple enough that it could be produced by commercial shipyards like those in Canada. At 55 metres in length, with a displacement of 683 tonnes and a top speed of 30.6 kilometres per hour, it was a third faster and nearly twice the size of the 355-tonne, 40-metre-long trawlers that had been the main strength of the Canadian anti-submarine fleet in 1918.

The corvette was larger still, at 965 tonnes displacement, 62.5 metres in length, and slightly faster with a top speed of 31.5 kilometres per hour. Built to commercial construction standards familiar to Canadian firms, the vessel was originally known as the "whale-hunting" type because it had been adapted by Smith's Dock Company from its whale-hunting vessels. It was an inspired development because the pursuit of whales required high manoeuvrability, an enormous asset in anti-submarine operations. The submarine's electric motors for underwater running had limited capacity, useful mainly for crash dives to escape pursuers; they were most effective when running on the surface with their efficient air-breathing diesel engines. Sad to say, whales and schools of fish were often the target of anti-submarine attacks, as they gave indications much like submarines on asdic, which projected high-frequency sound pulses through the water and picked up echoes from any solid objects.

The Royal Navy had led in the development of asdic, whose first practical designs had been ready shortly after the First World War, and it then became standard equipment in British warships. Canada first obtained asdic in the destroyers it purchased from Britain in the late 1930s and, at the outbreak of war, hastily began to equip its other warships (starting in 1940, Canada became a leading manufacturer of asdic). Great hopes among British and Canadian naval officers that asdic would provide mastery over submerged U-boats, however, would often be disappointed in wartime operations, particularly in the Gulf of St. Lawrence, where the complexity of the water conditions so interfered with the trajectory of sound beams that asdic proved to be nearly blind.

Although the naval staff quickly recognized that the asdic-equipped Bangor and corvette met Canada's needs and could be built by Canadian yards, the finance department insisted that the country could not afford to build more than a handful of the vessels. Finally, in February 1940, Mackenzie King himself insisted that orders should immediately be placed for the maximum number of ships industry could produce, sixty-four corvettes (fifty-four for the RCN and ten for the Royal Navy; the Admiralty placed the order to help stimulate Canadian capacity much needed for the Allied cause) and twenty-eight Bangors. Nelles' warnings were effective. Mackenzie King had, since 1936, repeatedly declared that his government's defence program was designed to meet just the kind of threats that German attacks on Atlantic shipping now suggested were imminent. Nelles, in pressing the program, had again played on the threat to the St. Lawrence:

> At the end of the last war, we had some 125 small craft based on Halifax and Sydney. The smaller number of craft now envisaged will look after Halifax and possibly the secondary convoy port of Sydney, C.B., which will be required next year.
>
> Until adequate naval protection is provided and depending on the action of the enemy, the defence of shipping in the St. Lawrence simply cannot be coped with, a situation I feel certain the Government would not wish to countenance.
>
> Such a situation might easily result in all overseas trade from the East Coast of Canada being routed by rail through Halifax, a most uneconomical procedure.[19]

Because it would take at least a year to complete the first of the new coastal defence vessels, the navy was forced to use the same desperate measures as in 1915–17 to obtain additional craft. Over the winter of 1939–40, patriotic yachtsmen, organized by the naval staff and the Department of External Affairs, travelled to the United States and purchased fourteen large pleasure craft.

Soon after the building program got underway, the navy's role was transformed by the swift German victories in France in May 1940. By the end of that month, four of Canada's destroyers—all the ones ready for extended service—had crossed the Atlantic in response to the Admiralty's pleas for help in the defence of the British Isles. At the same time, the RCAF's only fully equipped fighter squadron hurried overseas to assist in the defence of Britain against German bombing attacks. The Mackenzie King government accepted the advice of the chiefs of staff that Britain was Canada's first line of defence. If Britain resisted invasion and the Royal Navy remained an effective fighting force, then Germany could not mount major transatlantic attacks; the increased risk of hit-and-run raids in Canadian waters and on Canada's coasts as a result of the dispatch of defence forces overseas would have to be accepted.

For the Roosevelt administration in the United States, Canada now became the key element in hemispheric security, for assistance to Canada for its home defences would allow the Mackenzie King government to continue to send Canadian forces to Britain. On 17–18 August 1940, Mackenzie King and Roosevelt met in Ogdensburg, New York, immediately across the international border south of Ottawa, to establish the Canada–U.S. Permanent Joint Board on Defence. The board comprised senior officers of each of the armed services of the two nations, together with civilian officials. Their first order of business was to build up naval, air, and army base facilities in Newfoundland and Canada's maritime provinces so that large reinforcements from the United States could quickly help in the event of a major German attack.

One of the early results of the board's work was the dispatch of U.S. coast artillery armament that the Canadian Army installed in concrete fortifications at Shelburne, Nova Scotia, at Gaspé, and at St. John's and Botwood, the port on the north shore of Newfoundland that serviced the airport at Gander. These were strategically placed harbours that the RCN and RCAF intended to develop as bases for coastal defence forces, but in the summer of 1940 they had a more immediate importance as potential fleet anchorages for major U.S. warships. In the event of Britain's collapse, the fortified anchorages would also be available as refuges that could readily accommodate the largest vessels of the Royal Navy.

Expansion of the Canadian war effort and unfortunate chance brought changes in the defence portfolio in the Cabinet during the spring and summer of 1940. Since September 1939, the minister of national defence had been Norman Rogers, formerly minister of labour and a more capable administrator than Ian Mackenzie, whom Rogers replaced. The enormous scope of the British Commonwealth Air Training Plan resulted in the creation of a new portfolio, minister of national defence for air, in May 1940. The appointment went to Charles G. Power, previously postmaster general, an undemanding portfolio that had allowed him to focus his energy on political organization in Quebec and to assist with wide-ranging aspects of the war effort. Power was from a prominent Irish family from the Quebec City area, but he was fluently bilingual and had done his law degree in French at Laval University. In at least one important respect, Power served as a French-Canadian representative in the Cabinet. He had entered politics by running for the federal Quebec City seat formerly held by his father, also a Liberal, during the 1917 election as a loyalist to Wilfrid Laurier and opponent of overseas conscription. Power had been released from the military after being severely injured in September 1916 while serving in the front-line infantry; he had won the Military Cross for courage on the battlefield.[20] Power had a special interest in the defence of the

St. Lawrence, both as the minister responsible for the air force and a representative of Quebec City.

On 10 June 1940, when Rogers was killed in an air crash, Power became acting minister of national defence until James Layton Ralston took over the portfolio in July. Ralston, who had previously served as defence minister under Mackenzie King in 1926–30, had been intimately involved in the details of military mobilization as minister of finance in 1939–40. He was perhaps the most distinguished and decorated veteran in the Cabinet, having commanded the 85th Battalion from his native Nova Scotia during the First World War. Ralston made the army his main focus, and in July 1940 the government created yet another new portfolio, minister of national defence for naval services. This appointment went to Angus L. Macdonald, who had been Liberal premier of Nova Scotia since 1934. Mackenzie King lured him to Ottawa by recalling Macdonald's earlier pledge to come and help in any way he could with the war effort. Macdonald, at this stage, fully supported Mackenzie King's war policy, which emphasized industrial production and limiting the numbers of military personnel sent overseas, but that would change. Indeed, from the very outset Macdonald was not comfortable in Ottawa: he chafed under Mackenzie King's dominating leadership and, while willing to rely on the professional advice of the naval staff, soon questioned their tendency to mimic the Royal Navy in outlook and attitudes. Like the other ministers, Macdonald was a veteran of the Canadian Corps of the First World War. He had also served as an infantry officer at the front during the blood-drenched Hundred Days offensive in the summer and fall of 1918 and been badly wounded in the last days of the war.[21]

The Royal Air Force defeated the German bombing campaign that reached its peak in September 1940, but there was a danger Britain might yet be starved into submission. U-boats, which had begun to operate from French ports right on Britain's doorstep, destroyed 174 merchant vessels in the five months from June to October 1940, nearly double the ninety-seven sunk during the preceding five months.[22] Most of the heavy losses in the summer and fall—called the "happy time" by the U-boat crews—were from the transatlantic trade upon which Britain was utterly dependent for survival now that the whole of north-west Europe was occupied by the enemy. The British gathered additional shipping into convoys and, in July 1940, diverted them as far as possible from the new enemy bases in France. In an enormous logistical effort, ocean shipping shifted from the routes south of Ireland and the great ports in the southern part of the country to routes north of Ireland, with Liverpool becoming the main Atlantic port. This concentration of traffic to the north of Ireland allowed Coastal Command and the navy in turn to concentrate their thinly stretched anti-submarine forces in this one area to drive the U-boats back from the inshore waters and port approaches where it was easiest to find shipping.

Admiral Karl Dönitz, commander of the U-boat force, responded with tactics for coordinated attacks by groups of submarines—"wolf packs"—that he, as a young submarine commander, had begun to develop at the end of the First World War. He stationed several U-boats at maximum visibility distance from each other in a line or checkerboard pattern in the offshore areas where intelligence indicated major ocean convoys were likely to be routed. The first U-boat to sight the convoy radioed a report to headquarters, and then shadowed the convoy. The shadower would pass periodic reports to headquarters, which in turn sent the information to all the other U-boats in the area so that they could close to shadowing distance. After nightfall, all the submarines in the group attacked at once, remaining on the surface to use the speed—some thirty-three kilometres per hour—and manoeuvrability of their powerful diesel engines to fire torpedoes at multiple targets. They often closed from ahead of the convoy to combine their speed with that of the convoy. They raced between the columns of ships at fifty kilometres per hour or more, giving the escorts and defensive armament on the merchant ships no time to respond. If at all possible, the U-boats attacked in either moonless conditions or when the moon was behind the convoy so as to backlight the ships while the submarines were obscured in shadow. Effective as group tactics could be, the pursuit of a convoy required very large resources in what was a risky operation because of the presence of escorts. Dönitz's goal was to disrupt Allied seaborne supplies by sinking as many ships as possible with the least submarine losses. The ideal was to set U-boats loose on individual hunting missions in coastal waters where merchant ships sailed independently and could be readily located; each submarine could destroy two or three merchant vessels a day.

One of the key determinants in the vulnerability of a ship or convoy was its speed. Ships faster than twenty-eight kilometres per hour were generally not put in convoy because their speed matched or bettered a U-boat's best surfaced speed and thus could outrun the pursuer. HX convoys were reserved for ships that could make seventeen kilometres per hour or better, but less than twenty-eight kilometres per hour. Ships capable of less than seventeen kilometres per hour should in theory have been kept well clear of the main U-boat operating areas in the north Atlantic because the vessels' slowness allowed the submarines ample time to pursue and manoeuvre for an accurate torpedo shot, with possibilities of a second or even third try.

In the wake of the fall of France, however, Britain did not have the luxury of keeping slow ships away from dangerous waters. The nearest sources of essential bulky goods, such as timber, mineral ores, and grain, normally available on short hauls from the European continent, were now in North America. Thus every ship capable of the transatlantic voyage, including old and slow ships, had to be pressed into service. On 15 August 1940, SC 1, the first slow convoy, with forty merchant ships, sailed from Sydney as slow convoys had done during the First World War. Many of the bulk cargoes originated on the Great Lakes or in the St. Lawrence River and gulf, which made Sydney convenient and efficient for assembly. In theory, the slow convoys were open only to ships that could make at least thirteen kilometres per hour, but, in practice, ships still slower had to be accepted.

Nelles was in fact more than half right in his prediction of September 1939 that strengthened defences in British waters would bring the U-boats to search for unprotected shipping off Canada, as in 1918. That is what the German naval staff wanted to do in the spring of 1940, but Hitler would not allow it. An attack so close to the United States might bring war with that power, a risk that he did not wish to run for the time being.

Although operations against convoys inflicted far fewer losses than suffered by shipping that sailed independently, the successes achieved by Dönitz's wolf-pack tactics imperilled Britain. Britain's survival depended upon merchant vessels large enough to cross the Atlantic, and these were precisely the valuable vessels that were being lost in convoy. There was, moreover, no alternative to convoy for supply of the British Isles. Should the enemy achieve sustained successes that made convoy impractical, Britain's surrender would only be a matter of time.

The central issue in the Allied war effort in the fall of 1940 and the winter of 1941 became reinforcement of the anti-submarine escorts in the northwest approaches to the British Isles. So few were available that escorts would accompany an outbound convoy for only the first two days, and then break off to pick up an inbound convoy. Some of the worst losses in the fall of 1940 were suffered when the U-boats intercepted convoys before the anti-submarine escort was able to join them. At a time when there were as few as twenty-five escorts in the northwest approaches, Canada's four destroyers were an important augmentation.

It was the desperate situation at sea that led British prime minister Winston Churchill to redouble his attempts to draw the United States into the war. An early success was the "destroyers for bases" agreement of September 1940. Britain gave the United States ninety-nine-year leases on large sites for naval and air bases in Newfoundland,

Bermuda, and the British West Indies, and the United States Navy turned over to the Royal Navy fifty old destroyers, built at the end of the First World War.

Such were the strains on the Royal Navy for manpower that Canada, at the Admiralty's urgent request, took over six of the old U.S. destroyers and later a seventh. Mackenzie King and his colleagues initially hoped that these would be used on Canada's coasts to replace the River-class vessels engaged in the northwestern approaches. Nevertheless, and in a striking example of Canada's response to the crisis in Europe, the politicians accepted the naval staff's advice that the best four of the ex–U.S. destroyers should also go to the northwestern approaches. These additional Canadian ships arrived in January 1941. By that time, the first ten Canadian-built corvettes had been completed and were arriving in Britain. These ten vessels had been constructed on contract for the Royal Navy, but again the Admiralty asked Canada to provide crews, and again the RCN did so, expanding the Canadian escort force overseas to eighteen vessels.

The winter of 1940 and the spring of 1941 saw a continual push to the west of the battle for the convoys as the British and the Canadians tried to prevent German attacks in the mid-Atlantic. The British developed escort and air bases at Londonderry in Northern Ireland and in Iceland, which they had occupied after the Nazis invaded Denmark, and the new corvettes, including those from Canada, were among the craft pressed into ocean escort service. Although the vessels had been designed for coastal defence, the rounded hulls of their "whale-hunting" design rode on top of heavy seas, rather than cutting into the swell as finer hulls would do. They could navigate in extreme ocean conditions, even if the up-and-down bobbing and corkscrewing of the buoyant hulls convinced many of their seasick crews that death would be a welcome respite. The main tactical weakness of the corvettes was their speed, which was no better than that of a surfaced U-boat. For that reason, destroyers, although woefully short in number, were vital, for they had the high speed—as much as fifty-five kilometres per hour—needed to sweep out and attack shadowing U-boats.

Experience showed that the escort group for each convoy should include at least twelve warships, enough to ring the merchant ships so that there would be a full screen of coverage by electronic search devices that at that time had a range of, at most, a few thousand metres. These devices included asdic, which, as we have seen, projected sound beams down into the water to detect submerged targets, and radar, which projected radio emissions over the water to detect surfaced U-boats at night. The first radar sets, adapted in the fall of 1940 from a compact type developed for aircraft, worked on a wavelength of about 1.5 metres. It was not an entirely successful adaptation for anti-submarine work. When the sets were operated close to the water, as on the masts of escort vessels, waves on the ocean's surface absorbed much of the equipment's broad beam and masked the narrow hull of a U-boat. Still, the equipment was a godsend in plotting the position of the many ships in close quarters of a convoy in thick weather and at night. Through an emergency program in which industry applied radically new electronics engineering developed by university researchers, the Admiralty introduced short-wave radar in the spring of 1941. Type 271 operated on a wavelength of ten centimetres, which produced a fine search beam that could detect a submarine's narrow conning tower and low hull in most sea conditions.

Experience also showed the essential role of training. Crews of individual ships had to be able to carry out their duties instinctively if the escort was to maintain its correct position in the screen, keep a constant lookout over its entire sector, and be ready for instant action. Groups of ships had to be well-practised teams that could with a minimum of communication make a coordinated response to lightning-fast surprise attacks at night, whose main feature was chaotic confusion as merchant ships suddenly erupted in flames in different parts of the convoy and others fell out of formation to evade the enemy or rescue comrades.

Canada was ready to expand its force already committed to the northwestern approaches with the new corvettes that were beginning to come from the shipyards, but faced a daunting challenge in training the crews. The unexpected need to man the seven ex–U.S. destroyers and the ten corvettes built for Britain took up over 1500 of the most experienced personnel. The expansion of the shore bases and particularly training establishments—over 300 new personnel were entering the training system every week—had first draw on the remaining members with naval experience, essential for instructional positions and the senior staff positions. Crewing of the new ships therefore depended on the RCNVR, whose recruits usually had no previous marine experience. For many of the newly built warships, the only experienced office available was often the captain, a member of the RCNR—a merchant marine officer in civilian life—whose knowledge of naval operations relied on courses and some service in small coastal or harbour defence vessels. The personnel in the new ships therefore had to have some chance to become acclimatized to the alien environment of a warship at sea and to apply the technical skills learned in compressed courses before they could begin to operate as a team and the ship was efficient enough to make essential training in group manoeuvres worthwhile.

Starting in March 1941, the first ten corvettes ordered for the RCN received nine weeks of sea exercises at Halifax, including invaluable experience tracking a friendly submarine. They then began escorting the transatlantic convoys that departed from Halifax during their first two or three days of passage and mounting anti-submarine patrols in the port approaches. Only after they had gained some experience in these basic tasks, with ready access to support from the training and repair facilities at Halifax, would they be assigned to open ocean operations. This well-conceived program did not last through even the first cycle because of the urgent need for additional escorts in the rapidly expanding Atlantic war.

As the British reinforced the escorts in the northwestern approaches and extended anti-submarine protection for convoys further into the central Atlantic, the U-boats also moved westward to attack where the escorts for the convoys were weakest. More U-boats were needed for these distant operations, and they were available because additional submarines were now completing their own rigorous six-month "working up" training. From a low point of about twenty operational submarines in the winter of 1940–41, the fleet expanded to forty by May and eighty-five by the end of the year.[23]

By mid-April 1941, Britain's Western Approaches command, headquartered at Liverpool, had extended anti-submarine escort out to thirty-five degrees west, some 1100 kilometres west of Reykjavik, Iceland, but at a cost. Instead of twelve escorts per convoy, of which half were destroyers or other fast types, there were eight escorts, of which only two or three were destroyers. Even so, this considerable extension of escort to the west soon proved inadequate. On the night of 19–20 May, a U-boat group attacked HX 126 at forty degrees fifty-five minutes west, halfway between Reykjavik and St. John's and nearly 200 kilometres before the escort from Iceland joined. Over the next forty-eight hours, the U-boats destroyed nine ships in the convoy, five before escorts could reach the scene.

The Admiralty decided that continuous anti-submarine escort across the north Atlantic could no longer be delayed, much as that would strain the available forces. Immediately, the Admiralty created the Newfoundland Escort Force (NEF), based at St. John's, which would escort eastbound convoys to the vicinity of Iceland, refuel, and then bring westbound convoys back to the vicinity of St. John's. Previously, the convoys outward bound from the United Kingdom had dispersed in mid-ocean after their escort departed, with each of the merchant vessels making its own way to its destination. With the extension of the westbound convoys all the way to Newfoundland waters, they were designated "ON" (Outward-bound North); the convoys in the series alternated between fast and slow to accommodate the return passage of ships that had come to the United Kingdom in HX and SC convoys.

The Newfoundland-based force was intended to have sixty-three escorts, and the RCN agreed to provide about half of this strength by redeploying its eighteen ships from overseas and committing newly built corvettes. The Admiralty in turn agreed that a Canadian officer, Commodore L.W. Murray, RCN, would command the new force, and he arrived at St. John's early in June, by which time escorts were already beginning the long haul between St. John's and Iceland.

Arrangements never stabilized. The strength of the force was never much greater than fifty escorts because some of the more capable British ships initially assigned had to be redeployed to meet the movement of Dönitz's expanding U-boat force into new areas off Gibraltar and West Africa. Many of the destroyers that remained were the old ex–U.S. vessels, which had not been designed for the hard running across the north Atlantic and were prone to breakdown. Thus the stable escort-group organization that proved so vital in developing teamwork and coordinated tactics east of Iceland never existed west of it; ships were hurled into the breach at the last minute, and frequently they were newly arrived Canadian corvettes that had little chance for higher-level training or even enough time in port to correct builders' defects. The Canadian warships had already begun to fall behind their British counterparts in improvements to design and in the fitting of new equipment, such as radar. Because much of the work in upgrading the British escorts was the product of emergency programs and British industrial resources were strained to the limit, there were few sets available for Canadian ships, and there were not even the design specifications that would allow production in Canada.

The war was transformed on 22 June 1941 when German forces invaded the Soviet Union in defiance of the non-aggression pact concluded by the two powers in August 1939. Hitler's hope was to repeat the kind of lightning victory he had achieved against France, while the navy cut off Britain from the United States and Canada (since the German victories in Europe in the spring of 1940, North America had become the source of more than 50 percent of British imports). Thus weakened, Britain would be exposed to easy conquest when victorious German forces returned from the Soviet Union.[24] The Soviets suffered fearsome losses but held the German invaders just short of Moscow in December 1941. The Roosevelt administration, meanwhile, extended further assistance to ensure Britain's survival, despite the continued strength of isolationist opinion in the United States.

In July 1941, American forces relieved the British garrison in Iceland, a move that the president argued was essential to strengthen the defence of the western hemisphere. Roosevelt then used the necessity of protecting supplies dispatched to the American forces in Iceland as a political cover to relieve the strained Royal Navy of convoy protection in the western Atlantic.

The intention of the British Admiralty and the U.S. Navy Department was that the RCN should also be relieved from the Newfoundland–Iceland run so that it could once more send Canadian warships to the eastern Atlantic to help the British forces. Under the new arrangements, command of all escort operations west of Iceland came under Admiral Ernest J. King, commander-in-chief of the U.S. Atlantic Fleet. King, a fiery nationalist and a consummate professional who did not want to compromise the effectiveness of his forces by overextending them, decided to take responsibility for only the fast HX convoys and the return fast ON convoys. He asked the RCN to maintain its part of the Newfoundland Escort Force and escort the slow SC series and the return slow ON convoys, tasks that proved much larger and more difficult than anyone anticipated.

Only in the 1980s, when the British government released "ultra top-secret" intelligence files, did we learn that gaps in this vital information about German submarine operations occurred just when Canada took responsibility for the vulnerable slow convoy. During the spring of 1941, the Royal Navy had captured coding material from German warships that finally enabled British cryptographers to break into German U-boat radio traffic. This was the most challenging of the German military radio services to decrypt because of the rigorous discipline of the navy in employment of the Enigma encryption machines. The capture of the change lists for the machine settings gave British intelligence nearly instant access in June through August 1941, which largely accounts for the success of the early operations of the Newfoundland Escort Force: the Admiralty was able to route convoys clear of U-boat concentrations. By early September, though, British intelligence had to solve new changes in the settings, something which often resulted in blackouts for up to forty-eight hours.

It was during such a blackout, and as a direct result of it, that SC 42, a large slow convoy of some sixty-five merchant vessels, sailed directly into a group of twelve U-boats off the southwest coast of Greenland on 9 September 1941. The escort was a small Canadian group of one destroyer and three corvettes, and the only reinforcement available as the attack began was two additional corvettes, *Chambly* and *Moose Jaw*, the latter on its first ocean trip, in storm conditions that incapacitated much of the crew with seasickness. Although the group did better than should have been expected, damaging one U-boat and destroying another, the convoy lost fourteen vessels before it came within reach of British aircraft and escorts from Iceland on 11 September.

The Americans, who were just coming into action, had their hands full with the fast convoys, and the British had few warships to send (and even these few were delayed by essential repairs). Reinforcement of the escorts for the slow convoys could therefore only be achieved by Canada pushing newly built corvettes into action without full work-ups training or proper refits to complete their equipment and repair any but the most serious building defects. So thinly were Allied escort forces stretched that it was a question of Canada's raw, ill-equipped corvettes or nothing at all. There was no choice but to commit these ships. As a result of the gaps in Ultra intelligence and the burgeoning strength of the U-boat groups that made them more difficult to avoid, three more slow convoys with their insufficient escorts came under heavy attack in the fall of 1941.

The last of these attacks, against SC 52 on 1–3 November 1941, brought the enemy right to Canada's doorstep. With his growing fleet, Dönitz was able to make a stronger sweep towards Newfoundland than in the spring. He was always interested in the Strait of Belle Isle, the northern entrance to the Gulf of St. Lawrence, through which he knew that the Allies sailed ocean convoys to save about a day's sailing on the run to Iceland. The constricted straits, 125 kilometres in length and in most places less than 20 kilometres in width, could be kept under close surveillance and offered a good opportunity for ambush. Starting on 20 October, four U-boats took station within 200 kilometres north of the straits to watch for traffic, but they found only empty waters and patrolling U.S. and Canadian aircraft from Newfoundland. Because the fall storms and heavy fogs made the straits hazardous for navigation, the Allies had ceased to use the northern route over a week before the U-boats arrived. The U-boats' misfortune was only temporary.

SC 52 came from Sydney on the southern route and was picked up by a fifth submarine, U-374, on a lone patrol within a hundred kilometres of St. John's. The four U-boats off the Strait of Belle Isle had already begun to close with the convoy; also homing on the convoy were sixteen more U-boats that had been stationed in a large arc 550 to 750 kilometres off St. John's. When, late on 2 November while the convoy was still off the coast of Newfoundland, those gathering submarines sank two merchant ships, the Admiralty and the U.S. Navy Department concluded that the situation was hopeless. Current Ultra intelligence was not available, but there were indications of many submarines in the Newfoundland area, and their success in concentrating against the convoy at the very outset of its slow fourteen-day Atlantic crossing spelled disaster.

The U.S. Navy Department, with the Admiralty's full agreement, turned back the convoy. The U.S. convoy authorities ordered SC 52, then heading northeast off Newfoundland, to change course to the northwest to the Strait of Belle Isle and then slip south through the strait and back to Sydney. This was the quickest escape route from the enemy. On 3 November, as the convoy approached the strait in heavy fog, one of the pursuing U-boats sank two more ships. The escort commander, in the British destroyer HMS *Broadway*, concluded that he could not mount an organized defence in the fog and ordered the merchant ships to scatter, making their own way through the strait. In those difficult waters and difficult weather conditions, two ships ran aground and became total losses; one came to grief on the coast outside the strait, but the second, SS *Empire Energy*, struck inside the entrance. Because it was a marine accident and not the result of enemy fire, the ship has never been included among the German successes in the gulf, but her loss was in fact the first German victory in the St. Lawrence.

Fortunately the disaster was not immediately repeated. Continued bad weather and fresh breaks into German Enigma radio traffic kept the remaining convoys free from attack.

By the time of the SC 52 battle, Commodore Murray and his staff concluded that the Newfoundland Escort Force could no longer sustain the constant emergency efforts required to provide every slow convoy with eight escorts, the number experience showed was the bare minimum that had any hope of mounting an effective defence. Because the slow convoys were at sea for 30 percent—sometimes 50 percent or more— longer than the fast convoys, they were more prone not just to enemy attack, but delay and damage by the fall storms. Canadian ships were at sea fully twice as much as their British and American counterparts, with much less time in port to rest the crews, undertake training, and refit storm-tossed ships that in many cases had never had a chance for proper correction of builders' defects and which in all cases had never been fitted with the latest equipment.

In the case of radar, the National Research Council of Canada had done excellent work in quickly developing and arranging production of its own version of 1.5-metre radar for escorts to relieve pressure on Britain's overstretched industry. "Quickly," however, was not fast enough in the rapidly developing Atlantic war. When fitting of the long-wave radar in Canadian ships began in late 1941, many of the British escorts had already been upgraded to the much more effective ten-centimetre type 271. Most of the British corvettes had also been fitted with gyroscopic compasses, whose accuracy and precision were essential for the close manoeuvres of convoy work. Until 1943, most of the original sixty-four Canadian corvettes still had magnetic compasses whose wandering needles could indicate direction only to the level of the ancient sixty-four points of the compass as compared to the gyroscopic equipment which gave direction down to individual degrees in the 360-degree circle.

The British and the Americans, who worried about the Canadians and admitted they were carrying an unduly large share of the burden, were ready to revise the routes and reduce the strength of groups to allow Murray some breathing room. Yet within weeks, the expectation that the easing of the burden on the north Atlantic run would allow the RCN some space in early 1942 to improve its training and equipment was dashed. The pressures on the Canadian navy, far from lessening, multiplied. The need to get new escorts to sea as quickly as possible and drive the existing fleet on unrelenting schedules did not let up a whit. For that reason, the ships that could be cobbled together for the defence of the Gulf of St. Lawrence when the ice cleared and navigation opened in the spring of 1942 suffered from all the problems that had dogged the Newfoundland force: poor or missing equipment, inadequate training, and the impossibility of forming stable groups capable of coordinated action.

The new reality, improbable as it had seemed less than a year before, was that the RCN had become essential for the defence of the western Alliance's Atlantic shipping. Britain's survival depended on that shipping and the capacity of the western Allies to eventually strike back at the Axis. Modest as the Canadian warships were, they now filled a yawning gap in the arsenal of the western Allies. In these circumstances, the defence of the Gulf of St. Lawrence slid from the top of the RCN's priorities to near the bottom.

THREE

U–Boats Offshore, January–April 1942

One of the curiosities of the Second World War is that events in the Pacific Ocean, a third of the world away from Nova Scotia, brought the U-boat war to Canada's Atlantic seaboard. On 7 December 1941, the Japanese navy's aircraft carrier force made a devastating surprise attack on the U.S. Pacific Fleet at Pearl Harbor in the Hawaiian Islands. Hitler promptly declared war on the United States, even though he had no forewarning and was not obliged to do so under the Axis pact between Germany and Japan.

Admiral Dönitz seized the opportunity to turn his forces loose for a free-for-all hunt by individual U-boats amongst undefended shipping in North American waters. His original intention was to concentrate on the U.S. coast using big type IX long-range U-boats. These had been developed during the late 1930s especially for distant operations. The type IXC version available in early 1942 was seventy-seven metres in length, displaced 1232 tonnes when submerged, and had a range of 20,000 kilometres at a surface cruising speed of twenty-two kilometres per hour. It could achieve a top speed when surfaced of thirty-three kilometres per hour. There was a crew of forty-eight, and the main armament was four torpedo tubes in the bow and two in the stern, for which the boat carried a total of twenty-two torpedoes. These were enormous weapons, fifty-three centimetres in diameter, over seven metres in length, and weighing more than 1500 kilograms, of which 280 kilograms was the explosive charge in the warhead. The torpedo's on-board motor drove it through the water at a speed of seventy kilometres per hour; the range was seven~~.~~ kilometres, although in practice, with the fire control systems available in the early 1940s, it was best to shoot at a tiny fraction of that range, 2000 metres or less, if there was to be any good chance of hitting a moving vessel.[1]

Only five of the long-range type IXs were immediately available for operations, however. Thus the main weight of the initial assaults actually fell in the Canadian area, with two of the big type IX boats off Nova Scotia and twelve of the smaller type VIIs in the waters around southeastern Newfoundland, the limit of their estimated range. The type VII, the "medium" submarine that formed the largest part of the Second World War U-boat fleet, had also been developed in the late 1930s, with a premium on manoeuvrability and fast diving to ensure its effectiveness in the face of the main weight of enemy forces in European waters. The type VIIC that predominated in early 1942 had a length of 67.1 metres, displaced 865 tonnes when submerged, and carried fourteen torpedoes. Its range was only a bit more than half of that of the type IX, although in the transatlantic operations that got underway early in 1942 the crews would extend this limit by practising strict fuel economy.

The types VII and IX were the main types used by the German navy until the war's end. They were traditional submarines in the sense that they were most effective when running on their powerful diesel engines at speed on the surface. The limited performance of their electrical engines meant they were much slower underwater and could move at little better than a crawl for a period of more than a very few hours if they were not to deplete their batteries rapidly. Delays in the development of submarines that could move more quickly underwater were ultimately prolonged by Allied bombing operations against German shipyards and fabrication plants, so that the first type XXI and XXIII submarines designed for underwater speed just entered operations in the spring of 1945 as the war ended.

The northernmost of the type IX boats in the assault in January 1942 was *U-130*. This was the first war cruise for the submarine and the first combat mission in command for her commanding officer, Korvettenkapitän Ernst Kals. Kals, however, was one of the older U-boat commanders (36). Service, in cramped, physically stressful conditions, was a young man's game, and the U-boat arm was a young service, having been reborn only in the mid-1930s when Hitler threw off the restrictions of the 1919 Versailles Treaty that forbade submarines to the German navy. Kals had joined the navy in 1924 and had had a wide range of professional experience before entering the U-boat service in October 1940. He was extraordinarily aggressive. In December 1941, *U-130* was transiting from Germany to her operational base in France, a non-combat cruise, when she encountered convoy SC 57 off southern England; Kals attacked and sank three merchant vessels.[2]

Kals arrived off Sydney, his assigned attack area, on the morning of 12 January 1942. He never passed through the Cabot Strait, the waters between Cape Breton's Cape North and Newfoundland's Cape Ray, and thus technically did not penetrate the Gulf of St. Lawrence, but his presence, like that of the U-boats that had hovered off the Strait of Belle Isle two months earlier, showed German awareness of the important traffic that sailed from the St. Lawrence ports. As it was, Kals drew blood just outside the strait, a further indication that the enemy was drawing ever closer to Canadian territorial waters.

From first light on 12 January, *U-130* hovered less than forty kilometres off the Sydney headlands, patrolling back and forth on a north–south line so he could pick up any sign of a convoy departing.[3] Shortly before noon, the bridge lookout was surprised as a fast twin-engine landplane swept into view only about 6000 metres away. This was a Bristol Bolingbroke, piloted by Flight Sergeant R.L. Parker of 119 Squadron. The unit had just arrived from Yarmouth to replace 8 Squadron, which had departed to reinforce the west coast defences in case the Japanese followed up their success at Pearl Harbor by raiding the North American seaboard. Parker and his crew were making a routine patrol in the port approaches, one of the first by 119 Squadron aircraft since their arrival at Sydney, and were startled to see the conning tower of a submarine so close to the port. They were patrolling at an altitude of 213 metres and dropped to 76 metres to release two 113-kilogram anti-submarine bombs, an altitude that operational research would in the coming months show to be too high for the accuracy required to attack the tough, narrow hull of a U-boat. The U-boat crash-dived a full minute before the bombs fell, ample time to get to a depth safely removed from the explosion near the surface.

Even so, Kals was shaken, and his instincts for caution were reinforced by the subsequent appearance of additional aircraft from Sydney. The need to run submerged to escape the aircraft left little chance of accomplishing anything, so late that afternoon Kals pulled off to the southeast, into the route between Halifax and Cape Race. As night fell, he sighted the Norwegian freighter *Frisko* carrying supplies from Savannah, Georgia, to the U.S. Navy's base at Argentia, Newfoundland. The first torpedo hit had no noticeable effect, although the ship began to send radio distress calls. The torpedo had in fact, according to the ship's crew, "caused a large hole below water line. The explosion killed the lookout Seaman ([Herman] Urnheim). All hands were ordered aft to lifeboats, the Captain and Chief Officer going to Bridge and Second Mate (radio operator) to send S.O.S. Five minutes later 2nd torpedo struck amidships ... killing Captain, Chief Officer and Second Mate, and also set fire to ship."[4] Kals, now only 430 metres away, saw the fire break out as the crew boarded two boats. The fire spread rapidly: "the entire ship is brightly burning." An hour later, Kals reported, the flames were still visible. Kals thought he had hit a tanker; in fact, *Frisko* was carrying a load of lumber, which accounts for the fire.

Kals continued to the southeast, and about eight hours later, early on 13 January, he sighted the Panama-registered *Friar Rock*. She had sailed late from Sydney, on 10 January, and was attempting to catch up with SC 64, which had sailed on the ninth. Although the ship continued to manoeuvre after the first torpedo hit and dodged a second shot, it succumbed when Kals was able to deliver a final torpedo at short range nearly an hour after his first attack. The ship appears not to have dispatched a distress signal.

In fact, no word of *U-130*'s attacks had got out, for *Frisko*'s distress signals had not been heard ashore. News of *Frisko*'s loss—and hence intelligence about *U-130*'s whereabouts—did not get out until the afternoon of 14 January when the Danish schooner *Mjoaes* picked up the six survivors in one of the lifeboats. The second, in which there had been nine crewmen and which had separated from the first boat shortly after the sinking, was never found. Word of *Friar Rock*'s fate took still longer to reach the outside world. Perhaps the most fortunate among her people were those in one boat that capsized shortly after the sinking; they would not have suffered for more than few minutes before hypothermia numbed their senses. The second boat was finally sighted by the British destroyer HMS *Montgomery* on 17 January, four days after the attack. There were twelve frozen corpses; seven other occupants were still alive though most of them were unconscious. As a member of *Montgomery*'s crew later recalled, "One poor fellow ... was naked from the waist down and although still alive was coal black with frostbite, ice even covering his legs and lower abdomen." The half-naked man never regained consciousness and died in hospital in Halifax.[5]

On 15 January, Kals returned to the Sydney approaches and that night proceeded again to within forty kilometres of the entrance to the port. He noted that the "city is brightly lit"; this was at least in part because of the large steel mills there. He was startled by the sudden exposure of "several very powerful search lights" that "illuminate the entire shipping route offshore." These were big lights, 152 centimetres in diameter and with 800-million candle power, mounted in concrete emplacements at the harbour mouth and operated by the coastal artillery garrison of the port. Kals saw a merchant ship scuttling along very close to shore and guessed that the waters further off shore might be mined, which would account for the dearth of shipping out in the approaches to the port. In fact SC 64's sailing on 9 January had been the last from Sydney, whose harbour was already beginning to fill with floating ice. The limited traffic that remained for the most part used Louisbourg, around the Atlantic shore of Cape Breton.

On the evening of 17 January, Kals sighted a merchant ship about fifty-five kilometres northeast of Sydney. He tracked the vessel for nearly two-and-a-half hours and made two torpedo attacks, each of two torpedoes, all of which missed mainly because the ship was fast. The vessel moved at twenty-eight kilometres per hour, close to the U-boat's own best speed in the difficult sea conditions, which made it a challenge for Kals to get within range and complicated fire control because of the increasingly rapid rate of change in the relative position of the two vessels when the submarine did close. Kals had other problems that night. In making speed on the surface, *U-130* took a lot of seawater across the upper decks which began to freeze into a "thick coat." Indeed he was convinced that the merchant vessel saw the glint of the ice, despite the darkness, and was therefore able to evade his second attack. As he manoeuvred for a third attack, he suddenly saw what he thought was an American destroyer only 300 metres away and closing rapidly. "I tear the boat around with one screw at 'full speed ahead' and the other 'full speed astern' with the result that the destroyer speeds past the stern at a distance of roughly ten m[etres]." *U-130* made a crash dive, just as a second "destroyer" appeared near the merchant vessel. At that moment Kals discovered that the boat was plunging out of control, for the diesel exhaust valves were frozen open and water had rushed into the boat before he could seal off the valves. The boat crashed into the bottom, about forty-eight metres deep, and Kals switched off all systems to wait out the attack he expected. None came; no reports of the incident have come to light in Allied records and it seems unlikely the merchant vessel or the warships had actually seen the submarine in the darkness.

Kals did not surface until nearly five hours later and then made his way back out to Cape Breton's Atlantic coast. He was then grateful to receive a message from headquarters authorizing him "[i]f attack opportunities are unfavourable" to move to more southerly waters. Kals did so with pleasure for reasons he listed:

1. Limited amount of traffic.
2. Unfavourable weather ...
3. Good surveillance of narrow straits by fast land-based aircraft (conditions are like those encountered in the St. George Channel [heavily defended waters between southern England and Ireland])
4. Convoys appear to be heavily defended by destroyers.

U-109, the type IX assigned to the Halifax approaches, had similarly frustrating experiences, the product of successful defences. The Canadian navy had reacted to the offensive exactly as in 1918, by holding in port shipping that normally would have sailed independently along the coastal routes until escorts could be found, with priority to the route between Halifax and St. John's, where both the type IXs were hunting.

The most urgent need was to secure the western end of the main transatlantic convoys. The U.K.-bound HX and SC series had previously received only light escorts from Halifax and Sydney to the waters off eastern Newfoundland where NEF and U.S. groups based in Newfoundland joined. North America–bound ON convoys had dispersed off eastern Newfoundland with the merchant ships then making their own way to their destinations. A major Allied reorganization that began in late January 1942 combined the NEF and American groups based in Newfoundland into a single Mid-Ocean Escort Force (MOEF). By eliminating the northward diversion towards Iceland, the new force was able to escort convoys directly to Northern Ireland, thereby freeing some British escorts from the eastern Atlantic for the mid-ocean and western ocean. Reinforcements—British and Canadian—were also needed to replace American destroyers previously based in Newfoundland; by April 1942, all but a handful had to be withdrawn for the top priority task of escorting troopships that deployed U.S. land and air forces overseas.

A new Western Local Escort Force (WLEF), based in Halifax and commanded by Rear Admiral G.C. Jones, commanding officer Atlantic Coast, provided escort groups for the SC and HX convoys from Halifax out to the vicinity of St. John's and picked up incoming ON convoys, which now sailed through to Halifax. This commitment soon expanded, although the western force was even more under-strength than the mid-ocean force. The Royal Navy contributed thirteen destroyers to the WLEF, but these, together with the five provided by the RCN, were mostly the old vessels taken over from the USN in 1940 that were proving hard to maintain in the difficult north Atlantic environment. The RCN provided all twenty corvettes in the WLEF, and, to keep the groups up to a strength of at least four escorts each, had to assign recently built Bangor minesweepers.

The Canadians' immediate organization of improvised coastal convoys in January 1942 had persuaded the U-boats to shift the weight of their offensive into American waters. The U.S. Navy, whose escort building program was just getting underway, was loath to resort to the kind of desperate improvisation they had seen the Canadians employ in Newfoundland and so delayed the introduction of convoy until adequate escort forces could be assembled. Unfortunately, during 1942 the U-boat force more than doubled in size to some 210 submarines by the end of the year, and their capacity for long-range operations was greatly increased by the deployment of large tanker submarines in the central Atlantic. These "milch cows" replenished type VII U-boats at mid-ocean so they could make sustained patrols in the western ocean. Thus in 1942 Dönitz was able once more to do what he had done in the eastern and northern Atlantic in 1941: search out areas where defences were weak or non-existent, further and further south along the U.S. seaboard, and from there the Caribbean, the Gulf of Mexico, and the coast of Brazil. The U-boats inflicted heavy losses in every month of 1942 for a total of over 700 ships sunk in North and South American waters, fully a third of all Allied and neutral merchant ships destroyed by U-boats during the whole war.

In March 1942 the RCN started an important new convoy between Halifax and Boston to reduce losses among merchant ships making their way between northern U.S. and Canadian ports. In April, at American request, Boston replaced Halifax as the destination of ON convoys, adding the considerable burden of some 650 kilometres in each direction for the groups committed to bringing in the main westbound convoys from the waters off southeastern Newfoundland.

Thus was born the WLEF's triangle run. The first leg was from the Boston and Cape Cod area to Halifax (or Sydney) with northbound ships from U.S. ports. The second was the passage of 900 to 1000 kilometres from Halifax (or Sydney) to the western ocean meeting point southeast of St. John's, where the mid-ocean escort took over. At that point, the WLEF escort linked up with an incoming ON convoy for the 1500- to 1700-kilometre run back to Boston. It was a demanding schedule. Every week, two ON convoys arrived and two westbound convoys, one HX and one SC, sailed. The distance travelled, some 1700 kilometres in each direction, was half that of the run from Newfoundland across the central ocean. This task, together with keeping up the strength of the mid-ocean force as the United States pulled out most of its warships,

were the Alliance's top priorities and necessarily the RCN's top commitments. The next most pressing need was the coastal convoys that linked
Canadian and Newfoundland ports.

Far from having the planned respite starting in December 1941 to
allow improved training and upgrades to the equipment of the Canadian
escorts, the RCN's Atlantic fleet had remained on the treadmill—one
whose speed and uphill incline were increasing. All thirteen destroyers
and sixty-two corvettes on the Atlantic coast were assigned to the MOEF
and WLEF, together with ten of the twenty-two Bangors in service on
the east coast. The Bangor's construction to full naval specifications
posed greater challenges to Canadian industry than the corvettes, and
so the first vessel had not entered service until July 1941. Initially, the
new warships had been assigned to local defence at Halifax, Sydney, and
St. John's, but with the expanding needs in early 1942 the Bangors were
in turn diverted for coastal escort and to stand in for corvettes as ocean
escorts in the WLEF. Senior Allied staffs estimated that the RCN had
just a bit better than a third of the number of destroyers and corvettes
required for its responsibilities in the MOEF and WLEF, but in 1942
there was no source of reinforcements.[6]

Although the convoy system was successful in keeping shipping losses
to a minimum, the enemy was almost constantly present, and there was
no scope to reduce vigilance. U-boats bound for more southern waters
were routed through the waters near Nova Scotia to search for shipping
there, and groups of two, three, or four made sustained patrols in the
area. In the summer and fall of 1942, large groups of U-boats began to
gather again in the approaches to Newfoundland, as Dönitz's expanding
force allowed him to renew wolf pack operations against the mid-ocean
convoys, while also keeping up the coastal campaign in the western
Atlantic and Caribbean. This was the context for the first U-boat incursions into the St. Lawrence in 1942.

The Allies suffered from another disadvantage. At the end of
January, British intelligence lost the ability to decrypt signals by U-boats

operating in the Atlantic. The Germans introduced an improved version of the Enigma encryption machine that featured four rather than three rotors whose electrical circuits scrambled each letter of the original message, an innovation that multiplied the number of possible settings far beyond the capabilities of existing equipment to solve. The main source of radio intelligence, other than snippets of information from German networks that continued to use three-rotor Enigma encryption, was now direction-finding bearings on transmissions from U-boats. Stations in Britain, Canada, Iceland, Bermuda, the West Indies, West Africa, and now the United States maintained listening watches on frequencies used by the U-boats and took bearings on each broadcast. Bearings from two or more widely separated intercept stations were then plotted on special charts, and the intersection point of the bearings gave the approximate position. The position was very approximate—within ninety kilometres in any direction was a good result—but that still left a "probability area" of over 24,000 square kilometres. Messages were also recorded for analysis. Such analysis since the beginning of the war greatly helped when Ultra decrypts had been available by identifying the characteristic form of standard messages such as weather reports, and reports that enemy ships had been sighted. Even without being able to decipher the contents of such messages, knowing that a U-boat in a certain approximate position was carrying out the sorts of activities indicated by one or another of these types of messages fleshed out the picture of enemy deployments.

Among the many challenges that faced Commander Eric Brand on his secondment from the Royal Navy in 1939 to serve as the director of naval intelligence in Ottawa was to develop the Canadian navy's ability to gather radio intelligence. Brand selected for the task Commander Jean Maurice Barbe Pougnet de Marbois, Royal Naval Reserve. De Marbois had worked in British naval intelligence during the First World War and then, on returning to civilian life, settled in Canada and registered for service in an emergency. At the end of August 1939, he reported to

Brand in Ottawa who assigned him to create a new group, the Foreign Intelligence Section.

De Marbois' life bore more than a passing resemblance to a fictional adventurer in service of the British Empire of the sort that appeared in publications like *The Boy's Own Annual* (which was also very popular in Canada). He had been born in 1888 in the British Mascarene Islands (now Mauritius) in the Indian Ocean, where his father, a doctor, was surgeon general under the British administration in India. The family was Scottish, and de Marbois went to Scotland to stay with his older brother and then his grandparents after his parents died when he was about 12 or 13. Because of his Scottish roots, de Marbois was always known, at least later in his life, as "Jock." He embarked on a career in the merchant marine, which probably accounted for his tattooed forearms,[7] and joined the Royal Naval Reserve as an officer in September 1914. He had a gift for languages so, after service in the north Atlantic in the cruiser HMS *Donegal,* he was assigned to naval intelligence. His first posting, in the fall of 1915,[8] was as a liaison officer to the Russian naval forces that were participating in the failed Allied campaign to open the Dardanelles, and he eventually joined the staff of the British naval attaché in St. Petersburg. He escaped from Russia during the Bolshevik revolution and reached Britain in February 1918, suffering from what would today be termed traumatic stress. In the words of a medical report written soon after his return to Britain, he "had a very trying time during the last year, was blown up in a train, was shot at and stabbed on arresting a spy, and on many other occasions."[9] With him he brought his Russian fiancée, whom he married. De Marbois received the Order of the British Empire for his service in Russia and was demobilized from the navy at the beginning of 1920. He joined the colonial service and went to Nigeria in 1921, but had to leave after a few months because of severe tropical illness.[10] He came to Canada in 1923, initially to Alberta to try his hand in farming, but soon found his métier as a languages teacher at Upper Canada College in Toronto.[11] When de Marbois took up the intelligence appointment in Ottawa in 1939, among the first officers he recruited was one of his former language students from the college who had gone on to become a teacher there, Lieutenant C.H. Little, RCNVR.[12]

The Foreign Intelligence Section was responsible for analysis of foreign-language newspapers, other publications, and public radio broadcasts, tasks in which Little immediately found himself immersed. What consumed de Marbois' interest was the technical challenge of tracking German naval communications. The Canadian navy had virtually no resources of its own for this task, but Canada, because of its well-developed radio communications system and its vast territory that brackets the whole of the western side of the north Atlantic, had a vital part to play. Initially the Foreign Intelligence Section passed on instructions from the Admiralty to Canadian government radio stations, mostly operated by the Department of Transport, to monitor frequencies known to be used by the German navy. The Foreign Intelligence Section then passed the raw material—bearings and transcriptions of messages—to the Admiralty and also to the RN's America and West Indies command in Bermuda.[13]

De Marbois was not satisfied with this basic information-gathering role. He endeavoured to assemble the technical knowledge and skilled people needed to analyze the information and in particular to plot bearings to obtain fixes of the approximate location of enemy warships that were transmitting. The Admiralty provided full assistance starting in the summer of 1941, probably not coincidentally after the U-boat force pushed towards Newfoundland. The Canadian organization rapidly expanded, and just in time. When the German offensive into North American coastal waters began in January 1942, the Foreign Intelligence Section was becoming proficient in the science and art of plotting fixes, and the Admiralty authorized Naval Service Headquarters to broadcast fixes to ships operating in the western Atlantic. If fixes were possible with bearings from Canadian stations and from American stations that the United States had begun to dispatch to Ottawa in December 1941, then the plotting could be achieved in about an hour and a half, but if bearings from the Admiralty were needed, then delays in communications slowed the time to six to twelve hours. The big challenge was to do things faster as speed was of the essence in order to give shipping at risk the best possible warning.[14] In April 1942, a British delegation of direction-finding specialists visited Ottawa and Washington to coach the organizations and assist in the coordination of the two North American intelligence centres.

The arrangement reached in early May at the Admiralty's suggestion was that Ottawa would broadcast U-boat warnings to ships in the western Atlantic north of forty degrees north (the approximate latitude of New York), and the Navy Department in Washington to ships south of forty degrees, a dividing line that reflected the large role the RCN and RCAF had already taken on for the protection of convoys in U.S. waters north of New York.

Against the backdrop of the vast new responsibilities in the Atlantic battle that Canada assumed in the opening months of 1942, the naval and air force staffs updated the defence plan for the St. Lawrence in the coming shipping season. This had been an annual exercise since early 1940. Even then, the shortage of ships and aircraft and the obvious priority of the Atlantic had established the principle that there would be no attempt to introduce a system of convoys in the St. Lawrence until there was a confirmed enemy attack in the area. The 1940 plan also stated that if, once established, the convoys suffered substantial losses, it might be necessary to close the river and gulf, and route cargo by rail to the Atlantic ports. Although that contingency was not included in the 1942 version of the plan, senior officers understood that this was an option that it might not be possible to avoid as a "last resort," to use the wording of the 1940 and 1941 versions. Indeed, as we will see, with the extremely heavy losses to shipping, especially off the U.S. coast, in 1942 rail transport from the St. Lawrence area to Atlantic ports increasingly looked like a promising means of economizing by saving ships the week or more needed to do the round trip through the gulf.[15]

One of the main reasons for the navy's effort to obtain large U.S. yachts in 1940 was to provide some capacity in the gulf on the model of 1915 when exactly the same thing had been done. In October 1940, one of the yachts, HMCS *Vison,* took up station at Gaspé until the end of the season, and in the summer of 1941 four armed yachts, *Reindeer, Raccoon, Lynx,* and *Vison,* came up from Halifax to establish the "Gaspé Force."[16] Among the most capable of the yachts, they ranged from forty-three to fifty-five metres in length, displaced between 340 and 503 tonnes, and had naval crews of about forty personnel. Thus they were considerably smaller than the Bangor-class minesweepers and slower, with best speeds of only eighteen to twenty-two kilometres per hour. Each carried a single main gun, a 4-inch (10.2-centimetre) that fired a 9-kilogram projectile in the case of *Reindeer* and *Lynx* and a 12-pounder, which fired a 5.4-kilogram projectile, in *Raccoon* and *Vison.* The anti-submarine outfit was the basic type 123 asdic submarine detection device, and depth charges, the same as in corvettes. Although this was a useful armament, the ships were not built to robust naval standards and were lacking in such things as communications equipment, for which the new corvettes and Bangors had priority for limited supplies. It was a measure of the desperate situation among the Allied escort forces that the yachts continued in front line service through much of 1942.

The naval staff also looked to a new type of minor vessel just entering service, the "Fairmile B" motor launch, to help fill the gap. In the First World War, the navy had chartered civilian motor boats in an emergency effort to respond to reports of suspicious activities at the numerous inlets along isolated shorelines in the gulf; in the 1930s, the staff set a requirement for small combat vessels better able to carry out this close-in coastal defence role. Motor launches designed for the Admiralty by the Fairmile Engineering Company of England were better suited to the rough waters and long distances along the Canadian Atlantic coast than the smaller, higher performance motor torpedo boats that the staff initially considered. In 1940 the navy ordered twenty-four Fairmiles from Canadian yacht builders, and by the beginning of 1942 orders had been increased to a total of fifty-four. The mahogany-built craft were larger than the motor torpedo boats, thirty-four metres in length compared to twenty-one metres, and much slower, with a maximum speed of thirty-seven kilometres per hour. They had a longer range, and their larger, conventional hulls were better suited to asdic and depth charge equipment than the aqua-plane hulls of the torpedo boats that skimmed across the surface.[17]

There were delays in the Canadian construction pending the arrival from England of full drawings and specialized equipment. In the spring of 1942, the first nine boats were just working up at Halifax and St. John's; seven others were in Toronto, completing their equipment and waiting for the ice to clear from the St. Lawrence.[18]

Planning for the 1942 navigation season on the St. Lawrence took place in March 1942, in the near certainty that the intense U-boat operations would extend into the St. Lawrence in the coming late spring or summer after ice cleared from the river and gulf. The naval staff's estimate was correct, although Dönitz had no specific plans for such an operation. That was not how he worked. As we have seen, he probed for weak spots in the Allied defences, where his U-boats could sink the largest number of ships at the least risk. This would curtail the flow of supplies from North America that now not only sustained Great Britain, but also greatly assisted the Soviet Union in rebuilding its forces, which had endured enormous losses in the German invasion of 1941 and would face a renewed and massive German offensive later in the spring of 1942. During the first half of 1942, the U-boats enjoyed continued easy victories in the warm waters off the U.S. coast, but Allied staffs fully appreciated that, as soon as more effective defence measures could be organized along the American seaboard, the U-boats would probe elsewhere for soft spots, and that Dönitz, as always, would quickly reinforce any success.

A German thrust into the St. Lawrence would make the establishment of convoys in the river unavoidable, but it would be a large undertaking. Figures assembled by Brand's staff showed that, during the 1941 season, 750 ocean-going vessels had either arrived at Montreal from overseas ports or sailed for overseas destinations.[19] Figures for Quebec City showed that "approximately thirty-six" vessels had departed from that port every six days, a number that apparently included steamships sailing for ports within the Gulf of St. Lawrence as well as ships coming from Montreal for overseas. To move this traffic expeditiously would require convoys every three days in both directions, one outbound from the river to Sydney and one inbound from Sydney. U-boats were unlikely to penetrate beyond Rimouski, about 240 kilometres east of Quebec City where the river narrows and navigation becomes more difficult. Plans to have convoys assemble in the anchorage created by Bic Island, off the southern shore of the river about thirty-five kilometres west of Rimouski, would save escorts the half-day's steaming between Rimouski and Quebec City. Still, the run from Bic to Sydney is over 900 kilometres, some three full days for a convoy proceeding at thirteen kilometres per hour. Initial estimates were that thirty escorts would be required. Where were they to come from? Only the armed yachts and the first batch of Fairmiles were available, and neither type was capable of keeping the seas in the stormy conditions often encountered in the gulf.[20]

The naval staff signalled the Admiralty and the U.S. Navy Department, pointing out that the new arrangements on the Atlantic coast had taken no account of the St. Lawrence, and that there were no warships of the size needed, Bangor or larger, for all-weather escort duties. It was a hint that deployments on the Atlantic should be adjusted to free some of the larger escorts for the gulf. The Admiralty caught the hint: "the diversion of any [Atlantic escorts] from present duty ... not recommended." Better, the British staff advised, to rely on the air force: "A/S Air Patrol should prove considerable deterrent operation by U-boats in these waters."[21] That did not advance things much. Canadian planning for the defence of the gulf had always been for the air force to carry a good deal of the burden. In the scramble to expand escort services in coastal waters since January 1942, the navy had come to depend heavily on the all-out effort Eastern Air Command made to supply close air escort to every convoy.

Rear Admiral G.C. Jones, the commanding officer Atlantic Coast, came from Halifax to Ottawa to discuss the St. Lawrence problem with the naval staff in a meeting on 23 March. Jones, like Rear Admiral Murray, who held the navy's other major operational command in Newfoundland, had joined the service as an officer cadet at the age of 15 in 1911. Fierce career competition had developed between these two "comers," not at all uncommon in such a tiny organization as the early Royal Canadian Navy. In contrast to Murray and Nelles, who were fatherly in their manner towards subordinates, Jones, although no less genuinely concerned about the welfare and progress of those under his command, did not mask his ferocious temper. Jones was also a talented administrator; perhaps it was the impatience that sparked his clarity and decisiveness.[22] In the case of the St. Lawrence, he agreed with the Admiralty's advice. Any diversion of escorts from the WLEF and coastal convoys "would seriously endanger the East Coast." He also expected the air force to compensate for deficiencies in naval escort if U-boats should enter the gulf.[23]

The task of updating the plan for the defence of the gulf fell to the operations division of the naval staff, whose director was Captain H.N. Lay. He was a member of the regular RCN, a half-generation behind Admirals Nelles, Jones, and Murray. Born in 1903, Lay had joined the service as an officer cadet in 1918 and had commanded one of the River-class destroyers, HMCS *Restigouche,* during her hard service in British waters in 1940–41. Lay's given names, Horatio Nelson, seemed to make the navy his destiny. His memoirs, however, explain that he was named not for the famous British admiral who died victorious at the battle of

Trafalgar in 1805, but for his own grandfather, Horatio, whose middle name, Nelson, was that of his mother's family. Lay's grandfather and namesake had had a distinguished career in the British consular service in China in the mid-nineteenth century. Lay's mother had died only months after his birth. In 1907 his father married Jenny King, sister of William Lyon Mackenzie King, the future prime minister, whom Lay always knew as "Uncle Willie."[24] Although Lay did discuss naval affairs with his uncle, it was never, so far as revealed by Mackenzie King's diary, on matters of such detail as ship deployments. Still, Lay, as befitted Mackenzie King's nephew, was a passionate nationalist. During the negotiations with the British and Americans about the revised escort arrangements in the north Atlantic in the early months of 1942, he insisted that Canadian ships should be kept together in Canadian escort groups.[25] To the extent that the competition between Admirals Murray and Jones had divided the officers of Lay's generation into different camps, Lay was a member of the Jones group.[26] Jones' full agreement with the British Admiralty on the priority of the Western Local Escort Force and coastal convoys over the St. Lawrence would thus have carried particular weight.

There was one source of escorts that would not deplete the Atlantic forces. Newly completed warships from the shipyards on the Great Lakes and the St. Lawrence River had to traverse the gulf to reach Halifax for work-ups training and final fitting and adjustments of their equipment. Headquarters arranged for the new ships to have their main armament and detection devices installed and to receive initial trials at Montreal or Quebec rather than at Halifax so that the ships could act as escorts on their initial passage. Under the revised plan for the gulf, when new warships were ready to sail, merchant ships would be scheduled to sail with them in convoy whether submarines were known to be present or not.[27]

In the event of a confirmed attack by a submarine in the gulf, headquarters in Ottawa would broadcast "COMMENCE GL. 2," a signal for all ocean shipping bound for the gulf to enter Sydney and all outbound shipping to wait at Quebec until escort forces arrived to start convoy. The revised gulf plan cut the allocation of escorts to the bone, five Bangors, five armed yachts, and ten Fairmiles, which were to be organized into five escort groups, each consisting of a single Bangor, one armed yacht, and two Fairmiles. Only the Bangors had the capability to operate in rough weather and sea conditions, and the naval staff accepted the risk that only a single Bangor might be able to keep station with a convoy. The only reinforcements available would be new-construction warships that arrived at Quebec.

The RCAF would shortly be re-equipping 119 Squadron at RCAF Station Sydney with Lockheed Hudsons, more capable than the Bolingbrokes it was operating. There were also plans to strengthen a new squadron, 117, at the North Sydney flying boat station when the ice cleared from the port in the spring. It was to be equipped with Consolidated PBY flying boats, and the RCAF undertook to dispatch three of the 117 Squadron PBYs to operate from Gaspé. (The PBYs the RCAF received in 1941–42 were of three different variants with three different names: "Catalina" flying boats, built to British specifications in the United States and released by the British to Canada, and two variants built to RCAF specifications, known as the "Canso" flying boat and the "Canso A" amphibian version that had retractable wheels for operation from runways.)[28]

Work had begun in the summer of 1941 on a flying boat station and naval operating base at Gaspé, which were located together to allow the two services to share facilities. The main feature of the air station was a concrete apron on the shore that ran from the hangar out beyond the water's edge. Flying boats would taxi to the apron where crews in hip waders would put wheeled dollies under the hulls to allow the aircraft to be pulled up the apron and into the hangar for servicing. The naval part of the station included fuel tanks and warehouses for the supplies needed to replenish the escorts. There was also a small marine railway to pull the Fairmiles out of the water into a workshop for servicing under cover.

With aviation-style gasoline engines, high-speed propellers, and finely built wooden hulls, the Fairmiles had to be treated much like aircraft.

In 1940, the RCAF had started construction of an aerodrome at Mont Joli, Quebec, on the St. Lawrence River, about thirty kilometres northeast of Rimouski. Early in 1942, No. 9 Bombing and Gunnery School, a part of the British Commonwealth Air Training Plan organization, opened at Mont Joli. One of the considerations in the selection of the site was its suitability for air patrols over the St. Lawrence estuary and the western part of the gulf. In the event of a confirmed submarine attack, Eastern Air Command's plan was to move fast land-based bombers from the Atlantic stations to Mont Joli. The new facilities at Gaspé and Mont Joli superseded the pre-war plans to develop a base on Anticosti Island. The unexpectedly large scale of the British Commonwealth Air Training Plan had resulted in the construction of additional airfields in 1940–42 that were well placed to support operations in the gulf, at Charlottetown and Summerside on Prince Edward Island, at Chatham, New Brunswick, near that province's gulf coast, and in Nova Scotia at Greenwood in the Annapolis Valley and at Debert, near Truro.

Preparation for defence of the Strait of Belle Isle, the northern entrance to the gulf, was somewhat less urgent because of the persistence of ice that prevented navigation until late June or July. Plans for constant patrols by Bangors and corvettes were overtaken by the needs of the Mid-Ocean and Western Local Escort forces for these ships, and the task of covering the straits largely fell to air forces at Gander, in Newfoundland. In addition to the fifteen Digbys of the RCAF's 10 Squadron, the U.S. Army Air Corps deployed six four-engine Boeing B-17 Flying Fortress bombers at that airport.

Remarkably, when Admiral Jones was in Ottawa in late March to discuss the St. Lawrence plan, he and Admiral Nelles held a press conference in which they spoke freely about their certainty that the enemy would strike in the gulf during the coming shipping season. Jones, whom the *Globe and Mail* described as "[t]all, brisk and dark complex-ioned," explained that "It was perfectly feasible for the submarines now operating off the Atlantic coast to leave Bay of Biscay ports, cross the ocean in two weeks, spend another two weeks on this side and then return home." Nelles stated, "We will have submarines in the Gulf of St. Lawrence this summer, and they could place a supply ship here," which would allow the submarines to prolong their operations. He explained that although "Canadian aircraft would have a good chance to knock such [supply] vessels off ... it was quite feasible for them to come and operate there as the Gulf is a large body of water."[29] No specific evidence about why the navy's senior officers, normally noted for their reticence, should speak so openly has come to light, but more than ever the danger to the St. Lawrence was useful to the government.

In the latter part of 1941, as the number of voluntary recruits for the army sharply diminished, men drafted for service in Canada only began to replace general service personnel in home defence units, including those at Gaspé, Quebec City, and Sydney, so that the general service troops in the home units could go overseas. Nevertheless, pressure from the English-speaking provinces for overseas conscription had become so intense that, on the opening of the parliamentary session on 26 January 1942, Mackenzie King announced that there would be a plebiscite that would ask voters to release the government from its pledge not to send conscripts overseas. Mackenzie King, who was desperate not to alienate his party's supporters in Quebec, was at pains to explain that the govern-ment only wanted freedom to act in the event, which might never occur, that military circumstances made it essential to keep the overseas army up to strength. More than ever, Mackenzie King underscored the threat to Canadian waters and territory to respond to charges from supporters of overseas conscription that large forces were being kept at home only as a sop to Quebec, and at the same time to counter arguments from opponents of conscription that the war was a remote, purely British affair in which the danger to Canada was minimal. "I know some of our citizens were impatient with the government for insisting, from the outbreak of war, upon our responsibilities for the coastal and territorial defence of Canada.... Recent events in the Pacific, and the sinking of ships off Newfoundland and Nova Scotia, should serve to dispel any lingering belief that Canada is immune from attack."[30]

In a speech to Parliament on 25 March 1942, when an effective campaign to vote against releasing the government from its pledge was gaining strength in Quebec under the banner of *La ligue pour la défense du Canada*, Mackenzie King referred to the warnings that Jones and Nelles had given to the press only the day before. The prime minister observed that the emphasis in his speech of 26 January on the necessity for strong home defences had been vindicated by the subsequent "attacks by many submarines ... in coastal waters of Canada and the United States. In many cases these attacks have occurred within sight of the shores of this continent. There is no reason to believe that these attacks will not continue and probably become more intensive. Officers of the Canadian naval service have expressed the view that within a few months submarines may well be found operating within the gulf, and even in the St. Lawrence River. It is known that enemy submarines can leave their bases on the European continent, voyage to the shores of this continent, seek their prey for some days or weeks ..."[31]

FOUR

First Blood in the Gulf, May 1942

"Ironies of war" describes well the opening of the German submarine operations in the St. Lawrence in May 1942. But there is a better description by Karl von Clausewitz, the great Prussian military philosopher of the early nineteenth century, who caught the key idea in more practical and colourful language: "Everything in war is very simple, but the simplest thing is difficult."[1]

The Canadians had long expected a German attack, but it was by pure coincidence that an escorted group of shipping sailed down the St. Lawrence just as *U-553*, unknown to anyone including the German U-boat command, slipped into the gulf. As a result, the submarine was initially unable to find any shipping to attack. The group sailing was a trial carried out because newly completed warships happened to be ready to depart from Quebec City; there were no other warships available to escort the merchant vessels that sailed subsequently, and it was these later ships that *U-553* ultimately found. In another coincidence, a false U-boat warning by a civilian observer led to air searches by the Canadian and U.S. forces that had located *U-553* shortly after she entered the gulf. Further defensive patrols by the RCAF should have been effective in protecting the unescorted ships that followed the trial escorted group, but failed in the uniquely difficult conditions in the gulf.

U-boat headquarters had no plan for an early move into the gulf. The submarine commander acted on his own initiative. Unlike the Canadians, who were alerted by the air searches to the presence of a U-boat in the gulf, the German command was surprised by the news of the first sinkings in the St. Lawrence, which took place on the night of 11–12 May.

The final irony is that while U-boat headquarters was pleased by the initiative shown by the submarine commander, the Canadian prime minister was relieved by the news. An attack so deep in Canadian territorial waters, he hoped, would help bridge the large division between Quebec and the rest of the country revealed by the results of the recent plebiscite on overseas conscription.

On 19 April 1942, *U-553* sailed from St. Nazaire, France, for North American waters. She was a veteran boat under a veteran commander: this was her sixth war mission since commissioning in December 1940, and for that whole time she had been under the same commanding officer, Korvettenkapitän Karl Thurmann, who had joined the navy in 1928 and entered the submarine service in April 1940. This was the boat's second mission to Canadian waters; she had carried out a patrol there in January 1942 and sunk two tankers, her fourth and fifth successes, and the final ones before her spring 1942 mission.

On 5 May, when *U-553* was cruising westward south of Newfoundland's Avalon Peninsula towards the Halifax approaches, U-boat headquarters signalled orders to Thurmann giving him freedom to operate from the waters off Nova Scotia to the New York approaches or even further south. German intelligence knew that steamer traffic would begin to come out through the St. Lawrence route once the ice cleared in late April. Thurmann's initial intention therefore was to "Proceed towards Cape Breton, observe traffic in [i.e., coming out from] Gulf of St. Lawrence, then proceed southward along the [Nova Scotia] coast depending on weather conditions and enemy forces (convoy traffic),"[2] and so the boat turned towards the Cabot Strait. During the late morning on 6 May, when the boat was about 180 kilometres south of Newfoundland's Burin Peninsula immediately to the west of the Avalon Peninsula, *U-553* dived to attack what appeared to be a merchant ship. As the submarine fired a torpedo, which missed, it became clear that the vessel was a "Corvette or escort" and it headed towards the U-boat at high speed, firing a single depth charge that exploded at "moderate" range from *U-553*. After nearly an hour, the submarine surfaced, but then sighted the vessel five kilometres away. The escort closed at speed once more and dropped a second depth charge after the boat had again dived; this one exploded "at longer distance" from *U-553* than the first.[3] It seems unlikely that the warship definitely detected the submarine, for it otherwise would have dropped more depth charges and lingered to search the area. That may explain why no record of the incident has come to light in Allied archives.

Damage to the submarine was superficial. The one item of concern was that the attack periscope was out of action, but "provisional repairs" got it back into service. (The attack periscope had a small head, only 3.5 centimetres wide, to avoid detection, and a narrow field of vision but strong magnification for targeting ships, as compared to the larger main periscope whose wide-angle lens was designed for surveillance and navigation.) The next afternoon, while running submerged towards the Cape Breton coast, the submarine experienced "[t]hree separate explosions, moderate distance." Because there were no sounds of a ship on the surface, Thurmann concluded that they were "aircraft bombs dropped by chance." He may have been right, as there was a good deal of test flying taking place from the Sydney air station that day, and there is no evidence that the east coast commands suspected the presence of a submarine. The explosions, however, knocked the attack periscope out of action again, and the forward hydroplane, crucial for quick dives, developed severe defects. With the boat's combat readiness so diminished, Thurmann concluded, it would be "pointless" to move into the well-defended Halifax approaches, as he had intended. He decided instead to push into the gulf. He expected that the St. Lawrence area would not be well protected because no U-boats had yet operated there. Steamers might be sailing independently, without naval escort, en route to the convoy assembly ports of Sydney and Halifax. These would be easy targets.[4]

At about daybreak on 9 May, an observer on shore at Cape Ray, the southwest extremity of Newfoundland, reported a westbound submarine. It was a false report. *U-553* had passed the vicinity of Cape Ray at midday the day before, well out in the centre of the Cabot Strait, far beyond visual range of land and under the cover of poor weather. Nevertheless, the report, against all odds, led to firm contact with the U-boat. The air force took the sighting report seriously and ordered a search, even though the information grew stale as bad weather prevented flying for nearly thirty-six hours. Finally, on the afternoon of 10 May, two bombers, an RCAF Douglas B-18 and a U.S. Army Air Corps Boeing B-17, took off from Gander. Weather conditions were still marginal over the gulf. As the American aircraft reached its patrol area south of the eastern part of Anticosti Island, cloud forced the bomber down to an altitude of ninety metres. They were in luck. Although such a low patrol altitude gives a limited arc of visibility over the water, the co-pilot/observer sighted the surfaced submarine about nine kilometres away. The pilot increased speed to 342 kilometres per hour in the two-minute approach, swooping down to fifteen metres off the surface to release three depth bombs, about twelve seconds after the submarine crash-dived. The explosions seemed on target, and as the aircraft circled for three-quarters of an hour after the attack, the crew sighted debris on the surface, convincing them that they had destroyed the intruder.[5]

Although the U.S. Army command at Gander immediately reported the attack, they did not release any details until after the returning crew had all been debriefed. That decision, which the U.S. commander claimed was Army policy, left Canadian authorities in the dark.

Much more often than not, U-boat sighting reports in the fog-bound, flotsam-filled waters on the Canadian east coast proved to be false, and early details of a contact were essential to determine its possible veracity. Air Vice-Marshal C.M. McEwen, air officer commanding the RCAF's 1 Group in Newfoundland, did not finally get these details which confirmed the presence of a submarine until the afternoon of the eleventh, some twenty-four hours after the attack. "I had to extract the information myself," he complained.[6]

In Halifax, Eastern Air Command got a discouraging response from the navy's Atlantic Coast command. As one of the air force officers later recalled, "the Navy had nothing in the Gulf ... COAC said they could do nothing."[7] This was the bald truth. The already overstretched Western Local Escort Force at Halifax was struggling to respond to new sinkings off the southern Nova Scotia coast that revealed the presence on the main ocean convoy routes of the other U-boats with which U-553 had sailed. Despite the Canadian forces' long-held expectations of the arrival of U-boats in the gulf, U-553 had achieved tactical surprise by coming in on the heels of the retreating ice.[8] At snowbound Gaspé, there was still "heavy ice" in the harbour on 7 May, which did not clear until the tenth; work on laying the anti-submarine nets began only on the eighteenth,[9] and the port was not scheduled to be ready for operations until the end of May.

One important, though temporary, naval defence measure was in place. As U-553 made its way into the gulf searching for outbound shipping, outbound vessels were sailing in the first, trial, "escorted group." The group had passed around the Gaspé Peninsula and into the central gulf on the night of 9–10 May and by the time of the American attack were clear to the east of the submarine's westbound track.

The escorts, the corvette *La Malbaie* and the Bangor-class minesweeper *Granby*, had just been completed at St. Lawrence shipyards,[10] and it was their availability for passage to Halifax for final fitting out that occasioned the first group sailing. On the afternoon of 9 May, the two escorts had arrived from Quebec City at Father Point, near Rimouski, where four waiting Halifax-bound merchant ships fell in behind the warships. Aboard the escorts, the crews had been struggling to complete equipment trials in the last hours before the rendezvous, and *La Malbaie*, during the gulf passage, discovered defects in its steering gear.[11] Although the improvised nature of the group sailing underscored the extent to which the hard-pressed RCN had to scrape the bottom of the barrel, the gathering of outward-bound merchant ships into this group accounts for Thurmann's inability to find merchant ships during the first three days of his passage into the gulf.

The escorted group had air protection on 11 May as part of general coverage for the gulf. Eastern Air Command had not waited for the confirmation about the presence of a U-boat that the U.S. Army at Gander finally provided late in the day. In the dark early morning hours of 11 May, soon after the first unverified reports of the U.S. attack south of Anticosti, two 5 Squadron Canso amphibians trundled down the runway at RCAF Station Dartmouth for seventeen-hour missions over the gulf, from before dawn until after sunset.[12] Despite poor visibility off Cape Breton, short-ranged Bristol Bolingbrokes from 119 Squadron at Sydney flew patrols in direct support of the approaching escorted group.

In theory, these measures should have been effective. The hope of the Canso crews carrying out the long sweeps over the western gulf was that if a submarine was indeed present, it would be incautious enough to remain on the surface. That would allow the aircraft an opportunity to surprise it and attack. The more realistic expectation was that the presence of the aircraft would force the submarine to run submerged, in which state it had only a limited ability to locate shipping and was too slow to pursue any vessels but those that passed close by. All but the most foolhardy submarine commanders dived at the first hint that aircraft were in the area, whether by the distant sound of aero-engines or a speck on the horizon. Although the submarine could surface and run at speed during the dark hours, limited visibility then made it difficult to find ships.

This was all true in the open ocean, but not necessarily so within confined waters. After the attack by the American aircraft on the tenth, Thurmann had indeed run submerged during the daylight hours, but was able to surface and move at speed at night. By the time he surfaced at 9 PM on the evening of 11 May, he was well up the north shore of the Gaspé Peninsula in the estuary of the St. Lawrence River. In this area, the channel between the peninsula and western Anticosti Island is some seventy-five kilometres wide. He kept about fifteen kilometres off shore in the outbound shipping lane, the southern half of the passage. His timing was perfect. No new-construction naval vessels were available at Quebec City to organize another escorted group sailing of merchant ships following the trial group with *La Malbaie* and *Granby*, so cargo vessels had then departed independently, one by one as they completed loading, creating the stream of unprotected targets Thurmann had hoped to find. After surfacing off the Gaspé shore on the evening of 11 May, the submarine commander sighted a small coastal freighter, too small to be worth an attack. He then encountered a substantial vessel, the British merchant ship *Nicoya*, which had sailed from Montreal on 10 May en route for Halifax to join a convoy for Liverpool, England. On board were seventy-seven crew and ten passengers. Ironically, eight of the passengers were survivors of the large British steamer *Ulysses* that had been torpedoed off the North Carolina coast exactly one month before.[13]

Thurmann, on that misty moonless night, was able to close to only 400 metres without anyone on the big freighter catching even a glimpse. The first torpedo hit the after part of the ship at 11:52 PM and then, nineteen minutes later, at 12:11 AM on 12 May, a second "[c]oup de grace" hit amidships, and the vessel slipped under the surface just four minutes later. Immediately after the first hit, the *Nicoya*'s captain, Ernest Henry Brice, "signalled to the engine room for all hands to come on deck" to ensure that the men most at risk in the depths of the hull were not lost.[14] Of the four lifeboats, only two got away; one had been destroyed in the first torpedo attack, and a second, according to a crew member, broke against the ship's side, presumably because it caught against the canted hull of the sinking freighter while being lowered. The occupants of one lifeboat reported seeing the submarine only 30 metres away: "It was huge. Big enough to carry a plane."[15]

Before *U-553* launched the second torpedo, it was clear the ship was going down, and the crew and the captain jumped into the water. They got onto a life raft that had floated clear of the wreck. "As I was drifting on the raft," the captain later reported, "I saw six men clambering onto another raft near the ship. Before they could pull away, a second torpedo struck the vessel. Since they have not been seen again, it must be presumed they died in the explosion."[16]

U-553 continued on the surface, and less than two hours later, at 2:10 AM, sighted the Dutch steamer *Leto*, which was under charter to the British Ministry of War Transport. She had sailed from Montreal on 10 May, the same day as *Nicoya*, and was headed for Sydney to pick up a convoy for the U.K. Of the forty-three people aboard (thirty-nine crew and four passengers), thirty-one were Dutch and the rest British. As in the case of *Nicoya*, the passengers were merchant seamen who had survived the sinking of another ship, in this case seven weeks earlier. Thurmann fired from a much longer range than in his previous attacks, 1200 metres. This may have been because *Leto* was travelling faster than *Nicoya*, which made it more difficult to close; or it may have been because visibility had improved and with it the danger that the guns' crews that operated the vessel's self-defence armament might catch sight of the submarine. The torpedo hit square amidships at 2:28 AM, and *Leto* sank in only twelve minutes. Thurmann need not have worried about the vessel's armament. One of the gunners, Bill Middladitch,

25, of London, England, later told the press, "We had no gunners on watch ... We never used watches in the St. Lawrence river and we were only due to start them the morning after we were sunk."

According to the survivors, all of Leto's lifeboats were smashed in the torpedo explosion, and only a small "jolly boat" intended for use in calm harbour waters got clear. With a normal capacity for only twelve or thirteen people, the little water craft carried twenty-two. She was prevented from capsizing only because the occupants constantly bailed out the water that washed over the low-riding gunwales. One of the survivors, Jimmy Rudkin, 28, recalled the anguish: "It was maddening to see men floating by and be unable to help them. We couldn't have taken any more into our boat or it would have capsized."[17]

At 3:08 AM, less than half an hour after Leto disappeared, Thurmann sighted two more steamers. He was worried now because the sky had begun to brighten, so he manoeuvred to approach from the direction of the dark coastline to the south to ensure that the surfaced submarine's profile was not highlighted against the sky. As he closed, he realized it was still "too light" and therefore dove for a submerged attack. Now he found it was "too dark" effectively to track the ships through the periscope. At 3:20 AM, he was able to get off only a single shot, at the long range of 2000 metres at the second of the two ships. He was sure he got a hit but could not see the vessel sink through the periscope. These difficulties nicely illustrate why U-boat commanders preferred dark conditions that allowed surface attacks.

The two vessels Thurmann encountered were probably the steamers Dutch Maas and Titus. U-553's torpedo had in fact missed, fortunately for Leto's people. Leto had gone down so quickly that there had been no chance to send a radio distress signal. It was a matter of good luck that the vessels passed through the vicinity of Leto's sinking at about 5 AM and in the first morning light sighted the overloaded jolly boat. Dutch Maas took aboard the twenty-two men from the boat, and both ships searched the area for some two-and-a-half hours, according to Egbert

Hendrik Vanderveen, *Leto*'s captain. They recovered another twelve men from the water, one of whom, a Dutch sailor, later died of exposure. The decision of the captains of *Titus* and *Dutch Maas* to linger so long for rescue work in an area where a U-boat was likely present was courageous, particularly because *Leto*'s captain was convinced another ship had been sunk after his, a belief that can only be explained by the fact that *Leto*'s survivors, and thus certainly the crews of the rescue ships, heard the torpedo detonation of *U-553*'s failed attack.[18]

The inhabitants of the little fishing villages along the north shore of the Gaspé Peninsula immediately knew something dreadful had happened. RCMP constables who interviewed residents at Pointe-à-la-Frégate and Cloridorme reported that "all of them were unanimous in saying that the explosion [apparently the initial attack on *Nicoya*] was so violent that they were under the impression it was an earthquake."[19]

Well before dawn, one of *Nicoya*'s lifeboats which had a motor reached Cloridorme, about sixty kilometres by road to the northwest of the town of Gaspé, and the survivors alerted local authorities to the fact that another lifeboat and raft had got clear of the wreck. There was no telephone service along the coast, but an official got word out by telegraph. The nearest military base, at Gaspé, already knew about the sinking. Radio stations had immediately picked up *Nicoya*'s "SSSS," the code for submarine attack, broadcast at 11:55 PM on 11 May, and the Atlantic Coast command at Halifax had rebroadcast it to all naval authorities within minutes.[20] But there was nothing Commander W.B. Armit, the naval officer in charge at Gaspé, could do. The base still looked more like a construction site than a military facility. There were no fighting ships; there were no aircraft. Anything that could be done, and that was little enough, was being done by senior authorities. At Dartmouth, 5 Squadron was scrambling to get a Canso amphibian on its way to Gaspé. The nearest warship, the Bangor HMCS *Medicine Hat,* was at Sydney. She was one of the first escorts assigned to that base as it opened for traffic as the ice cleared. Orders had instantly gone out for *Medicine Hat* to respond, but she was twenty hours' steaming—more than 500 kilometres—away.

The only naval vessel available at Gaspé was the eighteen-metre-long *Venning*. She was the examination vessel intended only for local operations towards the mouth of the harbour to stop and identify incoming merchant ships. She had been laid up for winter, ashore on chocks, and just been launched as the ice cleared the day before. Hasty work got her underway. Armit meanwhile appealed to the army, which, with the help of the YMCA staff that provided amenities to the armed forces personnel at Gaspé, supplied additional trucks, medical personnel, and supplies that would be needed to assist survivors who had been injured or were suffering the effects of exposure.[21] There was no prospect for a speedy run, for the road approaching Cloridorme was still blocked by snow. Late in the morning the government radio station at Fame Point, about halfway between Cloridorme and Gaspé, sighted "life boat towing rafts [sic: there was only one] 6 miles [11 kilometres]" off shore.[22] *Nicoya*'s crew, tired out from rowing against the strong current, tidal pull, and winds through the night, were resting and allowing the boat and raft to drift. It was likely the Fame Point report, together with the poor road conditions near Cloridorme, that led Armit to direct the main part of the truck convoy towards one of the fishing hamlets, not snowbound, close to Fame Point.[23] Armit took to the water in a local fishing boat, crewed by Louis Huet and Xavier Colombe. They found the lifeboat and raft about nine kilometres off shore and pulled them in during the early afternoon at L'Anse-à-Valleau, a fishing village immediately southeast of Fame Point. Sub-Lieutenant Ian Tate, a young naval officer from Toronto, was part of the rescue party. An avid photographer, he took a shot that shows naval and army personnel carrying medical supplies down a coastal road at L'Anse-à-Valleau still covered in places by snowdrifts; the trucks had not been able to get through from the main highway to the shoreline.[24] The medical supplies were not, in the end, needed. The lifeboats were well equipped, and there were no severe injuries or serious cases of exposure. RCMP Constable J.A.E. Lacasse had managed to reach Cloridorme from the west on the afternoon of the twelfth: "Seeing that all the survivors were in good health and very well taken care of by the Rev. LeBlanc, Parish Priest of Cloridorme, and by the proprietor of Hotel Bernatchez, we left the place at 6 PM ...You will note that we have not seen the survivors who landed at L'Anse-à-Valleau as the road below Cloridorme was still closed to traffic. However, communications through the telegraph office reveal that they were all safe and very well taken care of."[25] Armit brought the thirty-nine survivors landed at L'Anse-à-Valleau back to Gaspé that evening in the truck convoy. At that time, the YMCA truck made it through to Cloridorme, and the YMCA arranged to bring the forty-one survivors there to Gaspé on the thirteenth by road. *Venning* had cleared Gaspé harbour and continued on to Cloridorme, the original plan having been to bring out the survivors there by sea, but she returned to Gaspé when the YMCA got through by road.[26]

BY COINCIDENCE, WORD OF *Nicoya*'s destruction reached Captain Brand, the member of the naval staff in Ottawa most directly concerned with such an event, almost instantly. Brand had been called into the office at 12:30 AM on 12 May to decode an unrelated top secret message that had just arrived. While he was working on this message, *Nicoya*'s SSSS signal reached Naval Service Headquarters. "About time too after all the years I had been expecting it," he later reflected in private memoirs he wrote for his children. "I got back to bed about 300 and subsequently there was a considerable newspaper flap of course."[27] That "newspaper flap" was the direct result of the actions of the naval minister, Angus L. Macdonald.

At 3:30 PM on 12 May, Macdonald's office issued a press release:

> The Minister for Naval Services announces that the first enemy submarine attack upon shipping in the St. Lawrence River took place on the 11th of May, when a freighter was sunk. Forty-one survivors have been landed from this vessel.

The situation regarding shipping in the river is being closely watched, and long prepared plans for its special protection under these circumstances are in operation. Any possible future sinkings in this area will not be made public, in order that information of value to the enemy may be withheld from him.

It is felt, however, that the Canadian public should be informed of the presence of enemy U-boats in Canadian territorial waters, and they are assured that every step is being taken to grapple with the situation.

Brand, in the 1946 historical report on the wartime activities of his division of the naval staff, stated that Macdonald had issued this statement for "political reasons." Brand was in a position to know: in May 1942 his division was responsible for the release of information to the public and the provision of guidelines to the censorship authorities to whom the media passed stories for vetting before publication or broadcast. It is likely that the minister's office consulted Brand about the press release, because Brand described the statement as "brief and carefully worded." Although such an early announcement of an enemy success flew in the face of the guidelines Brand had pressed on the censorship authorities time and time again, the announcement had been crafted to divulge the minimum amount of information needed to meet the government's requirements.

The government was facing collapse in possibly the gravest political crisis of the war at the precise moment of *U-553*'s trip into the St. Lawrence. The results of the plebiscite on conscription held on 27 April had revealed a deeply divided country. Over 70 percent of voters in the mainly English-speaking provinces had voted "yes" to release the government from its pledge against overseas conscription, but an equally resounding proportion in Quebec had replied "no." The Cabinet, as badly divided as the country, plunged into intense negotiations about how to respond to the vote. Finally, on Friday, 8 May, the day Thurmann pushed through the Cabot Strait, the ministers reached an uneasy compromise. The government would introduce legislation, Bill

80, to repeal the clause of the National Resources Mobilization Act that limited the service of conscripts to duty on Canadian soil, but take no action to send conscripts overseas unless and until there was a manpower shortage in the overseas army. That was sufficient, although barely, for the leading pro-conscription ministers, Ralston and Macdonald. It proved to be more than P.J.A. Cardin, minister of public works and the senior French-Canadian minister, could support. On Saturday, 9 May, he went to see Mackenzie King and resigned from the government. When announcing Cardin's resignation to the Cabinet on Monday, 11 May, Mackenzie King observed: "Our real problem today was not to allow a civil war to develop in Canada at a time we were seeking to fight an international war."[28] Later that day, Mackenzie King introduced Bill 80 in the House of Commons, as he had agreed with the conscriptionists. His big worry was that Cardin's departure from the government would trigger defections from the party by French-Canadian members. He had a restive night before meeting caucus midday on 12 May, where he immediately "could see from the looks on [the] faces of many of the French-Canadian members that they were deeply concerned and seemed to be facing a discouraging situation." Mackenzie King returned to the theme that he had first developed to justify rearmament in 1936–37 and had marched out in full dress during the plebiscite campaign: distant conflicts were no longer remote. Canada was not fighting Britain's war, but rather struggling for her own survival.

> I then spoke of there being no longer any such thing as overseas. Modern inventions had made it possible for submarines to cross the oceans, operate in our waters, and return for refuelling. The same thing was true of bombing planes and the like, use of explosives, etc. We could no longer consider the world today in terms of what it was like before the war. The war had become what Churchill termed a universal war. The President had termed it the war for survival....
>
> ... we had pretty good evidence of what I had been saying about space and time being eliminated. Matters were moving very rapidly and distances were being overcome.

Mackenzie King (speaking before Macdonald issued his press release) broke the news to caucus as dramatically as possible to drive home the necessity for the French-Canadian members in particular to support the government. He was at the same time delivering a message to those English-speaking members who were impatient with the government's caution in not immediately dispatching home defence conscripts overseas.

> I drew from my pocket a brown envelope with red seal and said that they would be surprised to learn that therein was word that an enemy submarine had torpedoed a ship in the waters of the St. Lawrence west of Gaspé and that this morning the survivors were being landed on the shores of the river in the province of Quebec. I said I hoped they would not imagine this was an isolated happening, and that they might expect to find it followed by further raids and the probable approach of the enemy into our country both on its waters and overhead, with the possibility of destruction of Canadian lives, homes, etc.
>
> I said I thought in view of this, the men who had stood by the government should now feel they had a complete answer to others who have been opposing and who have been saying there is no danger to Canada, Mr. King was exaggerating, etc., etc.

Mackenzie King felt he had "made a mess of my presentation" because of tiredness, but he was elated by "enthusiasm" for a resolution put forward by Ernest Bertrand, MP for the Montreal riding of Laurier, that caucus "desires to place on record its unbounded confidence in the leadership of our Prime Minister ..." Strikingly, the preface of the resolution paid tribute to Mackenzie King's wisdom in pressing for rearmament in the mid-1930s, which, as Mackenzie King had underscored in his own presentation, had emphasized the need for home defence, especially for the St. Lawrence:

> Very few public men have been criticized more, yet when the debatable issues were over, it was always found that he had been right and had foreseen fa[r]ther than his opponents and sometimes his own friends.

Amongst the statesmen of the world, he stands high, very high today. The second session after his re-election in 1935 he had the foresight[ed] ness of asking for a substantial increase in the National Defense estimates. When the depression was not yet over it took great courage to come before the public with such a measure at that time.

Mackenzie King reflected in his diary that he had had supernatural help with the political crisis. "This word [of the submarine attack] had come to me after I had reached the office and before going to caucus. When one considers the whole timing of events, it certainly was an evidence of guidance as to the moment to take the action I did with regard to the time for holding caucus and, particularly, having caucus today rather than later. No word, at the time, had appeared in the press or outside."[29]

Shortly, the sinkings would be very hot news. When, on the afternoon of 12 May, a few hours after the Liberal caucus, Macdonald issued his press release about the sinking of the first ship, he knowingly opened the door to media coverage. From the time of the first sinkings in Canadian waters off Nova Scotia in January 1942, Brand's staff had impressed upon the press censorship authorities that there must be no early coverage of sinkings in Canadian waters (in most instances, if the navy released information about a sinking and thus cleared the way for press reports, it was not until a week or more after the event), and in no case could stories mention the area in which the sinkings had taken place. Such stories would give the Germans early confirmation that the submarine had reached its patrol area and been successful, essential information for planning the dispatch of additional submarines. Equally important, the broadcast of this information by the media would remove the necessity of the U-boat itself reporting and thus deny Allied radio stations the opportunity to triangulate its approximate position.[30]

When on 12 May Macdonald himself released the two most important pieces of information—when the sinking had taken place and where—the press censorship staff immediately began to clear stories for publication. Reporters had quickly got word of the sinking and rushed to the scene or telephoned to interview survivors.[31] Media censorship, as a result of Mackenzie King's own determination to maintain as much freedom of the press as possible, erred on the side of openness. The organization was staffed by former journalists and media executives whose natural inclination was to clear news for publication. Censorship, moreover, was voluntary to the extent that the media was not obliged to submit stories for review, although they would be subject to prosecution if they violated regulations.[32]

Macdonald did not limit his revelations to the press release on 12 May, despite his warning that there would be no information given out on future sinkings. The next day, he rose in the House of Commons to announce that a second ship had been destroyed and supplied further information on the timing and location by arguing that it was part of a single incident that did "not come within the scope of the prohibition which I laid upon myself yesterday."[33]

The "press was running wild," complained Brand to a censorship official. While admitting that Macdonald's own statements had opened the door,[34] Brand and his staff soon produced a study of the press stories as the basis for tighter guidelines for the censors. From the survivors' reports in the press it was clear precisely how many torpedoes the U-boat had expended, the time of night and other aspects of the U-boat's tactics that had proved successful, the nationality of at least *Leto*, where in the St. Lawrence the attacks had taken place, and the shock of the crews in having been attacked in waters so far from the open ocean. Some of the details were of operational value to the enemy, and the points that weren't gave material of great use for propaganda, one of the key tools the Germans were using to undermine the morale of Allied merchant seamen.[35]

Yet the government had no reason to be unhappy about the graphic descriptions of the menace to the homeland. One major daily, the *Montreal Gazette*, which had supported the government in its appeal in Quebec for a "yes" vote in the plebiscite, printed on its front page an account of Mackenzie King's success at caucus on 12 May beside the report of the sinkings in the St. Lawrence and linked the events much as Mackenzie King himself had done:

> Stirred by the startling news of U-boat invasion of the river St. Lawrence, Liberal senators and commoners at a caucus today unanimously adopted a resolution expressing "unbounded confidence" in the leadership of Prime Minister Mackenzie King.
>
> Both the enemy undersea success within the province of Quebec and the action of the Government caucus ... were a fitting answer to yesterday's desertion of the Ministry by P.J.A. Cardin ...

The lead editorial was more explicit: "What will be the attitude now of the former Minister and of the members from the 'No' vote constituencies in the province? They have known all along, or should have known, the danger of waiting for the enemy to come as so many European countries waited."[36]

A week later in the Quebec legislature, Adélard Godbout, the Liberal premier, drew on the sinkings in the St. Lawrence to attack the opposition leader, Maurice Duplessis, and his Union Nationale party's opposition to the federal government's war effort. Godbout opposed overseas conscription, but he believed that only Mackenzie King among federal leaders could be trusted to respect Quebec's "no" vote in the plebiscite. Godbout's arguments echoed the points Mackenzie King had made in the Liberal caucus:

> The enemy is at our gates and what happens? The Opposition attack political opponents. While the Germans were preparing to invade us, the Dominion Government was doing its duty making cannons to defend us. While the Government was carrying out its effort the Leader of the Opposition (Maurice Duplessis) criticized it for making cannons instead of bread to feed the people.
>
> How many countries in Europe have fallen under Hitler's heel? We saw them fall and we saw them carry a yoke of slavery which is worse

than war. We heard them say that the war was that of the neighbor, and that they would not fight until it came to their borders. Hitler is controlling half of Europe. He is here in Quebec, he is in the St. Lawrence River attacking our ships and fishing fleets, and still some say that the war is not ours.[37]

THE ARMED FORCES' RESPONSE to the attacks was not as improvised as the struggle against ice and snow by the personnel at Gaspé suggested. There was a script, the gulf defence plan, whose revision had been completed only weeks before. The most important first step was to deny the enemy targets. Early on 12 May, within two-and-a-half hours of the attack on *Nicoya*, the navy's Atlantic Coast command (COAC) shut the gulf to incoming and outbound shipping. Approaching the gulf were three ships from the fast westbound transatlantic convoy ON 91. As the main convoy came in south of Cape Race on 11 May, it had been met by the Halifax-based corvette HMCS *Arrowhead*, which would normally have escorted the three ships for the St. Lawrence only partway to the Cabot Strait. Following a day behind ON 91 was the slow convoy ON 90, with seventeen merchant ships scheduled to break off on the afternoon of 12 May with local escort towards the Cabot Strait by the Halifax-based corvette *Kenogami*. Under the orders broadcast by COAC at 2:30 AM on 12 May, *Arrowhead* and *Kenogami* stayed with their charges through to Sydney; on 14 May, the two corvettes then carried on together into the gulf escorting a total of twenty-one merchant vessels. The convoy arrived at Bic Island on 17 May, where ten merchant ships bound for Sydney and Halifax were waiting. *Arrowhead* immediately took the vessels under escort, now joined by *Medicine Hat* and by *Burlington*, another Bangor-class minesweeper that had come from Halifax. This was designated convoy QS 1, and was a fast convoy with a speed of eighteen kilometres per hour. *Kenogami* sailed two days later with twelve slow merchant ships in a convoy designated QSS 1A, for "Quebec to Sydney Slow," with a speed of fourteen kilometres per hour.[38] The Bangor *Burlington* joined the escort, and the newly commissioned corvette *Woodstock* sailed as an additional escort. After *Arrowhead* and *Kenogami* reached Sydney with their respective convoys on 20 and 22 May, they continued to Halifax and returned to ocean escort duties.[39] Responsibility for the SQ–QS series passed to the Gulf Escort Force, the five Bangors that had come from Halifax and the armed yacht HMCS *Raccoon* all now based at Gaspé.

The scheme for alternating fast and slow convoys had been laid down in the defence plan for the gulf, but it proved impractical. To help replace ocean shipping losses, many vessels built for the Great Lakes had come out to supply industries in the gulf and for service on the Atlantic. A "good percentage of the traffic" in the gulf comprised "old, dirty bottomed, slow lakers," incapable of maintaining a 14-kilometre-per-hour convoy speed, the Trade Division's report for 1942 explained. "Consequently, the faster ships had to suffer as it was considered unwise and inexpedient to escort just the faster ships leaving the slow lakers to the mercies of the U-boats, since, if this plan were carried out, 80% of the shipping would still have been proceeding unescorted."[40] The preponderance of slow ships appears to be why the distinction between fast and slow convoys was abandoned with the sailing of SQ 3 from Sydney on 23 May under the escort of the Bangor *Drummondville* and *Raccoon*, and with QS 3 which sailed from Bic Island on 25 May under the escort of the Bangor *Medicine Hat*, with the new corvettes *Brantford* and *Noranda* joining as additional escorts.[41] Thereafter, all convoys had a nominal speed of fourteen kilometres per hour but in fact accepted slower ships, had the simple QS or SQ designation, and were numbered sequentially. Convoys departed from Bic Island at alternating intervals of four and five days and from Sydney at the same alternating intervals.

The prevalence of slow ships in the St. Lawrence was to have important consequences later in the 1942 season, when additional U-boats arrived. Slow convoys were much easier targets for U-boats, as had been well established on the Atlantic. In the gulf, where complex water conditions often blinded asdic, the Canadian warships' only equipment for underwater detection, and the geographically restricted shipping lanes gave little or no scope for evasive routing of convoys, the situation was in some respects even more difficult than on the open ocean. Still, the global shortage of Allied shipping dictated the use of old, slow ships, and they would have been infinitely more vulnerable sailing alone.

The air force was in much the same position, short of aircraft and pressing ahead with the completion of operating facilities. The rapid mobility of aircraft and the aerodromes of the British Commonwealth Air Training Plan (BCATP), however, allowed a quick response. A Canso amphibian from 5 Squadron at Dartmouth, already assigned before news of the sinkings to follow up the search of the western gulf begun on 10 May, took off before dawn on 12 May. Eastern Air Command now ordered the squadron to organize a detachment with ground crew to service the aircraft for extended operations in the gulf. Because the air station at Gaspé was not ready, the amphibian landed that evening at the Mont Joli training base. Earlier that day, two Lockheed Hudson bombers from 11 Squadron at Dartmouth had flown into Mont Joli for extended operations in the western gulf. During the afternoon, when it became clear that some of *Nicoya*'s people were still missing, three Lockheed Hudsons from the British operational training unit at Debert, Nova Scotia, searched from the vicinity of the sinking along the path of the currents out into the central gulf. At Sydney, 119 Squadron's Bolingbrokes continued to fly cover for the trial escorted gulf group as it passed through the Cabot Strait and also escorted *Arrowhead* and her three merchant ships from ON 91 as they approached Sydney. The 116 Squadron at Dartmouth dispatched a Canso flying boat to North Sydney, where both the aircraft and its crew transferred to 117 Squadron to hasten the rebuilding of that unit (whose aircraft and crews had been sent to reinforce the west coast late in 1941) for long-range coverage of the gulf and the ocean approaches to Sydney. Next day, this experienced crew patrolled the eastern gulf from Sydney to Anticosti for nearly thirteen hours, from before sunrise until after sunset on 13 May.

The modest buildup continued. A second 5 Squadron Canso amphibian from Dartmouth joined the Mont Joli detachment on 14 May. The 116 Squadron at Dartmouth dispatched additional Cansos and crews to 117 Squadron at North Sydney, strengthening that unit to six flying boats and crews by 29 May.[42] The British No. 31 General Reconnaissance School at Charlottetown, one of the Royal Air Force schools located in Canada under the BCATP, continued to exercise over the waters north of PEI to cover deep-water shipping routes. There were twenty-five and more flights by the station's complement of Avro Anson training aircraft each day, but these training machines had a short effective range, only to a line from the mouth of Baie des Chaleurs in the west to the Magdalen Islands and the Cape Breton coast. The RCAF suggested shifting the route for the SQ–QS through-gulf convoys from the north of the Magdalens to the south of the islands, to take advantage of the air cover, and on 14 May the navy agreed.[43]

The focal point of this expansion of Canada's maritime trade defences was Sydney. The sudden need to implement the plans for the gulf coincided with the reopening of the Cape Breton port for the assembly of transatlantic SC convoys and the reorganization of the coastal convoys on the Atlantic coast to protect the heavy summer traffic to and from Sydney. Commander R.B. Mitchell, the naval control service officer at Sydney, proudly reported that in the seventeen days from 12 to 28 May, "142 ships arrived at Sydney and 72 sailed in eighteen Coastal Convoys. The introduction of these Coastal Convoys ... has placed Sydney rather in the position of a railway junction as Convoys radiate from us in five directions." In addition to the main SQ–QS series through the gulf, there was a new service between Sydney and Corner Brook, Newfoundland, known as SB for the northbound run across the Cabot Strait, and BS for the southbound run to Sydney. The thrice weekly passage of the Newfoundland railway ferries between North Sydney and Port aux Basques had also now to be considered a protected convoy sailing, designated SPAB. On the Atlantic coast there was the Sydney to Halifax series, known as SH and HS, that, as we have seen, was inaugurated as extensions of the first Quebec to Sydney sailings for those ships needing through passage to Halifax. The CL–LC convoys from St. John's to Halifax on 14 May changed to Sydney as the Nova Scotia terminus.[44]

The Atlantic coast convoys were escorted by warships of the Halifax-based Western Local Escort Force, but the Quebec–Sydney series and the crossings to Corner Brook and Port aux Basques were the responsibility of the paltry forces at Gaspé and Sydney. By the end of May, these still included only the five Bangors of the Gulf Escort Force at Gaspé, the single Bangor, *Medicine Hat,* based at Sydney, and three armed yachts, two based at Gaspé and one at Sydney. Nine of the new Fairmile motor launches had reached Sydney, but were not yet ready for operations.[45] The air force stood in for the navy. In addition to flying escort missions for each of the convoys, the main operational units carried out daily anti-submarine patrols. The Cansos at North Sydney and Mont Joli, with their long endurance, swept the whole of the shipping routes from the river to the Cabot Strait, starting before dawn and landing after sunset. The Hudsons at Mont Joli concentrated on the river and the western gulf to approximately the eastern end of Anticosti Island. From 14 May, the Bolingbrokes at Sydney, with help from the flying boats at North Sydney, endeavoured to maintain a constant patrol of the Cabot Strait, the most heavily travelled focal point of shipping traffic in the gulf, from before dawn until after sunset.[46] In all patrol and escort missions, coverage at daybreak and sunset had priority to discourage submarines endeavouring to get into position for submerged attacks by day or fast surface runs in pursuit of shipping at night.[47]

The defence measures worked. *U-553* cruised along the north shore of the Gaspé Peninsula, expecting she could repeat her success against further sailings of batches of unescorted merchant ships timed to join the next big trans-ocean convoys from Sydney. But, as Thurmann tersely reported to U-boat headquarters on 21 May, there was "no shipping traffic, very alert air surveillance, warship patrols ..." The prompt introduction of convoy had eliminated the sailings of unescorted major vessels (Thurmann saw only a few "small coasters" in the distance), and the presence of the warships and especially aircraft forced him to run submerged except for the six hours of full darkness each night. The submarine was thus virtually immobile by day with only a limited search capability through the periscope and by hydrophones. Yet, as we have seen, more than twenty major merchant vessels passed around the north shore of the Gaspé Peninsula westbound to Bic Island and more than twenty eastbound to Sydney while *U-553* was on patrol, but they sailed in a total of only three convoys, which the submarine failed to detect. *U-553* departed through the Cabot Strait on 22 May. The Germans had discovered that radio reception in the gulf was often poor, and, as the submarine departed, the radio operator was finally able to pick up a number of messages, including some good news: "[t]he boat is named in the Wehrmacht News. Great jubilation." German propaganda broadcasts had begun to crow about the successful penetration of the St. Lawrence on 13 May, adding false information to the basic facts that had been gleaned from commercial radio broadcasts in Canada of Macdonald's announcements.[48]

The propaganda broadcast, in fact, accurately reflected Dönitz's reaction to *U-553*'s operation. What mattered was not Thurmann's report of how quickly and effectively the Canadian forces had responded to the sinkings on 11–12 May, but that a U-boat suffering from damage had succeeded in destroying substantial steamers. There was still a plenitude of easy targets in southern U.S. waters and the Caribbean, so Dönitz was not in a hurry to pursue opportunities in the St. Lawrence, but he was fully aware of the possibilities for further success there.

Holding the Home Front, July 1942

Convoy QS 15, which departed from Bic Island for Sydney on the afternoon of 5 July, was the sixth escort mission in the SQ–QS series for HMCS *Drummondville*, one of the five Bangors assigned to the Gulf Escort Force at Gaspé in May. With twelve merchant ships, the convoy was moderately large for the gulf series, but the Bangor was the sole escort, which was not unusual. Air escort by a Canso from Gaspé would begin at first light on the sixth. The air force had not received early notice that the convoy would sail, and the Gaspé air detachment was already busy covering SQ 16, which had sailed from Sydney late on the third. In any event, the river was heavy with fog when QS 15 formed up at Bic Island, which would have prevented air support.[1]

Drummondville groped through the fog around the merchant ships, coaxing them into position while carrying out an anti-submarine patrol.[2] Lieutenant J.P. Fraser had commanded the Bangor since she was commissioned in October 1941. A former merchant mariner, he had joined the

RCMP marine section in the 1930s. Like most of the personnel in the section, he had also become a member of the RCNR and been called out for active service at the outbreak of war. He had been almost continuously in command of small vessels since 1939.[3] Experienced and no doubt showing the habits of a policeman, he had little patience with the balky merchant ships of QS 15. "Convoy station keeping and smoke control were bad," he reported. "Example: On the afternoon of the 5th., a signal was made to S.S. *Prince Edward Island,* 'you are outside your distance.' The *Prince Edward Island* evidently thinking this an occasion for humour replied with a signal to the escort [which had dropped back to try to push the lagging merchants into position], 'You are astern of station.'"

As the convoy got underway at 1:36 PM, a Fairmile, attached from Gaspé to Rimouski for local river patrols, followed along "to round up stragglers." The sailing formation was two rows each with five merchant ships abreast and a third row in the rear with two merchant ships. At dusk *Drummondville* swept round astern of the convoy and discovered that it was still "spread back over a distance of about three miles [5.5 kilometres]," compared to about 800 metres if the ships had been in their proper stations.

The convoy was a slow one, only eleven kilometres per hour, making it easy to track. It was being tracked. *U-132,* like Thurmann's *U-553,* was a veteran U-boat under the command of an aggressive, skilful, long-service professional officer. Kapitänleutnant Ernst Vogelsang, born in 1911, had joined the navy in 1931. After service in destroyers, in June 1940 he began U-boat training, commanded a training submarine from December 1940 to May 1941, and in the latter month commissioned *U-132.* This was the boat's—and Vogelsang's—third combat mission. Allied vessels destroyed during the first two missions included a patrol boat, a freighter, and the U.S. Coast Guard Cutter *Alexander Hamilton.* The third mission started badly. On 13 June 1942, three days after departing from La Pallice, France, *U-132* was caught on the surface by a corvette and damaged. Headquarters advised Vogelsang to return to port, but he was determined to continue. On 20 June, in the north central Atlantic, he rendezvoused with *U-460*, one of the big "milch cow" supply submarines, refuelled, and was thus prepared for extended operations.[4] It may have been Thurmann's success in the St. Lawrence, even while damaged, that brought headquarters on 26 June to order *U-132* on a follow-up mission. Certainly Thurmann's experience was fresh to hand; *U-553* had just returned to port after her St. Lawrence mission on 24 June. Headquarters advised Vogelsang to head to the estuary of the river, where Thurmann had achieved his two sinkings. Information in headquarters' further signal of 27 June provides additional evidence about the impact of Eastern Air Command's efforts. Although defending naval forces were "weak" Vogelsang was to run submerged by day to avoid aircraft. Vogelsang followed this advice to the letter, running submerged except in the hours of darkness beginning on the morning of 30 June, when he approached the central part of the Cabot Strait. He surfaced briefly on the afternoon of the thirtieth to check his navigation, but within six minutes dived again when a "flying boat" suddenly appeared. Of the twenty-four days he spent in the gulf, he ran submerged fully 70 percent of the time. Vogelsang also observed radio silence after his exchange with headquarters on 27 June. The caution paid off: Allied intelligence had no clue that a submarine had entered the gulf.

By daylight on 4 July, Vogelsang had penetrated to the narrowest part of the estuary off Les Méchins, some 130 kilometres west of where Thurmann had had his successes. For about thirty-six hours he patrolled the waters off Les Méchins westward about twenty-five kilometres towards Matane. At 7:20 PM on 5 July, he finally saw through his periscope what he was looking for: a "convoy of 12 merchant ships is assembling." The description fits QS 15, and the timing is correct. The statement that the convoy was "assembling" corresponds to *Drummondville*'s sweep to the rear at about the same time to discover that the merchant ships were still spread out widely from their proper stations. There was not enough daylight left for Vogelsang to close at his slow submerged speed and still be able to track targets through the periscope. Only at 10:30 PM was it dark enough for him to surface to pursue the convoy. He soon saw two convoys passing each other: "5 merchant ships are inbound and 5 outbound." This was almost certainly SQ 16, under the escort of HMCS *Clayoquot,* passing westbound immediately north of QS 15.[5] The weather was now "misty," with "moderate" visibility. The water was phosphorescent, with the result, as Fraser remarked, that the "water line of the ships showed up clearly as if they were illuminated." These were "[i]deal conditions," as he later noted, "for short range torpedo firing."

When the convoy was about seventeen kilometres off Cap Chat, Vogelsang, as Thurmann had done, closed from the darkness of the coast towards the southern flank of the ships so he could shoot at their long side profiles. At twenty-one minutes after midnight on 6 July, when he was 1500 metres south of the southernmost ship in the first row, he fired a spread of four torpedoes. The reports of Vogelsang and Fraser agree that at that moment the first row of ships were fairly well aligned abreast. From Vogelsang's perspective as he approached from the flank, the broadsides of the ships overlapped to give him an extended target. At least two torpedoes found their mark. The Greek steamer *Anastasios Pateras,* carrying trucks and general cargo to Britain and sailing second in the row, suffered an explosion near the stokehold. The three firemen on duty there to feed coal to the boilers appear to have been killed instantly. The remaining twenty-six members of the crew immediately abandoned ship in a lifeboat, and the steamer sank within ten minutes. Two or three minutes after the explosion in *Anastasios Pateras,* there was an explosion square amidships in the Belgian steamer *Hainaut,* also carrying general cargo to Britain. *Hainaut* was at the far northern end of the row and, as Fraser reported, was "some distance outside of station," meaning she was still further to the north and several thousands of metres away from

James Phillip Fraser, commanding officer of HMCS *Drummondville*, one of the small force of Bangor minesweepers that carried out the bulk of convoy escort duties in the St. Lawrence in 1942. A professional merchant mariner, Fraser joined the RCMP marine section in the 1930s, and on the outbreak of war volunteered for duty with the Royal Canadian Naval Reserve. Photo taken in 1944, when Fraser was promoted to the rank of commander. Library and Archives Canada, e010859212.

Edgar G. Skinner, commanding officer of HMCS *Arrowhead*, one of the corvettes that reinforced the St. Lawrence in the summer and early fall of 1942. Skinner was another of the experienced merchant mariners who served in the Royal Canadian Naval Reserve and supplied most of the commanding officers for the corvettes and Bangors that were built in 1940–42. Photo taken in 1944, when Skinner was promoted to the rank of commander. Library and Archives Canada, e010859213.

Angus L. Macdonald, minister of national defence for naval services, and Vice-Admiral G.C. Jones, chief of the naval staff, in February 1945. In 1942, when Jones was commanding officer Atlantic Coast, he had supervised preparations for the defence of the St. Lawrence and operations against the first U-boats to attack. Macdonald aggressively defended the armed forces against charges in the press and by opposition politicians that more could and should have been done to counter the U-boats. Library and Archives Canada, e010859215.

Eric S. Brand, the Royal Navy officer on loan to the Canadian navy who organized and controlled merchant ship convoys, the most effective defence against U-boat attack. His advice and decisions shaped the defence arrangements in the St. Lawrence. Photo probably taken in 1940, after Brand was promoted to the rank of captain. Library and Archives Canada, e010859216.

HMCS *Magog*, motionless in the water shortly after the frigate was hit by a torpedo from *U-1223* on 14 October 1944. The explosion demolished the 20-metre-long after section of the hull, including the propellers and propeller shafts. Clearly visible are the buckled remnants of the upper deck of the stern part of the ship, folded overtop of the surviving superstructure. Library and Archives Canada, e010859218.

HMS *Salisbury*, one of two British destroyers ordered into the St. Lawrence by the Canadian navy in September 1942 to reinforce the defences. The lantern-like structure atop the bridge and ahead of the forward mast housed a short-wave radar that, unlike earlier long-wave types, could detect the low, narrow superstructure of a surfaced submarine. Library and Archives Canada, e010859220.

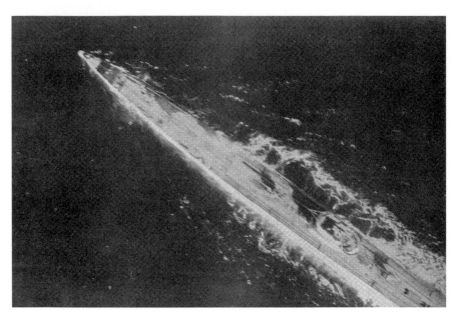

U-165 under attack on 9 September 1942 by a Lockheed Hudson of 113 Squadron, piloted by Pilot Officer Robert S. Keetley. Library and Archives Canada, e010859221.

Consolidated Canso or Catalina flying boat from the after deck of a Fairmile, showing the vessel's twin .50 calibre machine guns and depth charges, at Gaspé, June 1943. Library and Archives Canada, e010859223.

HMCS *Clayoquot,* a Bangor minesweeper that escorted Sydney–Quebec convoys from May to December 1942. In the foreground is one of the depth charge rails at the stern of another Bangor, with the hoist used to reload the rail with additional charges. Photo taken at the training area off Pictou, Nova Scotia, in July 1943. Library and Archives Canada, PA 116969.

A survivor of the torpedoed U.S. Army transport *Chatham* being rescued by personnel of HMCS *Trail.* The survivor appears to be coated with viscous fuel oil that was disgorged from the tanks of sinking ships and imperilled people in the water who could be choked or poisoned by the tarry substance. Library and Archives Canada, PA 200327.

Survivors of SS *Nicoya* coming ashore at L'Anse-à-Valleau from the local fishing boat that rescued them on the morning of 12 May 1942. The naval officer (with binoculars) is Commander W.B. Armit, RCNR, commander of the naval base at Gaspé. Photo by Ian Tate.

Personnel at the Gaspé naval base launch the harbour patrol craft *Venning* from the slip where it had wintered on the morning of 11 May 1942. This was the only naval vessel available on the Gaspé coast to respond to the news that SS *Nicoya* and SS *Leto* had been torpedoed off shore during the night of 11–12 May. Photo by Ian Tate.

HMCS *Q 090* and *Q 083*, two of the Fairmile launches based at Gaspé in 1942 for escort and anti-submarine patrol duties. Photo by Ian Tate.

The twin depth charge rails at the stern of HMCS *Hepatica*, together with their crew, at the naval jetty at Gaspé on 22 August 1942. Immediately behind is the Bangor HMCS *Chedabucto*, J168. Photo by Ian Tate.

"Although there had been some sort of a little establishment of the Navy before the summer of '42, HMCS 'Fort Ramsay' was officially taken over from the builders and 'commissioned' into the Navy on May 1, 1942 … Almost the entire personnel of the Base attended this ceremony, so you can see how few of us there were, just 11 days before the first ship was torpedoed." Photo and caption by Ian Tate.

"Burial of A.B. [Able Seaman Donald St. Clair] Bowser [RCNR], Sept 14/42, survivor from HMCS 'Charlottetown,' who subsequently died [at Gaspé] of injuries received when D/C's [depth charges] exploded while he was in the water." Photo and caption by Ian Tate.

Anastasios Pateras. The hits on two such widely separated targets led Fraser to conclude that two submarines must have attacked together. A fireman was killed in the explosion, and the other forty members of the crew quickly took to boats; the ship sank after about twenty minutes.[6]

The first that *Drummondville* or anyone in the convoy knew that anything was amiss was when the torpedo explosions shattered the night. There was pandemonium. "The convoy disperses in all directions," Vogelsang reported, "the larger portion turns inbound [i.e., back up the river in the direction of Rimouski]." Neither of the stricken ships had fired emergency rockets, the standard signal for ships in convoy to indicate that they had been hit, so Fraser had no idea what was going on. At first he assumed that the Fairmile from Rimouski, which had neglected to send a departure signal, was still following the convoy and that the explosions were its depth charge attacks on a submarine contact. *Drummondville* fired three star shells—projectiles that on bursting high in the air released powerful illumination flares attached to small parachutes that slowed their descent—to light up the area outside the convoy and dropped a depth charge in an effort to assist the presumed hunt by the Fairmile, which in fact had long since returned to port. The Bangor also attempted to illuminate the scene with its searchlight, but this proved ineffective because of the misty conditions. In the confusion, Fraser was finally able to find the convoy commodore's ship, *Fjorheim,* which had been sailing in the front row next to *Hainaut,* and the commodore signalled that he believed three ships, *Hainaut, Anastasios Pateras,* and, in the second row, *Panchito,* had been torpedoed. At fifty-eight minutes past midnight, thirty-seven minutes after the first attack, *U-132* fired at one of the dispersing merchant ships and three minutes later, at 1:01 AM, fired at another ship, but both shots missed and the torpedoes appear not to have detonated. At 1:45 AM, after closing to within 800 metres of the British steamer *Dinaric,* which had been the southernmost vessel in the second row and was now charging ahead on the convoy's original course, the submarine fired again, and this time hit *Dinaric* amidships, killing four of the crew. The ship rapidly listed, so the remaining thirty-four members of the crew took to a lifeboat. Meanwhile *Drummondville* rushed to the sound of the explosion, passed *Dinaric* with a huge hole in her side, and fired a star shell, which caught *U-132* in its glare, "distance about 900 to 1000 yards [820 to 914 metres]." The U-boat appeared to be stopped and did not dive until *Drummondville*, rushing in to ram, was "almost on top of her." The Bangor dropped three depth charges and then, astern, saw the "submarine surfaced ... apparently turning in a half circle before stopping completely and starting to settle." *Drummondville* swung around to make another attempt to ram, but the submarine was "sinking fast." The Bangor dropped more depth charges, which brought up "strong smelling oil." Believing that the U-boat had at the very least been driven out of action with severe damage and worried about the threat from a second submarine to the now scattered and utterly vulnerable ships of the convoy, *Drummondville* picked up *Dinaric*'s people and proceeded to try to reassemble the other vessels.

The U-boat had not been destroyed, but had had an exceedingly close call. When the Bangor appeared, *U-132* had in fact immediately crash-dived. The impression in *Drummondville* that the submarine had hesitated was the result of the unusual water conditions in many areas of the gulf. *U-132* had hit what felt almost like a physical barrier at twenty metres' depth and could dive no deeper. The submarine had encountered "density layering," heavy, cold, salt seawater underlying the warmer, lighter, fresh water from the river. At that moment the boat was severely rocked by the first three depth charges. Vogelsang does not mention having surfaced again, but noted that the dense water layer gave the boat "a tendency to rise"; the submarine was not in control and likely surfaced without the crew realizing it. In desperation, Vogelsang flooded the impulse tanks in the forward torpedo tubes, and with this additional weight in the bow, the boat broke through the density layer and went deeper as additional charges exploded in the distance. There was a new panic. The damage from *Drummondville*'s first three charges broke the main line for draining and flooding the buoyancy tanks. Only the smaller line for fine adjustments was functioning, and fine adjustments were not sufficient in these difficult water conditions. The boat plummeted to 185 metres, testing the limits at which the water pressure would crush the hull. Vogelsang blew water out of the buoyancy tanks, and the boat rose to 100 to 110 metres. It wouldn't hold there, even though the electric engines were running at three-quarters full submerged speed. This speed would normally give enough forward motion to counteract the tendency to sink, but it was a risky manoeuvre as such fast running would within a very few hours deplete the batteries, the only source of power with which to regain control of the boat. Still, the submarine drifted back down and down to 180 metres.

Staring death in the face, Vogelsang took an even greater risk. At least it had become quiet above, which gave hope. He blew out the buoyancy tanks and surfaced at 2:46 AM, fired up the diesels, and "[t]ook off at half speed." Again, he had to balance dangers and opportunity quickly. Vogelsang believed he saw "2 escort ships" 3.5 kilometres away and that one of them was following. Half speed, about seventeen kilometres per hour, allowed him to get away, but without broadcasting his position by the noise of the diesels at full speed and the bright sparkle the full-speed wake would create in the phosphorescent water. *Drummondville* in fact was still busy attempting to reorganize the convoy in the presence of what Fraser believed was a continuing threat from a second submarine. Finally, at 3:30 AM the Bangor's asdic operator heard the sound of diesels in the water. *Drummondville* rushed towards the position and briefly sighted a phosphorescent wake before the sound disappeared. Star shell revealed nothing. Fraser dropped depth charges and then returned to his priority task of gathering up and protecting the scattered merchant ships. He reasoned that the submarine he briefly sighted, whether it had in fact submerged or begun to run quietly to continue its escape on the surface, was no longer a threat and that he must not be distracted from the danger posed by a second U-boat. He was right that *U-132* was no longer a threat. Vogelsang reported that *Drummondville*'s star shell illumination had been short of the U-boat. *U-132* continued on the surface heading inshore towards shallower water, the line on the charts that showed 100-metre depth, where the submarine could rest on the bottom while carrying out repairs. The submarine remained submerged for over eighteen hours.

At 6 AM on 6 July, after daybreak, *Drummondville* finally sighted four of the merchant ships. A very heavy fog descended as she tried to bring the vessels into formation, and the Bangor was able to keep contact with only one merchantman, with which she reached Sydney the next afternoon. The convoy had been an endurance test from beginning to end. Commander Armit at Gaspé commended Fraser's "great zeal and ability," and with good reason. It is difficult to imagine a more chaotic situation than that as the sole escort of a moderately large convoy of ill-disciplined ships caught in the dead of night by a submarine in a perfect ambush position in an area that intelligence showed was clear of the enemy. Fraser had not only kept his mission clearly in view all through the chaos, but responded quickly and effectively when suddenly confronted by the enemy and driven him away with serious damage. In 1944 Fraser would receive command of HMCS *Waskesiu*, one of the RCN's powerful new frigates, and show similar grit and skill in destroying *U-257* during a prolonged nighttime hunt in the central north Atlantic that won accolades from the most senior British commanders in the Atlantic theatre.[7]

Drummondville's first broadcasts warning of the attack appear not to have been heard by some stations or to have been garbled in transmission. A general alert finally went out to the east coast bases from Atlantic Coast command at Halifax in a signal at 2:40 AM.[8] The nearest source of support was the two RCAF Canso amphibians at Gaspé, but the dense fog that would in a few hours engulf the estuary had already rolled in, making flying impossible. The training airfield at Mont Joli, just 125 kilometres west of Cap Chat, was clear, but the only combat

aircraft available there were Curtiss Kittyhawk fighters, not equipped
to carry bombs, of the recently established 130 Squadron. The unit was
not yet fully operational, and one of the pilots who flew that day later
recalled that none of the machine guns on the aircraft was loaded with
ammunition. Urgent efforts to overcome this difficulty got the first of
four aircraft, piloted by Squadron Leader J.A.J. Chevrier, the squadron's
commanding officer, into the air at 4:35 AM. The fighters searched the
Cap Chat area, where they saw boats of survivors still on the water and
the listing hulk of *Dinaric* kept afloat by her cargo of lumber. Shortly
after 6 AM, two Fairey Battle single-engine bombers from the training
school at Mont Joli also reached the scene. These aircraft had proved
too undependable for combat early in the war and therefore had been
relegated to training duties. The ground crew at Mont Joli hastily fitted
113-kilogram aerial depth charges in the aircraft for the patrol. True to
the Battle's poor reputation, one of the aircraft had engine difficulty that
forced its early return. The other machine completed a two-hour patrol,
refuelled, and then carried on with a second three-hour mission.[9]

Chevrier, commanding officer of 130 Squadron, was the first pilot
on the scene; he never came back. The only lead that air force accident
investigators got was from civilians near Cap Chat who said they had
seen an aircraft about three kilometres from shore suffer two explosions and plunge into the water at 6:30 AM. That would have been
very close to the limit of the Kittyhawk's fuel. Searches in the area,
including dragging operations in the water, found no trace of wreckage
or Chevrier's remains.[10] Rumours that he had been shot down either
by friendly fire or the Germans began to circulate. In 1982, one of the
squadron's former pilots wrote, "I heard from an independent informer
that his bullet-riddled body was found on the north Gaspésian Coast."[11]

During the afternoon when the weather began to clear, six Hudsons,
three from 119 Squadron at Sydney and three from 113 Squadron, a
newly formed unit at Yarmouth, re-established the anti-submarine
detachment at Mont Joli. One aircraft was always on patrol over the

estuary and the western gulf as far as Anticosti until 11 July. Shortage of aircraft on the Atlantic coast forced the return of the 119 Squadron Hudsons to Sydney, and the 113 Squadron aircraft kept up patrols for eighteen hours each day. The flying boats from 117 Squadron at North Sydney and Gaspé patrolled the eastern gulf as far north as the Strait of Belle Isle. The main body of 119 Squadron at Sydney patrolled the southern part of the eastern gulf, including the Cabot Strait and its approaches.

In response to the first news of the attacks, on the morning of 6 July, Gaspé dispatched the Bangor *Chedabucto* and the armed yacht *Raccoon* to assist the convoy. *Raccoon* took over the escort of three vessels from which *Drummondville* became separated in the fog. *Chedabucto* pushed on to the west searching for other dispersed merchant vessels.

The next day, 7 July, *Clayoquot,* following up air patrol reports that *Dinaric* was still afloat, located the wreck in the river off Mont Louis Bay. The Bangor attempted a tow that night, but had to abandon the effort as the hull began to settle and then turned over. Salvage experts confirmed that a tow was impossible. *Clayoquot,* assisted by several other warships, had to drop depth charges as well as pour in gunfire before the bow, still buoyed by the timber cargo, slipped below the surface.[12]

Admiral Jones at Halifax had ordered outbound shipping due to sail from river ports temporarily stopped, but he was anxious to keep the convoys on schedule. This he proposed to do by laying on additional anti-submarine searches and strengthened escorts.[13] At midday on 6 July, he had ordered three corvettes from the work-ups training area at Pictou, on the northern shore of Nova Scotia, into the western gulf. These were *Kamloops,* an experienced ship that was leading the exercises, and *Port Arthur* and *Ville de Quebec,* new ships commissioned at the end of May, that were working up. The group patrolled the convoy route as far as Gaspé, reached on the seventh, where the naval officer in charge ordered them to investigate a submarine sighting by an observer on shore at Sept

Îles on the north shore of the St. Lawrence.[14] Eastern Air Command
also responded and later that day a Hudson from 119 Squadron's Mont
Joli detachment dropped aerial depth charges on what appeared to be a
periscope. German records have confirmed that *U-132* was well to the
south at the time, and the aircraft likely attacked one of the many bits
of flotsam in those waters. That was not evident at the time, however.[15]

QS 16, comprising thirteen merchant vessels including two from
QS 15 that had turned back during the attack, would normally have
sailed from Bic Island on the afternoon of 8 July. The sailing was
delayed, but only by twelve hours to the morning of 9 July to allow the
three corvettes, after their patrol towards Sept Îles, to search the river
on their way towards Bic to meet the eastbound convoy. Even if the
warships did not locate the submarine, their presence would force the
enemy commander to exercise caution and keep back from the shipping
channel. The corvettes then joined the convoy, reinforcing the escort (the
Bangor *Burlington* and five Fairmiles) as the convoy left the river and
proceeded through the estuary.

Vogelsang's attack coincided with a new phase in the political crisis
over conscription, the vote on the second reading of Bill 80 which would
remove home-service limits on the employment of conscript soldiers.
Mackenzie King was tenacious in his efforts to respect Quebec's negative
vote in the plebiscite. Engaged against the pro-conscription wing of his
Cabinet, he had won agreement that the government would not send
draftees overseas unless and until the measure was a military necessity.
He was, however, determined to make a further commitment. Even if the
military situation overseas required dispatch of conscripts, the government would return to Parliament for a vote of confidence before acting.
This was, Mackenzie King wrote in his diary, "one of the most important debates ... of my political life."[16]

The prime minister got word of Vogelsang's attack on the afternoon
of 6 July, just when he was working on his speech for the Commons that
would immediately precede the vote. The submarine's success, he wrote,

"helps to bear out necessity of keeping one eye upon the forces that we must keep in Canada for our own country. It also helps to illustrate wherein, by degrees, the people in the province of Quebec will see the need for destruction of the enemy overseas ... I have felt today that there was a presence near that was giving me confidence in the course I was taking. I have no fears as to its consequences be they what they may. They will be, I believe, for what is best in the end."[17] Once more, as in the political crisis in May, the U-boat attack gave him reassurance that conscripts should be sent overseas only when and if there was a clear, urgent need to do so.

Mackenzie King acted forcefully the next day, 7 July. He called a meeting of the full Cabinet, in which the supporters of conscription had less influence than in the small Cabinet War Committee, and delivered a threat. If in the vote on Bill 80 that evening the party did not deliver a majority over the combined vote of the three opposition parties, he would resign. He then laid out the commitments he would present in his speech just before the vote. Defence minister Ralston, the central supporter of conscription, could not tolerate a return to Parliament for a vote of confidence, and he submitted his resignation. Mackenzie King, who got the majority he wanted in the vote on Bill 80, was confident he could persuade Ralston not to resign. He was right, although he and Ralston would be engaged in intense negotiations in the following days.

U-132's attacks had bolstered Mackenzie King's self-confidence, but he did not refer to them when he cajoled his colleagues. In fact, at the navy's request, the censorship authorities imposed a blackout on the news. Despite the best efforts of the telephone and telegraph censors to block reports from the St. Lawrence towns where the survivors of the stricken ships came ashore to warm succour from the local population, within forty-eight hours newspapers had the story, but they respected the publication ban.

Nevertheless, the news broke wide open on 10 July. J. Sasseville Roy, the MP for Gaspé, rose in the House of Commons to announce:

"According to information received from my constituency ... three ... ships forming part of a fourteen ship convoy were torpedoed last Sunday night opposite Cap Chat in the St. Lawrence river." Ralston, standing in for Macdonald, castigated Roy for revealing information of use to the enemy, but the government did not strike the statement from the published record of the debates or overturn the censorship authorities' ruling that Roy's disclosures cleared the way for the media to release the stories they had already gathered from survivors.

Roy, a native of the lower St. Lawrence and a businessman there, had been an organizer in the region for Maurice Duplessis' Union Nationale during the 1930s. In the federal election of March 1940, Roy was the only successful French-speaking candidate to run under the banner of the federal Conservative Party. When in November 1941 the federal Conservatives turned to support of overseas conscription, Roy left the party to sit as an independent. No French-Canadian, he declared, could be at home in an organization whose fundamental tenet was support for the British Empire.[18] Roy had then in the spring of 1942 co-operated closely with the eleven Quebec Liberal MPs who had supported former minister of public works Cardin in opposing conscription; among that group was J.F. Pouliot, MP for Témiscouata on the lower St. Lawrence.

By the time of the first sinkings in the St. Lawrence in May 1942, Roy had become a leader among the regional MPs in demanding improved defence measures. At the time of the first attacks, Roy demanded a special secret session of the House to consider the defences of the gulf. The government had refused, and Roy justified his revelation of the new losses as a demonstration of the urgent necessity for the secret session.[19]

When Angus L. Macdonald returned to the House on 13 July, he confirmed Roy's information, and the coverage that had appeared in the media: "three ships ... were torpedoed and sunk in the gulf of St. Lawrence about a week ago. I must add with regret that four members of the crews of those ships are known to have been killed, four are reported missing, and ninety-nine have been safely landed."[20] Macdonald explained that he was supplying this information only because Roy's actions had forced him to do so. The minister did not hide his fury. "If he thinks for one moment that the whole Canadian navy is going to line up along his shores and defend those shores only, letting the convoy system we have and the protection we have for all the rest of Canada go to the dogs, he is making a tremendous mistake. I am not ready to change the disposition of one ship of the Canadian navy for him or all the questions he may ask from now until doomsday."[21]

Undeterred, on 16 July Roy moved an immediate adjournment of the House to hold a secret session so that he could present evidence that "persons responsible for the protection of our coastal waters have been negligent in their duty." R.B. Hanson, leader of the Opposition in the House of Commons, who had previously doubted the utility of a secret session, now supported Roy, citing "numerous communications of a startling nature" he had recently received about what was happening in the St. Lawrence. The Social Credit and CCF also supported Roy, as did J.F. Pouliot, in speeches that castigated the government for using censorship to cover up the inadequacy of the country's home defences. Discussion dragged on for over two hours, with the opposition parties ultimately forcing the speaker to hold a recorded vote. The government won easily.[22] Still, Mackenzie King was alarmed at the manner in which Hanson was evidently forming an alliance of convenience with anti-conscriptionists to embarrass the government.[23] Mackenzie King's fears of conscriptionist plotting to paralyze the government were heightened by a report he received that Conservative leader Arthur Meighen (who did not have a seat in the House of Commons where Hanson served as interim leader) predicted he would soon be at the head of a new Union government in Ottawa:

> It is quite clear that a group in Toronto and Montreal think they are going to be able to bring this about—the combination being Meighen, Drew, Hepburn, McCullagh, John Bassett[24] and some other associated with them. Really a gangster gang with white collars. It seems to me

that the messages that are coming to me about staying on, meeting the challenge, etc to save great trouble in Canada have come to be a comfort and assurance in this crisis. These men are merely a Nazi Fascist output with characteristics and methods comparable to those of Hitler, Goering and others.[25]

Mackenzie King immediately shed his doubts about a secret session. He now thought it essential that the government respond to the charges of negligence in the defence of the St. Lawrence. He believed that the session, which sat the next day, Saturday, 18 July, for more than five hours, was a complete success:

> Took up statements of Roy and others about conditions in the gulf of St. Lawrence ... All kinds of rumours have been afloat....
>
> Angus Macdonald, with the aide [sic] of a map, showed how our Navy was employed. I thought he refuted completely all of the rumours. Power was able to tell of exploits of the Air Force and the probable sinking of a submarine in the St. Lawrence; of the death of young Chevrier ...
>
> I felt that the session was well worth while in helping to give Members a truer appreciation of what we are doing in Canada as well as outside of Canada. I think the Members are impressed. It was fortunate we had arranged for Saturday's sitting. It fitted in admirably.[26]

Mackenzie King's faith that MPs, having been taken into the government's confidence about the true situation in the gulf, would quash alarmist rumours in their constituencies would prove to be far too optimistic.

The naval staff was doing everything in its power to reinforce the gulf. As it happened, Admiral Nelles was on the west coast consulting with the commanders there about the dispatch of assistance to the U.S. Navy in the Aleutians. Early in June, the U.S. Navy had destroyed the main Japanese aircraft carrier force at the battle of Midway, but the decisiveness of this victory was as yet unclear, not least because at the same time another Japanese force had attacked Dutch Harbor in mainland Alaska and seized two islands, Kiska and Attu, in the Aleutian island chain off Alaska. Although the Canadian navy had kept the forces deployed on the west coast to a minimum in view of the priority for support of Britain on the Atlantic, the best of these few ships went north in response to urgent American appeals for escorts to protect merchant shipping that was building up U.S. forces to counter the Japanese in the Aleutians. In the midst of his work evaluating the needs of the west coast, Nelles instantly responded to messages from Ottawa that everything possible should be done to meet the crisis in the St. Lawrence.

Experienced ships from the Atlantic were immediately assigned to the St. Lawrence to relieve the training ships that made the initial emergency response. Most important were six corvettes that more than doubled the main escort force of five Bangors for the SQ–QS convoys. Each of these convoys was now protected by one or two corvettes in addition to a Bangor, together with two or three smaller vessels, the armed yachts and Fairmiles.

The readiness with which the navy redeployed the corvettes from the Atlantic, despite the priority of ocean commitments so bitingly thrown at Roy by Macdonald, requires some explanation. *U-132*'s attack was a rude shock. She had penetrated more deeply into the St. Lawrence than *U-553*, achieved more complete surprise, and inflicted heavy losses despite the implementation since May of comprehensive air patrols and convoy of shipping. These measures had amply demonstrated their effectiveness off Nova Scotia and Newfoundland. In the St. Lawrence, however, the same defences had no apparent effect.

Although the Canadian navy did not yet appreciate the full extent to which the peculiar conditions in the gulf favoured submarines, they had already designated Atlantic corvettes for assignment to meet this unexpected setback. The strong reaction by politicians and the media to the U-boat attacks off the Gaspé shore in May 1942—despite the repeated warnings by the prime minister, no less, that such attacks could and most likely would take place—drove home the fact that enemy operations so far within the territorial waters of the country had a far greater significance than the more serious and prolonged attacks that had taken place along the Atlantic seaboard.[27]

The realization that Canada would need some sort of naval force to meet these kinds of national priorities that the senior Allies could not or would not address had begun to take hold in Ottawa and Halifax a few weeks before *U-553*'s reconnaissance into the St. Lawrence. The issue was the defence of the oil tankers that fed Canadian refineries with petroleum from the Caribbean. Rob Fisher, who prepared the studies of Caribbean operations for the official history of the navy, discovered that it was no coincidence that the corvettes permanently assigned to the St. Lawrence after *U-132*'s first attacks in July came from a pool of escorts originally intended to protect oil tanker traffic from Trinidad.

Because of the vital importance of oil to all aspects of modern warfare, tankers were preferred targets for the U-boats that hunted in the poorly protected American waters during the first part of 1942. By mid-April, losses were so heavy that the U.S. Navy temporarily held tankers in port. Canadian supplies were already short, and by the end of the month naval stocks at Halifax and St. John's had dwindled to only fifteen days' supply. Admiral Nelles, as one staff officer later recalled, declared "to hell with that, we'll get our own," and had the Atlantic Coast command begin to run small improvised convoys of tankers to Trinidad with escorts from the hard-pressed WLEF early in May. It was a brilliant success; the convoys got through without loss, even as the U-boats moved into the Caribbean and the Gulf of Mexico and destroyed eighty-one vessels in these waters during the month of May. The Canadian navy was thus able to win the agreement of the British and Americans to bring in ten corvettes from the mid-ocean force (U-boat operations in the central ocean having fallen off as the Germans concentrated in southern U.S. waters and the Caribbean) to expand the Halifax–Trinidad tanker service. The senior Allies hoped that the Canadians would allocate their new tanker protection force to assist in development of convoys within the Caribbean, but the Canadians insisted on maintaining the direct Halifax to Trinidad run. It was much quicker than the very slow system of port to port convoys that the Americans were establishing along the U.S. coast and into which the new Caribbean convoys fed. The Canadian planners also wanted the warships to be based at Halifax so they could deploy in the St. Lawrence in the event of an emergency. Indeed, there was already a new requirement for the St. Lawrence, the protection of shipping from Quebec City to carry workers and building materials to Labrador for construction of a large new RCAF base at Goose Bay at the inner end of Hamilton Inlet, and two corvettes from the tanker force, HMCS *Trail* and *Shawinigan*, were assigned at the beginning of July for this service. Concern for the St. Lawrence accounts for the renaming of the tanker escort force, which in June had become the "Halifax Force," a designation that signalled its availability for service where needed.[28]

As it happened, *U-132* soon encountered the shipping on the northern route, and that would be important for future German operations. After the attack on QS 15, the submarine had withdrawn to the east along Quebec's north shore up into the southern approaches to the Strait of Belle Isle, where the boat patrolled from 8 to 12 July. Vogelsang sighted a small convoy headed south from the strait. Although the covering air patrols made it impossible for him to close to attack, he had the information he needed. Dönitz had long been interested in ambushing shipping in the constricted northern straits, and *U-132* confirmed that merchant vessels were still using the route. The ice had cleared only at the end of June, and the convoy Vogelsang saw was probably NL 1, the corvette *Trail*'s return passage with empty merchant ships that, under the designation LN 1, had just delivered the first cargoes of the season to the Goose Bay construction project.[29] Vogelsang had missed by only a day or so the first northbound convoy in another new series, SG, which stood for Sydney to Greenland. This was an American convoy that operated from Sydney to support the construction of U.S. airfields in Greenland. These, like the Canadian base at Goose Bay, formed part of a chain of landing facilities to ferry aircraft, including short-ranged fighters, from North American factories to Britain, thus saving precious time and shipping capacity.[30]

U-132 came back to its original hunting ground, re-entering the estuary west of Anticosti Island on 14 July. Vogelsang sighted a convoy by periscope on the afternoon of 15 July, but it was too far away (more than seven kilometres) for a submerged approach, and patrolling aircraft made a surfaced run impossibly dangerous. The convoy was likely SQ 19, escorted by the Bangor *Burlington* and two Fairmiles, reinforced by HMCS *Lethbridge* and *Summerside,* two of the six corvettes that the Atlantic Coast command had ordered into the gulf from Halifax to escort the Quebec–Sydney convoys.[31]

By late on 18 July, *U-132* had worked her way back east along the north shore of the Gaspé Peninsula, towards Cap de la Madeleine. It seems Vogelsang was seeking waters broader than the river. The relative narrowness of the river channel meant that every sweep by Eastern Air Command roared close by, whereas in the estuary the aircraft had to spread out their patrols. Just after sunrise on 19 July, *U-132* heard another inbound convoy, probably SQ 20, which had already passed by the submarine's submerged location. There were drifting banks of fog and mist on the water, so Vogelsang took the risk of surfacing to make a fast run to get into an attacking position ahead of the convoy. The convoy, about two kilometres away further out in the channel, was obscured in the fog, but the submarine found itself in a patch of clear visibility that extended right to the coastline; that made *U-132* vulnerable because of the "constant aircraft." Within the half hour before the submarine surfaced, in fact, two Canso flying boats from nearby Gaspé had taken off, one for area patrols of the Gaspé Passage and the other to escort SQ 20.[32] A minute after surfacing, the submarine dived again. Without realizing how close the convoy had come to the enemy, the senior officer of the escort, Lieutenant Commander J.W. Bonner, RCNR, commanding officer of the corvette HMCS *Charlottetown*, reported, "I consider that the aircraft coverage was unusually good during the entire passage ... There were always aircraft around during the hours of daylight and they arrived almost before there was any daylight to speak of and remained until late dusk."[33]

SQ 20's naval escort comprised the Bangor *Clayoquot* and the armed yacht *Raccoon*, together with *Charlottetown* and *Weyburn*, two more of the six corvettes ordered from Halifax, now carrying out their first run in the gulf. Just after midnight on 20 July, when SQ 20 was approaching Bic Island, *Weyburn* left the convoy and turned around to catch up with QS 19, which had sailed from Bic a few hours earlier. One of the advantages of the corvettes was that the navy had given them priority for the installation of radar. The 1.5-metre type available to Canadian ships, as we have seen, could not detect the narrow profile of a surfaced submarine, but was well able to pick up larger targets, such as surface ships and shorelines. In clear visibility, the radar could not match the performance of the human "eyeball Mark I," but in darkness or thick weather, it was a godsend. On that rainy, misty night, *Weyburn*'s first contact with the convoy was radar detection of two merchant vessels. The convoy of about ten ships had become "scattered over an area of ten [square] miles [eighteen square kilometres]" in the poor weather. By eight in the morning as the mist began to clear on the water, the ships were able to regain their stations with *Weyburn* in the lead. The original senior escort vessel, the Bangor *Chedabucto*, was on the port (north) beam, with Fairmile *Q 074* on the starboard (south) beam, and the Fairmile *Q 059* astern.[34] Eastern Air Command had ordered, in what was now routine, the same air cover that unknown to the Canadians had helped SQ 20. Bad weather conditions at Gaspé, however, prevented flying during the morning and early afternoon of the twentieth.

U-132 was well positioned, patrolling submerged in the area where it had seen SQ 20 the day before. It was now precisely two weeks since the submarine's encounter with QS 15. In preparing for that attack,

Vogelsang had seen that on Mondays a newly departed outbound convoy travelled down the river at the same time that an inbound convoy was arriving, the two following a similar enough track that they passed close by one another. Thus he had good reason to suspect, after seeing SQ 20 inward bound on the last leg of its journey, that the next day an outbound convoy would emerge from the river. At 11:37 on the morning of Monday, 20 July, he sighted QS 19 coming towards him, about an hour's steaming away; that would have been approximately thirteen kilometres, so the visibility on the water was good. He manoeuvred underwater for fully two hours. By now he was familiar with the density layering and appears to have kept down in the cold-water layer as *Weyburn,* in the van of the convoy, passed by him 700 metres away. As was not yet clear to the Allies, asdic was not able effectively to penetrate a cold-water layer, so the danger of sound detection was minimal. As *Weyburn* passed, Vogelsang came up to periscope depth: "I am inside the convoy," he wrote in his log. The convoy formation was like that for QS 15, two rows each of five ships sailing abeam each other. *U-132* was between the fourth and fifth ships in the rows; the ships would have been sailing perhaps 800 metres or further apart. Although *U-132* was now at periscope depth above the cold-water layer, the noise of the merchant ship engines would have masked her against asdic detection. At 1:39 in the afternoon, Vogelsang fired two torpedoes south towards the Gaspé coast at the southernmost ship in the second row from a range of 800 metres. The target was the British *Frederika Lensen,* which carried out a shuttle service to deliver coal from the mines at Sydney to Montreal. The vessel had brought a load from Sydney in SQ 18 the week before and was now travelling back empty.

Only one of the torpedoes hit and detonated, very low in the boiler room because the empty ship was riding high in the water. The four men on duty in the boiler room appear to have been instantly killed. The master of the ship, B.E. Russell, was "just finishing his lunch, when he heard the 'Whrr' of a motor. Jumping from his chair, and taking about two steps ... he heard a terrific explosion, and on rushing on deck, he was completely blinded with steam and smoke ..."[35] This would appear to be because the explosion blew off the hatch of at least one of the empty holds, allowing steam from the shattered machinery and coal dust from the cargo spaces to vent over the deck. The ship immediately began to list heavily, and the remaining forty-one members of the crew abandoned ship. The two lifeboats on the port side of the ship had been shattered in the explosion, but the crew was able to launch the boats on the starboard side.

For one of the ships in the convoy, the Canadian lake steamer *John S. Pillsbury*, the scene was too appallingly familiar. She, like *Frederika Lensen*, was a regular in the Quebec–Sydney convoys, shuttling mineral ores from the Maritimes to Montreal, and had been in QS 15 during *U-132*'s previous attack. As on that occasion, *Pillsbury* and another Canadian laker immediately broke out of the convoy at their best speed, rushing towards the coast hoping that their shallow drafts would enable them to reach shallow water where the submarine could not pursue them. *Q 064*, the Fairmile in the position astern, dashed after the vessels to try to coax them back into the convoy, but without success.

At the same time, *Q 074* on the southern flank closest to *Frederika Lensen* made an asdic contact and launched depth charge attacks. *Weyburn* handed control of the convoy over to *Chedabucto* and rushed to assist *Q 074* in the hunt, but was unable to pick up the asdic contact. There were "a great number" of dead herring floating in the area. *Weyburn*'s commanding officer, Lieutenant Thomas W. Golby, RCNR, concluded that the Fairmile's attacks had in fact been on a school of fish, which gave asdic returns similar to those of a submarine. Golby was right that there was no submarine on the southern flank of the convoy. Vogelsang had kept his position under the convoy, not daring to try to break away because the sound of his electric motors run at speed could well alert the asdic operators above. As he heard the explosions from the Fairmile's attacks, he plunged down to sixty metres depth and crept along slowly.

Master Russell of *Frederika Lensen* was surprised when after about twenty minutes the vessel's list did not increase. He was cheered and inspired when every member of the crew responded to his call for volunteers to reboard to see if she could be saved. Russell and a small party went below decks and saw terrifying evidence of the power of the torpedo. The heavy forward steel bulkhead of the boiler room had been driven nearly four metres forward, and the massive port boiler hurled upwards where it had smashed against the deck head above and deflected backwards on top of the engine with such force that it broke apart the engine's heavy steel structure, hurling some components to starboard and some backwards. Still, although the boiler room was flooded, two of the three holds were dry, and the third, next to the boiler room, was only slowly taking in water.

Weyburn then picked up *Frederika Lensen*'s people. Lieutenant Golby, a merchant mariner in civilian life, was instantly receptive to Master Russell's suggestion that they attempt to save the stricken vessel, and Golby had the marine skills to carry out the job. After *Weyburn* made an anti-submarine sweep, at 4 PM the corvette took the freighter under tow. A joint party from the crews of both ships had gone aboard the freighter to take up the tow line; *Q 074*, later joined by the Bangor *Clayoquot* that had rushed from Gaspé, provided cover, together with aircraft that had finally been able to take off with the improvement of the weather ashore. The unwieldy, canted hull lumbered along at no more than four-and-a-half kilometres per hour. Late that night, *Weyburn* towed the damaged ship into the small bay of Grande-Vallée. Following at a safe distance of just over five kilometres was *U-132*. Vogelsang watched every detail of the operation through his periscope.

The Canadians had no idea the submarine was so close. Because there had been no asdic contact and the explosion in *Frederika Lensen* was nearly at the bottom of the ship's hull, Canadian personnel concluded that the U-boat had initiated a new tactic in the St. Lawrence by laying mines that the ship had struck, or that the U-boat had had a lucky torpedo hit from a very long-range shot launched from far outside the escort screen of the convoy. An examination of the wreck by an explosives expert from Halifax subsequently ruled out the mine theory and the possibility of an accidental explosion of the ship's own boilers.[36] Still, the navy did not appreciate that the temperature layering in the water had blinded asdic and allowed the submarine to attack from inside the convoy and then hide under the merchant vessels.

Starting at first light next day, 21 July, the party of volunteers from *Frederika Lensen*'s crew together with personnel from *Q 074* and *Clayoquot* worked with anything to hand, including mattresses and bedding, to try to seal the bulkhead between the engine room, which had been ripped open by the torpedo, and the hold immediately forward. Water continued to rise in the hold. The bulkhead was giving way. That evening *Q 074*, which had the shallow draft to get close to shore, together with motor trucks on shore which took lines from the hulk, pulled her till she grounded and thus could not sink. When salvage vessels arrived the next morning, 22 July, it was clear *Frederika Lensen* was breaking up, so the main work was to strip her of self-defence guns, ammunition, and any other valuable equipment.[37]

After watching *Frederika Lensen* anchor in Grande-Vallée on the night of 20–21 July, Vogelsang started his departure from the gulf. The moon was waxing, making the nights, the only time he dared run on the surface, uncomfortably bright. In a further remarkable development in that remarkable cruise, U-boat Headquarters directed him to join the pursuit of the trans-ocean convoy ON 113 as it passed seaward of central and southern Nova Scotia. On the night of 29–30 July, *U-132* fired its last two torpedoes and destroyed the large freighter *Pacific Pioneer* and then endured a heavy counterattack by the escort. Despite reduced speed because of damage, the boat vainly attempted to regain contact with ON 113 as a "shadower" before heading for home; she finally reached La Pallice, France, on 16 August.

SIX

Squadron Leader Small Strikes; Admiral Dönitz Probes for Soft Spots, Summer 1942

Norville Everett "Molly" Small was a rarity in Canada's wartime air force, a seasoned professional pilot with considerable military experience. A native of Hamilton, Ontario, he had joined the RCAF at the age of 19 in 1928. He seems to have been a natural candidate. Sports, for the individual prowess, physical discipline, and team-playing they require, can be a good indicator of aptitude for military service. Small's appetite for physical activity was voracious, ranging from football, hockey, and baseball to golf, badminton, swimming, and fishing. He also had a bent for technology. He spent a year at the Hamilton Technical School and, as a hobby, built and operated an amateur radio station.[1]

In 1931, after training at Camp Borden where he qualified as a pilot and reached the rank of sergeant, he was posted to RCAF Station Vancouver. For the next six years he flew on the west coast, including much work in flying boats from temporary bases as far north as the Queen Charlotte Islands. In 1937, shortly after he had re-enlisted for another three-year engagement in the air force, he left to become a pilot with Canadian Airways. The offer must have been a lucrative one, for he had to purchase his release from the military for the then-considerable sum of $128. In July 1939 he moved to Imperial Airways, a British firm that operated large flying boats and had just the year before started a transatlantic service. Small took the three-month Imperial Airways navigation course, and this certainly contributed to his prowess as a navigator, an essential element in his success during the war. On conclusion of the course, he appears immediately to have accepted a position with Trans-Canada Airlines, the recently established government airline that later became Air Canada. Within a matter of weeks, in November 1939, he returned to the air force, this time as a commissioned officer.

A letter of reference from Canadian Airways in 1939 captured Small's combination of restless energy, intense application, technical skill, and qualities as a leader. He was "a pilot of outstanding ability and sound judgement," and also "an executive whose interest in his chosen work extends far beyond the limits of the ordinary 'day's work.'" He appears to have matured and developed an edge in the competitive world of commercial flying. The reports in his air force file from when he was an enlisted man and non-commissioned officer were favourable, but not glowing. That changed with his return to military service. His commanding officers' reports highlighted the same qualities Canadian Airways emphasized: "particularly keen and reliable as pilot"; "organizing ability"; "has initiative and a burning desire 'to get on with the job.'"

After a year of training and staff duties in Ottawa and Montreal, in January 1941 Small was assigned to transatlantic flying to deliver combat aircraft from their manufacturers in the United States to Britain. This was a new enterprise, started only in the fall of 1940, intended to avoid the delays of shipment of aircraft by sea and also help overcome the shortage of shipping capacity resulting from heavy losses to enemy attack. In this still experimental and dangerous work, Small was a standout. By July 1941, he had flown five Consolidated Catalina flying boats from Bermuda to the United Kingdom.

With this invaluable experience, Small was assigned to 116 Squadron at Dartmouth, newly formed to operate the RCAF's first Catalinas. It speaks volumes for Eastern Air Command's shortage of qualified people that he immediately put on three hats, as the squadron navigation officer, the senior instructor, and the commander of one of the two flights in the squadron. Only days after Small's arrival, Dartmouth felt the impact of his "get on with the job" approach. On 22 July 1941, he was taking a Catalina out for what was to have been an unarmed navigation training flight for several members of the squadron's flying personnel. At the last minute, as Small later reported, station control "advised that the aircraft should be armed. The crew as carried had at no time had the opportunity to receive any instruction in the use of the aircraft armament as their training had not reached a stage where it was practical." Small himself had "never flown in a Catalina aircraft with bomb gear fitted." Even as the crew was preparing the aircraft for takeoff, he "endeavoured to obtain information as to the operation of the electrical bombing instruments." During the flight, the crew sighted what appeared to be a submarine with decks awash, which then dived. This was certainly a false contact. Small swooped in to attack, but neither of the bombs dropped. He had one of the trainees go to the bomb aimer's compartment and flick switches. On the second pass, where the submarine had evidently dived, Small was able to drop a bomb, but it failed to explode. Unable to find the right entry in the reporting code book that he had picked up just before the flight, he improvised a radio report of the contact, partly in code and partly in plain language, which baffled the staff at Dartmouth.[2]

The can-do attitude was more important than the Keystone Kops quality of the attack. Small's improvisation had alerted Eastern Air Command's senior officers to the fact that the squadrons were receiving new aircrew with no armament and operations training, something that the units did not have the resources to provide themselves. The outcome of the failed attack was a demand from the command that Air Force Headquarters ensure that aircrew receive a course on reconnaissance operations before they were posted to the east coast.

Small plunged himself into the art and science of aerial anti-submarine warfare. From February to May 1942, he was posted to 10 Squadron at Gander, the best-established and most active of the command's units, to hone his knowledge. With this preparation and a promotion to acting squadron leader, in May he moved to Yarmouth, Nova Scotia. At first he commanded 162 Squadron, a new Canso unit. Because of delays in the delivery of aircraft, that unit was only at detachment strength. Less than a month later, on 13 June 1942, Small was reassigned to command another new unit at Yarmouth, 113 Squadron, which had a full complement of fifteen Lockheed Hudsons.

During 1941 and the first half of 1942 the RAF's Coastal Command undertook nothing less than a revolution in aerial anti-submarine warfare, from guarding convoys to actively seeking out their attackers. This was born of desperation and rigorous scientific analysis.

The RAF had pioneered operational research to make the most effective use of its limited fighter forces in the Battle of Britain in 1940, and did so as well for anti-submarine warfare. Scientists applied mathematical analysis to amassed data on air patrols and to results in terms of shipping lost or safely sailed and U-boats located to determine statistically what worked and what did not. Least efficient were efforts to provide air escort to all convoys. These "defensive tactics" wore out aircraft and exhausted crews, mostly in scouring waters where there were no submarines. By contrast, "offensive tactics" developed from the findings of the scientists used the most current naval intelligence about the possible locations of U-boats to concentrate a heavy effort in those areas and let go all the others. Aircraft on patrol pushed out to maximum range—then 1100 kilometres—over areas where U-boats were suspected to be approaching or on station. Convoys that intelligence suggested were threatened with attack received coverage by several aircraft. Increasingly, the aircraft assigned did not hover close around the convoy, but swept in all directions far beyond visibility range to catch U-boats lurking over the horizon and waiting until nightfall to approach and strike. In November 1941, the commander-in-chief of Coastal Command reported to Air Commodore N.R. Anderson, commander of Eastern Air Command: "It looks more and more as though the German submarines are fighting shy of aircraft patrols. It has been most rare to find a U-boat within 300 miles [555 kilometres] of shore-based aircraft...."[3]

One thing that Coastal Command could not do was destroy U-boats. Hundreds of attacks with aerial bombs and depth charges resulted in only a handful of "kills," several of these shared with warships that had reached the scene and finished off a submarine located by aircraft. Intense research and trials resulted in new Coastal Command tactical instructions issued in mid-December 1941 that emphasized surprise, speed, accuracy, and concentrated firepower.[4] So tough were the hulls of submarines, designed to withstand crushing pressures at depths of several hundred metres, that the standard 113-kilogram aerial depth charge could inflict serious damage only if it detonated within five metres. To achieve this kind of accuracy, the boat had to be caught while still on the surface. A crash dive could be completed within twenty-five seconds, and once under water the submarine would continue to move forward at a rate of four metres per second with the manoeuvrability to zigzag in any direction. Within forty seconds of the boat's submergence, according to the new instructions, the chances of placing the depth charges anywhere near the submarine were so remote that there was no point in dropping the weapons. In other words, an aircraft had to complete its attack within, at the very most, a minute from the German lookouts spotting the aircraft. Surprise was vital to gain the advantage of every additional precious second. Trials with submarines revealed that the optimum patrol altitude was 900 metres or considerably higher. From that height, aircrew had an excellent view of the ocean's surface over a wide arc. Equally important, lookouts on the conning tower, even with their superb binoculars, could scan for such high-flying aircraft only by straining their necks and were thus unlikely to keep as good a watch as at lower altitudes that could be more comfortably kept in view. Trials also showed that the standard dark colours of land planes made them stand out against the maritime sky. The best camouflage proved to be white. On reflection, that made perfect sense. This is the colour of the undersurfaces of seabirds that survive by conducting their own version of aerial submarine warfare by swooping down on unsuspecting fish.

Accuracy of attacks, as in all aspects of aerial warfare until the development of precision-guided munitions at the end of the twentieth century, was the greatest challenge. Existing fifteen-metre depth settings on aerial depth charges became obsolete with the realization that there was so little chance of success in an aerial attack on a submerged submarine. Early in 1942 a new fast-acting trigger, the Mark XIII, which was detonated by water pressure at shallow depths, became available. The new Coastal Command instructions were to "dive bomb" the submarine. No bombsight was equal to the task of accurately tracking the narrow, rapidly manoeuvring trace of a surfaced submarine. The only answer was to inundate the target with bombs from very close range. Aircraft were to plunge to an altitude height of only fifteen metres above the water and drop all charges carried (normally four in Eastern Air Command aircraft of the time) in a lateral "stick," with a spacing of eighteen metres between charges. The pilot was to endeavour to fly perpendicular to the submarine, attacking across the narrow hull, to maximize the chances of at least one of the four charges falling within lethal distance.

Coastal Command freely offered assistance to Eastern Air Command and also to the U.S. Army's anti-submarine air command. Early in February 1942, a mission led by Air Vice-Marshal G.R. Bromet, commander of Coastal Command's 19 Group, visited Eastern Air Command to promote the latest anti-submarine methods and gather information about the state of Canadian operations. He must have been taken aback by what he discovered. Eastern Air Command's geographical expanse in terms of the length of coastline and ocean area to be protected was comparable to that of Coastal Command. The volume of shipping and number of convoys in Canadian and Newfoundland waters was also comparable to those in British waters. Bromet, taking into consideration the level of U-boat activity in the western Atlantic, calculated that the command should have no fewer than eleven long-range squadrons. With this strength, the RCAF could imitate Coastal Command by pushing patrols over U-boat approach and concentration areas out to 750 to 1100 kilometres and providing a heavy schedule of wide-ranging sweeps all around convoys that naval intelligence showed were threatened. In fact, Eastern Air Command had only two long-range squadrons, numbers 5 and 116, with a total of twenty-five Catalina and Cansos, five below a full complement of fifteen per squadron. Bromet also discovered that the difficulties with aircrew training that Small's ill-fated attack of July 1941 had highlighted continued unabated. Because of the priority of the RAF's needs, the training system in Canada produced only eight pilots per month with full courses in maritime operations to feed both Eastern Air Command and Western Air Command. Most new aircrew for Eastern Air Command still received their maritime training "on the job" in the squadrons, which still lacked adequate training resources.[5]

With Bromet's mission came a supply of the new shallow-set Mark XIII depth-charge triggers under the charge of a senior Coastal Command armament officer who instructed RCAF armament officers in their installation and operation. Bromet arranged for a civilian scientist of the Coastal Command Operations Research Section, J.P.T. Pearman, to come to Halifax in March for a month-long tour of the command's units to learn how they were conducting flying operations and advise on improvements. His studies revealed that the vast majority of flying was within 370 kilometres of shore, focused on the close escort of the many coastal and ocean convoys in these waters. There was very little flying out to 750 kilometres and beyond to push U-boats out of coastal waters as Coastal Command had done in 1941, despite the fact that naval intelligence indicated that submarines were hovering on the outer reaches of Canadian and Newfoundland waters to track transatlantic shipping as it funnelled into approach routes for North American ports.[6]

The two most ardent students of the new British methods were "Molly" Small and Wing Commander Clare Annis, who had commanded 10 Squadron in Gander during Small's temporary posting to the unit in early 1942. In the spring, when Small went to Yarmouth to take up his first command, Annis went to Air Force Headquarters in Ottawa as staff officer (bomber reconnaissance) operations. Annis was especially interested in the use of naval intelligence, particularly recent direction-finding "fixes," to adopt Coastal Command's "offensive tactics." He arrived in Ottawa just when the navy was expanding the Foreign Intelligence Section with the assistance of British experts and as the organization's capabilities were improving dramatically. So excited was Annis with the possibilities that in June 1942 he arranged for Commander de Marbois, head of the Foreign Intelligence Section at naval headquarters, to organize a recurring three-week course on naval intelligence for air force officers assigned to the maritime commands.[7] This was one of the earliest and most important examples in Canada of institutional integration between the navy and air force for maritime warfare. Here lay the roots of the joint RCN–RCAF school established in Halifax in 1944–45, which, reborn in the early Cold War, still exists as the Canadian Forces Maritime Warfare Centre, the focal point for the development and teaching of doctrine for maritime operations in the face of constantly changing technology and threats. De Marbois was delighted at Annis' interest. Never one to hide his missionary zeal for radio intelligence or disguise his impatience for non-adherents to the faith, he contrasted the air force's positive attitude to the navy's own director of operations who "showed no inclination to understand or study the value of Operational intelligence and nick-named the organization the 'crystal gazers.'"[8]

From Annis' perspective, the most important result of recent improvements was the Foreign Intelligence Section's ability to obtain a direction-finding "fix" on a U-boat transmission within minutes rather than hours. If an aircraft was ready for takeoff at a nearby station or in the air in the vicinity, there was a real possibility it could locate the submarine while it was still on the surface. The difficulty was the absence of secure, fast communications links between Ottawa and the east coast. The solution worked out by Annis and de Marbois was to use commercial telephone which gave instant communication and to employ a word-replacement code to disguise the information. The naval intelligence staff telephoned "hot" fixes to Air Force Headquarters, which in turn immediately telephoned them to Eastern Air Command headquarters in Halifax. Annis arranged for fixes off southern Nova Scotia to be telephoned directly to Yarmouth.[9] Small, in his few weeks with 113 Squadron, had implemented the latest Coastal Command tactical instructions, and he was unique among Eastern Air Command squadron commanders in doing so. The squadron's Hudsons were painted white, patrolled at 900-metre or higher altitudes, and there was always an aircraft and crew ready for immediate takeoff in response to a hot "fix" by naval intelligence.

In the words of the RCAF official history, "[a]ll these elements came together on 31 July" 1942. Small himself piloted a Hudson in response to a fix south of Yarmouth, at an altitude of 900 metres. Conditions were nearly ideal for a surprise attack from this high altitude. "There was a slight haze near the surface, which made visibility from the surface upwards extremely difficult from the surface, while an aircraft at 3000 to 5000 feet [900 to 1500 metres] had a fairly clear view of objects on the surface with a horizontal visibility of approximately 5 miles [9 kilometres]." The aircraft sighted the fully surfaced submarine, *U-754*, 5.5 kilometres ahead. As the aircraft closed and rapidly lost altitude, the "submarine's crew was seen to be scrambling for the hatch ..." Small realized he was coming in too high and would overshoot the submarine as he approached it beam on. Showing superb tactical sense and remarkable airmanship, he swung around in a large semicircle to allow himself a few more seconds to drop for the low-level attack and then swept in almost parallel to the submarine from astern. This was a difficult angle from which to attack. The smallest slip would place all the charges too far off to one side, but Small planted them right along the hull and they exploded just as the submarine was slipping below the surface. Small made two quick passes, both times firing machine guns at the conning tower as it disappeared. Fifty-five minutes after the attack, the aircrew saw a heavy explosion nine kilometres away. Later in the day, warships that searched the area in case the submarine had only been damaged and was awaiting darkness to resurface discovered large amounts of oil where the large explosion had taken place. The U-boat had been destroyed.[10] Small's feat was the more remarkable because Coastal Command aircraft had just begun to sink submarines in the same month. One key to the RAF's success was improved aerial depth charges that were filled with Torpex, an explosive about 50 percent more powerful than the mainly TNT filling previously used, but the Torpex charges did not reach Eastern Air Command until later in the year. Small's marksmanship was extraordinary.

U-754 patrolled off southern Nova Scotia in search of poorly protected hunting grounds. This was a response to the sharply diminished results on the American seaboard as the U.S. Navy belatedly introduced local convoys in July. Dönitz had been expecting such defence measures and was pleasantly surprised at the long delay. The reconnaissance off southern Nova Scotia was an improvised response to employ *U-754* and other boats that were pulled back from American waters midway through their operations as it became clear that conditions had changed. The loss of *U-754* and meagre successes by three other boats showed that there had been no reduction in the effective defences off Nova Scotia.

Dönitz was more optimistic about prospects in the vicinity of the Strait of Belle Isle. *U-132*'s report on 20 July that traffic from the Gulf of St. Lawrence was being routed through the northern strait rekindled Dönitz's interest in the area. On 21 August 1942, he ordered three outward-bound boats, *U-165*, *U-513*, and *U-517*, to make for the strait. All three submarines had been commissioned early in 1942 under newly appointed commanding officers, and this was the first war patrol for the U-boats and their captains. Korvettenkapitän Eberhard Hoffmann of *U-165* and Korvettenkapitän Rolf Rüggeberg of *U-513*, both aged 35, were among the older U-boat commanding officers. They had joined the navy in 1925 and 1926 respectively, but had transferred to the submarine arm only in 1941. Kapitänleutnant Paul Hartwig of *U-517* was eight years younger, had joined the navy in 1935, and moved to the U-boat arm in the summer of 1940.

The timing of the mission was fortuitous for the Germans. Although the Allies routed only the irregularly scheduled convoys that supported construction of the northern air bases through the strait, a considerable volume of shipping was approaching the southern entrance as *U-165* and *U-517* entered through the northern entrance on 26–27 August.

Shortly after 3 AM on 27 August, Catalina H of 116 Squadron at Botwood, Newfoundland, flown by a crew captained by Flight Lieutenant G.M. Cook, RCAF, took off in darkness to provide coverage for the Canadian convoy LN 6, the small Great Lakes freighter *Donald Stewart* and the larger *Ericus* escorted by the corvette HMCS *Trail* bound for Goose Bay. At about first light, 4:45 AM, the Catalina crew sighted the U.S. Coast Guard cutter *Mojave* and the U.S. Army transport *Chatham* in the southern entrance to the strait.[11] (The U.S. Coast Guard had been integrated with the navy as a wartime measure, and coast guard personnel who were expert in Arctic navigation crewed the escorts for the SG convoys.) The Canadian convoy was further to the south and west, perhaps fifty kilometres, than the aircrew expected, and the Catalina found LN 6 only at 8:15 AM. All proved to be well, but at 9:40 AM when on an outer patrol leg, the Catalina crew "sighted ten or more lifeboats or rafts." There was no sign of *Mojave* or *Chatham*, and the Catalina sent a radio report that both U.S. vessels had evidently been destroyed. The Catalina flew back to *Trail* to alert the corvette to the danger and direct the warship to the survivors. The Canadian ships had now entered the narrow straits, where there was no room to divert around the area where a submarine might still be lurking, so *Trail* sent the two merchant vessels of LN 6 back along the Labrador coast to anchor in the shelter of Forteau Bay. The Catalina flew back to the lifeboats to direct *Trail* to the scene and at 1:26 PM also sighted *Mojave*, which had not gone down but had been conducting a hunt in the vicinity of the attack on *Chatham*; the Catalina immediately broadcast a new report to shore authorities, stating that only *Chatham* had been lost. The Catalina directed the U.S. warship to the lifeboats, dropped flares over the lifeboats to allow *Mojave* and *Trail to* quickly home in on them, and kept sweeping around the scene until recovery of the survivors was completed by 6 PM.[12]

U.S. authorities, and in particular commander task force 24 (CTF 24), the American naval headquarters at Argentia, Newfoundland, that was responsible for convoy protection, were in the dark about the circumstances. The transport and *Mojave* were supposed to be part of the slow convoy SG 6, a group of six merchant ships including *Chatham* under the protection of three USCG cutters, *Algonquin* and *Mohawk* as well as *Mojave*, and continuous daylight coverage by the RCAF's 10 Squadron at Gander. The main body of SG 6 was indeed where it was supposed to be, about twelve hours behind LN 6, well south of the Strait of Belle Isle. Why were *Chatham* and *Mojave* sailing on their own, so far ahead of schedule, and well beyond the air protection that CTF 24 arranged to be provided by 10 Squadron RCAF?

CTF 24 staff learned only two days after *Chatham*'s sinking that special sailing arrangements had been made at Sydney, the port where the Canadian naval control of shipping staff organized the Greenland convoys on behalf of the USN. *Chatham* carried 428 civilian workmen, 145 of whom were to be disembarked at Hamilton Inlet, Labrador, for the Canadian base at Goose Bay and the rest for the U.S. bases in Greenland. The difficulty was that one of the ships that arrived for the convoy had a maximum speed of only thirteen kilometres per hour, meaning that the convoy would be a slow one, and the side trip into Hamilton Inlet—required only to drop off the workmen in *Chatham*— would delay the passage still longer. The extended delays were a potentially critical problem because of the pressing construction schedules at the northern bases and the lateness of the season, which meant each day there was an increasing risk of ice pack movements near Greenland that would close navigation. The Canadian staff at Sydney and *Mojave*'s commanding officer agreed that *Chatham*, which could make as much as twenty-two kilometres per hour, should proceed ahead of the main convoy with *Mojave* as escort as far as Hamilton Inlet, drop off the workmen destined for Goose Bay, then come back out and rendezvous with the slow main body of the convoy as it proceeded northward off the Labrador coast. The Sydney command reported the division of the convoy in the sailing signal sent on 25 August to all authorities, including CTF 24,[13] but did not highlight the fact, and *Mojave*'s commanding officer did not make a report. CTF 24 staff failed to pick up the reference to the division of the convoy in the sailing signal and therefore called on the RCAF for air escort of only the main body of SG 6.[14]

The lack of direct air escort likely made little difference. The vessel had been ambushed in circumstances that overwhelmingly favoured the submarine. *U-517* had begun a submerged patrol of the southern entrance to the strait in the early dark hours of 27 August and never surfaced. She did not have to—*Chatham* had come into her sights. Her periscope would have been invisible to the surface ships and aircraft, and the water conditions were poor for asdic. One of the two torpedoes Hartwig fired at about 7:45 AM hit and burst two boilers. Even so, the ship did not slip below the surface for twenty-six minutes, allowing time for an orderly evacuation that was helped by the coolness of most of those on board and the fact that the master had held an abandon ship drill only two days before in which everyone had been assigned to a lifeboat station.[15] Of the 562 people aboard, including the passengers, crew, and naval armed guard, no more than fifteen were lost.[16]

With evidence of the peril in the Strait of Belle Isle and the inability of the coast guard cutters acting as escorts to counter the threat, CTF 24 diverted U.S. traffic. Convoy GS 6, southbound from Greenland with USCGC *Tampa* as the senior escort, was rerouted away from the Strait of Belle Isle out into the Atlantic, with passage to Sydney around Cape Race.[17] USCGC *Mojave* received permission to return to Sydney with the 293 survivors she had picked up. There was, however, further misunderstanding resulting from CTF 24's unawareness of the fact that SG 6 was sailing in two sections. The American headquarters, thinking *Mojave* was leading SG 6 as originally intended, believed the whole convoy was returning with her to Sydney. On the night of 27–28 August, only an hour after CTF 24 reported to the senior U.S. naval officer in Greenland that the whole of SG 6 had turned back to Sydney, a signal arrived that the convoy was again under attack.[18]

The main body of SG 6 comprised five merchant ships in two columns of two and a column of one following behind *Mohawk* and *Algonquin*, which sailed ahead on either flank. One can discern a growing sense of foreboding in the reports of proceedings as the convoy moved northward during the late afternoon and evening of 27 August. First they encountered *Mojave* and *Trail* heading south with their crowd of survivors from *Chatham*. Then the escorts picked up the signals diverting the southbound GS 6 away from the Strait of Belle Isle and *Mojave*'s report of the details of the loss of *Chatham*. Because no submarine had been seen or picked up by sonar, the convoy kept a close watch for mines. After darkness descended, the moon rose at 9:28 PM and almost immediately illuminated an oil slick, which likely marked the spot where *Chatham* had gone down. At around 10:30 PM, personnel below decks on the port (west) side of *Mohawk* "heard a marked hissing or whining sound that appeared to pass under the ship." There was no sighting of a wake or sonar contact to confirm the passage of a torpedo, but the crew in the port-side spaces were so convinced that they went to their action stations, while the engine room personnel switched over to the main burners so that they could deliver full speed at short notice. Moments later, at about 10:32 PM, there were explosions on the port sides of USS *Laramie* and SS *Arlyn,* the lead ships of the second and first columns of merchant ships.[19]

The crew of *Arlyn* immediately abandoned ship; she was carrying a lethal cargo of dynamite and high-test gasoline. *Laramie*, a gasoline-loaded tanker, was also a floating bomb, but she was commissioned in the U.S. Navy and crewed by naval personnel. Aside from two newly joined men who cut loose a large raft and made off, her people reacted with calm deliberation, even though the decks were awash in highly explosive fuel. She had been hit forward, and her engines and other equipment proved to be sound. The crew carried out effective damage control, got her underway, and fed sonar and radar contacts to *Algonquin* and *Mohawk* to assist them in the hunt for the attacker.[20]

U-165 had fired the torpedoes and, although her log has not survived, it appears that Hoffmann repeated Hartwig's successful ambush tactics at very nearly the same position. Like *Mojave* earlier in the day, *Algonquin* and *Mohawk* never got a trace of the submarine, suggesting that she may never have surfaced while enjoying the protection from sonar detection provided by the complex waters. Hartwig, who was hunting to the north, sighted star shells and rockets fired by the convoy after Hoffmann's attacks. *U-517* returned to the scene of her previous victory and in the early hours of 28 August sank the hulk of *Arlyn,* which, unknown to any Allied authority, had remained afloat after the crew took to the boats. Hartwig did not realize she was abandoned and barely moving. He had to fire a second time; his first torpedo ran clear because he had overestimated the vessel's speed.

When in the days following that attack U.S. Admiral R.M. Brainard, CTF 24, learned that SG 6 had been sailed in two parts apparently without his staff's knowledge, he sent a blistering message to the Canadian naval headquarters in Halifax, copied to Sydney and *Mojave*. The division of the convoy into two parts, he charged, was "never communicated to originator and were not known until approximately 48 hours after attack on S C [sic] 6." He never would have accepted the division of the convoy because that weakened the defences for both portions, "contrary to sound principles of employment of escort available for protection of shipping."[21] The Canadian authorities and *Mojave* had then compounded the error by keeping him in the dark and thus unable to countermand the division of the convoy. These errors "resulted in loss of 2 valuable ships and damage to third." Brainard somewhat moderated his criticism when he learned that the convoy staff at Sydney had indeed promulgated the arrangements to divide the convoy in the sailing telegram, but still insisted that the decision to split the convoy had been a grave error. "I am emphatically of the opinion that none of these acts or decisions were attributable to carelessness or neglect; in every instance they were the result of honest opinions and estimates and I do not consider that any of the personnel concerned can be charged with any fault more serious than that of error in judgment. However, errors in judgment can be costly ..."[22] Admiral Nelles responded personally to Admiral Brainard, pointing out that if the convoy sailing signal from Sydney of 25 August had been properly plotted by the CTF 24 staff, the arrangement to divide the convoy would have been perfectly clear. He also wondered if the responsible U.S. Navy authorities had informed CTF 24 that *Chatham* was to disembark workmen at Hamilton Inlet, which would have amply explained the decision to divide the convoy.[23]

The U.S. Navy's own analysis of the convoy showed that much of the confusion resulted from the inexperience of the coast guard cutters in anti-submarine and convoy operations. The officers did not understand that the need for radio silence ended the moment there was contact with the enemy, when the priority was for prompt broadcast of all information. The escorts for both parts of the convoy, moreover, had sailed too close in to the merchant ships to provide an effective screen and had allowed the merchant ships to proceed through dangerous waters on steady courses without zigzagging in the case of the faster ships or periodic evasive alterations of course for the slower vessels. This was no fault of the officers, who were master seamen with special expertise in Arctic operations, but had inadequate training in anti-submarine warfare. Brainard immediately arranged to have two coast guard officers with extensive escort command experience in transatlantic convoy operations assigned to the Greenland force as escort unit commanders.[24]

The new attacks near Belle Isle brought the Gaspé command immediately to turn around HMCS *Trail*'s little convoy, LN 6, to return to Gaspé. *Trail* had just disembarked at Forteau Bay the eighty-six survivors and one body she had recovered from *Chatham*. The diversion of LN 6 back south interrupted the schedule for supply of the Goose Bay air base project, as ships that had unloaded at Hamilton Inlet were waiting to make return passage with *Trail* in order to pick up their next cargoes. The Gaspé command therefore detached the corvette HMCS *Weyburn* from convoy SQ 32, and sailed the Bangor HMCS *Clayoquot* for a fast run to Hamilton Inlet to pick up the empty cargo vessels and bring them south. En route the two escorts did a sweep of the Strait of Belle Isle, and it was almost certainly these warships that Hartwig saw in the strait on 30 August. He attempted to attack, but the ships were zigzagging and forced him to dive deep when one ran right over him. Despite Hartwig's fears that he was under attack, the warships were unaware of his presence; asdic conditions thus appear to have been no better than they had been on the twenty-eighth. Hartwig himself had difficulties manoeuvring accurately underwater: "These water layers and unreliable depth information!"[25]

U-517 and the Canadian ships that she had encountered in her operations in the north would meet again within a few days over 300 kilometres to the southwest. This was no coincidence. Hartwig, seeing that traffic had dried up around the Strait of Belle Isle, headed south towards Anticosti Island where *U-553* and *U-132* had reported fairly heavy and regular traffic. Meanwhile, the Canadians, to compensate for the disruptions of supplies for the Goose Bay air base project caused by Hartwig and Hoffmann, were expediting shipments in convoys that sailed through Hartwig's new hunting area just at the moment he arrived there.

On 1 September, HMCS *Trail* and the two merchant ships of the diverted LN 6, *Ericus* and *Donald Stewart,* sailed from Gaspé and joined with LN 7 as it passed by en route from Father Point to Goose Bay. LN 7 comprised only the escort, the corvette HMCS *Shawinigan,* and a single merchant vessel, *Canatco,* so the combined convoy was well protected: three merchant ships, which sailed line abreast behind the two corvettes, which zigzagged ahead of each flank. Hartwig sighted the convoy east of Anticosti Island on the morning of 2 September but could not close because of the appearance overhead of a 117 Squadron Canso from Gaspé that was assigned as an escort.[26] Hartwig plotted the course of the convoy, pulled away to get clear of the aircraft, surfaced, and backtracked at speed to the northeast, planning to attack from ahead later in the day. He broadcast sighting reports in case *U-165* was nearby and could join in the attack. Naval intelligence intercepted two of the signals and correctly identified them as sighting reports, but was able to plot only very general positions; one placed the submarine in the Strait of Belle Isle, the other closer to the mark, on the southwest coast of Newfoundland. The submarine trackers in Ottawa correctly estimated that the submarine might have located either LN 7 or, coming southwestward in the reverse direction, NL 6. The latter was the special convoy organized by rushing *Weyburn* and *Clayoquot* northward following the diversion of *Trail*'s convoy back to Gaspé. *Weyburn* and *Clayoquot* had sailed from Hamilton Inlet on the morning of 1 September with three empty merchant vessels and were routed to pass close by LN 7 during the night of 2–3 September. Naval Service Headquarters warned both convoys that there might be a submarine on their tail.[27]

As luck would have it, the two convoys met at almost precisely the moment *U-517* was finally able to close with its prey, the Goose Bay–bound LN 7, shortly before 3:00 AM on 3 September. *Shawinigan* was patrolling off the southern flank of LN 7, ahead of the lake steamer *Donald Stewart,* and *Trail* was on the northern flank. At 2:40 AM, both corvettes made radar contacts about seven kilometres ahead. *Trail* advanced and saw that these were the vessels of the westbound NL 6, and that they would pass about 1460 metres to the north of LN 7.[28] *Shawinigan,* however, was alarmed to pick up a contact just 3.5 kilometres ahead of *Donald Stewart* and rushed forward at about 2:50 AM to see *Weyburn,* which was sweeping perhaps 2700 metres south of NL 6. *Shawinigan* warned *Weyburn* by blue flashing signal light that she was close to a collision course.[29] At about 5:54 the two convoys passed each other, NL 6 to the north, LN 7 to the south, with *Weyburn* westbound on the southern flank of the eastbound LN 7. At that same moment *U-517* raced in on the surface from astern of the southern flank of LN 7, to fire into the broadside of the three merchant ships travelling line abreast. *Shawinigan* had already passed, but *Weyburn* was only 550 metres away and appears to have sighted *U-517* just as the boat fired two torpedoes. Hartwig had seen the "guard ship" only a moment before and had increased to full speed for his attack run. *Weyburn* reported:

Speed was increased to emergency Full (C.E.R.A. [Chief Engine Room Artificer] reported later engine was turning 198 revs, which gives an estimated speed of 18.65 knots [34.5 kilometres per hour]), and course altered to ram Distance was about five cables [914 metres]. Once on a collision bearing, submarine altered course rapidly to port. About

30 seconds after altering, a ship was torpedoed and immediately burst into flame. Two white rockets were fired by WEYBURN. Course was again altered in an effort to ram, but submarine was too fast, moving away all the time. Its ability to turn rapidly was astonishing. Gun was brought to the ready and two rounds were fired. On the firing of the first round, S/M commenced to dive ... At the second round she was almost submerged.[30]

Weyburn made a snap depth charge attack and then began an asdic search, but could find no contact. The ship that had been hit was *Donald Stewart*: "flames burst out ... reaching height of 40 feet [12.2 metres] and rapidly spreading from stern to stem." *Shawinigan* briefly joined the hunt and then rescued *Donald Stewart*'s people; sixteen of her crew had got away in two boats, and three were lost, all engine room personnel as was so often the case.[31] Although the staff in Halifax was critical of the fact that the four escorts had not made a coordinated hunt based on *Weyburn*'s observation of the submarine's diving position—*Trail* and *Clayoquot* kept guard over the merchant ships—*Weyburn*'s action had been effective.[32] Hartwig was setting up for a second torpedo attack when the corvette's determined effort to close to ram persuaded him to dive to safety.

U-517 persisted. She followed the same course as LN 7 to the northeast towards the Strait of Belle Isle, using the cover of the hazy weather to move quickly on the surface. In the wake of the night attack, shore authorities arranged for reinforced air protection for LN 7 from first light on 3 September. By noon, visibility had improved and the air escort, a Digby from 10 Squadron at Gander captained by Flying Officer J.H. Sanderson of Dresden, Ontario, sighted *U-517* from a distance of twelve kilometres. The boat was able to submerge fully before the aircraft dropped four depth charges, whose detonation Hartwig described as "far off." One of the charges blew up prematurely when it hit the surface, and fragments perforated the wing of the Digby, which had dropped to an altitude of only forty-six metres. Damage was not serious, but the report ruefully noted that this was "the first occurrence of this nature in this Command." By the time Hartwig came up for a peek through his periscope about thirty minutes after the attack, he could see HMCS *Trail*, which had responded to the RCAF's attack report, and "an aircraft ... circling above the dive location." In fact, a second 10 Squadron Digby had arrived. With alert defences in the area and the weather clearing, Hartwig abandoned the chase and moved off again towards Anticosti Island. The RCAF was right to boast that the Digby's attack "was probably instrumental in keeping this submarine from attacking convoy LN-7 [sic] while passing through the Straits of Belle Isle." Both the navy and the air force had done well to limit the loss to LN 7 and NL 6 to one small freighter, but, with the blackout of intelligence from decrypted U-boat radio traffic, there was no way for the Canadian commands to know how well they had done, knowledge that would have helped boost spirits in the face of the difficult weeks to come.[33]

SEVEN

Crisis and Closure of the Gulf, 3–9 September 1942

Just hours before the destruction of *Donald Stewart* in the northern gulf, there was evidence of another threat, far to the west, in the river. On the night of 2 September, SQ 33, nine merchant ships under the escort of the corvette *Hepatica,* the Bangor *Red Deer,* and the armed yacht *Raccoon,* was proceeding up the river on the last leg of its trip. At twenty minutes before midnight, *Hepatica* saw two lights flash in the distance and rushed towards them—were these emergency rockets from a torpedoed ship? She searched for about twenty minutes, but the people on watch could make out nothing in the mist. A signal then arrived from *Raccoon,* on the northern flank of the convoy opposite to *Hepatica,* that she had dropped depth charges on a possible submarine contact. That explained the flashes, and *Hepatica* closed the convoy to see if any ships had been attacked, but was able to make out little in the murk. Only when the visibility cleared at 3 AM on 3 September was the corvette able to confirm that all the merchant ships were present.[1]

Raccoon's people had seen a torpedo track ahead of her bow and, shortly after, another that went right under the yacht. She immediately ran along the tracks, dropping the depth charges whose detonations *Hepatica* had seen, but discovered nothing.[2] There was good reason to suspect that the crew had not merely fallen for one of the many visual tricks the St. Lawrence waters can play, especially in conditions of poor visibility. At 12:33 in the morning, almost exactly an hour after *Raccoon* had seen the tracks, radio stations ashore intercepted U-boat transmissions that continued sporadically for over five hours. Direction-finding analysis, which appears not to have been completed until later in the day, showed that some of the transmissions came from the vicinity of SQ 33 and others further up the river, confirming that there was at least one U-boat moving up the river or possibly even two on station some distance apart.[3] U-boat headquarters' war diary shows that *U-165* radioed at about this time and that she was patrolling in the river.[4]

At dawn on 3 September, Eastern Air Command began round-the-clock coverage of the two convoys most at risk, QS 32 that had departed from Bic on the afternoon of 2 September and NL 6 westbound to the Gaspé Passage for Bic. To sustain constant daylight patrols over the river, 11 Squadron at Dartmouth sent three Hudsons on detached duty to Mont Joli (three Hudsons from 119 Squadron were already on station there).[5]

Soon a third threat appeared. Korvettenkapitän Rüggeberg in *U-513* had remained outside the Strait of Belle Isle after his consorts attacked SG 6, but saw nothing but aircraft on patrol. He therefore moved off, as headquarters had authorized, to the anchorage in Conception Bay, west of St. John's. His mission was to strike at the iron ore ships the Germans knew loaded at the Bell Island jetty.[6] It was not the sort of objective that would commend itself to cautious mariners who prefer sea room. Bell Island is located about twenty kilometres inside the southeast headland of Conception Bay. The island lies four to eight kilometres off shore, and the jetty and anchorage were on the shoreward side of the island. Still, the channel between the island and the mainland is deep, sixty metres and more, which commended it to submariners.

Rüggeberg was exceptionally bold. He first entered the bay on the night of 4 September, planning to make a fast surface attack on the ships at anchor between the island and the mainland. He was forced to withdraw, however, by the coast defence searchlights, crewed by the Newfoundland Militia, that periodically probed the entrance to the anchorage. He returned the next night and made a slow, submerged run right into the inner anchorage where he arrived in daylight on the morning of 5 September. He had to call off his initial attack on the two laden steamers at anchor because of mechanical failures. He lay there for nearly two hours while the crew completed repairs, and then began a fresh attack run. The torpedoes failed to launch from their tubes. Undismayed, he manoeuvred for another quarter of an hour to bring his stern tubes to bear. Finally, on his third attempt, at approximately 11:45 AM, two torpedoes ran, hitting *Sagana*. The boat had been struggling to maintain trim in the presence of density layering as pronounced as in the St. Lawrence. After the shots, the boat plunged "involuntarily," and as the crew regained control and brought the submarine back up from the depths, her conning tower collided with the bottom of the hull of *Lord Strathcona,* the second ore ship, and plunged again, right to the bottom, forty-four metres. Still undeterred, Rüggeberg brought the submarine back under control and, a half hour after the attack on *Sagana,* fired two torpedoes that ripped open *Lord Strathcona*'s hull.

On the surface there was pandemonium, and, from the townspeople and survivors of the sunken ships' crews, heroism. William Russell, head constable of the local detachment of the Royal Newfoundland Constabulary, reported: "At the time there were two other boats anchored in the road which kept up a rapid fire [with their self-defence armament] in all directions, and all the while everyone in Lance Cove that had a boat was searching for survivors together with a large number of people in lifeboats from the steamers. Everything possible was done by these people who were moving around in all directions amongst the shells that were bursting with no apparent regard for their safety."[7]

Rüggeberg had begun to backtrack and was disappointed to find that a steamer at the jetty that he had intended to attack as he left had got underway and was beyond reach. *U-513* crept out of the bay and did not surface until nightfall provided protective cover. The submarine had been below the surface for seventeen hours.

Shortly after noon the next day, 6 September, and 1200 kilometres to the west, the eight merchant vessels of convoy QS 33 departed from Bic Island. Senior ship of the escort was the corvette *Arrowhead*, with two Fairmiles, the armed yacht *Raccoon*, and, as an additional escort, the newly commissioned Bangor *Truro*, en route to Halifax for completion of her equipment and work-ups. Air protection was heavy, three Hudsons from Mont Joli, but they departed as darkness fell; that night, Eastern Air Command pulled back from the efforts at twenty-four-hour coverage begun on the third. Geoffrey Smith, the asdic operator on duty in *Arrowhead*, on the port (northern) bow of the convoy, vividly remembered forty-five years later the events that unfolded a half-hour after QS 33 passed Cap Chat. "The time was coming up 6 bells (11 PM) ... To starboard, out of the ASDIC cabin I could clearly see ... the silhouette of the Greek freighter 'AEAS' [carrying lumber and steel to the U.K. via Sydney]. Suddenly there was a terrible noise on the ASDIC that sounded like a train rushing through a tunnel. Remembering the various sounds we had been exposed to [on training recordings] at ASDIC school, I shouted 'Torpedoes.' Before I could say anything more there was a terrifying explosion that threw me off my ASDIC stool, out of the ASDIC cabin and across the bridge."[8] Ioannis (John) Skinitis, *Aeas*' master, later reported that she had been hit twice amidships, in the fuel bunker and number three hold. She immediately began to go down, and twenty-nine of the crew of thirty-one took to the boats; the other two crewmen were never accounted for.

Smith's recollection about *Aeas* sailing off *Arrowhead*'s starboard side is correct. The convoy was in two rows of four ships abreast. The Greek freighter was in "pendant" position 11, in the northernmost end in the front row. *Arrowhead* was zigzagging off the northern bow of the convoy to a maximum distance of about 4600 metres, next to *Aeas*. Captain Skinitis promptly fired two white rockets, leaving no doubt about what had happened, and *Arrowhead* was thus able to respond quickly, rushing towards the wreck, firing star shell to illuminate the scene. Nothing turned up. A call by radio-telephone to Fairmile *Q 065*, sweeping astern of the convoy perhaps 6500 metres or more behind *Arrowhead*, brought the laconic reply, "Saw nothing—did nothing." *Truro*, off on the southern flank of the convoy, was not fitted with radio-telephone and was therefore out of reach of quick communication. Commander Edgar Skinner, *Arrowhead*'s commanding officer, had, when the convoy sailed, instructed *Truro* to follow specific directions in the *Western Atlantic Convoy Instructions*, the bible for convoy operations. *Truro*, on seeing the emergency rockets, was attempting to carry out those instructions by closing with the merchant ships, like *Arrowhead*, while firing star shell. The Bangor, however, had to take evasive action to avoid collision with Great Lakes steamers that, as in the attacks during July, were dashing towards the protection of the shallow water along the shoreline. One of the lakers, *John S. Pillsbury*, was making its third such escape, having survived both QS 15 and QS 19. In the manoeuvres to avoid the charging lakers, *Truro*'s steering engine failed, so the Bangor pressed on as best she could with manual control and made an asdic search.

At 11:40 PM, after a forty-minute search, *Arrowhead* stopped and picked up *Aeas*' survivors from the freighter's "water-logged" boats. *Raccoon*, whose station was on the north side of the convoy at the rear, came forward to screen *Arrowhead* during the thirty-minute rescue operation. By 1 AM, 7 September, *Arrowhead* had regained her position ahead of the northern side of the convoy, and at 2:10 AM all the escorts heard what apparently were detonations of depth charges dropped by *Raccoon* and a blast on her whistle. *Arrowhead* swept back about four-and-a-half kilometres to the armed yacht's position in the screen, but could make out nothing in the now poor visibility: "Very dark with low clouds." Because the yacht had no radio-telephone, there was no method to communicate, aside from a general radio broadcast. Skinner expected *Racoon* would report in the morning. He suspected something might be wrong only when a radio message addressed to the yacht by Gaspé at 9:22 AM evoked no response.

The detonations from *Raccoon*'s place in the screen were almost certainly not caused by her own depth charges but by torpedoes from *U-165*, which reported shortly after the attack that she had sunk a total of three vessels in the convoy. The yacht's lightly built hull appears to have disintegrated. A fragment of her bridge and some naval signals washed up on shore a few days later. All thirty-eight of her people were lost. They were typical of the crews of Canada's citizen navy. The captain, Lieutenant Commander John H. Smith, RCNR, had been the first officer of Canadian National Steamship's small liner *Lady Rodney* before the war. Only four other members of the crew were RCNR, that is, had had professional marine experience before their wartime service. The rest were volunteer reservists from across the country. The navy announced the loss on 14 September, after the families had been informed. Press reports noted that one of the junior officers was Sub-Lieutenant Russell McConnell, RCNVR, of Westmount, Quebec, a star in McGill University's intercollegiate sports; he had been a back-fielder in the championship 1938 Redmen football team.[9] More than three weeks later, a "badly mutilated" body washed up at the western end of Anticosti Island. It proved to be McConnell, and he was buried at sea on 7 October.[10]

At the inquiry into *Raccoon*'s fate, the testimony of Able-Bodied Seaman Theodore Burton, the radar operator on duty in *Arrowhead*, provided a stark example of how in modern warfare a vessel can disappear unnoticed and without a trace within a few hundred metres of its consorts. It also highlights the extent to which warships groped on dark nights even with the early 1.5-metre radar set of the type fitted in *Arrowhead*.

> 68. From what you can remember, was the Raccoon in this position shortly before 0210?
>
> Ans. [Burton] Yes, sir she was. I could see her astern just before the two explosions occurred.
>
> ...
>
> 70. Did you pick up the Raccoon again?
>
> Ans. I saw the Raccoon for less than one minute after the explosion, then she seemed to fade away, and was not picked up again.
>
> ...
>
> 72. Is it correct that as you have a fixed set [i.e., the aerial did not rotate], no accurate bearing could be given particularly ... around the stern ...
>
> Ans. [Burton] Yes, sir.
>
> 73. Does it sometimes occur with this fixed type set, that echoes which you see suddenly die out for no reason although you know the object is still there?
>
> Ans. [Burton] Yes, this has happened in several cases when I have been on watch.
>
> 74. Can you pick up Fairmiles [approximately the same size as *Raccoon*] with your set?
>
> Ans. [Burton] Sometimes, but not at close range, inside a half mile [800 metres].[11]

From shortly after daybreak of 7 September, hours before anyone suspected anything was amiss with *Raccoon*, the convoy was again being tracked. Hartwig's *U-517* had just arrived north of Gaspé in the early hours of that day when Hoffmann radioed news of his success against the eastbound QS 33. Hartwig correctly estimated that the convoy would be closely following the coast north of Gaspé and rushed westward along the shore to intercept. He dived at first light, 5:55 AM, for safety against aircraft patrols, but a bit over three hours later sighted "Three fat steamers." He could not catch up at his slow submerged speed, but luck was with him. "Deterioration of visibility due to rain, mist, and fog" provided cover against aerial detection, so he was able to surface and move quickly to get ahead of the convoy. At 5:15 PM an aircraft's appearance forced Hartwig under, but he was able to track the oncoming vessels by sound, and the visibility then cleared enough that he was able to use his attack periscope. As the convoy passed over, he swung off to the north and quickly fired three torpedoes, two from his forward tubes and one from the stern, at close range and then plunged very deep, 120 metres.[12]

All three torpedoes found their marks. In *Arrowhead*, closest to the scene, it seemed the three ships—the Greek steamers *Mount Pindus* and *Mount Taygetus*, both carrying general cargo and deckloads of army tanks to the United Kingdom, and *Oakton*, a Canadian Great Lakes steamer carrying coal from Ohio—were hit almost simultaneously, "in about 15 seconds." *Truro*, on the southern side of the convoy, reported "Mount Pindus on the port [north] side of the Convoy was torpedoed, about two seconds later S.S. Oakton was torpedoed, and approximately forty seconds later third ship S.S. Tayget [sic] was torpedoed."[13] German historian Jürgen Rohwer, working from the torpedo firing records, concluded the shots were about one minute apart.[14] At the moment of the attack, the Bangor *Vegreville* was approaching, escorting the freighter *Sarnolite* from Gaspé, thirty kilometres away, to join the convoy. From the Bangor, six-and-a-half kilometres away as the attacks began, the action seemed to unfold like a slow-motion movie, with the first ship settling and disappearing as the "Escorts circled round dropping depth charges"; three minutes later the second ship went under, and five minutes later still, *Oakton*. From *Vegreville*, now closed to just under four kilometres, it looked like the laker took a second torpedo, but this was certainly an internal explosion: "the ship was seen to settle slightly amidships. Slowly the bow and stern rose until she finally broke in two, and sank swiftly." There was a particularly sad irony to *Oakton*'s destruction. She was one of the four lakers that had scattered from the convoy the night before. Three of the ships were headed for small ports around the Gaspé Peninsula and appear from aerial sighting reports to have sailed close along the shore to their destinations. *Oakton*, however, was bound for Corner Brook, Newfoundland, and was spotted on the horizon by *Arrowhead* which sent *Q 083* to round her up. She rejoined the convoy just two-and-a-half hours before *U-517*'s attacks. Normally, when a U-boat was known to be present, a ship was infinitely safer in convoy than sailing independently.

The escorts, as they rushed swiftly to the scene, made no asdic contact on *U-517*. They dropped depth charges as a deterrent to prevent the submarine from firing at *Bencas,* the sole remaining ship of the convoy. Among the four escorts, only the asdic sets in *Arrowhead* and *Q 065* were fully operational. In the newly built *Truro,* the search transmitter had failed the night before, so she was only able to listen through her equipment. *Q 083*'s set had failed a few hours before the attack. It did not really matter. Although asdic conditions appeared to be good in *Arrowhead,* "Average echo about 1600 yards [1463 metres]," that in all likelihood was returns in the top warm-water layer. *U-517* had immediately dived deep into the underlying cold-water layer.

Vegreville and *Truro* escorted *Sarnolite* and *Bencas* back into Gaspé. The Fairmile *Q 083* rescued survivors; seventy-eight people crowded the little vessel as she headed into port. *Arrowhead* and *Q 065* continued the hunt in the Gaspé approaches as additional support arrived, two aircraft, the Bangor *Chedabucto,* and the corvettes *Weyburn* and *Hepatica.* After the escorts' search of the approaches, the convoy was to continue, but the captain of *Bencas* refused to sail until daylight. In the early hours of 8 September, *Sarnolite* set sail once more with *Vegreville* as escort, and *Bencas,* screened by *Arrowhead* and *Truro,* followed after dawn.

During the early hours of 8 September, the Gaspé command launched searches of the Gaspé Passage that continued until 10 September and included twelve warships. Eastern Air Command weighed in with a total of forty-six patrols in the gulf over the three days.[15] The air coverage included an important new element. On 8 September, 113 Squadron at Yarmouth dispatched a detachment of three Hudsons to the training airfield at Chatham, New Brunswick, on the Miramichi River. Until this time, fast strike aircraft, able to respond quickly to U-boat intelligence, had been located at either end of the main convoy route, at Sydney in the east and at Mont Joli in the west. Chatham was right at the centre of the convoy route and, with the Hudson's speed, within a half hour's flying time of the Gaspé approaches. Immediately the detachment implemented the Yarmouth squadron's tactics of high-altitude sweeps that, while focused on positions where U-boats had been recently located, took in waters all around those areas to allow for the movement of the submarine.

On the morning of 9 September, the Hudsons began a search to the east of Gaspé. After eighty minutes on patrol, one of the aircraft, flown by twenty-two-year-old Pilot Officer Robert S. Keetley of Moose Jaw, Saskatchewan, sighted something about thirty-five kilometres south of the eastern tip of Anticosti Island. "At first did not think it was a submarine but mistook it for sail boat due to its excellent camouflage. The conning tower was painted white and the hull sea green ..."[16] Keetley had unusually good training for a new pilot in Eastern Air Command at this time in the war. He had completed a two-month maritime navigation course at the British general reconnaissance school at Charlottetown at the beginning of 1942 and then had training on the Hudson aircraft. He had, however, started operational flying only two months before, on 8 July 1942, and this was his first attack.[17]

Keetley dived from 1200 metres but was still at 245 metres as the Hudson passed over the U-boat. It appeared that the German crew had manned an anti-aircraft gun, so the Hudson sprayed the deck with machine gun fire as it whizzed over at 470 kilometres an hour. Keetley banked steeply and made a second pass, continuing his dive and dropping four depth charges at 9:55 AM, eight seconds after the conning tower disappeared. As Squadron Leader Small correctly concluded, the crew's inexperience had told in its initial hesitation in making an attack run, and the depth charges had been released a few seconds too late; the submarine was safely below and ahead of the lethal radius of the explosions.

The excellent photographs Keetley's crew took leave no doubt that they had attacked a U-boat. The target was *U-165*, and the attack almost certainly accounts for her withdrawal to the west into the river. Hoffmann later reported by radio to headquarters that he recommended operations in the river mouth in the vicinity of Matane because air patrols made it "difficult" to locate and pursue shipping in the Gaspé approaches and south of the eastern part of Anticosti, precisely the areas where 113 Squadron's offensive searches had taken place on 8–10 September.[18]

The Canadian navy also reinforced the defences in the gulf. The destruction of QS 33, despite substantial air cover and escort by a corvette, in addition to a Bangor and Fairmiles, showed that the substantial increases in the defence forces resulting from *U-132*'s attacks in July were not adequate. On 9 September, Naval Service Headquarters directed the Atlantic command at Halifax to assign to the gulf two of the thirteen old British destroyers serving in the RCN's Western Local Escort Force. Destroyers, with almost double the speed of the corvettes and Bangors, were able to pursue and overtake U-boats whose standard tactic was to shadow a convoy on the surface just beyond the visibility range of lookouts in the convoy escorts. These British destroyers, although old, had been fitted with the latest short-wave radar which, unlike the equipment in the Canadian warships, could dependably locate surfaced submarines. Although the effective range was limited to a few thousand metres, less than eyesight in clear weather, the new radar was invaluable at night and in foggy conditions when submarines were most likely to attempt a fast surface attack. Destroyers were also the scarcest and most precious resource in the Allied arsenal for the Atlantic war, and the allocation of these warships was one of the main sources of contention among the British, Canadian, and U.S. high commands. It was for this reason that the decision to assign the British destroyers came from headquarters in Ottawa, an intervention that showed the shock administered by the losses to QS 33.

Headquarters in Ottawa intervened again to delay the sailing of QS 34 from Bic Island for twenty-four hours until the morning of 11 September so that the first destroyer, HMS *Witherington*, could reinforce the escort. Similarly, instructions came from Ottawa to delay the sailing of the next convoy from Sydney, SQ 36, until the second destroyer, HMS *Salisbury*, could reach that port. No convoy in the Sydney to Quebec series was to sail without one of the destroyers in the escort. Such direct intervention by Ottawa in the particulars of operations was a rare occurrence.[19]

Naval Service Headquarters allocated the destroyers to the Gulf Escort Force only temporarily because the government had decided to close the St. Lawrence to overseas shipping. A signal dispatched from Ottawa to the Admiralty in London and the U.S. Navy Department in Washington on the evening of 9 September asked that all ships bound from the United Kingdom for St. Lawrence ports, including ships already at sea, be diverted to Sydney, Halifax, or Saint John. The intention was to shut down the Sydney to Quebec series of convoys within "about two weeks" and thus greatly reduce the defences in the gulf and river.[20]

The closure of the gulf at the moment of the U-boats' greatest success would seem to be definitive proof of a German victory. The whole purpose of the U-boat campaign was to prevent the shipment of supplies from North America to Britain, and the most important route from Canada had been shut down. That was the conclusion reached by Dr. G.N. Tucker's team in the official history published in 1952: "a defeat which had in reality been inflicted earlier in the summer."[21] Tucker's account, based on analysis of merchant shipping records, substantiated the similar conclusion reached in Joseph Schull's undocumented official operational history published in 1950.

More recent research has painted a quite different picture. The decision to close the gulf to ocean shipping in September 1942 was not anything like as precipitate as existing accounts suggest, and much more was involved than the U-boat attacks. In fact, Canada had begun to divert shipping away from the St. Lawrence months before the first attacks in May 1942 in order to meet more pressing Allied needs on the Atlantic, which had absolute priority over the gulf and river. In this light, the greatest danger posed by the U-boat attacks was to divert forces more urgently needed on the Atlantic. For this reason the naval staff was, by the early summer of 1942, already considering closure of the gulf to ocean shipping the following year. As it happened, the run of success by *U-165* and *U-517* in early September coincided with an Allied appeal to remove escorts from Canadian waters to support new operations in the Mediterranean, and these escorts could be found only by cancelling the main St. Lawrence convoys, a measure that the naval staff had already agreed should be taken in the near future. In other words, Canada closed the St. Lawrence for precisely the same reasons that priority for the defence of the area had been downgraded since the German conquest of northwest Europe in 1940 had thrust the Dominion into a leading role in the Atlantic war. Tucker was right that the closure of the superbly equipped St. Lawrence ports did, in the end, impose enormous burdens on other parts of the national transportation system, but these difficulties did not emerge until months after the closure. The foremost concern in September 1942 was to deploy Canada's navy resources best to support the common struggle, at a time when that struggle hung in precarious balance. Germany had yet to sustain a major strategic setback, and no major Allied counteroffensive had yet been launched.

Canadian policy towards the St. Lawrence began to change as a result of Britain's critical shortage of merchant vessels in late 1940 and early 1941. Losses in the intense operations in the spring of 1940 were compounded by the subsequent heavy German attacks from bases in France and Britain's dependence on overseas imports to the exclusion of short-hauls from Europe. An early Canadian response to British entreaties for help was a dramatic change in shipbuilding priorities from warships to merchant ships; one result of that decision was the delay in upgrading the RCN's hard-driven corvette fleet with improvements to existing ships and the construction of new types until late 1943 and 1944. Still more pressing than the construction of new merchant ships, a longer-term solution at best, was to overcome delays in the repair of merchant vessels.

By February 1941, the peak of the merchant ship repair crisis, some 25 percent of Britain's sea-going dry-cargo ships were in British ports undergoing or awaiting repairs. One answer to the crush of work that overwhelmed British yards was to have as many ships as possible repaired at overseas ports, and the British government made a special appeal to Canada. Halifax was particularly important as the main western terminal of the transatlantic convoys and Canada's principal year-round Atlantic port. Weather especially or accident (often the result of weather) damaged four times as many merchant ships as enemy action, in part because older ships had been pressed into ocean service for which they were not suited and, as luck would have it, the wartime winters on the north Atlantic were particularly fierce.[22] At Halifax by the end of February 1941, ninety-eight merchant ships were undergoing or awaiting repairs, as were another eighteen ships at Saint John, the other major year-round port on the Atlantic coast.[23] Although the Canadian government had begun work to expand the ship repair facilities, the more difficult problem was a shortage of manpower. In peacetime, the main shipping traffic at Halifax and Saint John was during the winter months when the more economical St. Lawrence route was blocked by ice. As a result, the waterfront workforce in the Maritime provinces was seasonal. Wartime did not change the pattern, for although merchant ships gathered for convoy at Halifax year round, except in winter most loaded or discharged cargoes at St. Lawrence ports and to save precious time underwent any necessary repairs while there. With the expansion of both military recruiting and war industry in 1940, many experienced workers found better opportunities elsewhere, and it was difficult to attract new workers to Halifax, where accommodation was overcrowded and expensive. The big challenge was to create year-round employment so that adequate labour would be available during the crisis periods in winter, such as that in February and March 1941.

Part of the solution urged on the British Ministry of War Transport by the powerful Canadian Department of Munitions and Supply, which was responsible for both shipbuilding and ship repair, was to divert some Allied merchant shipping from the St. Lawrence to unload and take on cargo at Halifax and Saint John in the summer months. Diversions in the summer of 1941 helped to keep the ship repair labour force at 1200 to 1300, the level it had reached with emergency efforts early in 1941 to deal with the repair crisis (and a dramatic increase over the 400 who had been on hand during the winter of 1939–40).[24] Still more men were needed, however, because "leakage" to other employment was a continuing problem, and the demand for repairs was still increasing. The Canadian government was taking extraordinary measures at Halifax and Saint John, including the recruitment of workers, training schemes for the skilled trades, and the construction of accommodation at public expense. These efforts would be of little use, however, without more employment for repair and other port services in the summer months. In the winter of 1941–42, Canadian authorities pressed the Ministry of War Transport for fuller diversions from the St. Lawrence for the summer of 1942. These diversions took place; early in August 1942, G. Huband, the British Ministry of War Transport representative in Canada, reported that the tonnage of cargo loaded and discharged at Halifax since the beginning of May "has been more than 250% in excess of the quantity handled during the corresponding period" in 1941.[25]

The arrival of the U-boats in North American waters in January 1942 and the necessity of a comprehensive system of port-to-port coastal convoys introduced an important new element into the equation, one that necessitated further diversions from the St. Lawrence to Atlantic ports. Although Canada's prompt introduction of coastal convoys prevented the wholesale slaughter of merchant shipping that took place in U.S. waters until the United States belatedly adopted a similar system in the spring and summer of 1942, the local convoys imposed very large penalties by delaying and slowing down the movement of shipping, thus greatly reducing its carrying power and the volume of essential supplies delivered to the U.K. The coastal convoy system also stretched the British and particularly the Canadian escort forces to the limit. The two Commonwealth navies had to run coastal convoys in U.S. waters while also replacing the destroyers the United States was forced to withdraw from the transatlantic run, which, at the same time, had to be extended south from Sydney and Halifax to Boston.

These pressures on the Atlantic, as we have seen, were the reason why the Canadian forces were so hard pressed to provide adequate defences in the St. Lawrence when *U-553* made its reconnaissance in May. One of the early results was further diversions to Halifax. Because the majority of ships using the St. Lawrence were slow—many of them very slow—the Canadians could run only slow convoys within the gulf, and the Atlantic coastal convoys were often not any faster. Fast ships suffered inordinate time losses, "in the neighbourhood of 12 [to] 14 days" Huband reported, for the vessels to make the run from Halifax, the fast convoy assembly port, to Montreal to unload and reload and back to Halifax. This span of time was equal to that for the full Atlantic crossing by a fast HX convoy. The British Ministry of War Transport addressed these unacceptable delays by diverting all fast ships from the St. Lawrence to Halifax early in August 1942.

Canada, whose escorts bore the brunt of the pressures created by the inefficient and incomplete convoy system in North American waters, took the lead in streamlining and fleshing out the organization. The naval staff hosted a conference in Ottawa on 23–24 July 1942 that was attended by Captain M.K. Metcalf, head of the Convoy and Routing section at the U.S. Navy Department, and British officers in the United States who organized shipping. Captain Brand, head of the Trade Division at Naval Service Headquarters, was the key Canadian participant, and the main result of the conference was to agree on a measure developed by Brand's division. Their analysis showed that, since the United States' entry into the war, the composition of the slow transatlantic SC convoys had changed markedly; only 30 percent of ships came from the St. Lawrence and fully 61 percent from U.S. ports. The assembly port for the SC convoys was therefore transferred from Sydney to Halifax starting with SC 95, which sailed on 4 August 1942. The change allowed a reduction in the Halifax to Sydney local convoys, and the conference looked for further savings, unanimously agreeing "that from the escort point of view it would be most desirable for the maximum number of ships ... to load in Nova Scotian or New Brunswick ports in summer as well as in winter."[26]

The Ottawa conference paved the way—as it was intended to do—for much larger changes in the North American coastal convoy system along the lines Brand urged. Most urgent was the continuing shortfall in deliveries of oil from the Caribbean to Britain. The Americans' institution of local port-to-port convoys up their seaboard had ended the heavy losses to tankers, but the necessity for U.K.-bound tankers repeatedly to put into port and await the sailing of a local convoy for the next leg imposed great delays, more than doubling the nine to eleven days' passage of the Canadian tanker convoys between Halifax and the Caribbean. All the Ottawa conference could do, however, was recommend a fast tanker convoy service direct from the Caribbean and southern U.S. waters to northern U.S. ports on the model of the Canadian oil convoys. Admiral King, who in the wake of the Pearl Harbor disaster had become commander in chief of the whole U.S. Navy,[27] was furious that the Canadians put the tanker issue on their agenda without working through the U.S. Navy Department, which under agreements with Britain and Canada had recently taken control over all merchant shipping in the ocean area off the American seaboard. The American admiral had nearly ordered his convoy and routing staff to boycott the Ottawa meeting.[28]

Still, King was coming round to the need for a complete, efficient system of coastal convoys in U.S. waters, including fast "through" tanker convoys. The U.S. Navy was the target of scathing criticism in the press—and from the U.S. Army—about the failure of the existing shipping defence measures. American industry, moreover, was now completing some of the additional escorts King had always insisted were essential to make coastal convoys effective. King called the British and Canadians to his own coastal convoy conference in Washington on 1 August; Brand was a leading participant. There was speedy progress in filling the gaps in the existing U.S. system and rearranging schedules so that ships could proceed in convoy the whole way from the Caribbean Sea and Gulf of Mexico to New York with reduced delays. There would also be a fast "through" convoy for tankers from Guantánamo in Cuba to New York that was larger and more frequent than the Halifax–Aruba run; Canada for its part shifted six corvettes from the Aruba run to help the Americans establish the new service.

The rearrangement of other convoys built on the analysis Brand had unveiled at the Ottawa conference. Because many more ships were now loading at U.S. rather than Canadian ports, more efficient employment of escorts and faster merchant ship passages could most readily be achieved by moving convoy assembly ports closer to the American loading ports. Thus the conference transferred the assembly of both HX and SC convoys from Halifax to New York, the northern terminal of the U.S. coastal convoys system, beginning with HX 208 (sailed 17 September 1942) and SC 102 (sailed 19 September 1942).[29]

The belated completion of the U.S. coastal convoy system depended not only on Canadian ideas, but on Canadian escorts. Able to trim the size and frequency of the Boston–Halifax and other convoys in Canadian waters, the Western Local Escort Force assumed responsibility for the escort of HX and SC convoys from New York to the waters off southern Newfoundland (where the Mid-Ocean Escort Force took over), and of ON and ONS convoys from Newfoundland waters south to New York. Because the shortest, most direct route to the United Kingdom took the big convoys close to Nova Scotia and the mouth of the Bay of Fundy, ships loaded at Canadian ports were able to efficiently join the main convoys in groups under the protection of two or three escorts that shuttled out of Saint John, Halifax, and Sydney. Similarly, ships from the ON and ONS convoys bound for Canadian ports broke off near their destinations and were met by the local escorts.

Not surprisingly, the Canadian naval staff was pleased with the outcome of the Washington meeting: "under the existing circumstances ... we are forced to escort ships up and down the American coast ... the new arrangement should very considerably speed up the movements of ships and might possibly result in a slight saving in escorts forces."[30] Brand noted one concern: "From about the middle of September roughly 65% of the ships at present coming to Halifax for convoy assembly will no longer go to that port, but will be assembled at an American port."[31] The reduction in convoy assembly work in no way diminished the need to increase year-round employment at Halifax, where, as experience in the winters of 1940 and 1941 had shown, the foremost priority was for labour to repair ships battered in the heavy winter seas. This need, together with the concentration of the escort forces on the main Atlantic convoy route between New York and southeastern Newfoundland, made still stronger the case for diverting St. Lawrence traffic to Halifax and Saint John for loading, unloading, and repair services. The most pressing issue, Huband informed his bosses at the Ministry of War Transport in London, was "to overcome the heavy loss of time consequent upon Coastal and river convoys." Much as the ministry valued the excellent timber- and grain-loading facilities at the St. Lawrence ports, Huband warned, the ministry should "lay ... plans in advance against the worst eventuality which will mean the virtual elimination of Montreal, Sorel, Three Rivers, and Quebec as loading and discharging ports during the summer season of 1943."[32]

Then, in late August, before the most important U-boat successes in the St. Lawrence, word reached Ottawa about dramatic developments in Allied war strategy that would require thinning the escorts in North American waters and the north Atlantic in order to deploy substantial forces to European waters.

On 27 August 1942, Churchill sent a cable to Mackenzie King reporting on Churchill's recent meetings in Moscow with Joseph Stalin, the Soviet leader. Mackenzie King immediately recognized the enormous importance of the message, which laid out Allied strategy for the coming year and in particular how the British and American forces would begin the counteroffensive against Germany. There were two main thrusts: a combined Anglo-U.S. strategic bombing offensive against German cities and industry, and a British and American invasion of French North Africa to destroy the German and Italian forces in that theatre.

This was an essentially British strategy that Churchill had persuaded the Americans to accept only with great difficulty. President Roosevelt of the United States was determined to have U.S. land forces engaged against German land forces by the end of 1942 to forestall strong public demands since the Japanese attack on Pearl Harbor for an immediate offensive against Japan. Such a major effort in the Pacific would have undermined the "Germany first" principle that was the basis of the Anglo-American alliance—hence Roosevelt's insistence on early action in Europe. Stalin had been demanding that his western Allies invade northwestern Europe to compel the Germans to withdraw forces from the east and relieve the nearly unbearable pressure on the Red Army. The American chiefs of staff urged precisely such a course, with the invasion of France to take place before the end of 1942 if necessary and certainly no later than the spring of 1943. Churchill and the British chiefs of staff, who remembered all too clearly the nightmarish four-year stalemate of

1914–18 in northern France and the Low Countries, precisely where a new invasion would have to be launched, were certain such premature action would result in a disaster. Thus they urged the bombing campaign and North African operations to wear down the forces Germany could deploy on the western front. So much at loggerheads were the British and U.S. chiefs of staff that Roosevelt had to intervene and direct his military advisors to join in the British plans.

Churchill's mission was then to persuade Stalin to accept the North African operation and the delay in an invasion of northwestern Europe. This was the reason for his extraordinary and arduous trip to Moscow. Stalin, after bitterly denouncing Anglo-American timidity in the face of the German Army, reluctantly acquiesced, thus clearing the way for the North African invasion, operation "Torch," which would take place in November 1942. Mackenzie King was delighted at the news: "Churchill has taken the right course in seeing Stalin, & having situation clearly understood."[33]

On Sunday, 30 August 1942, the same day the British high commissioner in Ottawa hand-delivered a fuller version of Churchill's Moscow report to Mackenzie King, Commodore R.M. Dick, chief of staff to Admiral Sir Andrew Cunningham, head of the British Admiralty Delegation in Washington, briefed Admiral Nelles in Ottawa about the North African operation. Cunningham had been designated as the naval commander for Torch, and had dispatched Commodore Dick to Ottawa to appeal for RCN escorts to help screen the invasion. It was to be the largest amphibious operation in history, with some 100,000 troops carried in three convoys, each of thirty to forty transports, for the initial assault alone.

Nelles immediately grasped the singular importance of the operation and the opportunities it afforded to promote the Canadian navy. (He in fact wanted to contribute destroyers from the RCN's mid-ocean force and had to be restrained by the British, who explained that it was essential the Canadian groups remain on the north Atlantic to help hold the line while Britain pulled out some of its own escorts for North Africa.) Nelles was sure—correctly—that the navy minister, Angus Macdonald, would be equally excited. Mackenzie King, however, would have to be approached more carefully. Nelles said he would share the information about the North African operation with no one but Macdonald and urged that Churchill should send a personal appeal to Mackenzie King for the escorts. Nelles suggested the wording that Churchill in fact used, "every ship capable escorting from both Canadian coasts," when he sent the cable on 5 September.[34]

Mackenzie King read Churchill's message appealing for the escorts to the Cabinet War Committee on 9 September. Macdonald then explained that the naval staff calculated that Canada could send seventeen corvettes. Admiral Nelles was in attendance, and he supplied the details. All five corvettes then in service on the Pacific coast could be spared without difficulty. The remaining twelve would have to come from the Atlantic coast. He then referred to the recent upsurge of sinkings by U-boats in the St. Lawrence and warned that the corvettes could be sent "only by closing the St. Lawrence to ocean traffic and thereby reducing escort requirements ..."[35] Mackenzie King alone, according to his diary, raised questions in general terms about the needs of Canadian home defence, not specifically about the closure of the St. Lawrence. As it was, all other members of the committee agreed that the corvettes should be sent, and Mackenzie King readily joined in: "personal appeal for this form of assistance from Churchill made it necessary to go as far as we could."[36]

The lack of discussion about the closure of the St. Lawrence suggests this was not an admission of defeat in an area of great political and economic importance to the country, but the confirmation of a consensus already achieved about priorities for the employment of Canadian forces to win the war. Since 1940, the Canadian military and government had shared the British view that the immediate protection of Canadian waters was secondary to the Battle of the Atlantic, and they now also shared the view that the offensive in North Africa, with precedence even over the Atlantic war, justified further cuts in Canadian home waters. C.D. Howe, the minister of munitions and supply and the economic czar of the Canadian war effort, had urged diversions of traffic from the St. Lawrence since early 1941, which the navy—and the other armed services—had fully supported both in the interests of increasing the capacity of the Atlantic ports and easing the grave shortage of escorts.

Mackenzie King's reference to the decisive importance of Churchill's appeal—which he did not know had been engineered and partly drafted by Nelles—needs to be approached with some caution in view of the prominent commitments he had repeatedly made about the defence of the St. Lawrence in Parliament, in Cabinet, and to the Liberal caucus. Mackenzie King's habit was to defer to such appeals or advice only when they confirmed his own instincts. In this case, it seems evident that Mackenzie King was above all else enormously relieved by Churchill's success with the Americans and Soviets in deferring the invasion of northwestern Europe. The whole purpose of the large army Canada had sent to Britain was to join in the invasion, and the horrific losses the 2nd Canadian Infantry Division had suffered only weeks before in the disastrous Dieppe raid more than substantiated the British caution about a large-scale cross-Channel attack. The government, moreover, had narrowly survived the recent political crisis on the issue of overseas conscription in large part by promising to dispatch conscripts only in the event of military necessity. Mackenzie King, of course, fervently prayed that day would never come because the opposition in Quebec was undiminished. Yet there was little doubt the conscripts would be needed at the front due to the heavy casualties that would result from a precipitate cross-Channel attack in which the Canadian Army was destined to play a central part.

Mackenzie King mentions none of this in connection with the news from Churchill about the North African invasion. He was, however, relieved that Canada had not been asked to supply ground troops, for he believed that the operation was risky and also unlikely to be effective in "defeating the enemy's land forces." For this reason, he was pleased at Churchill's clear assertion that Canada could most usefully contribute to the North African operation with naval forces, which had little chance of incurring heavy casualties. Mackenzie King had much greater hope in the commitment to the large combined bombing offensive. On 6 September, he read papers by Air Marshal Sir Arthur Harris, commander-in-chief of the RAF's Bomber Command, and retired Air Marshal Sir Hugh Trenchard, "both advocating a concentrated air attack on Germany." "I am sure they are right," Mackenzie King mused. "If we had concentrated on air, tanks, planes [that is, munitions production] & navy, instead of putting so much into the Army, our contribution would have been & would be today much more effective."[37]

Although the orders to close the St. Lawrence to ocean shipping were the result of a well-considered assessment of national and Allied priorities, they coincided with the beginning of the most dramatic successes by the U-boats, close along the Gaspé shore and deep into the river. It was this string of heavy losses so near to the centres of population that shaped public opinion, the views of the Canadian commanders, the reaction of the government, and, ultimately, the historical record. What was not noticed at the time—except by the Germans—was that the run of U-boat victories was short-lived, despite the departure of the principal escorts for service in European waters.

EIGHT

The Crisis Deepens but the Balance Shifts, 9–30 September 1942

While the Allied leaders in Ottawa, London, and Washington were making the decisions that were to change the role of the St. Lawrence, the life and death struggle in its waters went on. HMCS *Charlottetown* was the victim of an ambush in circumstances that gave the corvette no chance. On the evening of 10 September, *Charlottetown* and the Bangor *Clayoquot* had completed the escort of SQ 35 to Bic Island, and the two warships immediately headed back towards Gaspé. They groped through heavy fog and, because *Clayoquot* was low on fuel, did not zigzag and slowed from the normal transit speed of 26 kilometres per hour to a more fuel-efficient 21.5 kilometres per hour. After sunrise on 11 September, the fog partially cleared in the bright sunlight.

U-517 was making a submerged patrol back and forth across the shipping channel on the south shore near Cap Chat. Despite the misty conditions that would have masked the submarine against Allied detection while allowing it a much more effective hunting search on the surface, the submarine dived at first light, 6:27 AM, and stayed under. Hartwig had seen enough of patrolling aircraft and naval escorts on hunting patrols on the eighth and ninth that he was taking no chances. *Charlottetown* had the bad luck to come right into the sights of the submarine at 7:50 AM. It was a case of being in precisely the wrong place, for Hartwig never did sight or locate by sound *Clayoquot,* which was less than two kilometres further out in the shipping channel; Hartwig commented on the poor visibility through the periscope, and both *Clayoquot* and *Charlottetown* reported poor sound returns on asdic that morning. Unfortunately *Charlottetown*'s reduced speed and steady course made her an easy target.

At 8:03 AM, according to *Charlottetown*'s people, a torpedo tore into the starboard quarter [that is, on the right-hand side]; "it broke off the propeller."[1] Then a second torpedo hit further forward, in the boiler or engine room. "All I could see," reported *Clayoquot*'s commanding officer, Lieutenant H.E. Lade, RCNVR, "was flying debris."[2] The crew immediately abandoned the doomed ship with the captain, Lieutenant J.W. Bonner, RCNR, "urging all hands to get clear." *Charlottetown* went down in only three minutes,[3] and the sharp list towards the damaged starboard side made it possible to launch only the boat (a five-metre dinghy) on that side. One of the four large floats was destroyed in the explosion, but the other three got clear; each had the capacity for twelve men. "It is believed," Lieutenant G.M. Moore, RCNVR, the first lieutenant, reported, "that all except three hands out of sixty-four got off the ship and were free in the water before she went up by the bow."[4]

"As the ship began to settle," Moore continued, "a depth charge exploded." This, the detonation of the ship's own weapon, caused the largest number of casualties. Many of the men had managed to scramble onto the floats, but the bodies of those still in the water were crushed by the impact wave from the weapon's 172-kilogram high-explosive charge. Unlike the thin medium of air, in which the force of an explosion dissipates within a very short distance, the dense medium of water transmits the force efficiently for some metres. The charge that exploded would have done so at a depth of fifteen metres or less, a lethal radius for those in the water above. Among those killed was the captain, who had been among the last to leave the ship and was therefore close to the explosion. "All depth charges are carried at safe," Moore claimed, "and had been checked the day previous. It is believed that the force of the first torpedo explosion might have effected a pistol [trigger] in such a manner that water pressure could set it off."[5]

Clayoquot attacked two asdic contacts with depth charges, then proceeded to try to find the boat and rafts from *Charlottetown*. When nearing two of the rafts, the Bangor made another contact, but could not safely attack with the survivors so close to the position; *Charlottetown*'s people "were heard singing and a faint cheer was heard as CLAYOQUOT passed at full speed" to continue the hunt. The fog had meanwhile closed back in, reducing visibility to less than 200 metres. It was only by following in reverse the twists and turns of course traced on the asdic plotting sheet that recorded the manoeuvres made during a hunt for a submarine that the Bangor was able to find its way back to the vicinity of the sinking, locate the three rafts, and pick up the survivors at 10:10 AM.[6]

The single dinghy had been engaged in its own rescue work, under Lieutenant Moore, the senior survivor. The small boat initially had seventeen people on board, "but we managed to collect a few men in the water and transfer them to a float, and then go further afield after four more who were severely injured. This operation took up about one and one half hours and no dead bodies were seen except that of the captain ..."[7] The following is from the transcript of Moore's testimony at the inquiry into the sinking.

> 41. How many were in the dinghy at one time?
>   Ans. Twenty-one, five of whom were lying down.
>   ...

43. Where was the Captain's body picked up?

Ans. Seven miles [11.3 kilometres] from shore ... We ... lashed him to the rudder [because of the crowding in the boat].

44. How did you know he was dead?

Ans. He was lying back in the water and was cold. Everyone was convinced that he was dead. The rudder was [later] carried away with the weight of his body and we were forced to leave him, as we felt that we would make better time without the drag of his body.[8]

At 11:30 AM, *Clayoquot* located the dinghy; the survivors had been rowing for shore believing that the Bangor could not find them in the fog. During *Clayoquot*'s passage to Gaspé, Able Seaman Donald St. Clair Bowser, RCNR, of Halifax "died from internal bleeding"[9] caused by the shallow depth charge explosion when the ship was going down. During the following week at Gaspé hospital, two other seamen died of their injuries, Engine Room Artificer Thomas Allen Macdonald, a member of the regular navy who had been severely wounded by the second torpedo hit, and Leading Telegrapher Edmund Charles Robinson, RCNVR. Stoker Petty Officer John Alexander Grant was flown to Halifax for surgery in October, but succumbed to his injuries.[10] That brought the grim reaper's tally from the crew of sixty-four to ten killed or missing in action and believed killed; there were six others "seriously injured."[11] Lieutenant Moore noted that one of the missing, Ordinary Seaman John Harlie Garland, RCNVR, "showed especial gallantry in ... passing out life jackets from the lockers, giving them all away when he himself could not swim." Moore was profoundly moved by the "conduct of the crew as a whole. Their efficiency, coolness and cheerfulness ... have certainly been up to the highest standards of the Navy."[12] The board of inquiry into the sinking, presided over by Commander P.B. (Barry) German, who had succeeded Commander Armit as the commanding officer at Gaspé, commended the courage and professionalism of both crews.[13]

Distant from the events and the shaken survivors, the staff in Halifax was dispassionate and critical in their assessment of the reports.

Clayoquot was not too short of fuel to prevent zigzag, as demonstrated by the fact that she had had fuel to conduct the high-speed submarine hunt and still reach port without difficulty. In any case, the abundant intelligence about the presence of submarines in the St. Lawrence should have made zigzagging a priority. The fact that the "ready" depth charges on the quarter deck had not been checked to make sure they were set to "safe" since the day before the attack led the staff to doubt that all the trigger mechanisms had in fact been disengaged.[14] *Clayoquot*'s main radio had been knocked out by the detonation of the depth charges in the Bangor's first counterattack, and the ship did not send out a report of *Charlottetown*'s destruction until the set was repaired over three hours later. The staff in Halifax noted that *Clayoquot*'s first counterattack did not take place until eleven minutes after the first torpedo hit *Charlottetown*, more than enough time for a report that should have been broadcast as soon as the event took place. The staff anti-submarine officer in Halifax was very critical of the fact that *Clayoquot*'s initial hunt had not extended to the south of *Charlottetown*'s wreck when it was clear that the submarine had fired from that direction.[15]

SQ 36 was due to sail on 11 September, but was held in port until the thirteenth.[16] This was an unusually long delay. Despite the always urgent priority to keep merchant shipping moving, the Atlantic Coast command at Halifax was so concerned about the losses in the St. Lawrence that they ruled that the convoy should not sail until the second destroyer they had assigned to the gulf was available. This was HMS *Salisbury*, which the Royal Navy had only recently allocated to the RCN's Western Local Escort Force, and she arrived from Iceland at St. John's on 9 September.[17] *Salisbury* was one of the old U.S. "flush deck" destroyers, the former USS *Claxton*, which the Americans had transferred to Britain in the fall of 1940. The British had modified and updated her for escort duties, including notably the installation of short-wave (type 271) radar, the only type that could dependably locate surfaced submarines.[18] Like all the ex–U.S. destroyers, however, she was prone to breakdowns because of age and the hard pounding on the north Atlantic for which the ships had not been designed, and she reached St. John's needing repairs, which the base undertook as rapidly as possible.

SQ 36 sailed from Sydney at 5:30 AM on the morning of 13 September. It was a big convoy by gulf standards, twenty-two ships. Of these, thirteen ships were "in ballast," that is, running with their holds empty to pick up cargoes, mostly at Montreal area ports. Of the nine other ships, six carried coal and three carried paper, one of the latter for Buffalo, New York, the only destination west of Montreal. The initial escort included the corvette *Arrowhead*, the Bangor *Vegreville*, and three Fairmiles. *Salisbury*, her repairs at St. John's completed, was due at Sydney later that morning. After a few hours in port at Sydney, the British destroyer used her high speed to overtake the slow convoy. She joined the screen and took over the duties as the senior ship from *Arrowhead* at 5:45 in the evening.[19]

The timing of the convoy's early morning departure was likely a security measure. U-boat attacks on the SQ–QS route had all taken place in the confined waters from the vicinity of Gaspé and to the west. The sailing of SQ 36 early in the morning on the thirteenth meant that it would enter this danger area in full daylight on the fifteenth with seven or eight hours of daylight to make the passage around the north shore of the Gaspé Peninsula.

Air patrols continued on the heavy schedule established after the attacks on QS 33, with constant daylight sweeps of the river by the Mont Joli detachments, of the central gulf by the aircraft based at Gaspé and Chatham, and of the eastern gulf by the training aircraft from Charlottetown and Summerside and the squadrons at Sydney. SQ 36 had close escort by a Canso flying boat from before sunrise until after nightfall each day; Cansos from 5 Squadron in Dartmouth and Hudsons from the training unit at Debert had to carry out regular patrols over the St. Lawrence to relieve the strain on the gulf detachments.[20] The effects of the air patrols were beginning to be felt by the Germans. *U-517* ventured into the central gulf as far as Bird Rocks to the north of the Magdalen Islands on 13 September, but was disappointed: "Nothing observed under conditions of good vis[ibility]. and increasing seas; only heavy air cover encountered." Hartwig may have been unaware that the convoys invariably followed a route south of the Magdalens. He worked his way back to Gaspé, where he knew he could find shipping, on the fourteenth. At the same time, SQ 36 was travelling a nearly parallel course to the south, albeit more slowly than the submarine which, in its fast run through the night, made double the speed of the merchantmen.

At daybreak on 15 September when the convoy was off Baie des Chaleurs headed due north towards Gaspé, the corvette *Summerside* and the Bangor *Chedabucto* reinforced the escort, and soon after, a Canso flying boat arrived from Gaspé to provide close cover.[21] At practically the same moment when *Summerside* and *Chedabucto* joined the convoy, at 6:02 AM, U-517 dived "off Gaspé," about 110 kilometres north of SQ 36 and close by the track the convoy would follow. The elaborate defence measures were to no avail. With the technology available in the early 1940s, there was almost no hope of detecting a fully submerged submarine so familiar with local conditions and traffic that it knew when and where to wait without ever having to show itself above the surface. From his secure, submerged position, Hartwig correctly took the appearance of a "seaplane" at 10 AM as "advance notice of the convoy." At noon the convoy was in sight, and he used the same technique as in the attack on QS 33 eight days before, positioning himself in the convoy's path and allowing its speed and the current to bring him among the merchant ships.

The action that followed was confused, and Hartwig's log does not match up with the convoy records in some important particulars. Moreover, the chemically treated paper on which *Salisbury*'s asdic returns were plotted faded so quickly that this, the most important record for analysis, proved to be useless when the staff at Halifax endeavoured to piece together what happened. Although the Halifax staff did not, of course, have *U-517*'s log, their estimates, speculative as they were, seem a reasonable explanation of events that are obscure in Hartwig's account.[22]

The merchant ships of the convoy, as it headed north past Cap des Rosiers, were in seven short columns, each with three merchant ships following one after the other (the middle column had four ships). The columns were numbered one through seven, number one being closest to the coast and seven on the starboard wing furthest from the coast. As *U-517* neared the convoy it found itself out on the starboard (offshore) side beyond the seventh column and had to manoeuvre to avoid *Salisbury,* which was sweeping back down that side. In dodging the destroyer, Hartwig got too close to the seventh column, so he pulled off, and at 1:33 PM, by his account, fired four torpedoes into the convoy at two steamers in separate columns that, from his broadside view, seemed to be overlapping. He claimed only one hit, but had in fact fatally damaged two ships. The Norwegian *Inger Elisabeth*, the lead ship in column six, suffered a massive explosion amidships between the second hold and boiler room and went down in five minutes; twenty-three of her twenty-six people got away in boats. The instant after the hit on *Inger Elisabeth*, the Dutch *Saturnus*, the second ship in the fourth column, dead centre of the convoy, saw a torpedo track headed square at her. The ship increased to full speed and turned hard, but the torpedo struck the stern and demolished it. The ship went down in about fifteen minutes; one crewman had been killed in the explosion but the remaining thirty-five got away in boats. Several of the escorts and merchant ships heard two additional explosions as the torpedoes that missed detonated on the rocks below Cap des Rosiers, about 6.5 kilometres away.[23]

The convoy records tell a dramatic story. The lead ship in the fourth column, *Llangollen,* just ahead of *Saturnus,* sighted a periscope between the fourth and fifth columns a few minutes after *Saturnus* was hit. *Llangollen* opened fire on the periscope with her self-defence gun at approximately 1:45 PM, and other merchant ships saw a periscope and fired as well.[24] *Salisbury*, still outside the seventh column on the starboard flank of the convoy, came in response to the gunfire, saw the periscope, which disappeared at about 1:50 PM, but then made an asdic contact and followed with a pattern of five depth charges set shallow, fifteen metres, at 2 PM. *Arrowhead,* which had been patrolling ahead of the starboard side of the convoy, had by this time joined the destroyer and quickly followed with an attack by nine depth charges, some set to forty-six metres and others to ninety-two metres. *Arrowhead* and *Salisbury* made two more attacks before *Summerside* relieved the destroyer, which returned to the convoy. The two corvettes continued to scour the area until they were relieved in the hunt by Fairmiles; *Arrowhead* left to return to the convoy at 3:40 PM and *Summerside* forty minutes later.[25]

Hartwig does not mention entering the convoy after he fired or the gunfire from the merchant ships, only that depth charge attacks forced him to dive very deep. At 140 metres "there is a sharp metallic bang." The storage tubes for reserve torpedoes located beneath the upper deck but outside the pressure hull had been damaged, almost certainly in one of the two first attacks by *Salisbury* and *Arrowhead*. *U-517* did not surface until nightfall and for seven hours moved quickly around to the waters east of Cap Chat trying to catch up with SQ 36, but abandoned the chase as heavy fog set in.

U-165 was patrolling off Les Méchins at the far end of the Gaspé Peninisula's north shore, some 230 kilometres west of *U-517*'s attacks on the fifteenth. As the convoy approached the next morning, 16 September, Hoffmann was able to position himself for a submerged ambush, much as Hartwig had done the day before and, like Hartwig, achieved complete surprise. At 7:10 AM, in full daylight and clear visibility, a torpedo hit the British steamer *Essex Lance* between the rudder and the propeller. The crew of fifty took to the boats; one of the crewmen drowned and his body was later recovered. Although the stern flooded, the bulkheads held and the ship "settled down slightly." *Essex Lance* was the lead ship in the port-side column, closest to the south shore of the river, eight kilometres away. A few minutes later the Greek steamer *Joannis,* following *Essex Lance* in the same column, saw a periscope inside the convoy, and in the next instant, just as the ship turned hard away, a torpedo struck the after part of the ship. She sank quickly, but all thirty-two of her people got clear. *Salisbury,* which had been sweeping ahead of the centre of the convoy, dashed between the columns to where the periscope had been sighted and at 7:17 AM attacked a "good" contact, but then had difficulty manoeuvring within the convoy. *Arrowhead* and *Summerside,* which had been sweeping astern of the convoy, searched the area of *Salisbury*'s contact but came up empty-handed. *Vegreville* attempted to tow the hulk of *Essex Lance,* but could not make way with the unwieldy wreck. The merchantman's bow canted upward and the stern dragged down 11.6 metres into the water, perhaps twice the normal maximum draft of the ship, and the Bangor had to abandon the tow. The wreck drifted in heavy fog for twenty-four hours before tugs could locate her and take her under tow; they succeeded in bringing her into Quebec City on 22 September.[26]

The staff at Halifax who analyzed reports of the convoy in early November were scathing about the performance of the escorts and particularly *Salisbury*: the "absence of any escort organization is clearly shown." Although *Salisbury* had had to join the convoy at sea, giving no opportunity for a pre-sailing conference, the destroyer had passed no instructions by signal. "After realizing that a ship had been torpe-doed," on the fifteenth, "'Salisbury' failed to order 'Artichoke' or pass any instructions to the escort, and did not herself take any action until 12 minutes after the torpedoing ..." There was a similar "lack of any organized offensive action" on the sixteenth. "Artichoke" was a standard procedure where, at the first evidence of a U-boat within the convoy, the lead escorts reversed course and swept down between the columns of the convoy. The staff also criticized the fact that after both attacks *Salisbury* did not leave at least one escort to conduct a thorough search of the area and wait out an attempt by the submarine to surface.[27] The anti-submarine staff at Halifax completed the analysis of QS 33 after they had worked on SQ 36 and criticized *Arrowhead* for the "lack of a definite prearranged offensive action" in much the same terms as they had criticized *Salisbury*, even while admitting that in QS 33 *Arrowhead* was at a particular disadvantage because the only other full-sized escort was *Truro* which had not yet worked up or completed her equipment.[28] One can feel more than a little sympathy for the escort captains. Because of the shortage of warships, there was nothing resembling organized escort groups in the St. Lawrence; individual ships were assigned as they became available. The joining by *Summerside* and *Chedabucto* with SQ 36 only late on the second day (and as it turned out scant hours before the first attack) was typical of the constant shifting about of the few warships available. These circumstances, in confined and difficult waters, must have been entirely alien to the British ship, which had previously been employed in the well-organized groups of the British Western Approaches Command in open ocean missions.

The situation on the morning of 16 September allowed no time for reflection. At risk was another large convoy, QS 35 of twenty merchant ships, that had sailed from Bic Island the evening before. As luck would have it, the convoy was passing eastward to the north of SQ 36 right at the time of *U-165*'s attack and so close that QS 35's people could hear the explosions of the depth charges. The escort was substantial in number, including the corvette *Hepatica* and four Bangors. However, two of the Bangors, *Stratford* and *Sarnia*, had just recently been commissioned at Toronto and were on their way to Halifax for completion of their equipment and work-ups training. These ships were nothing like fully effective. *Salisbury* left SQ 36 at 11 AM and headed back to the east to catch up with QS 35.

U-165 had expended the last of its torpedoes and was headed for home, but *U-517* was searching for targets south of Anticosti. The 113 Squadron's Chatham detachment had flown three missions in pursuit of *U-517* after its attack on SQ 36 near Gaspé on the fifteenth, and at first light on the sixteenth, three aircraft renewed the search. The weather was hazy, which was probably why Hartwig, well offshore northeast of Cap de la Madeleine, continued to hunt on the surface. At 10 AM one of the aircraft, again with Pilot Officer Keetley at the controls, sighted the U-boat at the limit of visibility that morning, about five kilometres. The high altitude of the aircraft, 1311 metres, and its white camouflage delayed an alert by the lookouts on the conning tower. As the aircraft plunged, it opened fire with its machine guns at 460 metres, and the submarine was just submerging as the Hudson released four depth charges from a height of fifteen metres. The charges appeared to bracket the submarine as it disappeared, but if they were as accurate as they seemed, they were too late. *U-517* was undamaged. Keetley executed the best current tactics by dropping markers and sweeping the area for one hour and fifty minutes, thus keeping the U-boat submerged and immobile.[29]

There is a sequel, but its facts have come together only very recently. About two-and-a-half hours after Keetley's attack, Hartwig reported "aerial bombs, all of them scare-bombs," whose detonations continued for nearly fifty minutes (12:51 to 1:39 PM). Hartwig believed that aircraft summoned by Keetley's attack were randomly dropping charges to keep him down. There are, however, no references in Canadian records to aircraft dropping charges at this time in the area. Among my notes, I happened upon a battered print of a "report of proceedings" by the Fairmiles *Q 054* and *Q 055* that I had made from microfilmed naval records of convoys sometime in the 1980s or 90s, but whose significance was not apparent at that time.[30] In reviewing the records for the present account, the relationship between the Fairmiles' independent escort mission and Hartwig's report of mysterious aerial "scare bombs" finally became clear.

The Fairmiles *Q 054* and *Q 055* were bringing the merchant ship *Borgford* from the small port of Sainte-Anne-des-Monts on the north shore of the Gaspé Peninsula to rendezvous with QS 35 as it came from the west. At the time and near the position indicated by Hartwig's report of aerial bombing, *Q 055*, which was sweeping behind the merchant ship, attacked an asdic contact. The Fairmile continued the hunt while *Q 054* hurried ahead with *Borgford* towards the position that had been assigned for the rendezvous with QS 35. It seems unlikely that *Q 055* had in fact found *U-517*, as Hartwig's account suggests the depth charges were in the distance. Still, the Fairmile's initiative had precisely the effect desired from aggressive escort operations: the submarine kept its head down and did not detect the group of ships.

Equally interesting were the events that followed. When QS 35 did not appear at the assigned rendezvous position, the Fairmiles and their charge, *Borgford*, pressed further to the east towards the next position on the convoy's planned course. Shortly after 4 PM, the convoy escort signalled to the Fairmiles that there would be no rendezvous—shore authorities had diverted the convoy to the Jacques Cartier Passage, north of Anticosti, and well clear of the U-boats whose operating area in the Gaspé Passage had been revealed by Keetley's air attack. With the news that the main convoy had been diverted, the Fairmiles again showed initiative. They were already on their way to the east, and thus, in view of the fact that two submarines were known to be in the Gaspé Passage, pressed on at best speed to take shelter in Gaspé rather than attempt to backtrack and link up with QS 35 on its new course.

The Hudson attack and *Q 055*'s "scare bombs" had, unknown to anyone, done their work. *U-517* also moved east in the direction of Gaspé, keeping her head well down, not rising to periscope depth until 4:40 PM, when Hartwig heard the sound of propellers. He came up for a peek and saw a steamship, but it was too far off, eight kilometres, and he could not catch up, unwilling as he now was to run at speed on the surface and risk air attack. Only at 7 PM when fog rolled in did he dare surface in pursuit, but by then the steamer, which may have been *Borgford*, had disappeared. She later reached Gaspé with the two Fairmiles at midnight.

More significant than this example of a successful defence of shipping operation was the decision of shore authorities to make a radical diversion of QS 35, the first instance of such a diversion I can find for the St. Lawrence campaign. Clearly the grim experience of the past nine days had driven home the impossibility of effective defence against U-boats that had gained ambush positions on the confined traffic routes in the Gaspé Passage and river where deep water and difficult asdic conditions gave every advantage to the submarine. Heavy air cover and large escort groups, now including destroyers, had dismally failed to shift the balance. One of the advantages of moving ships in convoy is that it allows shore authorities even at short notice to divert all those ships away from danger, and this is what happened with QS 35 on 16 September, which from the moment it swung north of Anticosti was perfectly safe. Still, it was a fine judgment call. The great drawback of convoy is that it slows down the movement of shipping and thus reduces carrying capacity. Standard routes of the type introduced in the gulf in May 1942 allowed convoys to keep to tight schedules and thus minimize delays and lost carrying power.

Although it was not at all evident at the time, the heavy losses of 7–16 September marked a turning point in the St. Lawrence battle. The U-boats would never again be anything like as successful, despite larger efforts, at the very time the Canadian navy withdrew most of its escorts from the gulf to support the major western Allied offensive of 1942, operation Torch on the distant shores of North Africa. In retrospect, 113 Squadron's success in locating and attacking U-boats with the new offensive air tactics, the effectiveness of *Salisbury*'s and *Arrowhead*'s initial counterattack on *U-517* on 15 September, the initiative shown by the Fairmiles escorting *Borgford*, and the timely emergency diversion of QS 35 that ensured the safety of that large convoy foreshadowed the shape of future Canadian operations.

Despite the continuing threat, the Canadian navy pulled the corvettes from the Sydney–Quebec convoys on schedule; QS 35 was the last convoy in the series whose escort included a corvette (*Hepatica*). This was a question of the Alliance's highest priority, the buildup of forces for operation Torch. Nevertheless, the Sydney–Quebec convoys kept moving on schedule, each escorted by one of the destroyers (*Witherington* or *Salisbury*) and usually two Bangors and two Fairmiles, together with heavy cover from the air force. From Sydney, SQ 37, SQ 38, and SQ 39 sailed on 15, 19, and 23 September respectively. From Bic Island, QS 36 departed on 18 September, QS 37 on the twenty-third, and QS 38 on the twenty-seventh. Aside from the constant imperative of timeliness in merchant shipping movements, there was additional pressure to wrap up the program of ocean shipping into the gulf so that the two British destroyers, in their turn, could be released for higher Alliance priorities, in this case escort of the transatlantic convoys between the Newfoundland approaches and New York. As Churchill had underscored in his message to Mackenzie King earlier in the month, the reassignment of escorts from the transatlantic routes to Torch made it particularly vital that the already meagre destroyer strength of the transatlantic escort groups should be maintained.

Eastern Air Command pitched in still more fully to take up the slack and again developed new and effective tactics. The textbook answer— that is, the approach worked out by the Royal Navy and RAF Coastal Command—to the problem of defending confined waters like the St. Lawrence was to use naval intelligence for offensive sweeps against U-boats when they were still far out at sea and thereby discourage them from coming into the confined waters. That advice was not yet helpful to Eastern Air Command, which was short of long-range aircraft, had a vast ocean area and coastal zone to protect as compared to the much stronger, better-equipped Coastal Command, and was just beginning to get timely naval intelligence. For these reasons, the RCAF continued to give first priority to direct, close cover of convoys, especially in the St. Lawrence. Squadron Leader Small's pioneering effort of late July and early August to try out British offensive tactics against the U-boats then known to be located off Yarmouth had brought promising results. The available records suggest that 113 Squadron's new Chatham detachment undertook the very first sustained offensive operations in the gulf: the aircraft made prolonged, "offensive" searches over the entire "probability" area where recent intelligence placed a U-boat rather than providing "defensive" close cover of convoys. The main effect of the defensive convoy escort operations was to keep the U-boats submerged. This was a good result that reduced the number of attacks on shipping. But the lethal ambush attacks on QS 33 and SQ 36 by submerged U-boats that had used the geographical confines of the St. Lawrence route to pre-position themselves sharply demonstrated the limits of defensive tactics. Even if defensive tactics had generally succeeded in deterring U-boats, at least until the attacks on QS 33 and SQ 36, they had singularly failed to produce opportunities for aircraft to surprise submarines while they were on the surface in sufficient time to make an aerial depth charge attack that had any chance of effect. In this light, the achievement of the small detachment at Chatham was remarkable: promising attacks on two U-boats that had been surprised while running fully surfaced within a single week.

Eastern Air Command desperately wanted to reinforce the offensive effort, but it faced the perennial shortage of aircraft and aircrew. Already, on 3–4 September, in response to the intelligence that the U-boats operating in the Strait of Belle Isle were moving towards the Sydney–Quebec route, the command had stripped the coastal stations of all aircraft and personnel that could conceivably be spared for the gulf. The command, not surprisingly in view of the losses to SQ 36, was unwilling to run the risk of reducing defensive patrols by the detachments already in the gulf in order to assign more aircraft to the still experimental offensive operations.

On 17 September, Eastern Air Command made a bold proposal to headquarters in Ottawa: the remaining bombers at RCAF Station Yarmouth should be sent to the gulf. Other stations could cover the eastern part of Yarmouth's area, off southern Nova Scotia's Atlantic coast, but the waters to the south of Nova Scotia and west—including the approaches to the Bay of Fundy—would have to be entrusted to U.S. air forces. Air Marshal L.S. Breadner, the chief of the air staff, quickly agreed. He attached one stipulation. Knowing that the use of Canadian territory by the American military was a sensitive issue for national sovereignty, he laid down that U.S. aircraft should only visit Yarmouth for refuelling stops; they should not be based there.[31]

Headquarters in Ottawa telephoned Halifax with Breadner's approval, and the next day, 18 September, three 113 Squadron Hudsons flew from Yarmouth to Chatham, New Brunswick, to increase the offensive detachment there from three to six aircraft. The same squadron had already, on 16 September, sent three other Hudsons to Mont Joli to allow three Hudsons from 119 Squadron to return to Sydney and thereby strengthen coverage in the Cabot Strait and eastern gulf (a further three Hudsons from Dartmouth's 11 Squadron remained at Mont Joli, giving a total strength of six Hudsons at the Quebec station). Eastern Air Command had originally intended to send a new squadron at Yarmouth, No. 162, which still had only four Canso amphibians, to the gulf. Perhaps because of Breadner's ruling that U.S. aircraft could not take up station at Yarmouth, Eastern Air Command left the Cansos at Yarmouth to carry out long-range convoy support in the Yarmouth–Dartmouth area and shifted two additional Cansos from 5 Squadron at Dartmouth to North Sydney where they could support both ocean and gulf operations. As the last Hudsons from Yarmouth deployed to the gulf on 18 September, the U.S. Army's First Air Force took over the patrol area south and west of Yarmouth.

The redeployment gave a strength within the gulf of twelve Hudsons (six at Mont Joli and six at Chatham), two or three Cansos at Gaspé, and at Sydney, with responsibilities both for the gulf and the ocean convoys, six to eight Cansos and fifteen Hudsons. It was a modest force to achieve Eastern Air Command's goal: "to drive the enemy from the area."[32]

On 17–18 September, Hartwig pulled away to the quiet waters off the west coast of Newfoundland and on the night of 18–19 September surfaced to move the four reserve torpedoes from the sealed storage containers outside the pressure hull, just under the upper deck, into the boat and reload the forward tubes. The crew discovered what the loud noise had been when they were under attack by *Salisbury* and *Arrowhead* on the fifteenth. Two of the reserve torpedo storage canisters under the upper deck were flooded, and one of them had its "head pushed in." After an unfruitful reconnaissance of the Cabot Strait in heavy fog, *U-517* returned to her favoured hunting ground off Gaspé, arriving in the morning of 21 September.

Although the regular appearance of aircraft forced Hartwig to proceed cautiously below the surface, his knowledge of the waters and the convoy schedule did not let him down. At 11:42 AM he sighted smoke which proved to be a convoy, likely SQ 38, the only convoy on passage near Gaspé that day. He attempted to pursue for over three hours, but never got closer than ten kilometres. This was the benefit of the air coverage that prevented him from even considering a fast surface run, but only in part. Among the gems in the large collection of coastal convoy message sheets preserved at the Directorate of History and Heritage is a series of signals that shows that SQ 38 was the first of the Quebec–Sydney convoys to be routed with a diversion from the standard track, not as a result of recent U-boat intelligence as with QS 35, but as a matter of routine. The staff at Sydney had suggested concentrating the convoy defences by opening the schedule so that only one convoy would be on passage at a time. A further benefit would be that the dividing line between inward and outward convoys, whereby the Bic Island–bound convoys kept close to the north coast of the Gaspé Peninsula and the Sydney-bound convoys sailed further off shore, could be eliminated and all convoys given varying routes to deceive the enemy. The closure of the gulf to ocean shipping was reducing the schedule, and on 19 September the Atlantic Coast command approved diverse routes, to be assigned by the shipping control staff at Quebec for the eastbound convoys and by the staff at Sydney for those westbound.[33] In the case of SQ 38, the route was the standard one until it reached the Gaspé approaches. Then, instead of continuing along the coast north of Gaspé where the ambush attacks had occurred, it backtracked north-east clear of that dangerous shore until close to Anticosti Island's South West Point, the far side of the Gaspé Passage, and then headed north-west towards Sept Îles on the North Shore before dropping southwest through the centre of the estuary.[34]

At 3:19 PM, 21 September, soon after he lost sight of the convoy, Hartwig, swinging the periscope around, saw the "mastheads of an escort" coming up from behind.

> [The warship] suddenly turns away to port, increases to high speed and drops a depth charge; closes on my course at listening speed. The sea is smooth as a mirror. I try to knock off the escort which now is at bows left ... range 3000 m[etres]. I turn to port ... in order to achieve a position on her beam. When the range is roughly 800 [metres] ... she turns toward me and proceeds on my course line with inclination left 5. I observe men moving aft to the depth charge launcher; I therefore go to depth 120 [metres] at [3:30 PM].
>
> [3:32 PM] The first depth charge explodes. The boat drops to depth 100 [metres] at cruising speed. When I slow to listening speed, the boat climbs to 60 [metres]. These water layers!
>
> [3:32–7:29 PM] Depth charge attack. Depth charges were close by as long as it was light. I assume we had left an oil slick ... (presumably fuel oil test line from the inner bunker).

The encounter was with the Bangor HMCS *Georgian*. She had left the screen of SQ 38 the day before and sprinted ahead to refuel at Gaspé and was leaving that port to rejoin the convoy on the afternoon of the twenty-first. Hartwig, his attention on the convoy pulling away to the north, had not been aware of the Bangor coming up from behind. Here is *Georgian*'s account.

(2) At approximately [3:09 PM] ... submarine contact was obtained, indicated by good echoes and strong hydrophone effect. The submarine was then sighted on the surface off our port bow, at a distance of about 1000 yards [914 metres], the periscope and part of the conning tower was showing. H.M.C.S. Georgian closed at full speed with the intention of ramming but the submarine submerged and a full pattern of depth charges, set at 50 feet [15 metres], was dropped. Strong hydrophone and constant echoes were being obtained at the moment the charges were fired and one charge from the starboard thrower definitely dropped over the spot where the conning tower was observed to disappear. Asdic contact was still held after passing over the submarine to a distance of about 600 yards [549 metres].

(3) H.M.C.S. Georgian then turned towards the target at a range of about 1000 yards and a deliberate attack was carried out. This second pattern was set at 150 feet [46 metres]. After crossing the target at the time of deliberate attack the submarine surfaced astern about 900 yards [823 metres]. H.M.C.S. Georgian turned towards target again with the intention of ramming, but before reaching the position the submarine turned over on her side with definite wake astern and sank ... A full pattern set at 150 feet was then dropped ... huge patches of oil then appeared ... The time of sinking was at approximately 6:59 PM.[35]

The main discrepancy in the two accounts is that Hartwig believed he never rose above periscope depth, but *Georgian*'s people initially saw part of the conning tower and later a portion of the hull. The clue is Hartwig's lament about the cold-water layer that caused the U-boat suddenly and rapidly to rise as soon as he reduced speed. This is what happened to *U-132* in her action with *Drummondville* in July in similar water conditions, and *Georgian*'s account of the hull breaking surface matches what *Drummondville*'s crew reported.

Georgian's crew and the base staff at Gaspé celebrated what appeared to be a certain victory. It was all the more poignant because, when the Bangor returned to port that evening to replenish the thirty-four depth charges she had expended, her captain, acting Lieutenant Commander

A.G. Stanley, RCNR, had to leave the ship for hospital; he had suffered a heart attack.[36]

The staff at Halifax was not so quick to write off the submarine. They noted that the patterns quickly dropped directly on the swirl on the two occasions *U-517* dived, which from *Georgian* had appeared to be the most effective, did not take account of the U-boat's forward motion. That would have carried her clear of the lethal radius of the explosions.[37]

On the night of 22–23 September Hartwig made his way towards the north shore of the estuary, east of Sept Îles, to carry out repairs to the "inner exhaust vent flaps," one of which was frozen and the other difficult to move. He does not state whether this was damage from *Georgian*'s attack.

While hurrying to wrap up the repairs, late on the morning of 24 September *U-517* sighted smoke to the south. It was QS 37, another large convoy of twenty merchant ships, escorted by *Salisbury* and three Bangors. Hartwig had to make surface runs to keep the convoy in sight. One of 113 Squadron's Hudsons, piloted by Flight Sergeant Albert White of Windsor, Ontario, saw the submarine at 2:40 PM and was making an attack run when *U-517* dived. The RCAF crew showed good knowledge of tactics by aborting the attack—shallow-set aerial depth charges were useless if released more than a very few seconds after the submarine dived—dropping a marker, and flying off to warn QS 37, then about fifty kilometres away, about the danger.

Hartwig had not been aware that an aircraft was present. He dived because he was being approached by a steamer that had evidently fallen behind the convoy and was moving quickly to rejoin. *U-517* resurfaced after about half an hour, just as White returned from warning the convoy. The airmen, in the clear visibility, saw the submarine from twenty-eight kilometres and immediately closed. Hartwig's lookouts saw the "fast land-plane" at eight kilometres and completed the crash dive a few seconds before the Hudson streaked over at a height of only nine metres. A fuse had blown in the Hudson's bomb release gear, and only one charge fell: "lands above us," Hartwig recorded, "[i]t missed us." The submarine had already got down to forty metres.

QS 37 was not the only convoy threatened. Approaching the Gaspé Passage from the east was SQ 39, eight merchant ships escorted by HMS *Witherington* and the Bangors *Chedabucto* and *Clayoquot*. There was a slight advantage for the defence because the nights were illuminated by a full moon. This made night-flying practicable, and at *Witherington*'s request Eastern Air Command laid on a full program of close escort coverage and offensive sweeps.

At nightfall on the twenty-fourth, just three hours after Flight Sergeant White's attack, *U-517* surfaced in the "bright moonlight" and headed at speed towards the west end of the Gaspé Passage to catch up with QS 37. At 10:30 PM, a 113 Squadron Hudson, with Flying Officer Maurice Belanger at the controls, noticed what appeared to be a wake on the main shipping channel south of Anticosti Island's West Point, about a hundred kilometres east of the afternoon's attack. Whatever was on the water disappeared in the shadows. When, twenty-five minutes later, the crew saw something again, about two kilometres away, Belanger swooped towards it. Only at 460 metres could the airmen identify a fully surfaced submarine, but the aircraft was already well positioned and swept across the hull at twelve metres, dropping four depth charges. The night attack caught the *U-517* by surprise, and she remained on the surface long enough for the aircraft to circle and spray the conning tower with machine gun fire.

The aircrew reported that the depth charges had seemed to be perfectly placed "on each side and within ten feet [three metres] of the U-boat's hull, just ahead of the conning tower." However, "[n]o evidence of damage was seen following the attack," and "within five minutes the moon disappeared behind heavy cloud," making it impossible to see if there was debris from the submarine on the surface. Hartwig's report confirms that the charges were indeed on target: "2 powerful explosions astern. 3 bombs dropped; 3rd bomb right next to ship's side so that stern gets flooded over by impact. Presumably a dud." It thus appears that the charge within lethal distance of the hull failed to explode. This might be the occasion of a terrifying incident not included in *U-517*'s log, but which the U-boat's crew later reported to Allied interrogators: "a bomb fell on her deck near the 10.5-cm. gun ready-use locker. Fortunately for Hartwig and his men, it did not explode and he, the Engineer Officer and two ratings [seamen] threw it overboard."

This was a model attack which, but for the apparent depth charge failure, should have destroyed or severely damaged the U-boat. Belanger, whose francophone parents had moved to Vancouver when he was young, had only begun maritime patrol operations when he was posted to the newly organized 113 Squadron late in June 1942. He was a seasoned pilot, however. Such was his gift for flying that, after his own training, he had been retained as an instructor at No. 11 Service Flying Training School at Yorkton, Saskatchewan, from May 1941 to May 1942.

At the time of White's and Belanger's attacks, the officer responsible for the administration of 113 Squadron's Chatham detachment filed a report that captures the difficult conditions under which the personnel worked, but also the satisfaction from their extraordinary success in finding the enemy and striking back:

> The Detachment has no hangar, therefore the A/C [aircraft] stand outside. The use of an office in a hangar is at our disposal as are several rooms such as locker space, armament room and sleeping room for the ground crew. The idea of having the ground crew sleep in the hangar has worked very well since the men are able to do long shifts and be on hand for their duties.
>
> A gasoline tender has been placed at our disposal and a gas tank in front of the hangar is kept for our use. The gasoline situation is deplorable as we order three days in advance and the tank car usually gets lost on the way up from the United States. Gasoline has been begged and borrowed but the A.C. [sic] have been short on several occasions necessitating flying to Scoudouc [New Brunswick] for refuelling.

The A/C have to be flown to Yarmouth for checking as the civilian school here (using Ansons) cannot be expected to place their facilities at our disposal. The maintenance at Yarmouth has done exceptionally well in keeping our six Hudsons serviceable.

There is no motor transport available here for the use of the Detachment.

MORALE AND DISCIPLINE
Nowhere could one find a more enthusiastic body of men. The detachment is doing excellent work against the enemy and this tonic, of victory over enemy U-Boats in this area, has imbued all ranks with a devotion of duty which is magnificent. Flying personnel are on the alert all day and half of the crews every night. Ground crew are on shifts and maintain a round-the-clock service when this is necessary—for example on moonlight nights.

The Officer commanding [Small] has the full confidence of all his officers and men but when the occasion demands, he maintains discipline with a firm hand.[38]

Eastern Air Command followed up the attacks on 24 September with everything it had. There were twenty-eight air missions on 25 September, which included close escort for QS 37 as it continued southward towards the Magdalen Islands and for SQ 39 as it passed through the estuary into the river, together with the new-style wide-ranging sweeps. 113 Squadron's Chatham detachment, which flew ten missions on the twenty-fifth, continued to saturate the skies all around QS 37's route.

Hartwig was able to track QS 37 generally by following the air patrols, but was repeatedly blocked as he attempted to run quickly on the surface to approach the convoy and get into a position ahead from which he might develop an attack. Hudsons from 113 Squadron sighted U-517 at 8:16 and 9:45 in the morning, in the waters east of the mouth of Baie des Chaleurs and northwest of the Magdalen Islands, but both times the submarine dived before the aircraft could strike. On each occasion, Hartwig stayed under for an hour and a quarter, but then surfaced again to continue what was now a hot pursuit. He was on a course parallel to that of QS 37, perhaps forty-five kilometres from the convoy's track. By 4:00 in the afternoon, he was confident that he had pulled ahead of the convoy. He swung to a closing course for the final approach. Suddenly, at 5:03, "am surprised by a fast land-plane. 3 aerial bombs which are well-placed." Maurice Belanger was again at the controls, and he had done well to swoop down and release the depth charges while the U-boat was still on the surface, but the weapons overshot. The first was close to the hull, but the other three were spaced at twelve-metre intervals further away. The analysts at Eastern Air Command gnashed their teeth once more over the lack of Torpex-filled charges; if the single charge that landed close to the hull had more power, it could have inflicted serious damage. Even so, they took solace in the fact that the submarine "must have received a good shock."[39] They were right. *U-517* stayed under for over three-and-a-half hours this time, surfacing only at 8:40 PM as darkness descended.

Belanger's attack had driven the U-boat off the scent of QS 37 once and for all. While *U-517* was below the surface, the convoy, alerted about Belanger's attack, made an evasive change of course and safely reached Sydney twenty-four hours later, in the early evening of 26 September. *U-517* had dashed towards the Sydney approaches during the night of 25–26 September to try to intercept the convoy but was paralyzed by the heavy air coverage over the Cabot Strait. Hartwig saw smoke clouds on the horizon on the twenty-sixth, but every time he surfaced to pursue, the approach of aircraft forced him to dive once more.

In the midst of thick fog during the early hours of 28 September, Hartwig turned back to his favourite hunting ground off Gaspé. He was rewarded when in bright moonlight at 3:40 AM on 29 September he saw QS 38 further out in the shipping lane. There were about a dozen merchant ships, escorted by *Witherington* and *Salisbury*, and three Bangors, *Ganonoque*, *Chedabucto*, and *Red Deer*. The moon was behind Hartwig, which would backlight him in his planned surface attack. He therefore got well ahead of the convoy and moved further out into the shipping lane, in the shadows down moon from the convoy.

At 5:20 AM he began his attack run. He aimed to push "in between the forward and port-side [i.e., offshore] screen. As the port-side outer screen patrol was approaching rapidly and cutting off my route to the convoy," he fired his salvo of four torpedoes, early, from "2000–2500 m[etres]. Heard one detonation. After firing turned to port [further out into the shipping land] and tried to fire with after tubes. However I was forced away for the port screen and so I dived."

The short-wave radar in the destroyers picked up no trace of the surfaced submarine, and the first inkling they had of the attack was two "snowflake" rockets fired from one of the merchant ships on the rear offshore flank of the convoy. The Bangors on that side reported that they had heard two explosions, which had prompted the merchant ship to fire the rocket signal. *Witherington* realized the convoy had been attacked and called for additional air support. At about 3:20 in the afternoon, one of the Hudsons from 113 Squadron that had been flying sweeps was returning to base at Chatham when the crew was startled to see *U-517* fully surfaced only thirty-seven kilometres off Gaspé; Hartwig had not pursued QS 38, but remained in the Gaspé approaches. Once more it was Maurice Belanger and his crew, and they succeeded in dropping from 1500 metres altitude to eighteen metres or less off the water to complete the attack while the submarine was still surfaced: "The depth charges were seen to explode and they bracketed the hull slightly ahead of the conning tower, with the conning tower still visible. The U-boat's bow then came up out of the water; all forward motion seemed to have ceased, and it then appeared to settle straight down." Belanger patrolled in the vicinity for nearly two hours until two additional aircraft came out to take up the watch, but there was no evidence of wreckage.[40] Later analysis by specialists in Coastal Command and at U.S. Navy fleet headquarters concluded that the charges overshot slightly, and at most inflicted minor damage.

Commander C. Thompson of *Witherington*, who had been sharply critical of Canadian operations, was impressed by the nearly round-the-clock air coverage QS 38 and other convoys received in the latter part of September, and he suggested that air protection may have "deterred the submarine from pushing home his attack on the morning of the 29th." As we now know from Hartwig's log, he was unaware of any air patrols in the area and had actually been held back by the well-positioned and active escort screen. Lieutenant Commander M.H.R. Crichton of *Salisbury* had been critical of the Canadian ships for not maintaining their positions in the screen and thus leaving gaps. Thompson, on this, his last escort mission in the gulf, however, complimented the Bangors and Fairmiles, which "have shown themselves as efficient escorts and have done all that has been required of them." It was, in the matter of the defence of QS 38, truer than he knew. Still, he regretted that the little Canadian warships had to labour under the "great handicap" of not being fitted with radar, one of the several areas in which he found the Canadian home-waters forces to be ill equipped.[41]

After bringing QS 38—the last regular convoy in the series—safely into Sydney on the morning of 30 September, the two British destroyers headed off to Halifax in the afternoon and returned to ocean escort duty. That, the naval staff expected, should wrap up the St. Lawrence problem. With much less traffic in the gulf, it would scarcely be worth the substantial effort the Germans had evidently been applying. Although there is no evidence that the naval staff felt satisfaction— on the contrary, they were consumed by myriad challenges in the defence of the Atlantic convoys and the related difficulties in mustering resources for the offensive in North Africa—the senior officers could have been forgiven some sense of accomplishment. The final rush of loadings and sailings of ocean ships in the gulf during the two weeks since the SQ 36 battle had been a great success. Despite clear evidence of unrelenting German effort, seven convoys, most of them large, had made the passage without loss, and Canadian ships and aircraft had made five promising counterattacks, even as the corvettes were pulled out to get ready for Torch.

U-517 continued to hunt. Hartwig was determined to expend every last one of his torpedoes. *U-165*, however, had disappeared. On 26 September, ten days after the submarine's departure from the St. Lawrence, Hoffmann reported he was nearing the Bay of Biscay and was never heard from again. There are no records of Allied attacks on submarines in the area, so the best guess is that *U-165* was the victim of mines laid by British aircraft in the approaches to the French ports used by the German navy.[42]

Already the initial successes of *U-165*, *U-513*, and *U-517* and Hartwig's optimistic reports in mid-September—before the Canadian defences became more effective—had persuaded U-boat headquarters to send additional U-boats to the St. Lawrence. The first of a new wave of submarines reached the Cabot Strait at the end of September. The new assault was much stronger than the operation in late August and September. A total of four submarines would hunt in the St. Lawrence in October and November, and a fifth was assigned but only made a probe into the Cabot Strait's approaches; four other U-boats followed up *U-513*'s patrol in the waters off Newfoundland's Atlantic coast.

NINE

Achievement and Tragedy, October–November 1942

The story of the concerted German effort in the St. Lawrence during the fall of 1942 shows the fog of war and is laden with irony and with tragic consequences. The U-boats that came in the fall failed to achieve Dönitz's objective, to destroy large numbers of the ocean-going merchant ships that sustained the Allied war effort. Yet, as a direct result of that failure, *U-69*, while leaving the gulf to escape the Canadian defences, destroyed the coastal ferry *Caribou* with heavy loss of life, including women and children. This tragedy only tangentially supported Dönitz's objective.

The challenge for Admiral Dönitz and U-boat headquarters was always to make early decisions about where submarines should go to find the best opportunities for success. This was a special problem for operations in North American waters. It took about two weeks for submarines to cross the Atlantic at the moderate speeds—no more than twenty kilometres an hour—essential to conserve fuel needed for high-speed runs when pursuing shipping and dodging Allied anti-submarine forces. Thus, if Dönitz wanted to have U-boats take the place of *U-165* and *U-517* as they reached the limit of their fuel and supplies, he had to dispatch the replacement submarines in the middle of September or soon after.

At the mid-September decision point, Dönitz had heard nothing from *U-165* and *U-517* for a full week and suspected they had had no luck. Then, on 16 September, *U-165* broke her silence to report that she had just sunk a single freighter in the river (her attack on SQ 36). Within twenty-four hours, on the seventeenth, there was still better news from Hartwig, who reported the destruction of an "English auxiliary warship" (*Charlottetown*) in the river on the eleventh, and one, possibly two, steamers in a large convoy off Gaspé (the attack on SQ 36).

Hoffmann was cautious in his situation report. There were convoys along the coast between Gaspé and the river, but they were "[i]rregular" and it was difficult to contact them off Gaspé because of air patrols. However, the position from which he had ambushed SQ 36 in the river off Matane was "favourable." He had to remain submerged during the day, but there was "[p]atrolling only before convoy passed." Hartwig was more positive: "At present the use of two submarines should bring success."[1]

Headquarters seized upon Hartwig's optimism. "[T]he operations carried out by three boats [including *U-513*'s attack in Conception Bay] have been very successful. Defences proved comparatively weak and were limited to direct convoy escorts. Further boats are to be sent out to make the most of this situation." Headquarters was in fact anxiously looking for good news because at this very time success was drying up on the coast of the United States as a result of the American, British, and Canadian efforts that completed the convoy system along the American seaboard.[2] As always, Dönitz was searching for areas where defences were weak and shipping could readily be found.

On 19 September, U-boat headquarters directed *U-69*, which had recently laid mines at the mouth of Chesapeake Bay, to make for the Gaspé approaches. Headquarters also ordered *U-43* and *U-106*, outward bound from Lorient, to Canadian waters. On the twenty-fourth, headquarters directed *U-455*, which had laid mines off Charleston, South Carolina, to make for the Cape Race area, south of St. John's, in view of *U-513*'s report of steamer traffic in that area. On 1 October, orders went to *U-183*, then on an operation against a convoy south of Greenland, and *U-518*, recently sailed from Kiel, to head for the Strait of Belle Isle. A few days later, *U-520* and *U-521* sailed from Kiel for Canadian waters with the Strait of Belle Isle as their heading point, followed by *U-522*, which was later assigned to the St. John's area.[3]

The first of the new wave of submarines, *U-69*, entered the Cabot Strait on the evening of 30 September. On surfacing, the visibility was so clear the crew could see "both Newfoundland as well as Cape Breton." This was the boat's eighth combat cruise since she had entered service at the end of 1940, and the second under the command of 26-year-old Oberleutnant Ulrich Gräf, who had entered the navy in 1935 and joined the U-boat arm in 1940. In the previous mission under Gräf's command, the boat had destroyed three steamers and one sailing ship in the Caribbean.

U-69 soon encountered the improved defences in Canadian waters. While sweeping back and forth in the middle of the Cabot Strait during the early dark hours of 2 October, the boat sighted a small convoy heading south towards Sydney. She pursued it for over seven hours, but the vigorous zigzagging of the ships made a submerged attack impossible, and when Gräf surfaced, the frequent appearance of aircraft, despite low cloud cover and rainy weather, forced him back under. The air patrols were Gräf's own doing. Twice he made convoy-contact radio reports, and when he did not receive acknowledgment from headquarters, repeated the transmissions. (*U-517* and *U-165* had been much more cautious, broadcasting only after they had attacked and already

Commander J.M. "Jock" de Marbois, the officer who led the development of Canadian naval radio intelligence, which was essential for the defence of the St. Lawrence. After service with British naval intelligence during the First World War, de Marbois immigrated to Canada, embarked upon a teaching career at Upper Canada College in Toronto, and came out for duty with the Canadian navy in 1939. Photo taken in July 1940. Library and Archives Canada, PA 191706.

"Helmsman, Lyle Miller, [Fairmile] *Q-064*, Oct. 6 1942. A censorable, at the time, photo showing the helmsman wearing earphones on the Asdic set." Photo and caption by Ian Tate.

Rare photographs of a St. Lawrence convoy underway, taken on the afternoon of 2 October 1942 from the Fairmile HMCS *Q 064*, which was patrolling on the rear, southern side of the merchant vessels. This was the first "special" convoy, on the western leg of its trip, shortly after it departed from Gaspé for Bic Island. Photos by Ian Tate.

Pilot Officer Robert S. Keetley, 113 Squadron, RCAF, who made attacks on *U-165* and *U-517*, in the cockpit of a Lockheed Hudson bomber. Department of National Defence, PL 12617.

Squadron Leader N.E. "Molly" Small, commanding officer of 113 Squadron and the pioneer in Eastern Air Command of "offensive" anti-submarine tactics that helped turn the tide against the U-boats in the St. Lawrence in September and October 1942. Department of National Defence, PMR 77/177.

Flying Officer Maurice Belanger, 113 Squadron, RCAF, who made three attacks on *U-517*, exiting a Lockheed Hudson bomber. Department of National Defence, PL 12618.

Elusive target: *U-517* crash dives as Flying Officer Maurice Belanger's Lockheed Hudson makes its attack run on 29 September 1942. The Gaspé coast can be seen in the background. Department of National Defence, PMR 77-385.

A Lockheed Hudson of 113 Squadron, photographed before Squadron Leader Small had the machines repainted all in white, which British operational research demonstrated was most effective in preventing U-boat lookouts from sighting aircraft in time to allow the submarines to dive. Department of National Defence, PMR 77-191.

HMCS *Weyburn*, one of the corvettes assigned to the St. Lawrence in July 1942, and withdrawn in September for service in the Mediterranean, where the ship was sunk by an enemy mine on 22 February 1943. Department of National Defence, NP 1012.

Two views of HMCS
Springhill, one of the new
frigates that reinforced
the St. Lawrence in 1944.
Department of National
Defence, F-3079 and
F-3081.

Gaspé naval base, HMCS *Fort Ramsay*, 30 July 1942, still in the throes of construction. The large building in the centre is the main workshop, and the garage-like structure on its right is a covered work area into which Fairmile launches and smaller craft could be lifted on a marine railway on the foreshore. Department of National Defence, PMR 83-1248.

Gaspé naval and air base, 17 October 1944. On the right on the shoreline are the naval jetties and workshops. The large building in the centre is the RCAF hangar, with the flying boat apron descending into the water to the left. Department of National Defence, PMR 94-246.

FEB. 26, 1972

THE Canadian Magazine

THE WAR STORY OUR LEADERS KEPT QUIET

How Paul Hartwig and his U-boat attacked Canada and won

Also:
Punch Imlach's hat has made the Hockey Hall of Fame

French fries and fiddleheads from Florenceville, N. B.—a $60,000,000 business

The front page story in *The Canadian Magazine* by Peter Moon in February 1972 that did much to stimulate renewed interest in the St. Lawrence battle. Reprinted with permission—Torstar Syndication Services.

given away their position.) The RCN's intercept stations immediately noted the flurry of radio activity on the frequency used by the U-boats and plotted the source to the Cabot Strait area.[4] No. 119 Squadron dispatched three Hudsons on special search patrols in addition to four other Hudsons to escort convoys in the area, while 117 Squadron from North Sydney had a Canso on patrol over the straits all day.[5] Gräf's last attempt to approach the convoy, this time submerged, at midday was foiled when the convoy passed behind a schooner and a fishing trawler. The schooner was not moving and Gräf believed that this and other immobile schooners he had seen on the Newfoundland banks were "probably patrol vessels ... stationary guard ships,"[6] evidently placed to cover shipping routes. He seems to have been unaware that, in the North American Atlantic fisheries, dories carried in the schooners cast off in the morning to lay out fishing lines, while the mother ships dropped or reduced sail until late in the day when it was time to retrieve the dories and their catch.

As *U-69* arrived, the Canadian naval staff's intention of discontinuing the Sydney–Quebec series of convoys was coming unravelled. QS 38, which *Witherington* and *Salisbury* brought into Sydney on 30 September as they departed from the gulf, was supposed to have been the last convoy in the series. Already another dozen ships had come in from the Atlantic to Sydney carrying materials that were essential for industries in towns around the gulf. With all the available Bangors committed to QS 38 or refuelling at Gaspé, the navy took a chance. On 29 September, the merchant ships sailed from Sydney under the escort of only two Fairmiles, in a special convoy. The convoy had full air support and was routed evasively, hugging the coast around to Gaspé, into which the ships slipped from the south on 2 October. There, two Bangors, *Red Deer* and *Burlington*, reinforced the escort and took the convoy out of port on an evasive course similar to the one followed two weeks before by SQ 38 to avoid the coastal route along the north shore of the Gaspé Peninsula. The convoy headed northeast, back across the Gaspé

Passage, and then, when well out in the centre of the passage far off the Gaspé Peninsula's shore, headed west. It worked. *U-517* was patrolling out in the main shipping channel in the eastern approaches to Gaspé where the convoys had previously been routed and saw nothing. The main concerns of the escort were more prosaic: "problems anticipated on account of the large deck cargoes of pulpwood did not materialize as the wind died on the first evening."[7]

Meanwhile, three more ships bound for ports in the Gaspé area had come into Sydney from the Atlantic. They sailed as "Special St. Lawrence convoy No. 2" under the escort of the Bangor *Gananoque* in the dark early hours of 2 October, while *U-69*, whose presence no Allied authority yet suspected, was patrolling in the centre of the Cabot Strait; the convoy slipped unseen close around Cape North and reached Gaspé on the afternoon of 3 October.

The naval control service unit at Quebec City warned that substantial, essential steamer traffic would continue despite the closure of the St. Lawrence to ocean shipping. An analysis by the unit, whose efficiency Captain Brand commended, showed that only 60 percent of ships that had sailed in the outbound QS convoys since they started in May (286 vessels out of a total of 480 included in the convoys) were engaged in "Ocean Trade," largely to Britain. Of the remaining 194 sailings, sixty-one were for trade between Quebec ports and Newfoundland, both St. John's and Corner Brook, and they had gone through Sydney for onward routing in local convoys to those ports. A further forty-eight voyages were Great Lakes steamers that had come out for service on the Atlantic to help meet the shortfall of Allied shipping, and the remaining eighty-five voyages were Great Lakes steamers that linked the river and lakes ports with ports on the Gaspé coast and New Brunswick's gulf coast.

The naval control staff also reminded headquarters that a good deal of steamer traffic had never been included in the convoys, and the defence of this shipping should not be ignored. Since May, there had been a total of 197 independent sailings, "the majority lake vessels loading pulpwood on the North shore of St. Lawrence." The North Shore ports were distant from the convoy route, and unacceptable delays would have resulted from the inclusion of the vessels in convoy. "[S]o far by making their passages close inshore and by daylight, [the steamers] have escaped the attention of the enemy." The North Shore shipping, which sailed independently, included twenty-one voyages from those ports direct to Corner Brook. The ships scooted through the Jacques Cartier Passage north of Anticosti Island and thus avoided both the delays of the QS schedule and several days' waiting at Sydney for the Sydney–Corner Brook convoy sailings.[8]

Admiral Nelles circulated this information to the minister and the deputy minister and to the heads of all the staff branches to warn that the St. Lawrence would by no means be "closed down" as a result of the diversion of ocean shipping, even with the initiatives to increase the capacity of Halifax and Saint John for year-round loading. Further information sent by headquarters to operational commanders on the east coast listed over a hundred steamers that carried out transport services within the gulf, including many ships that had been regular members of the SQ–QS convoys.[9]

Thus the special convoys from Sydney became a continuation of the SQ–QS series, but at intervals of seven to ten days and so less frequent and less regular. The navy did not, however, reverse the deployment of corvettes away from the gulf that was the main objective in the diversion of ocean shipping. Escorts were limited to the Bangors and Fairmiles that remained at the end of September. More than ever, the protection of shipping depended upon the air force, which, still determined to drive the U-boats out of the St. Lawrence, kept up the additional Gulf detachments. The naval commands at Quebec, Gaspé, and Sydney also made greater use of evasive routing, for which there was more scope now that there was usually only one convoy on passage at a time. It was a gamble nevertheless.

QS 39 got underway at Bic Island late on the morning of 4 October 1942. The pre-sailing telegram listed fifteen merchant ships. Their

cargoes and destinations bore out the analysis of traffic made by the staff
at Quebec City: four vessels were carrying steel and lumber to the U.K.
(these were among the last of the ocean-trade ships to clear the gulf),
two were carrying general cargo to St. John's, and the rest were carrying
cargo between gulf ports. The escort included four Bangors, one of them
the newly completed *Westmount* on her way to Halifax for work-ups,
and three Fairmiles. The senior ship of the escort was the Bangor HMCS
Gananoque.[10]

Hartwig, frustrated at his inability to close with shipping off
Gaspé, had come west along the shore of the Gaspé Peninsula early on
4 October and surfaced to patrol the shipping channel off Les Méchins
at the mouth of the river on the night of 4–5 October. He sighted the
convoy shortly before midnight. During the next three hours, he applied
his favourite tactic, getting well ahead of the convoy and manoeuvring
slowly on the surface to allow the merchant ships to come to him. He
ran his quiet electric motors rather than the noisy diesels to avoid giving
himself away. Still, he was amazingly bold. There was bright moonlight
and further illumination from the northern lights, and two aircraft were
providing all-night coverage of the convoy.

At 2:49 AM, 5 October, Hartwig, still on the surface, fired two torpedoes in single aimed shots at two of the lead merchant ships from a range
of 2500 metres. Both missed and neither detonated. As Hartwig attempted
to run into the shadows of the Gaspé coast, one of the escorts on that
same side of the convoy began to close; all the while the submarine was
"being continually overflown by aircraft." *U-517* dived under the escort
to escape. Shortly before 4 AM, he surfaced again: "fortunately the moon
has disappeared behind the clouds ... the northern lights are very faint."
For two hours he again proceeded slowly, allowing the convoy to come to
him, even though "I am being frequently overflown by seaplanes at low
elevation." He was startled at 6 AM when one of the aircraft suddenly
turned on its lights to illuminate a sailing ship, but the aircrew did not
see the low profile of *U-517* in the surrounding darkness. A few minutes

later, as the sky began to brighten with first light, *U-517* dived and began a submerged attack. In the approach, she had to dodge the zigzagging escorts, a job complicated by the fact that the night periscope had been completely shattered, presumably in one of the earlier actions. Then, at the critical moment, the fire control calculator broke down. The salvo of two torpedoes missed, even though the target was "four overlapping ... merchant ships" at a close range of 600 metres.

The failure of these and the other torpedoes fired since 15 September to explode led Hartwig and his crew to blame the failure of the attacks on damage to the weapons that may have resulted from the battering their upper-deck storage tubes had suffered in *Salisbury* and *Arrowhead*'s counterattack during the SQ 36 action. That cannot be verified. What is clear from both the German and Canadian records is that cumulative damage inflicted by the defending forces' many near misses, intensified air cover with the new offensive tactics, more vigorous patrolling by the surface escorts, and evasive routing had together prevented *U-517* from achieving any success during its last three weeks in the St. Lawrence. The defending forces achieved these results despite the fact that Hartwig, who was a commander of exceptional skill and who had gained full knowledge of the convoy routes and schedules, was increasingly aggressive in his efforts to gain favourable attacking positions.

U-517 had fired her last torpedoes, and she headed for home.

QS 39 was still in danger. Gräf's *U-69* had come up from the Cabot Strait and was in the Gaspé Passage on a submerged patrol off Cap de la Madeleine. Shortly before 9 AM, 5 October, less than two hours after *U-517*'s final attack, the newly arrived submarine sighted the convoy and tracked it for four hours. Gräf seems to have been impressed by the numerous escorts and the close air cover by a flying boat. He did not dare fire because of the "glassy" water surface, which meant that the torpedo track and periscope could be sighted. He then abandoned the pursuit "because of unfavourable cloud ceiling; hilltops ashore are covered by clouds." He had seen enough of Eastern Air Command's patrols to worry that, should he need to escape at speed on the surface, he would be vulnerable to surprise attack by aircraft breaking through the cloud cover.

The convoy had no idea that it had been attacked twice and nearly attacked a third time. The first inkling of a threat came early on the afternoon of the fifth when Naval Service Headquarters warned that a U-boat had recently signalled from off the mouth of the Baie des Chaleurs, ahead of the convoy on the normal southerly route from Gaspé. This was the convoy-contact signal *U-69* had sent after breaking off from QS 39, and the submarine was still in fact on the north shore of the Gaspé coast, a good example of the limited accuracy of direction-finding plots, which normally could give only a general idea of the location of a transmitting warship. *Gananoque*'s commanding officer, Lieutenant E.M. More, RCNR, another of the former civilian merchant mariners who commanded so many vessels of Canada's anti-submarine fleet, showed initiative by quickly diverting to a new course. He directed the convoy eastward, instead of his assigned southerly route, to pass far to the north of the Magdalen Islands rather than the normal route to the south of them. This carried the convoy entirely clear of not just the reported position of the U-boat, but the normal shipping lane which the U-boat, from its reported position off the Baie des Chaleurs, seemed to be patrolling. Although the assumptions were erroneous and the convoy was already clear of the threat, NSHQ's swift plotting of *U-69*'s signal, the prompt alert to the convoy at risk, and More's energetic response— for which he later received plaudits from the senior commanders ashore—demonstrated the increased capabilities and readiness of the Canadian defences.[11]

Events during the next ten days severely tested the more vigilant and better coordinated Canadian effort. It must be underscored that Allied authorities had little idea that this period marked the beginning of the largest German effort in the St. Lawrence and adjacent coastal waters around the southern and eastern Atlantic shores of Newfoundland.

The 113 Squadron detachment at Chatham, New Brunswick, made a concerted effort in the waters south and east of Gaspé, off the mouth of Baie des Chaleurs. In one of the rare documents from 1942 that explicitly links particular operations to signals intelligence, the detachment reported that "[i]t appears that this U-boat is staying within a comparatively small area. Everything possible has been done at this station to attack this sub, so far without success."[12] There was nothing there. It would appear that NSHQ and EAC headquarters had combined direction-finding plots on *U-69*'s signals from near Gaspé on 5 October with *U-517*'s homebound broadcast of 6 October as that boat made its way eastward from Gaspé to conclude that a submarine was still hovering in the shipping lane off New Brunswick's gulf coast.

Air operations also took full account of the Germans' well-known fondness for ambush attacks in the river. There was a special reason to do so because two convoys, both in the continuing Quebec City to Goose Bay series, were in the river: the northbound LN 10 just departed from Bic Island, and the southbound NL 9 returning from Labrador. On 8 October, a Canso from Gaspé covered LN 10, while four Hudson patrols from the detachments at Mont Joli scoured the river and provided support to NL 9 from first light until nightfall.

After the failed operation against QS 39 on 5 October, Gräf in *U-69* had continued into the river. During the early hours of 6 October, he surfaced near Cap de la Madeleine to transfer torpedoes from the upper-deck storage tubes into the hull and partway through this task was startled to see the lights of cars travelling along the coastal highway nearby. By the night of 8–9 October, Gräf had penetrated further west than any other submarine, to the vicinity of Father Point, just east of Rimouski.

U-69 was the first boat to come into the St. Lawrence carrying the recently developed "radar observation equipment" (*Funkmess-Beobachtungsgerät*, or "FuMB"), known as "Metox" for Metox-Grandin and Sadir, the French manufacturers of the equipment. This was capable of detecting emissions by long-wave Allied radar, including the 1.5-metre sets in Allied maritime bombers and escorts.[13] On the dark, rainy night of 8–9 October, when visibility was virtually nil, *U-69*'s equipment proved tremendously useful.

At 8:38 PM on 8 October, *U-69*'s Metox suddenly warned of nearby transmissions, and the U-boat did an emergency dive. She then picked up propeller noises on her underwater listening equipment. Evidently it was radar in surface escorts and not the aircraft that had so often triggered Metox warnings. Thus assured that no aircraft were waiting to ambush him, Gräf surfaced again and pursued the sound bearings. Only with difficulty did he finally sight NL 9 against "the dark shore," which was about fifteen kilometres away to the south. He manoeuvred at a considerable distance ahead of the convoy—5000 to 6000 metres from the lead escort, which in turn was patrolling 2000 metres or more ahead of the merchant ships—because of the constant radar warnings from the Metox. At one point the equipment registered steady strengthening of the radar signal, which led Gräf to believe he must have been detected. Perhaps in relief when he realized that he had not in fact been picked up, he joked that the radar operators in the escorts must have been having a good snooze.

At 1:09 AM, 9 October, after tracking the convoy for over four hours and positioning himself on the offshore, northern side, Gräf quickly fired a salvo of two torpedoes immediately followed by a single torpedo. His target was the three merchant ships of the convoy, which were sailing line abreast, that is, one beside the other. From his perspective, the broadsides of the three vessels overlapped, making an excellent target, but the range was long, 2000 metres. Gräf fired early because one of the escorts—the corvette *Arrowhead* was patrolling ahead of the line of merchant ships and the corvette *Hepatica* was patrolling astern—suddenly changed course towards his position. After four minutes, Gräf heard an explosion and a minute later saw "a hit on a ... freighter, tall dark explosive plume with substantial flames, the target broke in two.

The fire is extinguished after two minutes, instantaneously. (The target was sunk.)"

The radar operators in the escorts were not asleep, as Gräf lightheartedly suggested. This was another example of the limited capabilities of the long-wave radar in the escorts against the slight profile of a surfaced submarine. Water conditions for asdic, moreover, were "very bad." Thus the first hint of trouble was the explosion in the freighter *Carolus*, and the corvettes reacted promptly, firing star shell to light the area. *U-69*, making a fast escape on the surface, was already clear of the illumination. *Hepatica* dropped a ten-charge pattern on an asdic contact, but when neither corvette was able to re-acquire the contact, they correctly concluded that it was "non-sub."[14]

Losses in *Carolus* were heavy, twelve of the crew of thirty, because she had gone down so quickly. *Carolus* was a Finnish ship. She had been at Montreal and was seized by the Canadian government after Canada and the other Allied nations declared war on Finland in December 1941 because of Finland's support for Germany's invasion of the Soviet Union. The Allies, not least Canada, did so reluctantly and at Stalin's insistence; Finland's heroic resistance to a Soviet invasion in the "Winter War" of 1939–40 had excited admiration and efforts at military aid among the western Allies. The crew of *Carolus* and at least one other Finnish ship, *Ericus*, had willingly carried on and, according to Captain Brand, given "excellent service." He asked that officials in the Immigration Service be alerted not to treat the survivors "as enemy aliens which, of course, they were technically." There was one cruelty that could not be avoided. The next of kin of the Finnish seamen who had died could not be notified because of the danger that the families might suffer if word leaked out to German authorities that members were helping the Allied cause.[15]

The destruction of *Carolus* was, Dönitz hoped, the opening blow in his new offensive in the St. Lawrence. *U-106* and *U-43* were approaching the Cabot Strait. *U-106*, a day ahead of *U-43*, was on its eighth war cruise since commissioning in the fall of 1940. Kapitänleutnant

Hermann Rasch, 28, had joined the navy in 1934 and served in *U-106* since she was commissioned; he had taken command in October 1941, and this was his fifth war cruise as her commanding officer. All of the boat's missions under Rasch's command had been to North American waters from Newfoundland to the Gulf of Mexico, during which the boat destroyed twelve merchant ships, including the Canadian National Steamship passenger vessel *Lady Drake* on 5 May 1942 near Bermuda. Rasch had good reason to respect Allied maritime air power. His previous mission, in July, had been cut short by an aircraft attack that damaged the submarine, killed one officer, and injured Rasch.

On the morning of 10 October, when *U-106* was westbound halfway between Cape Breton and the islands of Saint-Pierre and Miquelon, Rasch sighted a small coastal convoy and made a fast surface run in pursuit. An aircraft that was evidently screening the convoy suddenly appeared; Canadian records show that both 119 Squadron Hudsons from Sydney and 117 Squadron Cansos from North Sydney had a heavy schedule supporting several coastal convoys in the area that day. Rasch immediately dived; the convoy turned away, and he was unable to catch it at his best submerged speed.

Rasch headed towards the Cape Breton side of the Cabot Strait on the basis of Gräf's report of small convoys in those waters. Luck was with him. At 10:30 AM on 11 October, SB 31, on passage from Corner Brook to Sydney, came into sight; two merchant ships were headed directly towards *U-106*'s submerged hiding spot. The submarine only had to wait for thirty minutes and then, at a close range of 220 metres, fired two torpedoes into the Great Lakes steamer *Waterton*. Rasch immediately plunged deep. He was particularly worried about the 117 Squadron Canso that, in the cloudy, drizzling conditions, was flying close cover over the convoy at an altitude of only 230 metres. With the explosion of the first torpedo in the freighter, the Canso plummeted towards the ship and was "over the vessel at a height of 150 feet [45 metres] when a second torpedo struck the ship on the port side and the aircraft was enveloped in a shower of smoke and debris from the explosion." There was little to be done; the surface of the water was choppy and showed no trace of the torpedo track or of a periscope. The aircraft correctly did not drop its depth charges in the absence of a visible target, saving its offensive punch in case the submarine should come to the surface.[16]

The sole surface escort, the armed yacht HMCS *Vison*, rushed along the estimated track of the torpedo, the direction indicated by gunfire from the self-defence armament on the second merchant vessel, the tanker *Omaha*, which had had the clearest view of the attack. The armed yachts, intended only as a short-term emergency stopgap when taken up for naval service in 1940, had long since proven themselves unsuited for the rigours of escort work, as recently shown by the disintegration of *Raccoon* when hit by torpedoes from *U-165*. *Vison*'s counteraction on 11 October showed the hallmarks of the jury-rigged emergency conversion of these most civilian of vessels into warships and underscored the full extent to which the Royal Canadian Navy was scraping the bottom of the barrel to keep the coastal convoys running. On *Vison*'s initial run, the asdic set failed, and she therefore instantly made an unaimed attack with two depth charges to keep the submarine from firing again. Communications between the bridge and the depth charge position at the stern of the yacht were poor (faulty equipment appears to have been the problem), and the depth charge crew applied a deep setting of 107 metres instead of the shallow setting, fifteen metres, that the bridge had actually ordered. Meanwhile, the asdic operator plugged in a spare set of cables, the equipment began to function, and the yacht dropped two full depth charge patterns on a contact. The headquarters at Sydney subsequently requested full reports on the equipment breakdowns and miscommunication in *Vison*; one can imagine the senior officers cringing at the foul-ups.[17]

As we now know, the yacht's counteraction was effective and a nice example of what Canada's wartime sailors achieved with initiative despite the shortcomings of their tools and training. Rasch believed the first two depth charges in the snap attack came from the aircraft, whose presence made him nervous. Because of the choppy water on the surface, he had never seen *Vison*, only heard propeller noises that in the "very poor" listening conditions gave the impression that "two destroyers are at work." Those conditions would have greatly limited the effectiveness of the yacht's asdic; nevertheless, Rasch described the first of the two full depth charge patterns as "well placed." The U-boat continued its dive to 145 metres and stayed under for over eight hours.

The sound conditions were poor indeed, for Rasch heard nothing of the response launched by the Sydney command: two Bangors, two Fairmiles, and another armed yacht, with air support, screened *Omaha* and carried out a search for the submarine. Despite the severity of the explosions in *Waterton*, the steamer did not sink for eight minutes, and all twenty-seven of her people were rescued by *Vison*. The staff officer at the U.S. Navy Department who analyzed the Canadian reports assumed that the Germans had better intelligence than was actually the case and had been pursuing the large, valuable tanker *Omaha* but had been deceived by the structure of the smaller Great Lakes steamer.[18] *Waterton*'s funnel was at the stern, much like an ocean tanker. This analysis was half correct; in the limited visibility through the periscope in the rough seas, Rasch had believed *Waterton* was the larger of the two vessels.

When Rasch finally surfaced on the evening of 11 October, he received two messages from headquarters. One warned of "standing U-Boat pursuit patrols ... with continual surveillance of adjacent areas" in the Gaspé approaches. The headquarters war diary does not state the source of the information, but perhaps German intelligence had picked up radio traffic from the Gaspé base or 113 Squadron's Chatham detachment, which had been so active in the area. The second signal gave freedom of action to *U-106* and to *U-43* in the Gulf of St. Lawrence and particularly commended the river: "promise of success in the new moon period." This advice undoubtedly reflected *U-69*'s report of recent success; Gräf's radio message claimed that, aside from the destruction of

Carolus, hits on other ships in the convoy were "probable." Rasch was encouraged: the river "combines the depths of water that we require with its constriction which limits the opportunities for evasion open to the enemy."[19]

U-43, which passed through the Cabot Strait on the night of 12–13 October 1942, followed *U-106* towards the river. The newcomer was another veteran boat, under the command of Oberleutnant zur See Hans-Joachim Schwantke, 24. He had joined the navy in 1936 and served in *U-43* since January 1941 before taking command of the submarine in March 1942. During Schwantke's first war cruise in command, the boat had joined in the attack on the transatlantic convoy ON 115 east of Newfoundland and on 3 August 1942 been damaged by one of the Canadian escorts, the corvette HMCS *Sackville.*

As *U-106* and *U-43* were making their way towards the river, *U-69* vacated the area in the face of the "continuous heavy air cover using radar"[20] following the sinking of *Carolus.* Part of the difficulty was the primitive nature of the Metox receiver, which gave no indication of the distance from which the enemy radar transmissions were emanating. When the equipment sounded an alarm, the U-boat had no choice but to dive. With the round-the-clock patrols by Eastern Air Command triggering the Metox every few hours, *U-69* could not make sustained surface runs even at night. The boat was having difficulties with its air compressor,[21] which could only work with electrical power. So frequently did the boat have to dive that the diesel-run generators could not drive the compressor long enough to ensure a sufficient supply of compressed air with which to control the boat. (This forced water from the buoyancy tanks should the submarine have to make extended under-water manoeuvres in the event she was pursued by escorts or aircraft.) Gräf arrived back in the Cabot Strait on 12 October. There was no night flying in the area, and he was able in the dark, moonless conditions to patrol on the surface, heading towards an encounter in the early hours of 14 October with the ferry *Caribou,* whose destruction was the single worst disaster in Canada's naval war. The ferry, while under naval escort on a run within Canadian and Newfoundland territorial waters, was destroyed with the loss of 136 people, nearly two-thirds of those on board, including twenty-eight women and young children. It would be more than forty years before research in German documents revealed that this defining event in Canada's apparent defeat in the St. Lawrence was the result of effective defences which drove *U-69* and other German submarines from the gulf. If they had remained there, the Canadian losses would have been even greater.

Gräf, at least, had achieved one sinking inside the gulf before the defensive patrols made those waters untenable for him. Rasch in *U-106* and Schwantke in *U-43* came away empty-handed. Rasch felt uncomfortable from his first night in the gulf, 12–13 October, as he approached Anticosti Island. "Even when there is no moon, it is not at all dark. The stars are continually bright and the bright northern lights annoy us."[22] By the morning of 15 October, he was off Matane, in the river, making a submerged patrol. "I am close to the shore, distance off 2–3 nm [nautical miles—3.7 to 5.5 kilometres]. The visibility is so good that the northern shore can also be distinguished clearly through the periscope. No smoke plume can pass through this area without being noticed. But none comes."[23] By the evening of 16 October, he had lost patience, but as he pulled back to the Gaspé area, his Metox constantly screamed out warnings, and on the evening of 17 October he got down just in time to avoid two escorts that "circle around me." It was not a graceful manoeuvre. Because of the density layering in the water the "boat falls back on the bottom in depth 90 m [metres]." On 18 October, when he was passing south of Anticosti, he was annoyed to receive a message from headquarters demanding a situation report and citing the directive for such regular reports from "'Command Officers' Handbook Para. 354." One can sense that Rasch was by now fed up: "I will ... not transmit a situation report until when I am clear of this gully because the reception and transmission conditions are thoroughly miserable here." He reported only on 22 October when he had pulled out past Cape Breton's Atlantic coast: "Have shifted from BA 35 and 38 [St. Lawrence River] ... because of moon and defences. Nothing sighted in BA [St. Lawrence River and estuary]. Strong defensive forces since 16:10. Search units using asdic in Qu [BB] 14 [off Gaspé], air surveillance co-operating with surface search forces and also operating everywhere without surface forces."[24]

U-43, which began to patrol in the estuary and river along the north shore of the Gaspé Peninsula on 15 October, had exactly the same experience. Schwantke was just as discouraged as *U-106*'s Rasch, but decided to remain because of the previous reports of "heavy shipping traffic in this area." His patience paid off when at midday on 21 October he sighted SQ 43 coming towards him, off Les Méchins. He moved very slowly and kept his periscope down except for occasional short peeks because of the "mirror-like sea." He was confident, however, because of the strong density layering; since he arrived in these waters it had helped him maintain a steady submerged depth and very clearly blinded asdic in the several patrolling escorts he had encountered. He was in the midst of his final approach towards two merchant ships when he became aware of "5–6 depth charges which explode almost simultaneously. The battery circuit automatic breaker is knocked off. The torpedo in Tube V is activated in the tube. Several light bulbs etc. are knocked out." Schwantke immediately plunged to 130 metres to escape what he feared was a coordinated air–sea attack. Like Rasch, he had been impressed by the fact that, when escorts were patrolling in an area, they were almost always preceded by about an hour by air patrols. He had not heard any escort approaching and therefore assumed he had been detected by aircraft. He stayed deep for over seven hours.

This, one of the most effective counterattacks during the St. Lawrence battle, was an almost casual affair, and it reflected the improved readiness on the part of the escorts. In this case, for a brief period, the density layering appears to have favoured the defending forces. Although Schwantke heard no escort above him and thus feared detection by aircraft, the attack had come from the Bangor HMCS *Gananoque*, which had been patrolling ahead of the convoy. The asdic made a "doubtful" contact, the second of the day. In both instances, *Gananoque* was careful to investigate with the help of sister escorts, but in both cases the contact disappeared. When the asdic set was unable to regain contact after encounter with *U-43*, Lieutenant B. Williams, the anti-submarine control officer in *Gananoque*, concluded "that this attack was made on a shoal of fish or tide rip."[25] In fact, the Bangor had not only prevented an attack on the two merchant ships in SQ 43, but ensured the safe passage of a second convoy. At Bic Island, *Gananoque* and the Bangor HMCS *Burlington*, which had assisted in the search after the attack on *U-43*, formed up QS 40 and sailed at midday on 22 October. *U-43*, operating extremely cautiously after the depth charging the day before, did not detect the eastbound convoy.

When the boat finally received headquarters' demand for a report on the morning of 24 October, Schwantke flashed "Advise against despatching further boats to this area. Numerous unexercised naval units working in good co-operation with air forces. Attacked with aircraft bombs during submerged attack on convoy ... on the 21st." Because of the bad radio conditions, the message did not get through, and Schwantke did not risk repeat transmissions. After daybreak on 25 October, Schwantke sighted an eastbound convoy off Cap Chat; this was probably LN 12, bound from Bic Island for Goose Bay under the escort of the corvettes *Trail* and *Shawinigan* and, as Schwantke noted, a Canso flying boat. The events of 21 October then virtually replayed themselves. As he made a submerged approach, suddenly four depth charges exploded "fairly close." *U-43* went deep, the convoy passed overhead, and then, as he was rising to periscope depth to renew the pursuit, there were "4 well-placed depth charges," and the boat plunged to hide at a depth of 120 metres. There is no record of the attacks in the report for LN 12; presumably the ships once again dropped charges on uncertain contacts purely as a precaution.[26] *U-43* remained on patrol at the mouth of the river until 4 November, but with no result. She later reported that both traffic and patrols had stopped after 25 October; in fact at least two other convoys, SQ 44 and QS 42, safely got past the U-boat.

The submarines found conditions little different along Newfoundland's Atlantic coast and in the waters south of Newfoundland and east of Cape Breton. *U-69* pulled out to sea south of Newfoundland in the face of the "continuous heavy air cover" following the destruction of *Caribou*. In the early hours of 20 October in wild seas off the mouth of Conception Bay, the boat made a torpedo attack on the ore carrier *Rose Castle*. During the storm, the vessel had lost contact with its convoy, BW 9, from Sydney to Wabana on Bell Island. The crew of the ore carrier heard the torpedo hit the hull; Gräf reported that the steamer "sounded her whistle continually for one minute, stopped ... and showed distress lights." But there was no explosion. "Twenty minutes later the steamer continues her passage." The torpedo had failed, and it was the submarine's last. "Employment of gun not feasible," Gräf remarked, "because of the weather conditions." Gräf turned southeast to clear the coast and head for home. That evening he radioed a report of his attack on *Rose Castle*—the submarine had identified the vessel from her distress broadcasts. Next afternoon, the twenty-first, a Hudson from 145 Squadron, based at RCAF Station Torbay near St. John's, swooped on the submarine from an altitude of 760 metres, just under the cloud base. The lookouts spotted the "very fast" aircraft in the nick of time, and the boat had submerged when the four depth charges exploded astern. This unwelcome farewell from the Canadian coastal area was the result of the navy having plotted *U-69*'s radio report of the night before and Eastern Air Command's dispatch of aircraft to scour the most promising area of probability.[27]

At the same time, *U-106*, after its departure through the Cabot Strait, had found no relief from the "heavy surveillance," even in the

Atlantic waters off Cape Breton's eastern coast. Part of the problem was the bright moonlight, which brought night air patrols. Rasch therefore headed further out to sea: "The ship's company has to get some fresh air for a change. (Too much operating submerged spoils the fighting spirit.)"[28] *U-455*, the boat assigned to replace *U-513* off St. John's, had already been and gone. In a nine-day vigil, she had seen little shipping and then had to head for home on 14 October because of equipment problems. *U-183* and *U-518*, which arrived on their station at the northern entrance to the Strait of Belle Isle on 18 October, were having no more luck finding targets. The strait was "completely dead," *U-183* reported on 27 October.

With the failure to find shipping close in to Newfoundland's shores, Dönitz cleared both *U-183* and *U-522*, the latter previously assigned to the St. John's area, to make instead for Halifax. Early on 30 October, *U-522*, en route to its new station, sighted SC 107 south of the Avalon Peninsula. Dönitz ordered *U-520* and *U-521*, then approaching their coastal-waters patrol areas off St. John's and Conception Bay, to join in the pursuit of the transatlantic convoy. Canadian naval intelligence, which had been plotting the radio chatter among the U-boats, had already alerted Eastern Air Command, which made an all-out effort with the squadrons of 1 Group in Newfoundland. Later on the morning of the thirtieth, a 145 Squadron Hudson, searching at the limits of its range, 538 kilometres from its base at Torbay, destroyed *U-658*, a member of group "Veilchen," thirteen U-boats coming in from the Grand Banks in response to *U-522*'s radio reports. "The D.C.s [depth charges] straddled the U-boat, two falling on the port side, one apparently hitting direct, rolling off and exploding; the fourth one was seen to explode six feet [1.8 metres] off the starboard bow. These explosions lifted the submarine right out of the water—it then settled straight down finally disappearing, showing an estimated one third of its hull towards the stern ... An oil patch immediately showed which developed in ever growing intensity ..." There were no survivors among the submarine's forty-eight crew.

Later that day, a Douglas Digby of 10 Squadron from Gander, returning from a mission in support of another convoy, made a chance sighting of *U-520* 212 kilometres east of St. John's and attacked. The submarine managed to get under as the depth charges fell. The Digby, however, carried 204-kilogram naval depth charges, not the aerial 113-kilogram version that armed the smaller Hudson, and the more powerful detonations showed immediate results. "A dark object came to the surface but quickly disappeared; this being followed by large air bubbles and oil in quantity. Darkness was spreading over the scene and the Digby had to leave thirty minutes after the attack, at [that] time oil and air bubbles were still coming to the surface—the oil having spread into a patch about 100 by 300 yards [91 by 274 metres]." The bubbling oil—its vast quantity in comparison to the smaller amounts often left by a boat as it crash-dived showed that the attack had been successful— marked the grave of all fifty-three German crew. The next day, 31 October, one of four 145 Squadron Hudsons patrolling the convoy's course in poor weather made Eastern Air Command's first confirmed radar contact on a submarine, in this case *U-521*, although the resulting attack did not do serious damage.[29]

In contrast to the patrols in coastal waters by single U-boats in search of unprotected or poorly protected shipping, the submarines operated in large groups on the open ocean. These were needed to fan out and search the broad seas for convoys and then to concentrate in order to counter the numerous escorts around the big ocean convoys. The groups could search—and attack—most effectively when surfaced, so they avoided areas covered by the increasingly effective Allied shore-based aircraft. The successful operation by Eastern Air Command against the lead U-boats searching on the surface for SC 107 was a stark demonstration of the command's achievement of top-level performance and why the U-boat groups hovered well off shore. Unfortunately, the best of the aircraft available in Newfoundland and eastern Canada could reach no further than about 900 kilometres out to sea, and often, because of the poor weather conditions, much less. Thus, as SC 107 moved beyond the range of the aircraft, the large U-boat group assembling further out to sea was able to overwhelm the RCN escort group, which comprised only a single destroyer, HMCS *Restigouche*, and four corvettes. Experience showed that the group should have had at least twice that number of escorts, and at least two should have been destroyers or other fast warships. High speed, which the corvettes lacked, was essential in order to dash out in response to radio intelligence, radar, and sighting reports to put down U-boats before they had a chance to close and strike, much as the offensive air sweeps had done in the St. Lawrence. As it was, the escorts were outnumbered almost three to one, and the convoy's slow speed, about nine kilometres an hour, allowed the submarines to readily stay in contact and get into favourable attacking positions. By the time the convoy moved within range of British air support from Iceland on 5 November, fifteen of the forty-two merchant ships had been destroyed.

The story of the German interception of SC 107 is a striking example of an important shift in the Battle of the Atlantic in the fall of 1942. The U-boats that made the initial contact south of St. John's stumbled on the convoy when they were changing stations in coastal waters because the more effective Canadian defences made it impossible for them to find shipping. The U-boats' effort to pursue the convoy in coastal waters had been defeated by strong air patrols, but, once the convoy was beyond the range of the aircraft, the U-boats had a field day because of the weakness of the naval escorts for the mid-ocean run. Since the U-boats had moved into North American waters in January 1942, the Allies had had to transfer Canadian and British warships from the mid-ocean force to build the vast coastal convoy system required to stop the slaughter of unescorted shipping along the American coast and in the Caribbean.

The U-boat force, which had increased in strength from 91 fully operational submarines in January 1942 to 203 in December 1942,[30] was able to continue to press into poorly protected coastal areas in distant waters while concentrating its main effort in group attacks against mid-ocean convoys. Significantly, however, the poor results of the October offensive in the St. Lawrence brought U-boat headquarters to rule out the area for the ongoing coastal operations.

While disaster overtook SC 107 far out in the central Atlantic, *U-518* delivered the parting blow of 1942 in the Canadian coastal area.

U-518, like her sister *U-517*, had been commissioned in the spring of 1942, and this was her first war cruise. The commanding officer, Oberleutnant zur See Friedrich-Wilhelm Wissmann, 25, was a few months younger than *U-517*'s Hartwig. Wissmann had also entered the navy in 1935 and joined the U-boat arm in the spring of 1941, the best part of a year after Hartwig. Wissmann had served as first officer in *U-109* during her mission to Canadian and U.S. waters in January–February 1942. Like Hartwig, Wissmann was on his first operation in command, and like Hartwig he proved to be skilful and bold.

Wissmann learned from the radio traffic that *U-520* and *U-521* had been diverted away from their patrols off St. John's and Conception Bay to pursue SC 107. He decided to probe the area himself and attempt to duplicate *U-513*'s feat at the Wabana ore-loading anchorage. Korvettenkapitän Rüggeberg's exploit there had brought the Canadian forces to reassess the defences of the ore ships. The coastal battery, at the north, seaward, end of the island had been sited to protect the northern entrance to the anchorage against attack by a surface warship, and it was not well positioned to deal with an attacker that had got into the anchorage. Little could be done to improve coverage within the anchorage itself, short of building and garrisoning an additional battery, an effort that the army judged impractical given the shortage of coastal defence equipment and the pressure of needs for other higher-priority sites on both coasts of the country. The navy, however, assigned two Fairmiles to maintain a patrol of the anchorage and established the Wabana–Sydney series of convoys to protect ships as they arrived at and departed from Wabana; while ore ships were loading, one of the convoy escorts remained on patrol at the anchorage to augment the Fairmiles.

These were considerable efforts and a reasonable response to *U-513*'s submerged attack through the northern entrance to the anchorage, but they did no good. Wissmann did everything differently. On the night of 1–2 November he came on the surface through the broad expanse of Conception Bay, passing well to the south of Wabana, and then entered the anchorage from the southern entrance. The coastal battery's searchlights, which were periodically illuminated to sweep the anchorage very briefly so as not to provide a beacon for an attacker, caused the U-boat commander considerable anxiety and forced him to manoeuvre carefully. The lights would have been more effective still but for an error in procedure by the garrison. Instructions were to illuminate the lights and sweep at very irregular intervals to prevent an attacking vessel from dodging them, which was precisely what Wissmann was able to do as soon as he saw that the lights came on every ten minutes.

The corvette *Drumheller,* the escort on duty, was on patrol outside the north entrance. The duty Fairmile was patrolling the anchorage off the loading pier, inside the north entrance. Shortly after 3:30 AM, 2 November, Wissmann fired from the south, hitting *Rose Castle* and the French ore carrier *PLM-27,* which were moored 800 metres from him off the southern part of the island. He made a longer shot at *Flyingdale,* which was alongside one of the loading piers to the north; the torpedo missed the ship but detonated on the corner of the pier with a huge explosion that blew a chunk out of the massive concrete structure. The Canadian warships rushed to the stricken ships, while Wissmann, in the darkness well to the south, took off at full speed the way he had come in. Loss of life in the stricken ore carriers was heavy because they were loaded and went down quickly. *Rose Castle*, which had had an eerie premonition of her fate with *U-69*'s faulty torpedo less than two weeks earlier, lost twenty-eight people; twelve of *PLM-27*'s crew died.[31]

Late in the morning of 3 November, when *U-518* was south of Cape Race making her way towards the Cabot Strait, a Digby from Gander attacked, dropping four big naval depth charges shortly after the boat dived. The submarine had got deep enough that she did not suffer any damage. Fog rolled in shortly after the attack, leaving the aircraft no choice but to return to base. The Digby was performing a sweep, likely in response to a naval direction-finding plot of Wissmann's radio report the previous day of his success at Wabana.

U-518 was now on a "special mission" to put ashore an agent tasked to carry out espionage and organize sabotage. The U-boat cruised submerged through the Cabot Strait on the night of 6–7 November, and on 8 November made an extended submerged run that brought her into the Baie des Chaleurs after nightfall. Once certain the bay was empty of shipping, Wissmann surfaced and made his way towards New Carlisle, Quebec, on the north shore of the bay. About 700 metres off shore, he let the submarine settle to the bottom to reduce its profile, and at 12:30 AM, 9 November, a dinghy, rowed by a crewman and carrying the agent, cast off. There was then an anxious moment. "An automobile appears on the road ... the road curves directly ahead of us so that the car's headlights sweep across the water ... I hold my breath. Involuntarily, I quickly order heads down before the light hits us. The automobile continues turning and then passed by directly ahead at a distance of roughly 800 m[etres] ... The scattered houses and all small details ashore can be clearly seen in the car's headlight beams." Wissmann was not charmed by his first close look at Canada's Maritime region: "The houses make a miserable impression." When the dinghy returned at 1:20 AM, the U-boat lifted off the bottom and, running on the surface on its quiet electric motors, departed from the bay. Wissmann was reassured by the "peacetime-like" calm on shore: "I am firmly convinced that the Special Agent got through subsequently."

The agent, Werner Janowski, was an experienced saboteur and a committed, long-time supporter of the Nazi party. He had moved to Canada in 1930 and lived in Toronto before, in 1933, abandoning a Canadian wife he had married for her money and returning to Europe.[32]

Janowski spent a cold night on the rocky beach before, at sunrise, he could make his way up the coastal bluffs and hitch a car ride into New Carlisle, six kilometres away. At 9:00 AM, he appeared at the Carlisle Hotel, asking for breakfast and a room where he could bathe before going to the railway station. The Annett family who ran the hotel, and especially the eldest son, 20-year-old Earle Jr., were suspicious of this lone stranger who appeared early in the morning in clothes not tailored in a North American style when no bus or train service operated. The father, Earle Sr., was convinced by his son's suspicions because of the peculiar smell about the stranger. Mr. Annett had been to sea in his youth and always remembered the pungent odour that permeated every-thing in the hold of a ship after a few weeks at sea. Janowski had been in *U-518* for forty-four days. He and all of his belongings were ripe with what the Germans called "submarine stink," a combination of diesel fuel, briny damp, and the cumulative aroma of the bodies of over fifty men in crowded quarters who could not bathe because of the limited amount of fresh water produced by the distillation equipment. The Annetts' suspicions were heightened when the stranger paid in oversize pre-1935 banknotes of a kind that the new Bank of Canada, founded in 1937, had been withdrawing from circulation and replacing with its own smaller notes. The stranger, a heavy smoker, also dropped a box of matches, which Earle Jr. saw were manufactured in Belgium, an occupied country. Young Annett followed the stranger to the train station and, when the train arrived, went aboard to find the naval shore patrolman who travelled on each train to keep order among the military personnel. The patrolman had no authority over civilians, so he and Earle Jr. rushed to La Maison Blanche, another hotel where members of the local Quebec Provincial Police detachment had rooms.[33] The detectives required some convincing. U-boat operations so near the coast had heightened spy fever among the population, and the police had been bombarded by reports of suspicious characters and incidents, including one from the Annett family, that had proved groundless. Ultimately persuaded something might be amiss, the policemen confronted Janowski on the train and, on seeing anomalies in his identification cards, asked to examine his suitcase, at which point he admitted he was a German officer.

The policemen kept Janowski at La Maison Blanche that night. He claimed to be the captain of a U-boat and that he had come ashore for a short reconnaissance. It was evidently to sustain that story and avoid execution as an agent that he played out a drama at 11 PM that night. "The prisoner ... started up in bed with a cry of 'My God! My boat!' and ... rushed to the window. The detectives on guard state they had clearly heard a sound like diesel engines. They had then taken the prisoner down to the local wharf prior to midnight and ... used a flashlight to signal to seaward to endeavour to get an indication if a submarine was in the vicinity. After some time they gave up the attempt, although they stated they had seen lights which may have been a reply from seaward; they then took the prisoner to the court house where he was locked up in a cell ... apparently as a precaution against possible rescue by a landing party from a submarine." The detectives were so surprised that they did not initially alert two naval officers whom Commander German, the commanding officer at the Gaspé base, had sent the previous afternoon as soon as the Quebec police reported Janowski's apprehension. The naval officers, on belatedly learning of Janowski's performance, spent the rest of the night on the wharf vainly looking for signs of a submarine, but were powerless to do much else: the telephone service at New Carlisle was shut down until 8 AM. When the officers were then able to report to Commander German, he dispatched two Bangors, HMCS *Red Deer* and *Burlington*, to search Baie des Chaleurs.[34]

During the first three years of the war, German had worked in naval intelligence with Captain Brand in Ottawa, and it was likely Brand's high opinion of Commander German that resulted in his being selected to command at Gaspé. On learning of Janowski, German appealed for expert help, and his old office in Ottawa put Lieutenant Wilfred Samuel, RNVR, on the train for Gaspé. Samuel, who was in his mid-fifties and in civilian life a businessman in England, had done part of his education in Germany and was fluent in German. During the First World War, he had served in the British Army and later the air force. His passion was history; he published articles in professional journals. The language and research skills resulted in his becoming a specialist in U-boat intelligence when he came out for service at the outbreak of the Second World War. Early in 1941 the Admiralty sent him to assist Brand. Samuel took over the censorship of—and information gathering from—letters of German naval personnel among the enemy prisoners of war whom Britain sent to Canada for internment. Samuel was also responsible for interrogation of German navy prisoners, work that he had done in the U.K.[35]

While Samuel was on his way to Gaspé, the Department of Justice intervened and ruled that the prisoner should be turned over to the RCMP, not the navy. Samuel got off the train in New Carlisle where Inspector Clifford Harvison of the Mounties had arrived by car, and the group drove back to Montreal, with Harvison and Samuel grilling Janowski. Janowski, fearful for his life, was devious and skilful, but Samuel's questioning soon cut through his claim to be a submarine officer.

The RCMP, enlisting the help of British intelligence, attempted to run Janowski as a double agent. From an apartment the RCMP set up in Montreal, he made radio contact with his controller in Germany; the RCMP hoped to capture additional agents that he said would be following him to carry out sabotage. It became evident from the cautious responses from Germany that his controllers were probably aware that he had been captured—he may have tipped them off by code words in his messages—and the RCMP and British intelligence shut down the operation. Harvison escorted him to Britain in August 1943 so that he could serve as a source for British intelligence.

Dean Beeby's *Cargo of Lies*, an account of the case based on his determined and ultimately successful efforts to gain access to the large RCMP file, highlights the amateurism of the Canadian police. They had had little experience of intelligence operations and none with such a hardened—and desperate—agent. The naval intelligence side of the story is a bit different, and perhaps not surprisingly so. Samuel had considerable experience in the interrogation of German prisoners and had access to banks of information gathered by Canadian and British naval intelligence which helped guide his questions and verify answers. Samuel, in a series of interviews, assembled what has proved from the German sources now available to be a generally accurate picture of *U-518*'s full operation, including the frustrating vigil off the Strait of Belle Isle by *U-518*, the names of *U-518*'s and *U-183*'s commanding officers (Wissmann and Schäfer), the diversion of the U-boats on the coast to pursue an ocean convoy, Wissmann's decision to go to Wabana, and an account of that attack. Samuel's further research in his files about *U-518*'s commander provides an example of how British and Canadian intelligence collected personal details about the U-boat crews to assist them in interrogations; casual references to such details by interrogators encouraged prisoners to talk in the belief that the Allies already had fuller information than in fact was the case. "It seems likely that WISSMANN is Friedrich-Wilhelm WISSMANN of the 1935 entry, who is known, from a [prisoner of war] letter intercepted at Ottawa, to have attended a party on 9.12.41, at the U-boat base of La Pallice, with 12 other U-boat officers, mostly commanders or prospective commanders." Wissmann was indeed taking his commander's course at that time. One early practical result of the interrogation came from Janowski's description of the manner in which *U-518* was able to dodge the sweeps of the coast defence searchlights at Wabana; the naval staff in Newfoundland alerted the army about the need for proper tactics, that is, exposure at irregular intervals and with varying sweeps.[36]

U-518, after creeping submerged out of Baie des Chaleurs in the early hours of 10 November, followed the shipping route north to Gaspé and patrolled off the port. En route, at periscope depth, Wissmann had a jolt when the "boat is sucked upwards and comes clear of the surface.

Nothing to be seen. Thank God." The same thing happened again two-and-a-half hours later, "despite correct measures by the Engineer Officer."[37] These unusual events, he concluded, were probably the result of "very pronounced variations in water density." U-518's experience may explain why Drummondville, during her attacks on U-132 in July, and Georgian, in her encounter with U-517 on 21 September, reported that the submarines broke surface when the U-boat commanders were endeavouring to make an underwater escape.

The submarine had only one opportunity to shoot during its patrol off Gaspé, at a tanker in the early hours of 15 November. Wissmann had to fire hastily, as the tanker was about to enter into the waters covered by the searchlights of the Gaspé defences; the two torpedoes missed and did not detonate. Wissmann departed through the Cabot Strait on 17 November. "Only ships sailing singly may be encountered," Wissmann concluded, "and ... these proceed close inshore or else seek shelter in bays, so that the prospects for successful attack are only very limited and are more or less a matter of luck." His experience off Gaspé, he noted, confirmed what Schwantke had recently reported about the river and Rasch about the Cabot Strait and its approaches.

Meanwhile, U-183, which headquarters had cleared for the St. Lawrence River on 29 October, did not enter the gulf. The boat was a new one, commissioned in April 1942, on its first war cruise. The commanding officer, Kapitänleutnant Heinrich Schäfer, was older, the same age as Hoffmann of U-165 and Rüggeberg of U-513, who had entered the navy in 1925, the same year as Hoffmann and, like him, had transferred to submarines only in 1941. Unlike Hoffmann and Rüggeberg, Schäfer was cautious. He must, Dönitz concluded after this first patrol, "act more tenaciously and aggressively."[38] Late on the afternoon of 4 November, U-183 was west of Saint-Pierre and Miquelon, south of Newfoundland, in the outer approaches to the Cabot Strait when the boat suddenly had to dive when "three aircraft" appeared. Schäfer was nervous about detection by aircraft while he was close inshore, and this unpleasant surprise may explain why he then headed south along the Atlantic coast of Cape Breton. He attacked a lone freighter and a Sydney to Halifax convoy, but hit no targets; he described the convoy as "strongly protected." By that time, 6 November, one of the propeller shafts was making a loud knocking noise which increased Schäfer's caution, and he made no other attempt to go into the gulf. This was not just the end of the 1942 campaign in the St. Lawrence. U-boat headquarters had no intention of renewing operations in the future because of the disappointing results of the fall offensive.

TEN

The Politics of Defence and the Ultra Top-Secret War, November 1942– December 1943

The Canadian forces shut down the U-boat assault in the St. Lawrence. The U-boats' run of sustained success was less than three weeks in duration, 31 August to 16 September. Thereafter, the five U-boats that reinforced the effort found conditions so unpromising that they withdrew. This result was achieved in spite of the defending forces' lack of training, equipment, and adequate numbers of ships and aircraft. The forces were modest because the Canadian military and the government held firm to higher Allied and national goals despite alarming and tragic losses within sight of the country's shores.

Yet the armed forces had little sense of accomplishment—quite the reverse. Because of the Allied inability to decrypt the German radio signals generated by the more sophisticated Enigma machines introduced early in 1942, there was no intelligence that suggested the defences had driven out the U-boats. For Canadians, the defining moment in the campaign was *U-69*'s destruction of *Caribou*, and there was no way of knowing that the submarine struck this heavy blow even while retreating from the effective defences in the gulf for the safety of open ocean.

In fact, the armed forces faced a public relations disaster. Word of the *Caribou* spread like wildfire in Newfoundland and on the mainland. In view of the loss of 136 people, the navy released full information immediately to spare the families of survivors and those lost the agony of uncertainty. The timing could not have been worse. The navy had just announced the loss of *Carolus*, and under the censorship regulations this official notice freed the press to publish their own coverage. The stories the journalists had gathered emphasized the terror experienced by people on shore as the roar of depth charges and the glare of star shell cut through the night and stressed the fact that the sinking had taken place only 320 kilometres from Quebec City—the enemy's deepest thrust towards the country's heartland.

On 14 October, the day *Caribou* went down, the nationalist Quebec newspaper *L'Action Catholique* published "Ce qui se passe en Gaspésie" ("What is happening in the Gaspé"), the first of a series of three articles on the *angoisse collective* (collective anguish) of the coastal communities who witnessed the summer battles, helped survivors struggle ashore, and tended their wounds. The pieces reported the more plausible rumours among the wild stories circulating in the villages along the river and around the gulf. These painted a devastating picture of the armed forces: incompetent, undisciplined, and mired in red tape. Shame at this embarrassing record, the articles concluded, not the need to keep military information from the enemy, was the real reason for government censorship. People were living in the grip of a cover-up, a denial of truth that made the tragedies unfolding along the shores still more difficult to bear.

Joseph W.G. Clark, director of public relations at the Wartime Information Board, hurried a copy of the first *L'Action Catholique* article to Charles Power, minister of national defence for air, and Angus Macdonald, minister of national defence for naval services, urging that they carry out immediate investigations to collect information that might counter the specific allegations against the air force and the navy. The board, established only in August, was an expanded and reorganized version of the Bureau of Public Information. These changes were a response to widespread criticism of the government's "business as usual" approach to public information and in particular the utter failure in Quebec of the campaign for a "yes" vote in the plebiscite on conscription. The architect and head of the new board was Charles Vining, a former lobbyist with close ties to the newspaper community, who urged the cultivation of influence with opinion leaders through personal contact.[1] Vining agreed with Clark that open rebuttal of the *L'Action Catholique* articles would only stir up more controversy. Better to privately provide the information gathered by Power and Macdonald to the journalist Edouard Laurent, and to other newspapers to inspire more factual coverage. As Clark explained to the ministers, "We consider it significant that Mr. Laurent is, or has been, associated with Mr. Duplessis," leader of the Union Nationale opposition in Quebec.[2] He and his party were virulently opposed to federal government authority in general and in particular to the large scale of support to Britain, threatening as it did to require conscription.

Academic psychologists who urged "scientific" information management through such methods as public opinion polling had already warned about the corrosive effects of the wild U-boat rumours circulating in Quebec and the Maritime provinces. One of these, still told in Halifax, was that German submariners captured when their unnamed U-boat was sunk in the mid-Atlantic were found to have ticket stubs from the city's popular Capitol movie theatre in their pockets—it was that easy for the Germans to make clandestine visits ashore while operating along

Canada's weakly protected coasts. Systematic collection and analysis of rumours like this, the psychologists argued, would highlight the kind of public information needed to counter defeatism. J.T. Thorson, the minister responsible for the Bureau of Public Information, had in May 1942 established the Committee on Morale, a group of the leading university psychologists, to carry out such studies.

Early in September 1942, morale committee member J.A. Irving, professor of psychology at the University of British Columbia, produced a report based on rumours collected in May through August.[3]

In recent weeks the loss of a small number of ships in the St. Lawrence River and Gulf has been admitted. These admissions have led to the wholesale development of rumours that indicate wide-spread fear and anxiety.

These rumours express the wishes and hostilities of the social groups through which they are transmitted. They may, therefore, be taken as an indication of the emotional state of the people among whom they are current.

On the one hand, rumours exaggerating shipping losses express anxiety and fear—a very great threat to security. On the other hand, rumours denying that there have been any shipping losses whatever express a mood of smugness and complacency ...

During the height of the debate over Bill 80, rumours denying that any ships at all had been sunk developed very extensively. At the same time other rumours express a pronounced hostility to the British, in their assertion that if ships had been torpedoed it was by British submarines [to stimulate a greater Canadian war effort].

The rumours gravitating around the case of Squadron-Leader Chevrier bid fair to make him a legendary figure. The attribution of an heroic death to him—a French-Canadian—is countered by other rumours charging gross neglect of duty and drunkenness to English-speaking air-officers during the night of the sinkings at Cape-Chat. These sharply contrasting rumours point up the racial antagonism existent in Canada.

The rumours regarding Germans in our midst follow a pattern that became very familiar in the last war. The Halifax theatre-ticket stubs story is a direct "revival" of an old act. The story about German officers mixing freely with girls in a St. Lawrence River town, and entertaining them, suggest that Nazi submarine officers can come and go at will ...

... Newspapers always try to give exact figures—so do the rumour-mongers ... [W]hen a statement is expressed in terms of exact figures, it seems to carry ... a superior certainty, and it passes without question. The rumour about exaggerated shipping losses must be true since exact figures are given! "Figures do not lie!"[4]

The appearance in October of the "Ce qui se passe en Gaspésie" series in *L'Action Catholique* amply confirmed Irving's conclusion: "The prevalence of these rumours on the Atlantic coast indicates that the people in Eastern Canada are not satisfied with the formal system of communication. The radio and the newspaper do not satisfy their need for information. They also distrust the statements made by Cabinet Ministers or other spokesmen of the Government regarding shipping losses." Further confirmation came from a public opinion poll held on 19 September 1942 by the Canadian Institute of Public Opinion, the Canadian arm of the American Gallup organization. The question "Do you feel that Ottawa is giving the people enough information about the sinkings in the St. Lawrence River?" yielded a "no" response from 58 percent of Quebec respondents, as compared to only 40 percent in the whole national sample.[5]

Laurent's pieces reflected not only the anxiety among the coastal population. Adélard Godbout, premier of the Liberal administration in Quebec and an essential ally of the federal government, sent translations of all three articles to Mackenzie King with the endorsement that they were "the most complete and objective articles I have seen ... [The] confidence of the local inhabitants ... is severely shaken."[6] Mackenzie King brought Godbout's letter to the Cabinet War Committee, where it triggered sharp discussion: "Macdonald was most unreasonable about the criticism of the French-Canadians concerning the sinkings in the St. Lawrence and Gulf. St. Laurent was very outspoken and pretty hot at any reference which implied that Godbout was not co-operating in every possible way."[7]

Angry as Macdonald was at Godbout's alarmist tone—a display of incomprehension about Quebec that helps account for the cooling of the naval minister's relations with Mackenzie King—he could only agree with Godbout's request for fuller information. The Quebec premier wanted to be able to reassure the population and also facilitate fuller co-operation between provincial agencies involved with defence measures, such as the police. Macdonald and Power had the naval and air staffs investigate the specific instances of confusion, incompetence, and indiscipline among the services cited in the *L'Action Catholique* articles and prepare detailed reports which in almost every case disproved the allegations. The results of the investigations, together with a full explanation of the defence arrangements for the St. Lawrence, went to Godbout.[8]

In the management of the media, the government was low key, as the Wartime Information Board recommended. Moreover, Louis St. Laurent, as the senior minister from Quebec and Mackenzie King's Quebec lieutenant, played a leading role. He took the rebuttals of the Laurent articles prepared by the naval and air staffs to the editor of *L'Action Catholique*.[9] Later, on 2 November, when making a speech in Quebec City that was well attended by the national media, St. Laurent mentioned that he had heard rumours that forty ships had been sunk in the St. Lawrence. He had consulted Macdonald and the real number was "between 10 and 15."[10] Macdonald followed up with his own press conference in Ottawa on 24 November: a total of fourteen ships had been sunk in the river and the western gulf, and another six in the Cabot Strait and the Strait of Belle Isle.[11] The defence department also issued positive press releases, including a detailed account of the two attacks on submarines in the gulf by Flying Officer R.S. Keetley's Lockheed Hudson: "'It was a beautiful attack,' said [navigator, Flying Officer P.G.] Hughes, '... He was really clipping it off, but I don't think he spotted us until we were on his tail and opened fire. While he was trying to crash dive I could see the tracers splashing all about the conning tower. It was just like the 24th of May.'"[12]

Controversy flared up again early in March 1943. At the opening of the Quebec legislature, Onésime Gagnon, the Union Nationale member for Matane on the south shore of the river near the scene of some of the heavy losses, claimed that "more than thirty" ships had been sunk by the Germans in the St. Lawrence in 1942, not twenty as Macdonald himself had again recently stated in a speech at the Canadian Club in Quebec City. Godbout responded with the assurances he had received from the federal government, but Duplessis retorted that "Ottawa never did anything to prevent sinkings in the St. Lawrence but to censor letters."[13] The issue took hold again. In Ottawa the Conservative opposition supported MPs Roy and Pouliot's calls for a formal inquiry into the events in the St. Lawrence; members in both the federal and provincial capitals brought up stories of armed forces negligence or incompetence that had been published by Laurent in *L'Action Catholique*.

Macdonald responded in the House of Commons on 10 and 17 March 1943, now fully deploying the material the military staffs had gathered months earlier in their investigations of Laurent's stories. He took particular care in responding to charges that he was lying about the number of ships sunk in 1942. As he explained in a message to the Admiralty asking permission to name the British ships lost, Gagnon's allegations had caused "tension in Quebec, despite minister's denial ... It is considered essential to restore now Quebec confidence before this year's expected enemy action develops."[14] Macdonald then went ahead, before the British responded, and listed the names of all twenty ships sunk. He was forthright, admitting there was no definite information about *Raccoon*'s fate and that another ship, the twenty-first, had been lost—*Frederika Lensen*, which had made port but then proved unsalvageable.[15] The British in fact refused permission to name ships on grounds that it would "give information useful to the enemy,"[16] but the signal arrived two days after Macdonald had spoken.

Macdonald did not hesitate to draw comparisons between the Canadian and larger Allied navies. Many more vessels had been sunk in the Gulf of Mexico than in the St. Lawrence, but no American suggested that "the whole United States fleet should be diverted from its other duties to protect the Gulf of Mexico."[17] He also referred to the failure of the British forces to prevent the escape of the German battle cruisers *Scharnhorst* and *Gneisenau* from Brest in France through the English Channel back to Germany:

> The St. Lawrence River, at the point furthest inland where an attack was made last year, is thirty miles wide. This is almost like the open sea. It is wider than the straits of Dover between England and France. If the great British navy with all its experience and skill and strength and devotion to duty ... was unable to prevent certain great enemy ships from going through the straits ... is it to be wondered at that we cannot guarantee complete immunity to ships in the river St. Lawrence?[18]

Early in December 1942, the armed forces chiefs of staff had created a powerful tri-service committee to review what had happened in the St. Lawrence and coordinate plans by the military and other agencies for 1943. A top priority was to address the government's concerns about the alarm in Quebec. The chair was Air Vice-Marshal N.R. Anderson, the air force's senior planner.[19] Captain Lay, who as the navy's director of operations worked out the assignment of warships to the various commands and bases, was also a member. Although Anderson's committee reported through the chiefs of staff, guidance came directly from the Cabinet War Committee, which also reviewed Anderson's reports and authorized quick action on the military committee's recommendations. During the first six months of 1943, the Anderson committee was the centre of what today would be called an "all of government" approach to the defence of the St. Lawrence. Its work involved public information, collaboration with provincial agencies, and relations with the civilian population as much as strictly military issues. Although scarcely recognized in existing accounts, the committee was a significant example of the government's initiatives in the latter part of 1942 and early 1943 to exercise more effective control over the country's war effort.

AS LARGE AS THE ST. LAWRENCE loomed in public relations, more than ever it took a distant back seat to the battle in the Atlantic in terms of the country's war effort. During the winter of 1942–43, Canada's maritime forces faced their greatest crisis of the war. That crisis, unlike the setbacks in the St. Lawrence, unfolded in the remote vastness of the central ocean and in top-secret messages and meetings, far removed from public or journalistic scrutiny. Indeed it was something of a public relations success story, because it was kept quiet at the time and for many years after the war. The first published account of the difficulties that would have most deeply embarrassed the government was naval historian Marc Milner's *North Atlantic Run*, which only appeared in 1985.

The U-boat force, at its peak wartime strength of more than 200 combat-ready submarines, concentrated against the transatlantic convoys at mid-ocean, at the moment when escort forces were weakest. Escorts and aircraft had been diverted to protect the North American coast, the Caribbean, and the large convoys from Britain to the Mediterranean that sustained operation Torch, the Anglo-American offensive in North Africa. As losses to the strategically vital trans-ocean convoys mounted, the Canadian effort, always shoestring because of the desperate Allied calls for help since 1940, came under critical scrutiny by British and American authorities. In an urgent search for greater combat effectiveness, the U.S. and British navies proposed to integrate the Canadian operating forces more completely under Allied command, thereby sidelining Canada from direction of the Battle of the Atlantic. That would have been a major setback for Canada. Participation in higher-level command had become one of the navy's and the government's leading priorities because of the enormous Canadian commitment and contribution to a struggle whose battles unfolded on the country's ocean frontier.

Nevertheless, the heavy losses to SC 107 while under a Canadian escort group early in November 1942, together with comparable losses to the slow westbound convoy ON 154 under another Canadian escort group in late December 1942, left the navy no choice but to comply with a British request to transfer all four mid-ocean Canadian groups to British control on the run between Britain and the Mediterranean in early 1943. The idea was to have the Canadian groups mentored by expert British staff, while better equipped and trained British groups filled in for them on the tough Atlantic crossing.

In the event, the Canadian groups performed well on the run to the Mediterranean, while convoys in the Atlantic continued to suffer heavy losses. Clearly the difficulty in the Atlantic was not the exhaustion or lack of training of the Canadians, but the need for more escorts. The British hurried back three Canadian groups to the mid-ocean force by April 1943; the fourth group never did leave for the Mediterranean run. While reinforcing the Atlantic in the spring of 1943 by every means possible, the British also organized some of their best anti-submarine warships into five new "support groups." These were so named because they did not escort convoys, but rather rushed to support any convoy that intelligence showed was at risk of attack. The Americans adopted the more brutal term "hunter-killer" groups, which described what these new units did: use their excellent detection equipment and weapons to search out and destroy U-boats in the big groups or "wolf packs" that the Germans were using to overwhelm the six or eight warships escorting each of the ocean convoys.

Other U.S. and British proposals in the winter of 1942–43 were to streamline or even unify command of the whole Atlantic theatre. One initiative was to cut Ottawa out of its role in gathering and analyzing U-boat intelligence for the waters north of New York and to centralize intelligence operations for the whole of the western Atlantic in Washington. Related proposals were to combine the patchwork of Canadian and U.S. naval and air force commands in Newfoundland, the Canadian east coast, and the northeastern U.S. seaboard under a senior U.S. headquarters. The result if these changes came into effect would be to squeeze Canada out of the significant part in direction of the Atlantic war that Ottawa had successfully demanded in view of the essential contribution of Canada's seaports and air and naval forces. Admiral Nelles and the Canadian naval staff stoutly resisted the British and American initiatives, with support from the RCAF. The air force, a young service like the navy and, like the navy, anxious to establish a national and international presence, had previously insisted on the independence of Eastern Air Command from control by the navy. In early 1943, however, the prospect that both Canadian east coast organizations would become subordinate parts of a U.S. or British super command instantly dissolved the air force's resistance to the unification of national command. In February 1943, Rear Admiral Murray at Halifax became the commander-in-chief of all of Canada's maritime forces on the Atlantic, including Eastern Air Command and its 1 Group in Newfoundland and both the Atlantic Coast and Newfoundland naval commands. This change, a dramatic one in view of the long-standing determination by both the navy and the air force to assert their independence as distinct armed services, was a matter of closing national ranks to show the British and the Americans that Canada could streamline its organization without the intrusion of a new American or British super command.

Admiral Nelles at the same time persuaded U.S. Admiral King that the most efficient means of rationalizing the multiplicity of commands in the western Atlantic was for the United States to withdraw from control of Allied convoy operations north of New York and turn that responsibility over to Admiral Murray, who would function as a senior Allied commander. Most U.S. naval escort forces had withdrawn from the northern ocean early in 1942, leaving the bulk of the escort work to the Canadian and British navies, and the historic ties between these Commonwealth forces had always ensured effective co-operation. There was an important trade-off. The United States had begun to run its own transatlantic convoys during the fall of 1942 for the American part of operation Torch in North Africa and to build up forces in Britain for the combined bomber offensive and, ultimately, the invasion of occupied France. Under existing arrangements, control of these U.S. convoys passed to the Royal Navy at mid-ocean, just as control over the northern convoys passed from the U.S. admiral in Newfoundland to the Royal Navy. If the Canadians and British took full control over the northern routes across the Atlantic, as Nelles proposed, then the United States could exercise complete control over their own convoys on the more southerly routes.

Admiral King liked Nelles' suggestion, and it became the basis for the Allied Atlantic Convoy Conference that King hosted in Washington in March 1943. The broad results were those that the Canadians had recommended. On 30 April 1943, Admiral Murray at Halifax became commander-in-chief, Canadian Northwest Atlantic, a new Allied theatre in which Murray controlled all Allied convoy operations; Murray was the only Canadian officer to command an Allied theatre in either of the world wars.

At that moment, the tide was turning in the battle on the convoy routes. Between 29 April and 24 May 1943, an all-out push by the U-boats against convoys in the central ocean sank nineteen ships, but at the cost of seventeen submarines lost to Allied attacks, most by the Royal Navy's support groups, convoy escorts, and the aircraft of the RAF's Coastal Command.[20] Britain's desperate measures to strengthen the forces in the central Atlantic and concentrate reinforcements as quickly as possible around threatened convoys paid off. On 24 May, Dönitz pulled back his submarines from the transatlantic convoy routes to regroup and re-equip. The U-boats would nevertheless remain a formidable force, using new methods and technology to strike again on the main convoy routes and in the very mouths of Allied harbours right till the war's end. Allied countermeasures, much as they grew in scale and sophistication, could not destroy the U-boat force completely. The Allies' maritime forces were, however, able to contain the submarines so that they never seriously impeded the flow of supplies from North America to Britain and to the Allied forces that later liberated Europe. Canadian escort and maritime air forces played a major part in achieving that result, not least in the St. Lawrence.

There was much more involved in Murray's new Allied command role than Canadian officers initially realized. At the end of 1942, British code breakers had begun to crack the German U-boat signals generated by the four-rotor Enigma machine introduced at the beginning of the year. In a deepening intelligence partnership, the United States joined the effort; only American resources could quickly produce the massive and complex computing machines and thousands of specially trained personnel needed to analyze messages enciphered in the four-rotor version of Enigma. One immediate result of the Washington conference of March 1943 was that Canada became a partner in the Ultra secret, among the most closely guarded of the Second World War. Although the navy had regularly received British estimates of German U-boat positions based on decrypts of German Enigma messages, the source of this intelligence had always been carefully disguised for security reasons as the product of direction-finding bearings, radar contacts, or sighting reports. Now Canadian naval intelligence was to receive the decrypted messages as soon as they were available and immediately join British and U.S. submarine tracking experts in analyzing and interpreting the information. British experts swept into Ottawa and Halifax to spur on the expansion and reorganization of intelligence and communications staffs necessary to receive and employ the decrypts with the necessary speed and security measures.

In Ottawa, the Foreign Intelligence Section was expanded into a new division of the naval staff, the Operational Intelligence Centre, and Commander de Marbois was promoted to captain. Lieutenant Commander J.B. McDiarmid, RCNVR, head of the centre's submarine tracking room, received an Ultra indoctrination course in England. He joined in daily discussions by secure undersea cable and landline with his counterparts in Washington and London to assess the latest decrypted German signals. McDiarmid, typically of officers engaged in high-level intelligence work, was a language specialist, in his case ancient Greek and Sanskrit. He entered the navy shortly after obtaining his Ph.D. at Johns Hopkins University and continued with a distinguished academic career after the war. He was for many years a professor and chair of classics at the University of Washington in Seattle.[21]

Changes on the east coast were equally important. At Halifax, Eastern Air Command headquarters and the headquarters of the navy's Atlantic Command were joined into a large "area combined headquarters," on the model pioneered by the British. Admiral Murray and Air Vice-Marshal G.O. Johnson, who was now under Murray's direction and commanded all maritime air forces in eastern Canada and Newfoundland, shared a common operations room with a single plotting map that showed all current air, naval, and shipping movements in the northwest Atlantic. Previously the naval and air staffs at Halifax and St. John's had each organized operations on the basis of their analysis of intelligence obtained locally and from the intelligence section in Ottawa. Starting in July 1943, the Operational Intelligence Centre in Ottawa became *the* clearing house for all information. This measure ensured that every scrap of evidence—directional bearings on possible U-boat transmissions, U-boat sighting reports, and any unusual occurrences—would immediately be collated and checked against the latest Ultra decrypts by the most expert analysts to create the fullest and most accurate picture possible as quickly as possible. The Ottawa centre dispatched a message code-named "Otter" each evening that defined search areas for the following day for each submarine believed to be within the Canadian command area.

The new intelligence resources and the integrated command structure provided the means for the east coast commands to implement more generally and effectively the "offensive tactics" that 113 Squadron had pioneered at Yarmouth and in the Gulf of St. Lawrence in August and September 1942. Eastern Air Command also acquired the means to strike much further out into the Atlantic and eliminate the gap in coverage between Newfoundland- and Iceland-based aircraft where U-boats had been able to organize group attacks, as in the assault on SC 107. In the spring of 1943, 10 Squadron RCAF at Gander was finally able to retire its heavily worn twin-engine Douglas Digby bombers and re-equip with fifteen Consolidated Liberator four-engine bombers. These big machines—the wingspan was thirty-three metres, and unloaded they weighed more than fifteen tonnes—were fast, with a cruising speed of 370 kilometres per hour. They had been modified with increased fuel storage among other features to give them "very long range" capability.[22] The Liberators could and on occasion did patrol across the whole breadth of the Atlantic.

The improved and timelier intelligence available also made possible the assignment of warships to offensive searches in close co-operation with the air patrols. Still, with the perennial shortage of warships in the Canadian command, the navy's first priority continued to be escort of convoys, the most basic and essential protection for merchant shipping. Indeed, the effect of the elevation of Murray as an Allied commander-in-chief and the important operational reforms that resulted was to allow the Canadians to secure the northwest Atlantic more efficiently and thus commit still greater forces to overseas operations in support of Britain's overstretched Royal Navy. The increased emphasis on current signals intelligence about enemy movements as the basis for operations underscored the need for fast, dependable communications which did not exist in the sprawling land mass of eastern Canada. Inspired and successful as the improvised use of commercial telephone circuits had been in the offensive air sweeps undertaken in 1942, these desperate measures proved the need for large-scale redevelopment of existing facilities. The leading requirement was for secure landlines or cable capable of carrying a high volume of traffic between the main headquarters at Ottawa, Halifax, and St. John's and the naval and air operating bases.

Early in 1943, the Department of Munitions and Supply created a new crown company, Defence Communications Limited, to carry out this work. The new company drew on the expertise available in Canadian National Railways, one of the country's leading telegraph companies. The project was immediately expanded to take in the coastal areas around the Gulf of St. Lawrence on the recommendation of the Anderson committee. Poor communications, the committee noted, had not only hindered military operations in 1942, but played a large role in shaking the confidence of the civilian population. Along the shore of the Gaspé Peninsula, there was an incomplete patchwork of local telephone and telegraph companies, most of which did not have twenty-four-hour service; on the north shore of the gulf, there were no landlines at all. Several of the stories reported by Laurent in *L'Action Catholique* concerned the frustration and fury of civilians who, in endeavouring to report suspected submarines or survivors of attacks, could not get a message through to authorities for hours. For example, the Aircraft Detection Corps was the network of volunteer civilian observers recruited by the air force who had instructions to report anything unusual whether related to aviation or not; however, they sometimes discovered that the police or military authority they finally reached had no knowledge of the organization and the procedures for quickly passing information to reporting centres. Defence Communications worked with the small telephone and telegraph companies to expand their service and create dedicated circuits that ensured civilians could quickly reach the Aircraft Detection Corps centres. On the north shore where there was no infra-structure of landlines to build upon, Defence Communications greatly improved radio communications for civilian observers.

The bitter struggle on the ocean routes and in European waters to ensure the continued containment of the U-boats set tight limits on the forces that could be allocated to the St. Lawrence for 1943. The air force would again carry a large share of the burden. The naval commitment would include only warship types that were not capable of long-range ocean escort—Bangors and Fairmiles. Indeed, to allow the RCN to allocate all of its corvettes to ocean duties, the Royal Navy lent a group of its own anti-submarine trawlers to the Canadians. The trawlers, approximately the same size as Bangors but slower, with a top speed of only twenty-two kilometres per hour, were suitable for local escort duty.

The RCN, fearing a still greater German assault in the St. Lawrence in 1943, wanted to continue the closure of the gulf to ocean shipping. That was not possible, responded the British Ministry of War Transport. Overcrowding of the single rail lines to Halifax and Saint John had resulted in those ports failing to dispatch sufficient quantities of timber and grain, commodities desperately needed in the United Kingdom that were normally shipped from the St. Lawrence. Under this pressure, the Canadian staff finally agreed that twenty-two ships a month could enter the St. Lawrence to load these bulky cargoes.

Canadian caution came from the lack of high-grade intelligence in 1942 that would have revealed the effectiveness of the defences and the fact that the Germans had withdrawn. Ironically, the fortuitous receipt of excellent, but incomplete, information about enemy operations in 1942 deepened Canadian pessimism. On 21 November 1942, when *U-517*, with Kapitänleutnant Hartwig still in command, was four days out of port in France on the beginning of her next mission, she had the bad luck to encounter an anti-submarine aircraft from the carrier HMS *Victorious* that fatally damaged the U-boat. All but one of the crew got clear and were rescued by the destroyers that screened the carrier.

British interrogators could get little from Hartwig, "a cold and calculating young Nazi, filled with ideals of false heroism and unyielding devotion to his Führer."[23] Other members of the crew provided a wealth of information, however. The final interrogation report was twenty-one closely printed legal-sized pages that included an account of the St. Lawrence operation that in some respects is fuller than Hartwig's own log, and, as we now know, is confirmed in most details by the log. The report shows the enormous strain endured by the crew as they narrowly escaped destruction on several occasions and how damage inflicted by these near misses rendered the submarine ineffective during the last three weeks of its mission. These, however, were not the points that struck Canadian officers who received the report. The salient facts were that much of the carnage in the St. Lawrence had been caused by a single submarine that was on its first combat mission, with a crew who were mostly inexperienced, under a captain who was making his first cruise in command. The submarine had pressed on in the face of attacks by what the crew calculated was a total of 145 depth charges dropped by aircraft and warships. As Admiral Murray commented in an appreciation of the gulf situation that served as the basis for the 1943 plan, "Especially in view of the successes last year of U-517, we must expect increased U-boat activity."[24]

The interrogation report had an equally great, and similar, influence on the historical record of the St. Lawrence campaign. It was one of the few pieces of high-level intelligence available to the navy's own historical section. Joseph Schull made the report the centrepiece of his chapter on the St. Lawrence in *Far Distant Ships*, relating the highlights in some detail in the course of more than five printed pages. He concluded, on the basis of the report, that although the defending Canadian forces were "not inactive," they were "meagre and unsuccessful."[25]

In the spring of 1943, the armed forces hurried the dispatch of forces to the St. Lawrence. Fears of a repetition of *U-553*'s entry before full clearance of the winter ice in May 1942 were apparently confirmed when on 24 April a shore observer at New Carlisle, Quebec, reported he had seen a submarine about two kilometres off shore in the Baie des Chaleurs. Eastern Air Command thought the report should be "viewed with reserve," perhaps because of the spy and submarine fever that had been rampant at New Carlisle since Janowski's landing there a few months before. Nevertheless, the report could not be entirely discounted, because ice was already clearing from the gulf. The command diverted two aircraft from Dartmouth to investigate and ordered 119 Squadron at Sydney to deploy detachments of its Lockheed Hudsons to Chatham, New Brunswick, and Mont Joli.

Stronger evidence that a submarine might be present came in a message from the Admiralty on 29 April 1943. Mail censors in Britain had intercepted a letter sent from Germany through the Red Cross to a prisoner of war held in eastern Canada and decoded a message hidden in the innocuous text. A U-boat would be arriving in early May to "wait quote 'in place described in your letter of September' unquote for several days." The Admiralty guessed that the pickup might take place in the Gulf of Maine.[26] Naval Service Headquarters, possibly thinking of the Janowski operation whose failure was still apparently unknown to the Germans, drew its own conclusions and flashed a warning to the east coast: "There is reason to believe that a U-boat will enter the Gulf of St. Lawrence ... presumably to land or pick up enemy agents. May four [sic] is most likely date but there is no indication of place operation will take place."[27] On 30 April fishermen reported a submarine off the north shore of Prince Edward Island, and that same day a training aircraft sighted what appeared to be the wake of a submarine in the Northumberland Strait to the west of the island. These areas came under heavy surveillance in the following days.

U-262, under the command of Oberleutnant Heinz Franke, had indeed entered through the Cabot Strait on the night of 27–28 April on a mission under sealed written orders to rescue prisoners of war who were to have escaped from Camp 70 near Fredericton.[28] Franke, 27 years of age, had entered the navy in 1934 and served in the battle cruiser *Gneisenau* before transferring to U-boats in 1940. This was his first combat cruise in command. No doubt he was hoping even more than usual for good luck; he had taken command of the submarine shortly after her first combat operation in September 1942 had been cut short by a British air attack that badly damaged the submarine.

U-262 was in fact the "back-up" U-boat, and Franke received word to open the instructions only when the boat originally assigned, U-376, failed to report. In a heroic effort, described in detail in historian Michael Hadley's *U-boats against Canada*, U-262 pushed into pack ice that clogged the Cabot Strait. When unable to make headway in the ice on the surface, the boat dove under it. This was an extremely risky manoeuvre because of the submarine's limited underwater endurance. Franke then carried on, despite serious damage, displacement, and bending of the watertight doors to three of the torpedo tubes. Inside the gulf, he was able to keep clear of the "drifting fields of ice," but as he cruised south of Anticosti towards Gaspé on 30 April to 1 May, he saw no vessels whatever: "[t]hese waters are like a morgue." He was killing time until he was due at the rendezvous point, North Point, Prince Edward Island, which ironically was midway between the positions of false sightings reported to the Canadian command on 30 April. When during the late morning of 2 May, U-262 arrived, submerged, off North Point and made a preliminary search of the area by periscope, he found it "very suspicious" that three aircraft "are flying surveillance precisely above my rendezvous position." He allayed his worries with the thought "it is also possible that there is a training base not too far away in Nova Scotia." He was right on both counts. There was still special coverage of the area around Prince Edward Island because of the earlier sightings and the Admiralty warning. Although air patrols were becoming more wide ranging through the gulf when nothing further turned up after the rather tenuous sightings on 30 April, both training bases now operating in Prince Edward Island, at Charlottetown and Summerside, were saturating the shipping routes north of the island with a total of over a hundred flights per day.

Franke hovered to the east of North Point until 6 May. He surfaced and closed the coast only at night—the RCAF undertook no night operations—and pulled out into deep water before first light. The prisoners had not in fact escaped, and Franke, seeing no signal at the rendezvous, reluctantly pulled away and passed out of the Cabot Strait on the night of 7–8 May.

On the morning of 7 May, less than twenty-four hours after *U-262* departed from the North Point area, one of the season's first "escorted groups" of shipping passed through the waters where the submarine had been lurking. In this case it was a single merchant ship, *Essex Lance*, on her way from Quebec City where she had been repaired following severe damage by one of *U-165*'s torpedoes in SQ 36 on 16 September 1942. The escort was three corvettes recently completed in St. Lawrence shipyards for the U.S. Navy, USS *Alacrity*, *Haste*, and *Intensity*. Whether because of ice conditions or the intelligence about a possible U-boat in the gulf, the group was routed through the Northumberland Strait, south of Prince Edward Island, rather than north of the island. As the ships passed North Point into the western entrance of the strait, the newly commissioned warships tried out their guns and anti-submarine weapons, the latter producing spectacular upsurges of water in the shallow seas. Soon after, a 119 Squadron Hudson from Chatham, New Brunswick, arrived to supply cover. This dramatic action made an indelible impression on observers ashore, vividly remembered by some of them more than fifty years later. Thus was born the local story that there had been a battle in which a U-boat was destroyed by a combined air–sea strike force. The story gained credibility when in 1985 Michael Hadley published the first full account of Operation Elster and revealed that *U-262* had waited in precisely the waters where the "battle" had taken place. Although Hadley's account showed that *U-262* had returned home, it also mentioned that the first boat assigned to the mission, *U-376*, had disappeared and never been accounted for. Could the submarine in fact have come in to the rendezvous and been destroyed or lost? The German and Allied records now available show that the possibility is infinitesimally remote, but the existence of an outcrop on the seabed off shore, which one diver in the late 1980s reported looked like the wreck of a submarine, has kept the story alive.[29]

In fact, the Admiralty's warning of 29 April tentatively listed two U-boats, with question marks, that might be connected with the mysterious mission. It may have been this suggestion that brought the Canadian services to estimate in mid-May—a full week after *U-262* had departed—that there might be two submarines in the gulf. Certainly there had been enormous activity with no fewer than eleven reported submarine sightings from 14 to 16 May alone, many of them north of Prince Edward Island and south of the Magdalens.[30] All the sightings were by fishermen or by training or transport aircraft, and the pilots of 119 Squadron had doubts as they scrambled to respond to report after report. "On each and every occasion a large school of porpoise was met ... all the crews ... were staunchly of the opinion that all of these sightings were probably porpoises diving as it presented a very realistic picture of a submarine if the crews were not familiar with submarine silhouettes ... The complete Gulf was covered by our a/c [aircraft] for 36 hours without let up and nothing was sighted except schools of porpoises."[31] The crews were almost certainly right, and Eastern Air Command headquarters later concluded that the events in 1942, intensive press coverage, and, rather paradoxically, the large efforts by the air force and other agencies to recruit and train civilian observers in coastal areas while also providing good communications to military establishments for civilian observers had "impressed the local inhabitants so that every possible image is reported as a submarine."[32]

Frustrated as the aircrews might have been, emergency searches in quick response to civilian reports were not a bad thing from the government's perspective. On 8 June 1943, the prime minister himself rose in the House of Commons to review what had been done to improve the defence organization in the St. Lawrence for the coming shipping season. The statement was in fact the government's response, crafted over the preceding months, to the articles that had appeared in *L'Action Catholique* in October 1942 and more particularly Godbout's warning that they accurately captured the mood of the population. Mackenzie

King's statement, which was supported by a tour for the press of the military bases in the St. Lawrence,[33] bore all the hallmarks of the government's more comprehensive and strategic approach to public information.

Mackenzie King described the work coordinated by Air Vice-Marshal Anderson's committee. He highlighted the greatly improved communications, close co-operation with Quebec authorities, recruitment of thousands of new civilian observers for the Aircraft Detection Corps, and the special training in identification of U-boats by four travelling teams who were working with municipal leaders and parish clergy in all parts of the region.

> To get action, any resident of the region who sights a submarine ... has only to go to the nearest telephone and ask the operator for "Aircraft Detection Corps" ...
>
> A point which I wish to emphasize is that the report goes from the reporting centre directly to operation units which not only have full authority but the duty of taking instant action ... without waiting for instructions from any higher authority ...
>
> Thus, the moment a report is received at an operational station, planes of the air force that are already in the air on anti-submarine patrol are directed by radio to the spot where the U-boat was sighted. Ships of the navy already on patrol in the same area are also directed by radio to the location ... Meanwhile other planes at aerodromes in the district and additional naval vessels at local harbours are in constant readiness.[34]

Mackenzie King's statement coincided with the end of serious controversy over the defence of the St. Lawrence. The information campaign and activity by the training teams and communications construction crews throughout the region contributed to that result. Even more so did the absence of any sinkings by the enemy during the 1943 season. There was a bit of irony in these good results, considering the widespread charges of incompetence and negligence that helped produce the larger defence effort of 1943. The expansion of the organization of civilian watchers, together with projects by the military to place shore-based army radar along the Gaspé coast, were designed to prevent U-boats from moving quickly on the surface to search out shipping and then take up submerged ambush positions ahead of the vessels. Yet, as the Allied commands did not realize as a result of the blackout of Ultra intelligence, the more aggressive tactics of the RCAF and RCN surface escorts had achieved that result during the last three weeks of *U-517*'s mission and against the submarines that followed in October 1942.

Although the new intelligence resources that Canada acquired in the spring and summer of 1943 were an enormous asset, their capabilities must not be exaggerated. That was especially the case for coastal waters. The Germans, rightly suspecting that the Allies were taking bearings on submarine radio signals to direct land-based anti-submarine aircraft with devastating effect, reduced radio transmissions to the barest minimum when U-boats approached closer than a few hundred kilometres from the North American coast. Moreover, submarines that had to linger at a specific point on the coast to land agents or lay mines sailed with sealed written orders that were opened only when at sea to avoid possible leaks through radio security lapses. That was why radio intelligence played only a small part in the operations against *U-262* even though the Allies had regained the ability to decrypt U-boat signals.

The only other U-boat to enter the gulf in 1943 was also on a clandestine mission, which again produced little radio intelligence but good material from more traditional methods. This was a second effort by the German submarine service to rescue members who had been captured and were held in Canadian camps. The focus was Camp 30 at Bowmanville, Ontario, whose inmates included some of the most distinguished U-boat officers, including Otto Kretschmer, the "ace" whose *U-99* had been destroyed by British forces in March 1941. Kretschmer was the leader of the scheme, which the prisoners coordinated with U-boat headquarters through coded messages in letters and documents hidden in the bindings of books mailed through the Red Cross. Canadian naval intelligence appears to have picked up the trail through the censorship of the German letters and brought in the RCMP for assistance. Technicians in the RCMP crime detection laboratory discovered documents in the bindings of several suspect books, including Canadian currency, forged Canadian identity papers, and a map showing precisely where a U-boat was to pick up the escaped prisoners, at Pointe de Maisonnette on the south shore of the Baie des Chaleurs. The technicians made photographic copies of all the papers they found and replaced the originals by rebinding the books. This was a delicate process; the original covers had disintegrated in the unbinding because of the low quality of the paper, so the police technicians had to find comparable paper and reprint the covers by a photographic process. The books were delivered to the prisoners so that they would not suspect the plan had been discovered and alert U-boat headquarters by a message the censors might not detect.

Admiral Murray's staff in Halifax organized an elaborate plan to trap the U-boat when it came in to shore. The army moved two of its mobile anti-aircraft radar sets to positions hidden off to either side of the landing place so the equipment could sweep the surface of the water to detect the submarine when it surfaced at night. The job of coordinating the operation on the beach went to Lieutenant Commander D.W. Piers, a young but extremely experienced officer of the regular navy who had recently come ashore to a training position at Halifax after nearly two years of constant service on convoy escort; as commanding officer of the destroyer HMCS *Restigouche*, he had been the senior officer of the ill-fated SC 107. Piers recalled in an interview in 1982 that the Admiralty discouraged the RCN's initial plan to attempt to capture the submarine with a boarding party led by a German-speaking Canadian naval officer. Thus the final plan was to destroy the enemy vessel by a hunting group of warships that would hang back offshore until alerted by Piers that the submarine had been detected, by sight or the army radar, when it surfaced to take on the escaped prisoners of war. Piers and his party set up an operations room, with communications, in a lighthouse near the landing spot, using as a cover the explanation that they were searching for coastal-waters areas suitable for warship training.

On 6 September, the Admiralty submarine-tracking room reported to its American counterpart—and presumably the Canadian one as well, although those records have not yet come to light—that U-boat headquarters had sent unreadable special "officer" cyphers to three U-boats outward bound in the eastern Atlantic. These were often an indication that the submarine was undertaking a secret mission, such as landing agents or planting mines, and the Admiralty asked for the Americans' views as to whether this might be linked to an "operation which appears possibly aimed at Canadian area."[35] By 20 September the Admiralty, probably on the basis of the fuller information the Canadian navy and the RCMP had gathered from the intercepted documents, were confident that one outward-bound submarine was headed for the St. Lawrence and identified U-536 as one of the boats assigned to special missions, but believed that she had been assigned to the Caribbean.[36]

On 24 September, Admiral Murray's headquarters ordered HMS *Chelsea*, one of the British (ex-U.S.) four-stack destroyers assigned to help the Canadian western Atlantic escort force, the corvette HMCS *Lethbridge*, and the Bangor HMCS *Granby* to pick up sealed written orders at Mulgrave on the Canso Strait entrance to the gulf. On 26 September, the warships began a patrol off the headlands of Baie des Chaleurs, far enough out, they hoped, not to alert the U-boat, but close enough to rush towards Pointe de Maisonnette when Piers' group signalled that the submarine had been detected. The ships were met off the bay by HMCS *Rimouski*, a corvette that had been fitted with an experimental lighting system that matched the ambient light conditions in poor visibility and at night so that the vessel showed little silhouette against the sky and was nearly invisible.

Already in late August, the German prisoners' original plan for a breakout from the camp at Bowmanville had been thwarted. On 28 August, guards discovered that there was a space between the ceiling and the roof of one of the large camp buildings. Above the ceiling, a great deal of earth was carefully spread between the rafters. In a search of the building, the guards found the entrance to a tunnel, concealed under a clothes cupboard, but the tunnel was only forty feet long and had evidently been abandoned. There was a ready explanation: in the spring of 1942, the barbed wire in the vicinity of the tunnel had been moved further out, making the project impractical. After two days of searching, the guards found the entrance to a second tunnel, which was a masterpiece of engineering. The prisoners had cut through the concrete floor of one of the rooms to create a removable slab that nearly perfectly concealed the entrance.

> The Tunnel was about 2 ft [61 centimetres] high and 22 inches [56 centimetres] wide, and at the deepest point about 12 ft [3.7 metres] under the surface, shored in places with the lumber taken from the roof of this same building, and fitted with electric lights, with bits of wire stolen from various Buildings, and the usual slush boxes for hauling out the dirt, which was then pulled up in sacks and dumps ... above the ceiling ...

The tunnel, seventy-six metres long, extended forty-six metres beyond the outer wire, and was within forty-six metres of a depression in the ground outside the camp where the escapees would have been concealed from the sentries.[37]

The German officers were nothing if not organized, disciplined, and tenacious. Wolfgang Heyda, formerly commanding officer of *U-434* (sunk in December 1941), escaped on the night of 24 September by scaling a power pole, rigging a sling chair over the power line, and pulling himself "hand-over-fist" to another power pole outside the barbed wire.[38] The guards soon discovered someone was missing at the head count before lights out, but could not identify who it was. The prisoners answered for each other's names and some of the air force and navy officers had exchanged uniforms to increase the confusion.

Photographs in the prisoners' files did not resolve the difficulty as many of the photographs were "now two or three years old" and there had been "great change ... in the appearance of many of the Prisoners during their confinement." Late on 25 September, after the prisoners had been held on parade for five hours, they agreed to answer to their correct names, and it was only then that the Canadian authorities were able to determine that it was Heyda who had escaped.[39] An all-out hunt had already begun on the twenty-fourth, and the authorities now released Heyda's photograph and description to the press for general publication. Even though the Mounted Police and the military knew where he was headed, Heyda led them, as they admitted to the press, on an "870 mile [1400 kilometre] chase."[40] He duly appeared on the beach at Pointe de Maisonnette, where he was picked up by the army personnel attached to Piers' group, probably on the evening of 27 September. Piers recalled:

> About eight or nine o'clock in the evening, as we were having a little game of cards in the lighthouse, we got a telephone call from the sentries on the shore that they had a man who said he was a tourist ... so they brought this man in and I took one look at him and, of course, immediately I knew that he was one of the German U-boat captains ... In fact, I had received a cryptic message indicating that the Germans had attempted a mass break out of ... Bowmanville and one of them, in fact, had got away ...
>
> He feigned annoyance, said he was a tourist ... He showed me a letter indicating that he had been discharged from the Royal Canadian Engineers in order to join Northern Electric company to make anti-submarine equipment to help the allies in the U-boat battle in the North Atlantic, which was rather a neat little twist of things. He showed me a letter of thanks from the Chief of the Naval Staff for the good work ... I could see that it was all hand done, but beautifully done. The only thing that was really wrong—the signature was absolutely nothing like Admiral Nelles' which I happened to know ...
>
> He showed me his ID card. Once again, beautifully done exactly like the Canadian model but all done by hand ... [O]f the real give-aways, the one that broke him down to admit that he was a German

U-boat Captain, was the fact that he had some German Red Cross chocolate in his bag ...

Piers recalled that, even as he was questioning Heyda, word of a surface contact came from the Army radar sets, and he called in the warship group lurking off the mouth of the bay.[41] Piers' memory is confirmed by the log of HMCS *Lethbridge*, which shows that the warships increased speed and headed into the bay shortly after midnight on 28 September in response to a radar contact.[42] Although the warships found nothing, the timing of the evident appearance of the U-boat was precisely what intelligence had predicted. Confirmation came later on that same day when British intelligence intercepted instructions from U-boat headquarters to *U-536* to listen for a radio signal from station "Kiebnitz"—German for the plover seabird—on a particular frequency at certain times of day until 6 October. The reference to "Kiebnitz," which was the code word for the operation to rescue the escapees, baffled Allied intelligence.[43] The important thing, however, was the timing of the message, which showed that the Allies' information about the timing of the mission was correct.

In fact, *U-536* had come in to Pointe de Maisonnette "some days earlier" than 26 September. Since the submarine was commissioned in January 1943, she had been commanded by Kapitänleutnant Rolf Schauenburg, and this was the second mission for both the boat and her commanding officer. At 30 years of age, Schauenburg was older than many U-boat officers; he had joined the navy in 1934 and transferred to the submarine arm in 1941.

On entering the Baie des Chaleurs, *U-536* never showed anything more than the top part of the conning tower even in the hours of darkness. Early on the night of 26–27 September, Schauenburg left the confines of the bay for a respite in the gulf where he could fully surface and recharge the batteries, having the sea room to dive and escape if there were any sign of Allied forces. As he was departing the bay at periscope depth, he sighted the Canadian warships and concluded the operation was blown. He dropped to the bottom and on the night of 27–28 September began a slow, quiet, submerged run; the submariners could clearly hear the warships in the vicinity. Thus, the radar contact by the Army equipment was almost certainly a false one; the U-boat had not broken the surface for some twenty-four hours. The U-boat crew heard depth charges, but they were distant.[44] *Chelsea*'s group, with support from Bangors and Fairmiles from Gaspé, kept up the watch off Baie des Chaleurs until 8 October.[45]

Only eight weeks later, on the night of 19–20 November 1943, the Royal Canadian Navy participated in the destruction of the submarine on the far side of the Atlantic. *U-536* joined a pack attack on the combined Gibraltar–U.K. convoy MKS 30/SL 139. Canada's first "support group," EG 6, which had been strengthened by the British frigate HMS *Nene*, reinforced the convoy. *Nene* and the corvette HMCS *Snowberry* made an asdic contact on the submarine, and *Nene*'s depth charges blew her to the surface about 800 metres from *Snowberry*, which raked the submarine with gunfire. *Nene* and the corvette HMCS *Calgary* joined in the bombardment. Only Schauenburg, two other officers, and fourteen seamen from the submarine's crew of fifty-five survived.[46]

Schauenburg passed his account of the failure of the rescue mission back to U-boat headquarters through another captured officer who was repatriated to German hands early in January 1944. According to this account, when *U-536* entered the Gulf of St. Lawrence "the coast was bustling, a lot of shipping traffic."[47] *U-536* may have encountered the many small vessels that were never convoyed and kept close to shore, but she may also have sighted ocean-going freighters. Naval Service Headquarters had cancelled the Sydney–Quebec and Sydney–Corner Brook convoys two weeks before the submarine's arrival and allowed the vessels previously included in these series to sail independently. The Canadian staff was exceedingly reluctant to reduce the defence measures in this way, fearing a fresh run of losses such as those suffered in 1942, with the political consequences of alarm among the coastal population that had so profoundly concerned the government. The British insisted, however. They urgently needed to make the most efficient use of the St. Lawrence by avoiding the delays of convoy in order to expedite grain and timber shipments that had been tied up by the inadequate rail service to Halifax and Saint John and the shortage of stevedores at those ports.

The fact that the Canadian authorities did not restart gulf convoys during *U-536*'s mission indicates that the high quality of intelligence about her clandestine task gave confidence she would keep her head down and not attack shipping. Still, such was Canadian caution after the experiences of 1942 that neither the RCN nor the RCAF reduced the forces assigned to the gulf, but continued to track shipping closely so that convoy could be reinstituted at short notice. That happened with the sailing of QS 68A from Quebec City on 20 October, which put into Gaspé on the twenty-second to pick up additional eastbound merchant ships. *U-536* had dropped out of sight, and Ultra revealed that U-boat headquarters had given her freedom of action to attack shipping after her rescue mission.[48]

At this same time, there was other striking evidence of the Germans' continuing interest in Canadian waters and their ability to act. *U-220*, operating with sealed orders and under radio silence, had slipped in to lay a widely dispersed field of sixty-six magnetic mines south of St. John's on the night of 9–10 October. Local minesweepers quickly located one of the mines on 11 October, and Ultra soon provided fuller information when the U-boat broke radio silence to report success in laying the field. Nevertheless, the Germans had achieved complete surprise. Even as the minesweepers carried out the difficult and very slow task of clearance, on 19 October two steamers in a Wabana–Sydney convoy hit mines well beyond what had been believed were the southern limits of the field. Both ships went down, one of them, *Penolver*, with the loss of twenty-seven of her crew of forty-one, adding a chapter to the sad record of heavy casualties suffered by the ore ships that shuttled between Wabana and Sydney.

A new threat appeared during the last week of October, when Ultra revealed that *U-537* had completed a clandestine operation off the coast of Labrador. She was within reach of the Strait of Belle Isle, and the submarine trackers in Ottawa warned of the danger that she might press through to the gulf as *U-517* and *U-165* had done to initiate the worst period of the assault in 1942. The likelihood of that danger passed when Ultra revealed that U-boat headquarters gave unusually specific orders for *U-537* to operate off St. John's. The operating area assigned the boat was large, several thousand square kilometres, but it was well defined enough for Admiral Murray to make the east coast commands' first attempt at a concerted coordinated air–sea search. Bad weather and the challenge of new procedures required to precisely coordinate ships and aircraft in the systematic search of vast ocean areas resulted in gaps in coverage. Nevertheless, 1 Group aircraft located and attacked the submarine twice, on 31 October and 10 November 1943. The damage inflicted was slight, but the U-boat's captain was so alarmed at being located in the open ocean that he operated very cautiously and accomplished nothing.

The story of *U-537*'s mission off Newfoundland came to the attention of the Directorate of History at National Defence Headquarters in 1981 in unusual circumstances. Franz Selinger, a retired engineer in Germany who was researching wartime automatic weather stations, contacted Alec Douglas, director of history, with information about the installation of such a station on the far northern tip of Labrador by *U-537*. (German meteorologists needed readings on westerly weather fronts to supply forecasts vital for military operations in Europe.) One of my early assignments was to look into the voyage of the submarine, and this work confirmed Selinger's research. Douglas and Selinger travelled to Martin Bay, Labrador, on the Canadian Coast Guard icebreaker *Louis St. Laurent* in the summer of 1981 and discovered the rusted remains of the station. The Coast Guard crew lifted the components with the ship's helicopter and delivered them to the Canadian War Museum, where the refurbished station is now on display.[49] I was deputy director at the museum when the remains were refurbished in 2002 and helped with the research. In Ultra intelligence material released by the United States in the late 1980s, I discovered that Allied submarine trackers had immediately known about the station in 1943. Unusually for such a secret mission, U-boat headquarters had incautiously referred to the "weather apparatus" in a signal that had been promptly decrypted. From other information, however, Allied intelligence concluded that the reference was to a floating station installed in a buoy that had been dropped somewhere in northern waters.[50] Still, the purpose of U-537's mission had not been unknown to the Allies; rather, that knowledge had been locked up for decades in the "Ultra Top-Secret" archives.

During 1943, the course of the war turned decisively to the advantage of the Allies. The Anglo-American campaign in North Africa, which began with operation Torch in November 1942, ended in complete victory with the surrender of over 250,000 German and Italian troops early in May 1943. The Anglo-American forces in the Mediterranean, now including the 1st Canadian Infantry Division, then took the island of Sicily in July and August 1943 and landed in mainland Italy early in September. On the eastern front, the Soviet Army smashed what would prove to be the final German offensive, at Kursk, in July 1943 and began to push the German forces back to the west. Forces and supplies were all the while being built up for the final campaigns against Germany, including the liberation of northwest Europe beginning with the invasion at Normandy, France, in the spring of 1944 by British, Canadian, and American ground forces.

The victory over the U-boat group—or wolf pack—attacks against the main transatlantic convoys in May 1943 ensured the timely delivery of vastly increased supplies and forces from North America that sustained the widening Allied offensive. The supply lines were kept open, however, only by constant vigilance by Allied anti-submarine forces that continued to expand in scale and grow in technical and tactical sophistication. Not only were new submarines entering service to replace those lost, but the U-boat arm pursued technical and tactical innovation in repeated efforts to regain the initiative.

Although the U-boats that came into Canadian and Newfoundland coastal waters in 1943 were on clandestine missions and accomplished little, their ability to evade the increasingly effective Allied anti-submarine forces held out the prospect of renewed success in 1944. Single U-boats— protected from Allied countermeasures by the fact that they could operate in radio silence and run submerged in daylight hours in contrast to the surface patrols and constant signalling essential to group operations on the high seas—might once again be able to ambush shipping close to Allied shores and ports. This is what the U-boats endeavoured to do, with a remarkable tenacity that resulted in some of the most intense combats of the war with Allied warships, not least those of the Canadian navy.

ELEVEN

Supporting the Liberation of Europe, April 1944–May 1945

When the ice cleared from the St. Lawrence at the end of April 1944, the armed services and civilian shipping agencies were making an all-out push to hurry cargoes overseas for the long-awaited Allied invasion of France, which would take place at Normandy on 6 June 1944. The landings were a success, but the need for supplies from North America was unrelenting and ever increasing. Determined German resistance delayed the Allied breakout from the Normandy area until the end of August and in the fall and winter stalled the advance in the Low Countries. Hopes for ending the war in 1944 vanished as both the western Allies and the Soviet armies pressing against the eastern borders of Germany had to launch fresh mass offensives early in 1945.

Canada's navy continued to expand dramatically, and the service took on greater commitments for the protection of transatlantic shipping and new roles in European waters. The navy achieved these important results by keeping the forces in the country's home waters at a bare minimum as it had done in 1942 and 1943, even though the U-boat force made a fresh assault on Canadian waters during the late summer and fall of 1944. In the St. Lawrence, that assault matched the scale of the offensive in 1942. This time, however, because of the pressing needs of the campaign in Europe, Canada had no choice but to increase the flow of overseas shipping through the St. Lawrence. Even so, the Canadian forces prevented the U-boats from ever gaining the initiative.

The navy grew from about 28,000 personnel in January 1942 to 48,693 in January 1943 and kept expanding to 71,549 in January 1944 and 87,141 in January 1945.[1] The continued rapid growth was largely the result of the new wave of escort construction started during the crises of 1942 in yards at Quebec City, Montreal, the Great Lakes, and Victoria, British Columbia. The ocean-going fighting fleet nearly doubled in size from late 1943 to the end of the war. Notable additions included seventy-two frigates. This new type of vessel was a development of the corvette design expressly intended to meet the needs of extended ocean escort duty. At 1400 tonnes displacement and a length of 91 metres, frigates were 50 percent larger than corvettes and, with a top speed of thirty-five kilometres per hour, somewhat faster, a critical advantage in anti-submarine operations. In addition, forty-three improved corvettes and twelve Algerine escorts, a development of the Bangor design into a much larger and more ocean-capable ship, joined the fleet. Shipbuilding, based on expansion of the few firms that had existed before 1939, and the creation of new yards by companies with experience in heavy engineering and construction became one of the largest wartime industries in Canada. Production also included 400 ocean-going merchant ships in addition to hundreds of tugboats, barges, and small vessels.

Virtually all of the navy's important new forces were committed overseas, where Britain's Royal Navy needed them to augment its flagging resources. Britain had begun to run short of manpower by the fall of 1943 and needed help to meet its obligations for the impending liberation of northwest Europe which started with the D-Day landings. Beginning in January 1944, the RCN's mid-ocean groups took over all responsibility for the escort of north Atlantic convoys between Newfoundland and the British Isles to relieve the British groups for invasion duties. Many of the most experienced ships from Canadian waters and the mid-ocean force deployed to British waters to join in the invasion and were replaced in convoy duty by new ships; 100 Canadian warships crewed by 10,000 personnel would participate in the invasion.

Expanding commitments overseas raised challenges in Canadian home waters, especially the St. Lawrence. How were more merchant ships to be loaded and dispatched to Britain and Europe more rapidly when the local escort forces on the Canadian coast were barely adequate for the existing schedules? During the early months of 1944, British shipping authorities made it clear that the St. Lawrence ports would have to be used in the coming season to lift essential bulk cargoes, particularly timber that could be most efficiently loaded at various smaller ports close to the producers and grain, through the excellent terminals at Montreal. Overloading of the rail system in eastern Canada and the northeastern United States meant it would be worth the extra shipping capacity needed for the voyage up the St. Lawrence, but only if the ships moved promptly without delays for convoy.

The answer was to do again what had been done in response to British pleas during the 1943 season: to let gulf shipping proceed independently, without convoy, so long as there was no immediate threat. On 29 April 1944, a new system came into force for coastal convoys in the Canadian–Newfoundland area. Building on the experience in the St. Lawrence in 1943, Captain Brand's Trade Division at headquarters divided Canadian and Newfoundland waters into twelve zones, one of them being the whole of the St. Lawrence gulf and river. If intelligence gave no indication that a submarine was present, shipping was free to move independently and by the quickest route. The most important intelligence was the Ultra decrypts of tasking orders to submarines.

Ultra in fact reinforced the caution of Canadian commanders and particularly their concern about a fresh disaster in the St. Lawrence. Decrypted German signals revealed renewed interest in the North American seaboard. From February 1944, there were usually one or two submarines on extended patrols in Newfoundland and Canadian waters. They took such care to evade defences and the decrypted tasking messages from U-boat headquarters designated such broad operating areas that extended searches in these vast expanses of ocean by the air force and naval groups came up empty-handed. The U-boats very seldom inflicted losses, only when shipping had the bad luck to stumble into the submarine's crosshairs. On the night of 5–6 May 1944, however, the victim was the new frigate HMCS *Valleyfield*. Ignoring warnings (based on Ultra) to avoid a suspected U-boat operating area south of St. John's, the big warship passed close by *U-548* when she was submerged in a field of ice fragments that shielded her from detection. The torpedoes broke the frigate in half and she went down quickly; only 38 of her company of 163 survived.

One challenge that the Canadian planners did not face in preparing for the real danger of similar ambush tactics was the public alarm and political controversy of 1942 and early 1943. Onésime Gagnon, in the Quebec legislature on 11 February 1944, referred to his charges of the year before that forty ships had been torpedoed in the St. Lawrence in 1942. He did so, however, to claim credit for the successful defence in 1943 when "no ship was torpedoed." Gagnon recalled that the demands he and other members from the region had made early in the war for improved communications and transportation facilities had been ignored. Finally, in the wake of the disasters in 1942, the federal government had acted, notably with the expansion of the telephone services, and thus made the defences effective. He now urged Godbout's government to join with federal authorities in improving road and rail service essential for economic growth. Perrault Casgrain, member for Gaspé-Nord, joined the debate to urge that the Gaspé naval base be made a permanent establishment, part of a redevelopment of the harbour that should include new commercial port facilities.[2]

In the Quebec provincial election, called by Godbout on 28 June 1944 for 8 August, the adequacy of defence in the St. Lawrence was not an issue. The Union Nationale under Duplessis narrowly defeated Godbout's Liberals, but Mackenzie King was philosophical. Although Duplessis continued to attack the federal government on the issue of conscription and an excessive military effort overseas, more extreme attacks by a new party, the Bloc Populaire created in the wake of the 1942 conscription crisis, brought Duplessis to position himself as a moderate.

A FRESH OFFENSIVE IN Canadian waters on the scale of the attacks in 1942 took shape as a result of the Allied landings at Normandy. There was more than a faint echo of events in August and September 1918, when U-boats had run amok amidst the fishing fleets off Cape Breton, Newfoundland, and southern Nova Scotia even as the Canadian Corps led the victorious Hundred Days offensive that resulted in the armistice of 11 November 1918. In late summer 1918, however, the tide was just turning in the Allies' favour, and there was still hope that the U-boats could seriously hinder the arrival of Allied reinforcements. By 1944 there was no such possibility. The objective was thus to "tie down" the thousands of ships and aircraft and tens of thousands of personnel in the Allied anti-submarine forces to prevent them from being reassigned to the assault on the German homeland.[3]

Technology was the key to the new German effort. During the U-boats' periods of greatest success from 1940 to early 1943, they had depended upon fast surface runs to locate shipping and get into favourable attacking positions, a tactic countered by improved radar on escorts and more comprehensive air patrols. "Schnorkels," air tubes on extendable masts, were the German answer. With the mast fully deployed, the U-boat could run about five metres below the surface almost indefinitely on its powerful air-breathing diesel engines which took in fresh air and vented exhaust fumes through the small masthead, a metre or less above the surface. The first schnorkel-equipped U-boats proved themselves during the Normandy invasion. Allied air and surface anti-submarine forces inflicted heavy losses on conventional U-boats, but the schnorkel boats were able to strike and escape. The small schnorkel mastheads were all but invisible to the naked eye and radar. Without an initial visual or radar contact on a surfaced submarine before it dived, asdic proved almost useless. Its range was too limited—a maximum of 2000 or 3000 metres in the best of conditions—for an effective search of a large area, and conditions in the complex coastal waters of the English Channel greatly diminished the performance of the equipment, although not so dramatically as was often the case in the St. Lawrence.

Submarines running on schnorkel could, more effectively than the submarines that had patrolled off Nova Scotia and Newfoundland in the first part of 1944, hide submerged for days or even weeks close to ports and in constricted waters where targets would come to them. Experience in 1942 suggested that the Gulf of St. Lawrence offered precisely these conditions, as Dönitz explained to the commanders of the U-boats he dispatched there:

1) Area was evacuated in 1942 in view of the appearance of A/C [aircraft] and location [radar], which impeded battery charging [by making surface runs impossible]. But area is easily navigable with "schnorchel" (see also English Channel experiences). Make approach unseen. Advisable to pick up traffic in the narrow sounds, in particular in BA 30 [the St. Lawrence estuary].

...

3) Traffic situation 1942 ...

A) Very heavy traffic, almost without exception in small weakly escorted convoys.

...

4) Countermeasures: situation in 1942

Medium to strong air with and without location [radar], especially after being observed. Sea countermeasures relatively slight and unpractised. Location conditions [i.e., by sonar] very unfavourable to the enemy, as there is marked underwater density-layering. Find out about this density-layering, even for considerable depths, before a depth-charge hunt starts.

In general: Main defences by A/C. Sea defences little to be feared. Situation thought to have altered little since 1942. Land location stations [radar] are to be assumed.

...

IV) Surprise appearance after so long a time promises wonderful success if defences are slight.[4]

This message is particularly noteworthy because it explains that Canadian defences forced the U-boats to abandon the St. Lawrence in 1942. It also shows the extent to which the Germans underestimated the effectiveness of the naval escorts as a result of the poor sound conditions. As we have seen, commanders mistook naval attacks for air attacks because they could not hear the escorts moving through the water.

U-802, newly equipped with schnorkel, set out from Lorient in France on 16 July. She had been commissioned in June 1943, and this was her second combat cruise. Her first, in late January to early May 1944, had been to the Halifax approaches where she had escaped extended hunts by the Canadian air force and navy, but had to lie low and was able to sink only one small steamer during the long mission. Her captain from December 1943 was Kapitänleutnant Helmut Schmoeckel, who had joined the navy in 1936 when he was 19 years old and served in large warships until entering U-boat training in 1942.

On 20 July 1944 headquarters ordered Schmoeckel to make for the St. Lawrence, with an initial approach point off central Nova Scotia about 330 kilometres southeast of the Cabot Strait. Allied intelligence decrypted the message within twenty-four hours.[5] Thus the submarine tracking rooms in Ottawa, Washington, and London were able to plot *U-802*'s estimated progress across the Atlantic as accurately as U-boat headquarters. The escort aircraft carrier USS *Bogue* and her supporting group of destroyers was northwest of the Azores in the eastern Atlantic, and the U.S. Atlantic Fleet assigned the group to follow *U-802*'s track towards her approach point south of Newfoundland. (The Royal Navy had in 1941 operated the first small "escort" carrier for convoy defence, but others only became available from U.S. shipyards, in the spring and summer of 1943, when they were assigned to the new "support groups" to hunt U-boats.)

While *Bogue*'s group closed from the east, on the evening of 9 August, Admiral Murray at Halifax launched a search of the estimated track starting about 830 kilometres southeast of St. John's, falling back according to the estimated advance of the submarine, about 150 kilometres a day. Murray committed his only naval support group, the newly formed EG 16 of five recently completed frigates, which swept, line abreast, back and forth across the estimated track. It was not an adequate response; two groups at least would have been needed to cover the wide area through which the submarine might pass in the vast approaches south of Newfoundland. EG 16, moreover, was still in the midst of shakedowns. It had completed basic work-ups only in late July, and there were shortcomings in the radar and communications equipment that had yet to be addressed; in truth the hunt for *U-802* was a training cruise.

As was so often the case in the Canadian area, Murray relied on the air force to make up for the shortage of warships. From 9 to 13 August, the big Liberators from Gander, supported by Cansos from Torbay near St. John's, flew thirty extended missions. These flights covered at intervals of two to four hours all parts of the entire probability zone of approximately 180 kilometres by 180 kilometres.

The Allied estimates of *U-802*'s track were excellent, almost identical to the plot at U-boat headquarters: both agreed that the submarine would pass south of Cape Race on 13 August. The search ordered by Admiral Murray should have been right on target, but the estimates were wildly wrong. Schmoeckel had had a difficult crossing: "Remarkably active air surveillance over the whole outward-bound route. Apparently my whole route was followed by enemy DF [radar]." Instead of making fast runs on the surface at night, Schmoeckel, in his fear of air attack, ran on schnorkel for all but a few hours; he also headed far to the south of his assigned track—the one U-boat headquarters and Allied intelligence were both following—presumably to keep clear of land-based aviation in Newfoundland.

During Schmoeckel's brief surface run on the night of 11–12 August, his radar detector picked up nearby emissions, and he was certain he had been located. His position already compromised, he made a radio report the next night, as was standard practice. No ship or aircraft had in fact made a contact, but the Allies took accurate bearings on his radio signal. This placed the boat 900 kilometres to the southeast of the position estimated by U-boat headquarters and the Allies—far out at sea on the latitude of New York rather than south of eastern Newfoundland on the latitude of Halifax. So greatly had Schmoeckel deviated from his assigned course that for a few hours, before decryption of Schmoeckel's signal revealed his identity, the Allied submarine trackers believed a second previously undetected submarine was following *U-802* by several days.

Murray ordered EG 16 to the southeast to patrol the track from the new position towards the Cabot Strait, but a succession of weather fronts prevented any but a few air patrols in support on 14–19 August. *Bogue*, further out at sea, was able to manoeuvre clear of the fronts and launch her aircraft, one of the great advantages of carrier aviation. On the night of 18–19 August, about 550 kilometres southeast of St. John's, a searchlight-equipped aircraft from *Bogue* sighted the U-boat during her brief surface run and made a depth charge attack that was wide of the mark. Then, at midday on 20 August, one of *Bogue*'s pilots was startled to see a fully surfaced U-boat in broad daylight, which initial reports identified as *U-802*, the only submarine known to be in the area. The aircraft damaged the submarine with rocket and depth charge attacks, and additional aircraft swarmed in soon after. Depth charge attacks forced her to the surface, and the aircraft made attacks with wing-mounted unguided rockets—a new weapon for air strikes on surface targets—until the German crew began to abandon ship; American warships rescued forty-two survivors from the crew of sixty.[6]

The war diary of Admiral Murray's headquarters reveals how rapidly and flexibly high-grade intelligence was applied to the control of shipping in order to minimize delays. It was a striking contrast to the situation in 1942 when the earliest dependable information about the presence of a submarine was usually its first attack on shipping. On 12 August, when it looked like *U-802* was approaching the Cabot Strait, Murray ordered recommencement of the Sydney–Quebec convoys for the first time since the fall of 1943. Murray promptly cancelled the convoy order the next day: the bearing on *U-802*'s radio report showed she was still far out at sea. On 19 August, following *Bogue*'s unsuccessful attack on *U-802*, Murray closed the routes between Halifax, Sydney, and St. John's to independent shipping. *Bogue*'s successful attack the next day evidently eliminated the only known U-boat in the Canadian area, and Murray immediately reopened the routes to independent sailing. Then, on 22 August, Murray shut down both the coastal routes and the gulf to independent sailing and reinstituted the Halifax–Sydney, Sydney–Wabana, and Sydney–Quebec convoys. To help protect them, Murray dispatched to Sydney the six corvettes of group W-7 of the Western Escort Force, responsible for escorting the main ocean convoys between New York and southeastern Newfoundland.[7]

Why had the confidence following *Bogue*'s victory on 20 August so quickly turned to the imposition of full convoy? Interrogation of the survivors of the boat destroyed by *Bogue*'s aircraft revealed that she was not *U-802*, but *U-1229*. Allied intelligence knew from decrypted radio traffic that *U-1229* had put to sea, but the radio traffic gave no clue as to her destination. The submarine trackers correctly concluded that she was on a secret mission, promulgated only by written orders for security, but where was she headed? The coast of Maine, the survivors revealed, to drop off an agent, and then carry out anti-shipping operations off Halifax. The boat had been unaware of the hunt for *U-802* nearby and had made the mistake of thinking that the poor flying conditions resulting from the weather fronts moving through had made it safe to proceed on the surface in daylight.

That meant *U-802* had been free since 19 August to continue to the Cabot Strait. On the evening of 22 August, Liberators and Cansos began intense coverage of a probability zone extending from about 220 kilometres seaward of the Cabot Strait back into the eastern gulf. The next day EG 16 sailed from Sydney to patrol the seaward approaches to the strait, while in the following days Fairmiles established patrols in the strait. On 28 August the air patrols began to fall back, westward, into the gulf; during the period 22–30 August, the air force carried out more than sixty missions to cover probability areas and support convoys in the gulf and the approaches to the Cabot Strait. These operations showed the flexibility and mobility the air force had gained with the further development of stations and communications since 1942. Early in August, additional Cansos had moved from Nova Scotia to Newfoundland to support the hunt for *U-802* as she entered the Canadian Northwest Atlantic area; from 22 August, additional Cansos and also Liberators from Gander moved down to Sydney to cover the Cabot Strait and eastern gulf. Thereafter Cansos moved back to Summerside, PEI, Gaspé and, on the north shore, a new airfield at Sept Îles. As in the initial search for *U-802* off Newfoundland, the aircraft patrolled back and forth to cover all areas of probability zones of up to 160 kilometres by 160 kilometres every four hours by day and every two hours by night.

The Canadian submarine trackers estimated that *U-802* entered through the Cabot Strait on about 26 August and by 28 or 29 August would reach the St. Lawrence estuary, the objective indicated in the orders radioed by U-boat headquarters and decrypted by Allied intelligence. These estimates were better than U-boat headquarters' own, which plotted the submarine through the Cabot Strait on 24 August, but even so they were wrong. Terrorized by the encounter with *Bogue*'s aircraft, Schmoeckel crawled, never surfacing and at most showing his schnorkel mast. He passed through the strait only on the night of 30–31 August. Although pleasantly surprised at the "extraordinarily weak defences," he still did not dare surface and had a quiet—though dead slow—passage to the estuary, which he reached only on 6 September. He had been following three days or more behind the main concentration of the Canadian search.

Allied intelligence already knew that *U-802* was not coming alone. Ultra decrypts promptly revealed that *U-541*, after departing the French coast on 6 August, was assigned a route similar to the one given to *U-802* and on 25 August received the same orders for the St. Lawrence. The submarine had been commissioned in March 1943, and this was her third war cruise. She had the same commanding officer through the whole of her service, 27-year-old Kapitänleutnant Kurt Petersen, who had joined the navy in 1936 and transferred to U-boats in 1940. The submarine had seen some intense action, but had not yet destroyed any shipping.

On 28 August, USS *Bogue* and her destroyers, having refuelled at Argentia, Newfoundland, departed to begin pursuit of *U-541*. That same night, Petersen, having been overflown by aircraft and assuming (incorrectly) that he had been located, sent a short radio report. Allied radio stations took bearings, which showed *U-541* was about 740 kilometres southeast of St. John's, right on the course she had been assigned and slightly ahead of schedule.

Petersen, possibly encouraged by the periods of poor flying weather that hindered the Newfoundland-based Canadian air patrols assigned to his track, made long fast surface runs at night and ran still further ahead of the plots at German and Allied headquarters. In the pre-dawn darkness on 3 September, the boat was 180 kilometres east of Sydney, about thirty-six hours ahead of the "furthest on" Allied estimates, when Petersen sighted the small Newfoundland steamer *Livingstone* on independent passage between Halifax and St. John's because she was too slow for convoy. One of the torpedoes from the first salvo of three detonated prematurely, with "a flash of flame followed by a huge column of water." Alerted, the steamer manoeuvred to escape while Petersen pursued for a full half-hour, firing a fourth, then a fifth torpedo. The last found its mark and blew the ship apart. Only fourteen members of the crew got clear and into a lifeboat; the other fourteen were lost, an indication of the terrible effect of the explosion on the small steamer. Although the ship had dispatched distress signals, none was heard ashore. Luckily for the survivors, their boat was sighted by the corvette HMCS *Barrie* at noon, about seven hours after the sinking. *Barrie*, together with *Shawinigan*, was escorting the troopship *Lady Rodney*, which had full medical facilities and an army doctor aboard. Several of *Livingstone*'s people were too badly injured for transfer, however, and remained in the care of Sick Berth Attendant Stanley Mosher. One man, Mosher recalled, "had been blown through a space between two bulkheads studded with bolt ends ... He had large patches of flesh missing as if someone had clawed out handfuls of meat." Another had a "bad break" in his leg: "you could see the jagged ends of the bone under the skin." A third survivor had "broken ribs and possible back injuries," and a fourth "had a large scalp wound about five inches long and down to the bone." When the doctor from *Lady Rodney* was able to visit *Barrie*, he found that Mosher with the help of the crew had done such good work with the limited resources in the corvette that nothing more needed to be done; Mosher was decorated with a "Mention in Despatches" for "outstanding devotion to duty and determination in administering medical attention."[8]

Livingstone came to grief so far ahead of the "furthest on" estimate for the incoming *U-541* that Allied submarine trackers concluded the attacker must have been *U-802*, which was apparently hovering outside the Cabot Strait even as *U-541* approached south of Newfoundland. As a result, Admiral Murray's headquarters threw everything that was available into the area from the Cabot Strait eastward to the south of Newfoundland. The frigates of EG 16 sailed from Sydney to re-establish a patrol in the Cabot Strait. Another group, C 8 of the mid-ocean escort force, came in to patrol to the seaward of the position where *Livingstone* had gone down, while Eastern Air Command, including Liberators from Gander, patrolled the whole area. *Bogue*'s group continued to hunt to the east of the Canadian patrols, on the estimated track of *U-541*. In fact, *U-541* was now far ahead of the estimated track and went through the Cabot Strait on the night of 4–5 September as fog rolled in that would ground most of Eastern Air Command's patrols for the next three days.

On the night of 7–8 September, when *U-541* was passing south of the east end of Anticosti Island, Petersen was lured to the surface by hydrophone sounds of a large freighter without any trace of the distinctive sounds of escorting warships. The vessel, *Fort Remy*, had broken off from the Quebec to Sydney convoy QS 89 two hours before to make for Sydney at best speed. Once surfaced, Petersen saw the freighter in the distance—he estimated 6000 metres—and there were no warships in sight. He therefore ignored "blaring" warnings on his radar detection equipment.

> Steamer then dead ahead ... Suddenly starboard ahead muzzle flashes can be seen and gunfire heard. Behind the boat five star shells go off and light up the water surface as light as day. In the meantime a destroyer comes at me from the bow starboard side at high speed, approximately 20 knots on a course almost parallel to the boats and passes by at 300 m[etres] abeam on the starboard side. I turned immediately off to port. On my beam the destroyer begins firing 2 cm guns.

Later, the submarine crew discovered shell holes in the conning tower. As the submarine made a crash dive, she fired a torpedo and then heard what sounded like a ship breaking up and sinking; Petersen claimed the destruction of a "destroyer." Then what was evidently a second "destroyer" could be heard overhead, which made only one inaccurate depth charge attack.

The "destroyer" that illuminated and then shot up *U-541* was the corvette HMCS *Norsyd*, one of the Western Escort Force ships Admiral Murray had assigned for convoy duties in the gulf. She had left the screen for QS 89 to protect *Fort Remy*. *U-541*'s torpedo had been far wide of the mark. In the difficult water conditions, however, neither *Norsyd* nor the Norwegian escort *King Haakon VII*, which had rushed from QS 89 in support, could make any asdic contacts. The warships stayed over the position, carrying out a continuous search whose radius expanded according to the submerged speed of a U-boat. This was a "hunt to exhaustion," a tactic adapted from the effective practices developed by the British forces that was designed to prevent the U-boat from surfacing and escaping at speed. Ideally, the U-boat would, within twenty-four hours, be compelled by loss of electric power to surface right in the midst of the patrolling forces. From Sydney, four frigates of EG 16 came to join the expanding search. The remaining two frigates from EG 16 reinforced by two other frigates created a temporary group, W 13, which maintained the patrol in the Cabot Strait. Fairmiles from Gaspé ran a barrier patrol to cover the escape route north of the Gaspé Peninsula, while Fairmiles from Sydney helped the frigates keep watch in the Cabot Strait. Cansos and Liberators supported the naval barrier patrols north of Gaspé and in the Cabot Strait, while other Cansos flew continuous patrols as part of the expanding hunt to exhaustion. By the time the hunt to exhaustion was called off after forty-four hours, five Cansos were on station at a time, constantly patrolling at different distances from the initial contact to keep the whole probability area, now a good part of the western central gulf and the waters north of the Gaspé Peninsula, under constant surveillance.

Designed to counter conventional submarines that had to come to the surface to run their diesels and recharge their batteries, the hunt to exhaustion was much less effective against schnorkel-equipped boats, especially in the water conditions of the gulf that blinded asdic. After the encounter with *Norsyd, U-541* crept submerged north to the southern shore of Anticosti and, to conserve the batteries, came to rest on the bottom, at a depth of over 100 metres. She gingerly schnorkelled west along the southern shore of Anticosti for a few hours on the night of 8–9 September and bottomed again until late on 9 September, then began a submerged passage towards the estuary.

The poor sound conditions in the gulf waters and the fact that *U-541* showed nothing more than the top of her schnorkel above water, and that only during dark hours, meant the searching forces had no chance of finding her. Still, the strong countermeasures triggered by Petersen's attempt to close with a target at speed on the surface, even in the middle of the night, made the U-boat commander extremely cautious, much as the encounter with *Bogue's* aircraft south of Newfoundland had persuaded Schmoeckel that he dare not surface.

The Canadian hunt all but paralyzed not only Petersen but Schmoeckel as well. In the wake of the hunt to exhaustion on 8–9 September, the air and naval patrols concentrated on the waters to the west of Gaspé on the correct assumption that the boat that had attacked *Fort Remy* was incoming towards the river estuary. Schmoeckel, who had not been able to pick up any radio messages because of poor reception in the gulf, had no idea *U-541* was following him and was deeply alarmed about the increased defence activity over his submerged position north of the Gaspé Peninsula, off Cap Chat. On 13 September—when the westbound *U-541*, unknown to Schmoeckel, passed within a few kilometres of *U-802*—Schmoeckel brooded:

> It appears that the enemy may after all have picked up some indication of my presence. After all, there hasn't been any other boat in this area for the last two years. Perhaps he was able to pick up my schnorkel with his land-based equipment. It strikes me as odd that the aircraft are always flying back and forth over the area on a north–south course, while I have also been standing to and off land on north–south courses for the last seven days.[9]

Now very nervous about being trapped in the narrow waters north of the Gaspé Peninsula, Schmoeckel decided to move east of Gaspé out into the gulf where he would have more sea room. He was just beginning his submerged passage in the late morning of 14 September when he sighted "three destroyers" in line abreast (each ship keeping station about four kilometres to the side of its neighbour) about 4000 metres ahead. In fact these were the four frigates of the new temporary group, W 13, that were doing continuous patrols at the mouth of the estuary. *U-802* swung north to try to get around the group, anticipating that a convoy of merchant vessels was behind the warships. At a range of about 650 metres, HMCS *Stettler*, second from the northern end of the group, made an asdic contact and increased from twenty-two to thirty-three kilometres per hour on a depth-charge attack run.

Schmoeckel, seeing the puff of smoke from the warship's funnel that could only mean an increase of speed to attack, let fly an acoustic torpedo when the frigate was 500 metres away. Within seconds, the right time delay for such a short range, there was a satisfying explosion and other noises in the water like a ship breaking up. Schmoeckel later reported the destruction of the warship. Aboard *Stettler*, the crew heard an explosion in the ship's wake "somewhat similar to a very shallow Depth Charge, the detonation and a column of dark coloured water which rose to a height of about 20 feet [6 metres], occurring almost simultaneously." The captain, D.G. King, one of a small group of talented volunteer reserve officers who had been promoted to corvette commands in 1942 and were now being given commands of larger ships, assumed that the depth charge crew had begun to fire early and telephoned them to stop firing. King quickly realized from the bewildered response that the explosion had likely come from an enemy torpedo. The asdic crew still had the contact, and King now manoeuvred to fire his hedgehog anti-submarine mortar. This discharged a pattern of twenty-four small contact-fused charges ahead of the ship, thus allowing the asdic crew to keep the contact without interruption (in a depth charge attack, contact was lost as the ship swept over the target to drop the charges). None of the mortar bombs exploded, meaning they had not found the target. The contact disappeared after a further attack with depth charges. The frigates continued an expanding search for another seven-and-half hours, but without result.[10]

U-802 crept north to within 3000 or 4000 metres of the north shore of the St. Lawrence, west of Anticosti, and dropped to the bottom for six hours. It was not a secure resting spot—the boat began to slip down what appeared to be a precipice—so U-802 began to inch her way eastward towards the gulf. Periodically the crew heard the sounds of "destroyers" through the water, and when the boat came up to periscope depth there seemed always to be aircraft overhead. Twice during the submarine's slow passage on 15–18 September midway between the north shore of the Gaspé Peninsula and Anticosti, Petersen shut down his engines and let the current carry the boat along. He was particularly worried about draining his depleted batteries and not having the power to manoeuvre should he be discovered. Aircraft and escorts were so frequently in evidence that he concluded it was not safe to schnorkel even at night; the water was often flat calm and phosphorescent, so he dared schnorkel for only a few hours in late twilight. U-802 finally passed out from the Cabot Strait on the Cape Breton side on the night of 22–23 September. U-541, whose experiences were similar, passed out the same night on the Newfoundland side.

By this time, U-boat headquarters was dispatching signals demanding reports from the submarines, having heard nothing from them in a month and urgently needing information for the tasking of follow-on boats. The submarines heard little or none of this radio traffic because of poor reception and difficulties with the schnorkel-mounted aerials. Neither Schmoeckel nor Petersen gave any thought to surfacing in order to make a signal because of the strength of the defences.

No less anxious for some word from the submarines was Allied intelligence. The confusion caused by U-541's attack on Livingstone on

3 September when that submarine was still supposed to be far out at sea had continued. There was nothing to suggest that the attacks on *Fort Remy* and HMCS *Stettler* within the gulf had in fact been carried out by two submarines, and thus these incidents seemed to show the presence in the gulf of only one boat. Apparent confirmation came on 8 September when aircraft from USS *Bogue*, which was still searching for *U-541* on the basis of serious underestimates of the speed of her passage, sighted what appeared to be a schnorkel mast or periscope about 280 kilometres south of Cape Race, Newfoundland. This was the beginning of a series of convincing—but false—visual, radar, and sonar contacts that would lead *Bogue*'s group and much of the RCAF's strength in Newfoundland on a week-long chase of a phantom. It was, as the historian of the U.S. Navy commented, "probably the most frustrating time of the war for ... the *Bogue* group,"[11] which, unlike the Canadian forces, had little experience of the extremely difficult operating conditions in these coastal waters.

When finally, on the night of 6–7 October, Petersen signalled a report of his experiences in the Canadian area, Allied code breakers had the clear text within forty-eight hours. (Schmoeckel, suffering from continuing problems with his radio antennae, did not in the end get a signal through to U-boat headquarters until 20 October, much to the relief of headquarters, who assumed from the nine-week silence that *U-802* had been destroyed.) The new information, however, served only to obscure the intelligence picture.

Petersen advised there was little traffic in the St. Lawrence and that he had his best hunting outside the Cabot Strait against shipping between Halifax and St. John's. U-boat headquarters, in a message Allied intelligence quickly decrypted, authorized two U-boats in the southern approaches to Halifax to take advantage of Petersen's information by shifting north towards the Cabot Strait. These two submarines were *U-1229*, whose destruction was unknown to the Germans, and *U-1221*, which, as the Allies knew from decryption of tasking signals, had likely arrived off Nova Scotia late in September. Petersen's information also might have changed the operating area of another submarine, *U-1223*, under Oberleutnant Albert Kneip, which Allied submarine trackers estimated had arrived in the vicinity of the Cabot Strait only a few days before.

U-1223 had been commissioned in October 1943, and Kneip had taken command in March 1944 while the boat was still preparing for operations. This was the submarine's first war cruise. Kneip had joined the navy in 1939, entering directly into the U-boat arm. He had served in three other submarines; this was his first command on a combat mission, and it was to be a successful one.

Allied intelligence knew from Ultra decrypts that Kneip had received orders for the Gulf of St. Lawrence identical to those given to *U-802* and *U-541*, orders that were based on experience in 1942 and therefore badly out of date. The fresh assessment broadcast by Petersen and endorsed by U-boat headquarters—that hunting was better on the Halifax to St. John's route than in the St. Lawrence—raised the strong possibility that Kneip might not enter the gulf. Rather paradoxically, the timely decryption of German radio traffic, in which U-boat headquarters gave the commanders a great deal of latitude in choosing their operational areas, rendered the Canadian intelligence plot very hazy indeed. *U-1221* and *U-1223* might be found anywhere from the waters off southern Nova Scotia east to the vicinity of St. John's and west as far as the St. Lawrence River. Indeed, the submarine tracking room in Ottawa was not able to define probability areas for the focused air and naval patrols that had been so effective in suppressing *U-802* and *U-541*. Defences were therefore concentrated around convoys to endeavour to hold back the submarines wherever they attempted to attack shipping.

EG 16's task was to shuttle convoys back and forth between Sydney and Father Point. Since convoy had been reinstituted in the gulf in late August 1944, ships in westbound ON convoys from the United Kingdom bound for the gulf had broken off under local escort south of

Newfoundland and, instead of putting into Sydney, continued directly through the Cabot Strait and on to their destinations. If there were ships at Sydney ready to enter the gulf, they came out and joined the ON group rather than waiting until the next SQ convoy. This method avoided several days of delay for incoming ships, an urgent priority in view of the need to keep bulk cargoes of timber and grain moving to the United Kingdom. During the late morning of 14 October, five frigates from EG 16 together with HMCS *Shawinigan,* one of the Western Escort Force corvettes assigned by Admiral Murray to local escort duties out of Sydney in August, were escorting the ten merchant ships in the gulf section of ONS 33 on a course that lay about eleven kilometres off the north shore near Pointe des Monts, where the estuary narrows. Suddenly the frigate HMCS *Magog,* screening the northern side of the convoy, suffered an explosion that demolished twenty metres of her stern. The blast cleanly ripped off her propellers and their shafts just behind the bulkhead of the engine room and hurled the after part of the deck, still attached to the ship, up and over the rear gun platform in an arc, much like the open lid of a tin can. A few seconds later, there was a second explosion about fifty metres behind the crippled ship; *U-1223* later reported that she had fired two torpedoes. *Magog* and the other escorts had been actively searching with asdic, but none of the warships made any contact. *U-1223* had good luck. The convoy passed within firing range of the submarine's submerged position, and she was able to hide in the cold-water layer safe from sonic detection.

Magog's crew, despite the fact that the immobile ship was a sitting target and work below decks was perilous, responded quickly and effectively. Damage control parties immediately began to shore up the engine room bulkhead, which, now exposed to the sea and in effect forming the stern of the hull, was the key to the warship's survival. *Magog,* whose asdic was still functioning, kept an anti-submarine watch to assist her consorts in the hunt for the attacker. In the afternoon, three-and-a-half hours after the attack, *Shawinigan* took the frigate under tow into nearby Godbout Bay. Casualties were mercifully light—three dead and three seriously injured—in view of the massive damage to the ship. The navy requested the air force's help in evacuating the injured, and a Canso from Gaspé set down beside the frigate in the mouth of Godbout Bay, seven hours after the attack. Although the sea was by no means calm, *Magog*'s crew and the airmen managed to get the injured, secured on stretchers, into the frigate's boat, over to the Canso, and then through the small access way created by opening the transparent blister on the side of the flying boat. The Canso rushed the injured to the hospital at Mont Joli.[12]

Admiral Murray ordered a hunt to exhaustion in the vicinity of the attack on *Magog*. During the next forty-eight hours, Cansos made twenty-six extended flights over the expanding probability area. EG 16 carried out the naval side of the hunt for the first twenty-four hours and then screened QS 97, a convoy of twenty-eight merchant ships outbound from Bic Island. Although the hunt found no trace of *U-1223*, the large convoy passed through the danger area without incident: *U-1223* had been suppressed.

Allied intelligence believed—erroneously—that *U-1223* was the only U-boat remaining in the Canadian area when in fact two were still there. The intelligence staffs had incorrectly estimated that *U-1221* had departed from the Nova Scotia coast in mid-October. When *U-1221* broadcast her actual "homebound" radio message on the night of 30–31 October, the Allied submarine trackers concluded that the message came from *U-1223* and thus declared Canadian waters clear of the enemy.

Admiral Murray's headquarters allowed merchant ships to begin sailing independently once more, and the air force began to pull back from the St. Lawrence. Fall storms in the gulf, including snow and freezing conditions, were making air operations from Gaspé and Sept Îles exceedingly difficult, so 161 Squadron withdrew its Canso detachments from both places to Yarmouth, the unit's winter base, leaving only the detachment at Summerside, PEI.

Late in the afternoon of 2 November the grain-filled freighter *Fort Thompson*, sailing independently down the St. Lawrence River and only about seventy kilometres east of Father Point, suffered a "violent explosion." The forward holds were flooding, and it looked like she might go down. The master told the crew to make the boats ready in case of the worst. As the damaged ship lurched over to port, one of the boats, with seventeen men aboard, broke free and was caught by the strong river current. With no hope of recovering the boat, the master shouted for the men to head for Matane, a few kilometres to the east, which they did. *Fort Thompson* radioed a submarine warning and headed for shallower water on the south shore of the river, where she anchored. An attempt to pump out the forward part of the ship went well. She was able to swing around and make port at Quebec City.

Eastern Air Command had responded swiftly to the initial submarine report. A Canso from Summerside patrolled that same night, while a total of nine Cansos came from Yarmouth and Sydney to operate from Mont Joli. The aircraft did a round-the-clock hunt to exhaustion until the weather closed in at midday on 4 November. The weather cleared on 7 November, and the Mont Joli detachment carried on with patrols, including escort of the convoys the navy had immediately reinstituted after the attack on *Fort Thompson*.[13] The caution was correct. Kneip did not leave the gulf until about 21 November. Although he reported the defences were weak, he never had another opportunity to attack.[14]

Kneip's departure was not the end of the offensive in the St. Lawrence. At this stage in the war even the limited (but inflated) claims reported by Petersen for his two-month mission—the destruction of *Livingstone* and, incorrectly, a "destroyer" (*Norsyd*)—counted as a major success. U-boat headquarters, in signals Allied intelligence immediately decrypted, ordered no fewer than three boats outbound from Norway, *U-1228*, followed by *U-1231* and then *U-806*, to make for the area east of Cape Breton, where *U-541* had destroyed *Livingstone*. All three boats had the freedom to press into the gulf or remain south of Newfoundland and hunt the St. John's–Halifax traffic Petersen had reported. The events that unfolded in the latter part of November, in part because of the haziness of the intelligence picture, uncannily echoed those of October 1942. The defences kept the boats at bay, but one of them, in retreat as *U-69* had been two years earlier, happened upon a target of opportunity in the dead of night—and only a few kilometres from where *Caribou* had gone down.

The lead submarine in the new group was *U-1228*, commissioned in December 1943 and commanded during her whole service by Oberleutnant Friedrich Wilhelm Marienfeld. He had joined the navy at the age of 18 in 1938 and transferred to the U-boat arm in 1940. *U-1228* arrived at the approach point off Cape Breton on 14 November, just as U-boat headquarters broadcast Petersen's report of his good hunting in that same area. Marienfeld's intention was to follow Petersen's advice and remain off Cape Breton "until my first success and then, after the anticipated strengthening of the defences and increased protective measures for shipping in the coastal area, to penetrate into the Gulf." As he began to hunt, he was struck by the stark contrast of his combat mission with the peaceful cavorting of a school of porpoises, which were "putting on a running show. A great deal of squealing, crackling and humming, sometimes to be heard with the unaided ear."[15] Marienfeld made a submerged patrol for a week, with occasional contacts on shipping that proved too distant for attack.

On the night of 22–23 November, the schnorkel malfunctioned. "No air coming into boat. Float valve jammed in closed position. By raising and lowering the mast several times, valve does let in air now and then but always closes up again at periscope depth." Marienfeld understandably reacted with some alarm. *U-1228*'s previous mission in September 1944, his first in command, had been cut short when the boat was attacked by a U.K.-based Liberator bomber and the schnorkel was damaged. The entire crew fell into a torpor ("exhausted condition"), and one man died of carbon monoxide poisoning. Fortunately the boat was close to the coast of Norway, and Marienfeld dodged further air attacks, taking refuge in a fjord where the crew was able to make emergency repairs that enabled the boat to make port at Bergen.[16] Now Marienfeld again sought the shelter of an isolated fjord—Connoire Bay on Newfoundland's thinly populated southern shore, about 110 kilometres east of Cape Ray. On the night of 23–24 November, he surfaced nine kilometres off the bay to lubricate the schnorkel valve and see if extensive repairs would be needed. Apparently not, as the valve began to work. "It's clacking again!" he noted in his log, referring to the sound of the valve lifting and falling. *U-1228* schnorkelled its way towards the gulf, running only 5000 metres off the south shore of Newfoundland. She was near Channel Head at the southwest tip of Newfoundland when Marienfeld checked the gyroscopic compass, which had been giving trouble, and discovered it was deviating wildly. That settled it. He was not going to risk the gulf with schnorkel and compass problems. He turned to depart: "Coast shining beautifully in moonlight, Table Mountain, Sugar Loaf, Cape Ray beacons showing up as gleams on the horizon." At that moment there was a hydrophone contact, and he rose to periscope depth and saw a "destroyer" moving across his stern at a range of only 3000 metres. Marienfeld swung around, closed the range to 2500 metres, and fired an acoustic torpedo aimed at the warship's propellers. "Torpedo and screw noises merge. A hit after 4 min[utes] 0 sec[ond]s. High, 50 m[etre], large explosion column with heavy shower of sparks, after collapse of explosion column, only 10 m high now, then smoke cloud, destroyer disappeared."

The stricken vessel was the corvette HMCS *Shawinigan*. On the evening of 23 November 1944, she had sailed from North Sydney as escort for the Newfoundland Railway ferry *Burgeo,* the vessel that had continued the service to Port aux Basques, Newfoundland, after the loss of *Caribou*. When the little convoy reached the approaches to Channel–Port aux Basques on the afternoon of 25 November, *Shawinigan,* as was standard procedure, had remained at sea keeping a patrol until *Burgeo* came out at 7:15 the next morning for the return passage to Cape Breton. An observer on shore reported the death of the ship through the Aircraft Detection Corps. "Loud explosion followed by 3 min[ute]s. silence followed by roar like thunder" was the entry in the operations log at naval headquarters in Ottawa. It didn't seem significant at the time, however: "American blasting operations in progress day and night in vicinity."[17] No one was aware that anything was amiss until *Burgeo* appeared at Sydney alone on 26 November. The ferry reported that she had repeatedly called the corvette by radio telephone when she failed to appear at the rendezvous, but had to proceed because of a stiffening gale. A call to the Americans about the work near Channel Head then revealed that there had been no blasting on the night of 24–25 November, strongly suggesting that the reported explosions had signalled the death of the corvette.

Marienfeld's sojourn to the Newfoundland coast had taken him well clear of the operational areas recommended by U-boat headquarters that, picked up by the Allies in Ultra intelligence, formed the basis for the Canadian patrols. Eastern Air Command now shifted its searches to the Channel Head area. The aircraft located an oil slick on the morning of 27 November and homed in on EG 16's frigates.

> Oil, apparently boiler fuel, covered a considerable area, and in searching further, six bodies wearing R.C.N. life belts were located floating in the sea ...
>
> The oil slick ... resembled chunks of mud floating on the water.
>
> Each body was wearing a life belt when recovered, and appeared to be floating upright in the water, with the face submerged.
>
> A portion of a ship's bridge was recovered ...
>
> From the evidence of ratings [seamen] on board it is considered that the bodies were from H.M.C.S. "SHAWINIGAN."[18]

No one in the crew of ninety-one officers and ratings had survived. The navy released the news for publication on 8 December. The *Toronto Telegram* headed its report "Loss of H.M.C.S. Shawinigan Strikes All

Canada." "With parents and relatives all across Canada, the country mourns the loss of the gallant company of H.M.C.S. Shawinigan. The members of her crew hailed from all nine provinces, and there is no part of the Dominion that does not know sorrow for the loss of those who will never come home from the sea."[19] "Thirteen Toronto Men Shawinigan Casualties," reported the Toronto *Globe and Mail*. Some of the men had been expected home on leave just when their families received the news. The *Globe* ran biographies of each of the thirteen, leading with a local hockey star.

> AB [Able Bodied Seaman] Dudley (Red) Morine Garrett, 23, former Toronto Maple Leaf hockey player, was killed in action. He had hobbled to a naval recruiting office with his foot in a cast to keep his rendezvous with death ... AB Garrett was the son of Mr. and Mrs. D.M. Garrett, Balsam Ave., and had played hockey for Sudbury junior teams before [c]oming here to play with Toronto Shamrocks, Marlboro Juniors when they won the O.H.A. Championship, and for the Leafs. He went to New York Rangers and several months later broke his ankle. Enlisting here, he played with the Toronto Navy team. He took an officers' training course and was putting in "sea time" before receiving his commission.[20]

The *Hamilton Spectator* ran a sombre account of how a sailor in one of the EG 16 frigates recognized a friend among the bodies recovered and thus provided the first confirmation that the wreckage was *Shawinigan*.

> Boys stationed on the recently-built frigate Antigonish are no longer "green" after their experiences searching for the Canadian corvette Shawinigan, said Sick Berth Attendant Edward D. Rasky, of Toronto ...
> "There wasn't a sound throughout the whole ship except for the faint throb of the engines," he said. "The sea had calmed. The men stood about the deck with tight lips. Then one of them suddenly dropped on his knees beside the body. He had recognized it as that of his buddy from Shawinigan.

"He started to pray—there on his knees on the deck. It got us, all of us, I can tell you. We bared our heads—well, it gets you."[21]

U-1231 heard the destruction of *Shawinigan* as the submarine entered the gulf on the night of 24–25 November. The boat went up the river as far as the vicinity of Matane and on 3–4 December made no fewer than four submerged torpedo attacks. All were wide of the mark. The intended targets, the merchant ships and escorts of convoy QS 107, heard "mild" or "very mild" explosions on only two occasions. The explosions were so distant and indistinct that the Canadians wrote them off as one of the "unexplained" phenomena encountered in these complex waters.[22] The U-boat's commanding officer, Kapitän zur See Hermann Lessing, was an older officer, 44 years of age, who had transferred from the air force only eighteen months earlier. Whether because of age or inexperience, he was extremely cautious and had not pressed anything like close enough to his targets for the torpedoes to have a chance of hitting. *U-1231* departed the gulf on 7 December when ice began to encrust the schnorkel, threatening critical malfunction. The last convoy of the season, QS 109, two merchant ships escorted by the Bangor HMCS *Melville*, reached Sydney on 16 December, battered by a gale with wind gusts to more than eighty kilometres an hour.[23]

The threat to the St. Lawrence and preparations of defence measures to meet that threat continued until the very end of the war in May 1945. Canadian and Allied command staffs believed that the U-boats would return to the gulf in 1945 in numbers at least as great as in the fall of 1944. Although German successes had been meagre, decrypts of radio traffic revealed that the submarine commanders, who now had to trust to hydrophone indications of ships sinking rather than direct observation, inflated their claims. They also reported the extent to which the unusual prevalence of cold-water density layers in the St. Lawrence provided protection against Allied defences. At this stage in the war, as the decrypts also revealed, U-boat headquarters was elated at any success and especially one in which the submarine was able to escape Allied hunting forces.

Achievements by the last boats of the fall offensive into Canadian waters underscored what boldly handled schnorkel submarines could accomplish in favourable water conditions.[24] On 21 December, *U-806* severely damaged a freighter right under the noses of escorts, only eighteen kilometres from the Halifax headlands. On the morning of Christmas Eve, the boat then destroyed the Bangor *Clayoquot,* a veteran of the St. Lawrence, still closer in to the port and escaped another prolonged hunt. In January 1945, *U-1232* destroyed four merchant ships, severely damaged a fifth in these same waters, and got away even though escorts had been present and immediately launched hunts. Chill winter air created a surface cold layer of water over warmer water just below, the reverse of the situation in the St. Lawrence, but equally effective in blinding asdic and screening a submarine.

British shipping authorities insisted that Montreal and gulf ports would have to be even more fully employed in the coming season than in 1944 because of the railway and other bottlenecks that continued to interfere with increased use of Canadian Atlantic ports. The Canadian chiefs of staff agreed that the risk had to be taken. The naval and air staffs made plans to deploy the same level of forces that had been in place in 1943 and 1944 to allow comprehensive convoy of shipping in the event of a new U-boat assault. In addition, the navy won the Admiralty's agreement to pull corvettes out of the mid-ocean escort groups so that six would be available in the gulf to reinforce convoy escorts, as had been done when the U-boats arrived in late August 1944. The Admiralty also agreed that the Canadians should be allowed to pull one experienced support group, EG 6, from British waters to reinforce the two support groups under Admiral Murray's command. This too was based on experience in 1944 when two support groups had been needed in the gulf to cover the eastern and western areas and had had to be improvised by creating the temporary W 13 group so as not to denude Halifax.

The 1945 shipping season in the St. Lawrence got off to a "flying start." Very early clearance of ice allowed the first incoming ocean-going ship to reach Montreal on 9 April, and both port and naval control of shipping authorities pushed loading and sailing operations to full speed to meet British demands for still greater deliveries from the St. Lawrence than in 1944, ninety ships a month. Fortunately, there was no indication of U-boats in the gulf, so shipping moved independently, without the delays of convoy.[25] Nevertheless, the air force and navy hurried the dispatch of escorts and bomber aircraft to the gulf stations, for the German effort in North American coastal waters was unrelenting. Ultra showed that as many as six U-boats were en route to the Halifax area and waters to the south. Very general tasking orders made it impossible to determine which boats were headed where and when they would arrive. It was in this confused picture that *U-190*, in ambush position close off the Halifax headlands, sank the Bangor HMCS *Esquimalt* with heavy loss of life on 16 April.

On 8 May, the day after the German surrender, U-boat headquarters radioed orders in clear text for the U-boats at sea to surface, broadcast their positions, and give themselves up to Allied forces. In the northwestern Atlantic, six U-boats surrendered, four to U.S. forces, including Marienfeld's *U-1228*, *Shawinigan*'s killer, which was outward bound from Norway on a new mission, and two to Canadian forces. *U-190*, which had pulled back from Halifax into the open ocean southeast of Cape Race, surrendered to the frigate HMCS *Victoriaville* and the corvette HMCS *Thorlock*. The warships brought her into Bay Bulls, the base facility near St. John's, on 14 May. *U-889*, closer in to Newfoundland, was sighted by Liberator "X" of 10 Squadron, RCAF. The aircrew homed in on the Western Escort Force group W 6, which took the submarine into the base at Shelburne, Nova Scotia, on 13 May.[26]

Still, naval control of shipping and ocean convoy continued until the end of May as a safeguard against any U-boats that either did not receive the surrender orders or chose to ignore them. For the naval control staff at Sydney which had a hectic time in April and May, hurrying merchant ships into the gulf and then expediting the organization of ocean convoys for outbound ships, the end came in June 1945: "Reductions in staff progressed—office space was reduced and equipment turned in. Sydney, which existed by virtue of being a convoy assembly port, relapsed to quieter ways of life ... the job was done."[27]

THE CANADIAN FORCES' achievement in the gulf during the German offensive in 1944 was a significant one. The most important objective was to increase loadings at St. Lawrence ports of merchant ships bound for overseas destinations. The total for the 1944 season was 346 ships, more than double the 178 that had sailed in 1943 when overseas traffic was restricted and a substantial increase over the 278 that had sailed in 1942 when ocean traffic had been restricted during the last third of the season.[28] Moreover, most of the increased traffic in 1944 sailed during August and later, precisely when the new U-boat offensive in the St. Lawrence took place. Yet none of these merchant ships was lost to enemy action, the sole casualty being damage to *Fort Thompson*, which occurred as a result of Allied intelligence making an incorrect assessment and declaring the St. Lawrence free of submarines.

Despite the advantages conferred by Ultra intelligence, the net effect was to require greater, not less, effort on the part of the defending forces because of the opportunity the intelligence afforded for "offensive" patrols over the operating areas ordered by U-boat headquarters. Certainly it was an effective effort; the U-boats were all but neutralized by these patrols. Most of the German commanders did not dare even to raise their schnorkel masts except for a few hours at evening and morning twilight when visibility conditions on the water offered greatest protection and thus were unable to get into attacking positions. Yet those patrols told heavily on the limited forces available in the Canadian area. Because U-boat headquarters often designated two large operating areas for each boat and the boats themselves almost never gave away their actual positions by signalling, vast areas had to be patrolled. That effort moreover was in addition to the direct escort of convoys, which had to be comprehensive and strong because the operating areas designated by U-boat headquarters covered the main shipping routes outside as well as within the gulf.

The air and naval forces based in eastern Canada were desperately frustrated at their failure to sink a U-boat, but they should not have been. Canadian policy was to concentrate the country's striking forces overseas. Many of the new-construction warships that Admiral Murray's command prepared for service went overseas to hunt U-boats in British and European coastal waters, where the weight of the German submarine campaign in 1944–45 was heaviest. The RCN continuously maintained four and later five support groups of destroyers and frigates in these waters, sending out replacement groups as others came home for refits. These groups destroyed nine German submarines in British waters from June 1944 to March 1945, while RCAF squadrons serving in RAF Coastal Command destroyed another six, five of them by Eastern Air Command's own 162 Squadron, deployed overseas as part of the buildup for the invasion of Europe. In 1944–45, as in 1942 and 1943, the St. Lawrence took a distant second place behind Canada's large contribution to the main Allied effort.

CONCLUSION

The battle of the St. Lawrence was a small corner of the battle of the Atlantic, itself the longest and arguably most important campaign of the Second World War. During the ten months of offensive operations in the St. Lawrence, five months in 1942 and five months in 1944, the Germans committed a total of thirteen submarines. They destroyed eighteen merchant ships, a U.S. Army transport, and three warships. They also damaged a fourth warship beyond economical repair and damaged two merchant ships and a U.S. Navy tanker that later returned to service. In these ships, approximately 366 lives were lost. During the course of the whole battle of the Atlantic, the Germans committed 859 U-boats[1] and sank 2772 merchant ships; losses to British merchant marine personnel alone numbered 22,858.[2]

The principal British Commonwealth anti-submarine escort forces in the Atlantic, that is corvettes and larger types, included about 1000 warships,[3] of which more than 200, over 20 percent, were Canadian. There were never more than ten corvettes stationed in the St. Lawrence and for long periods of time only four. There was a temporary reinforcement by two destroyers for three weeks in 1942. From September to October 1944, four to eight frigates, the roving striking force of the Canadian Northwest Atlantic command, carried out specific missions in the gulf but also wherever else in Canadian and Newfoundland waters intelligence indicated the presence of a submarine. Otherwise the defence of the gulf was carried out by the smallest classes of warships, a half-dozen Bangor minesweepers, a half-dozen trawlers (only in 1943 and 1944), and a maximum of two dozen Fairmile motor launches, minuscule forces for a sea space fully half the size of the Baltic. Increasingly skilful use of aircraft from the Royal Canadian Air Force's Eastern Air Command was what allowed the navy to keep the St. Lawrence defences at such a modest level.

In terms of the German "tonnage warfare" against Allied shipping, there was nothing exceptional about the St. Lawrence. This was just one of the many areas where U-boats suddenly appeared in search of unprotected or weakly protected shipping that could be destroyed most efficiently and at least risk to the submarines themselves. Nor was the course of events much different than in other areas. Surprise allowed the U-boats to initially achieve significant successes, which rapidly diminished as defence measures came into effect. Only the first five U-boats to enter the gulf achieved two or more sinkings per submarine. So discouraging was the experience of the last four U-boats to operate in the St. Lawrence during the fall of 1942 that U-boat headquarters did not attempt any further offensive operations until the late summer of 1944, in the hopes that new technology, the schnorkel, had evened the balance. It did not, and the five boats that undertook extended patrols in 1944 succeeded only in sinking one warship, damaging another, and damaging a single merchant ship despite heavy merchant ship traffic in the river and the gulf.

For Canadians this "business as usual" submarine warfare had special significance because the initial run of German success in 1942 took place so far inside the country's territorial waters, within sight of villages on shore, where houses were violently shaken by the explosions of torpedoes and depth charges and residents had to succour hundreds of seamen who struggled ashore. Emotions were already running high in the St. Lawrence region, and in Ottawa as well, because these enemy successes took place during a grave national crisis over the question of compulsory overseas military service. The strongest opponents were French-speaking Quebeckers, who were prone to believe that home defences had been compromised by the government's too-willing and generous help to Britain. Even so, English-Canadian supporters of conscription and French-Canadian opponents quickly found common cause in bashing the government for its apparently inept defence effort in the St. Lawrence. Proof soon came to hand: the sinking of the railway ferry *Caribou* with heavy loss of life. The government's hope of inspiring united support for the war effort by making early releases of full information on the German attacks thus backfired. One result was that the St. Lawrence defences became a focal point in the government's efforts to revamp its public information program and to revise home defence measures by including a major public relations effort and co-operation with provincial authorities, especially in the St. Lawrence region. The success of this effort and, more importantly, the fact that the armed forces had unknowingly convinced the German U-boat command not to attempt a fresh offensive in 1943 appears to have removed the issue of St. Lawrence defences from the list of Quebec's grievances with the federal government.

Yet, the "fog of war" had indeed shaken the confidence of even senior Canadian military officers and would distort the historical record for decades to come. Because the 1942 incursions took place during the nearly year-long blackout of high-grade intelligence from decrypted U-boat radio traffic, senior commanders had no idea that *Caribou* had been sunk by a submarine fleeing the defences in the river and gulf. Nor did Canadian authorities have any idea that as many as four submarines operated in the St. Lawrence in the fall of 1942, nor that all four made discouraging reports to U-boat headquarters, advising against further operations in the now dangerous and unproductive St. Lawrence area. Only in 2000 did historians discover that the offensive in the fall of 1942 had included a fifth submarine that did not enter the gulf because of the effective defences she encountered off Cape Breton Island.

The only good intelligence came to hand early in 1943 when U-517, the most successful of the submarines to operate in the St. Lawrence in 1942, was destroyed by British forces in the eastern Atlantic. Most of the crew survived and provided Allied intelligence with a detailed and accurate—and gripping—account of their exploits in Canadian waters. The main message distilled by the Canadian command, that the defences had singularly failed to deter the enemy and that he would return in greater strength, was the opposite of the truth. This fact was not discovered for decades, however, because of postwar cutbacks in the official histories program. As a result, accounts of German proficiency and Canadian fumbling persisted in official and popular accounts until the 1980s. If there was one hero to emerge from the St. Lawrence campaign in Canadian publications, it was Paul Hartwig, the commander of U-517. Certainly he deserves the recognition. The full sources if anything enhance his achievements. However, the full sources also show that U-517 accomplished nothing in the last half of its long mission because of effective defences and particularly new efforts by the air force, forgotten because the history of Eastern Air Command was cancelled before serious research got started.

Further apparent evidence of the German victory in 1942 was the government's decision to close the St. Lawrence to ocean shipping on 9 September 1942 in the midst of the greatest German successes. This was the conclusion reached by the original team of official historians under Dr. G.N. Tucker in their study of merchant shipping operations published in 1952. The enemy had forced Canada to abandon its main summer shipping route and, in particular, Montreal, the best-equipped port for the efficient dispatch of such bulk cargoes as grain that Britain urgently needed. Yet the detailed findings in other parts of Tucker's account and a further official history published in 1970 suggested quite different reasons for the closure of the gulf, which have been confirmed by further research.

Diversions of shipping from the St. Lawrence to Halifax and Saint John actually began in 1941 as a result of urgent appeals from Britain for these ports to undertake repairs of damaged merchant ships that could not be accommodated in U.K. shipyards. The greatest need was in the winter months when severe weather battered many vessels and the main Canadian shipyards on the St. Lawrence were closed by ice. The winter workforce at Halifax and Saint John, however, could only be increased by providing more stable year-round employment, which could most readily be achieved by having ships normally loaded and serviced at St. Lawrence ports during the summer months go to the Atlantic ports instead.

In the early summer of 1942, the Royal Canadian Navy successfully urged a much greater diversion of merchant shipping—the transfer of transatlantic convoy assembly from Sydney and Halifax to New York—to ease the Canadian service's desperate shortage of escorts. The bulk of transatlantic shipping now originated from U.S. ports, and the shuttling of merchant ships from American ports to Nova Scotia and back was an inefficient use of the limited pool of escorts that resulted in many convoys being protected by under-strength groups. During the summer of 1942—some weeks before the major U-boat successes in September— the Royal Canadian Navy proposed completely closing the St. Lawrence to ocean traffic in the 1943 shipping season so that the escort protection of the vital Atlantic convoys could be further strengthened. The early implementation of the closure in September 1942 was then triggered by an urgent British appeal for Canada to release as many escorts as it could from North American waters to participate in the forthcoming Anglo-American invasion of North Africa, operation Torch. This was far and away the top Allied priority, not least because President Roosevelt insisted U.S. ground troops had to be engaged against the German Army in 1942 so that he could resist enormous pressure from the public for early offensives in the Pacific. Such an effort in the Pacific would have profoundly compromised the "Germany first" strategy that was the foundation of the western Alliance. So important was Torch that the Allied navies accepted great risks by reducing coverage of transatlantic convoys to build up escort strength in the Mediterranean theatre. This was perhaps the most important reason for increased German successes in the central Atlantic in late 1942 and early 1943, one of the great crises of the Atlantic campaign that saw imports to Britain plunge to their lowest levels of the war.

Canadian forces in the St. Lawrence became more effective even as the main escorts were withdrawn in late September 1942. Strikingly, the smaller forces kept the U-boats at bay despite the fact that it proved impossible to reduce shipping to the point where the convoy system could be shut down, the original intention in closing the gulf to ocean vessels. The extent of the improved performance and the reasons for it were dimly appreciated at the time and have been clarified only by recent research. Although the Canadian command knew that asdic conditions in the St. Lawrence were poor, they did not realize how poor and what an enormous advantage that was for the U-boats. By running in the cold-water layer below the surface layer of warmer water, the U-boats were safe from detection by asdic, the principal means by which warships protected convoys. In these conditions, the U-boats were able to submerge well ahead of approaching convoys at the first sight of air or surface escorts and take up ambush positions from which the U-boats could launch torpedoes at close range as the convoy passed by. The U-boats were able to position themselves well even before the escorts appeared because the convoys followed regular schedules, a measure to minimize the sailing delays that were the main drawback of convoy, and followed standard routes in order to receive as much coverage as possible from short-range aircraft at the various training air bases around the gulf.

When the main escorts departed the gulf and there were still unexpectedly large numbers of merchant ships needing protection, local commanders organized convoys as they were needed, on an irregular schedule. In an effort to compensate for the weakness of the surface escorts available, the local commanders also sailed the convoys on diverse routes. In this routing, they took advantage of the new ability of the Foreign Intelligence Section to produce timely reports on possible U-boat locations based on direction-finding bearings on their radio transmissions. The air force also exploited this new capability by concentrating air patrols in wide-ranging searches around suspected U-boat locations and in the broad vicinity—to a radius of seventy-five kilometres or more—of any convoys in the area, a considerable change from the previous emphasis on close-air escort near the convoy. Unable to locate convoys according to the previous schedules and on the standard routes, the U-boats were forced to search more widely in fast runs on the surface, but then were repeatedly forced to dive—and thus lose their ability to search out and attack targets—by the new offensive air patrols. Unknown to the Canadians, U-boat headquarters decided to abandon the St. Lawrence as a hunting ground because of the effectiveness of the defences. U-boats did not return in strength to attack shipping until the late summer and fall of 1944 when new technology—schnorkel breathing tubes—gave them an advantage. Defending forces were still limited because of greatly increased commitments overseas, including a major role by the Canadian navy in the Normandy invasion that began on 6 June 1944. It was not possible, moreover, to limit ocean shipping traffic in the St. Lawrence; support for the liberation of Europe required full use of the St. Lawrence ports to load bulky cargoes of grain and timber. Nevertheless, by using high-grade Ultra intelligence to refine techniques developed in the fall of 1942, the defending forces limited losses to the heavy merchant ship traffic to only one ship damaged. The warships that screened the merchant vessels, however, suffered more heavily owing to the extremely elusive schnorkel-fitted submarines—with HMCS *Shawinigan* destroyed and HMCS *Magog* damaged beyond repair.

CONSIDERING THE TIGHT LIMITS on the naval effort in the St. Lawrence, warship losses were indeed heavy. During the course of the war, enemy action destroyed a total of nineteen Canadian warships, and three of these were in the gulf, including the two, *Raccoon* and *Shawinigan*, that had no survivors. These figures do not include the severe damage to *Magog*, one of only three Canadian frigates put out of service by the enemy. There were 142 personnel killed in these ships, more than 9 percent of the 1534 fatalities the navy suffered as a result of enemy action during the whole war,[4] a large number considering the small portion of the fleet that was deployed in the gulf, and a testament to the difficult water conditions that allowed submerged U-boats to strike with near impunity against patrolling warships that had the bad luck to come within torpedo range.

Some prominent veterans of the gulf later became casualties in the wider war. Squadron Leader N.E. Small died on 7 January 1943 as a result of his vigorous determination to get at the enemy. He had moved to Gander and was working with Canso amphibians, stripping them of non-essential equipment so they could carry additional gasoline to extend their range into the north Atlantic where U-boats were intercepting the main trans-ocean convoys. A Canso piloted by Small on one of these missions crashed on takeoff, and he did not survive. *Weyburn*, one of the corvettes dispatched from the St. Lawrence to the Mediterranean in the fall of 1942, struck a mine in the Strait of Gibraltar on 22 February 1943. In an uncanny echo of *Charlottetown*'s loss in the St. Lawrence River, *Weyburn*'s depth charges detonated as the hull slipped below the surface, inflicting heavy casualties on the men in the water and severely damaging the British destroyer HMS *Wivern* which had closed for rescue work. As in the *Charlottetown*'s sinking, the commanding officer, Lieutenant Commander Thomas W. Golby, RCNR, did not survive. He had been among the last to leave the ship while attempting to save a seaman. As already described, *Clayoquot*, one of the small group of Bangors that had held the line in 1942, fell victim to an ambush attack by a schnorkel-equipped submarine off Halifax on Christmas Eve of 1944.

The navy's senior leadership underwent upheavals during the latter part of the war. These changes were not the result of the controversies raised by the U-boat assault in the St. Lawrence, but rather the larger problems that attended the rapid, massive expansion of the tiny peacetime service that in 1939 possessed so little of the technical and managerial expertise that would soon be demanded by the Atlantic war. Admiral Percy Nelles, who, as chief of the naval staff, was the senior military authority responsible for planning and operations in the St. Lawrence, was shuffled to a largely symbolic position as the senior Canadian flag officer overseas in January 1944 and forced quietly to retire early in 1945. His unceremonious departure after ten years' service as professional head of the navy was the product of unpleasant politics. Protests from seagoing officers of the main mid-ocean escort force in 1943 that their ships were still lagging in acquisition of the latest equipment and enduring punishing schedules that precluded essential refresher training and rest raised fears in the office of Angus Macdonald, the navy minister, about a public scandal.[5] Macdonald pinned the blame on Nelles, making sure there was a full record of his accusations on the official files. Nelles was no equal to the minister, a Harvard graduate and law professor before he entered politics, in the battle of memoranda, but there was little justice in the accusations. The navy was desperately strained by overcommitment in the Atlantic war, but the minister had participated in every significant discussion and decision. The government, moreover, had consistently supported the navy in its pursuit of a prominent place in the Atlantic. In the instances in which Nelles had worked behind the scenes with his British counterparts to press the Canadian Cabinet for a larger naval effort, as in the dispatch of the corvettes to Torch, Nelles had kept Macdonald fully informed and received his support. Macdonald, it is true, had on important occasions reacted against the elitist attitude of Nelles and the tiny regular naval officer corps, insisting upon fuller opportunities for promotion among the citizen sailors of the volunteer reserve. These were heartfelt convictions that appear to have originated in the minister's impoverished childhood and his service as a citizen soldier during the First World War. This may account for the minister's acute sensitivity in late 1943 to the effects that publicity regarding the problems of the Atlantic fleet, overwhelmingly crewed by volunteer reservists, would have had for his image as a man of the people. Yet until this confrontation, Nelles and Macdonald were an effective team, not least in the evidently seamless agreement and co-operation in the direction and political management of the St. Lawrence operations in the difficult circumstances of 1942 and early 1943. Ironically, at the very moment of Nelles' departure, the industrial bottlenecks in Canada, Britain, and the United States that had hindered the modernization of the Canadian Atlantic fleet were being overcome. In retirement, Nelles withdrew from public life and died in 1951 at the age of 59.[6]

Nelles' replacement as chief of the naval staff was G.C. Jones, promoted to vice admiral. When commanding officer Atlantic Coast, he had commanded operations in the gulf until September 1942, and he then became vice-chief of the naval staff in Ottawa. An ambitious and ruthless administrator in contrast to the more collegial Nelles, Jones abetted criticism of his chief. As chief of the naval staff, Jones saw the navy through the rest of the war and the first months of peace, but on 8 February 1946 suffered a fatal heart attack; he was 50 years of age.[7]

Jones' great rival in the navy, Rear Admiral L.W. Murray, had succeeded Jones in the Atlantic Coast command in September 1942, and then, when named commander-in-chief Canadian Northwest Atlantic in April 1943, directed all Allied convoy operations in the western North Atlantic. His career was abruptly ended by the riots that broke out in Halifax on 7 and 8 May 1945 on the announcement of victory in Europe. Naval personnel, poorly disciplined because of the inadequate base facilities and organization and frustrated by the costly, overcrowded conditions in the city, were prominent in the riots. Murray took responsibility, resigned from the service, and left for England, where he began a new career as a lawyer. He returned to Canada later in his life and in May 1970, wearing his wartime uniform, unveiled the Sailors' Memorial in Point Pleasant Park in Halifax. He died the following year at the age of 75.[8]

Angus Macdonald had already thrown off the reins of federal office before the war's end. Macdonald had been an effective advocate of the navy in Cabinet, and the prime minister was pleased with the manner in which the minister deployed detailed information from the naval staff in responding to criticisms of the St. Lawrence defences in 1942–43. Yet Mackenzie King mistrusted Macdonald's ambition and in particular his support for the dispatch of conscripts overseas. On that issue and on Mackenzie King's close control of Cabinet, Macdonald's dislike of the prime minister became ill-disguised hatred. In April 1945, Macdonald left the federal Cabinet and returned to Nova Scotia, where he again became premier until his death in 1954 at the age of 63.

J.M. de Marbois, whose inspired leadership in the development of naval operational intelligence was central to the effective defence of the St. Lawrence, received the least public recognition because of the top-secret nature of his work. He was also the oldest of the senior officers, 56 at the war's end. After leaving active naval service in 1946, he returned to teaching at Upper Canada College for a year, but his health, compromised since the injuries and traumatic stress he had suffered in Turkey and Russia during the First World War, appears to have deteriorated. In 1972, when he was 84 years of age, he died as result of injuries received when he was struck by a car in Mississauga, Ontario, where he had been living with his daughter in the wake of the death of his beloved wife Tatiana in 1965. He had taken care, before his retirement from the navy, to record the development of the Operational Intelligence Centre and its widespread activities, but his reports were not declassified and thus did not become available to researchers until the early 1980s. Only then did he begin to receive the recognition that, he complained in his later years, had been denied him.[9]

Eric and Margaret Brand, by contrast, realized the new opportunities they had hoped for when they came to Ottawa in 1939. Despite periods of strain when Brand rightly thought he was being treated as an Admiralty interloper, he remained at Naval Service Headquarters until he retired from the Royal Navy in 1946. Ottawa became the Brands' permanent home as he embarked on a new career in the federal civil service and Margaret carried on with the extensive charity work she had begun during the war. Brand drew on his wartime experience in a succession of positions for the administration of maritime affairs, ultimately as director of marine operations in the Department of Transport. He oversaw the reorganization of that department's fleet as the new Canadian Coast Guard in 1962. After his first retirement in 1963, he came back to help organize the new Coast Guard College that opened in Sydney in 1965. Brand kept meticulous records of the wartime Trade Division, which have long been important resources for research, and assisted several historical projects in his later life. Brand died in 1991 at the age of 95; Margaret followed him in 1993.[10]

Commander Nelson Lay, who as director of the operations division had overseen the making of the gulf defence plans and the allocation of warships to carry them out, returned to sea duty in 1943. Promoted to captain, he commanded HMS *Nabob*, a British escort aircraft carrier that was crewed by the RCN to allow the Canadian service to gain experience in carrier operations and help relieve Britain's critical manpower shortage. On 22 August 1944, when *Nabob* was off the Norwegian coast as part of a naval air strike against the German battleship *Tirpitz* in port at Narvik, the carrier was torpedoed by *U-354*. So too was the British destroyer *Bickerton* as it came in support. Conditions in the chill northern waters were similar to those created by the Labrador Current in the St. Lawrence, and the U-boat had thus been able to escape asdic detection, despite the presence of well-equipped, experienced British escorts. Outstanding damage control efforts by *Nabob*'s crew under Lay's cool leadership enabled her, although severely damaged, to return to port in Scotland. Lay's naval career continued to flourish in the postwar years. He reached the rank of rear admiral and became vice-chief of the naval staff in 1954, his last appointment before retirement in 1958. He was one of the very few senior Canadian officers of any service to write his memoirs, published shortly before his death at the age of 85 in 1988.

The impetus for fuller commemoration of Canada's maritime war came from the younger personnel who had served in the ships, aircraft, and coastal bases. These people, in their twenties during the war, quickly returned to civilian life to get on with their lives—the consuming challenges of careers and raising families that pushed their few years in uniform into the deeper recesses of memory. By the time they reached their late fifties and sixties in the 1970s and 80s, many had more time and inclination for reflection, particularly about the legacy of the wartime effort among younger generations who had no memory of the 1940s and had come to adulthood amid the anti-military culture inspired by the protest movements against the American war in Vietnam that resonated so powerfully north of the border. This was why the St. Lawrence veterans gathered at Gaspé in 1979 welcomed the CBC production on the events by Brian McKenna and published their memories in *Victory in the St. Lawrence: Canada's Unknown War*. The Gaspé commemoration was one of a number of significant projects by veterans of all phases of the maritime war. Veterans, including those who had served in the German forces, also assisted and encouraged academic work by scholars such as Alec Douglas, Michael Hadley, and Marc Milner, who were mining the newly opened wartime naval archives of Canada, Great Britain, the United States, and Germany. Douglas, as director of history at National Defence Headquarters, was able to draw on this support to help win the defence department's approval of a new history of RCN operations in the Second World War to update Joseph Schull's incomplete account.

One result of the new research into the maritime war was the creation of a distinct "Battle of the St. Lawrence" battle honour, the lack of which had so troubled the veterans who gathered at Gaspé in 1979. The Canadian navy had always adopted British naval battle honours, and these included only a general one for the "Battle of the Atlantic." By the mid-1980s, with the revelations of the belated work on the importance of the St. Lawrence operations, senior officials and military officers agreed that adherence to British naval honours had become anachronistic.[11] A great deal of research was needed in the scattered records of St. Lawrence operations to determine precisely which ships—those operating in the gulf during the periods in 1942 and 1944 when German records showed that U-boats were operating offensively in those waters—were entitled to receive the new honour. In 1992, when the considerable staff work was completed, the governor general and commander-in-chief of the Canadian Forces, Ramon Hnatyshyn, approved the new battle honour. It is carried by eight warships of the current Canadian navy fleet, including the frigate HMCS *Charlottetown* and the maritime coastal defence vessel HMCS *Shawinigan*.[12]

The St. Lawrence battle has always been best remembered in the towns of Channel and Port aux Basques, Newfoundland, devastated by the loss in *Caribou* of thirty-one crew based in those small communities. The Newfoundland Railway Workers Welfare Association raised funds to erect a memorial in Port aux Basques on which the names of all those who had perished were engraved. It was unveiled on 14 October 1947, the fifth anniversary of the sinking. In 1986, the new 16,000-tonne super ferry on the North Sydney–Port aux Basques run was named MV *Caribou* in memory of the earlier ship. She carried fourteen survivors of the sinking on her inaugural voyage who gathered to drop a wreath on the position of *U-69*'s lethal attack. At that same time, the memorial was moved to the ferry terminal at Port aux Basques as part of a new memorial park designed for remembrance ceremonies. In 1999 Governor General Adrienne Clarkson unveiled a special St. Lawrence memorial flag at whose centre is a maple leaf in flames; MV *Caribou*, the only ship in service with the same name as any of the merchant vessels lost in the St. Lawrence battle, flew the memorial flag until she left service late in 2010.[13]

THE CANADIAN ACHIEVEMENT in the St. Lawrence battle was to ensure that it was never more than a small corner of the Atlantic war. Minor naval forces, supported by air forces that during the crucial struggle of 1942 were nearly as thinly stretched and ill-equipped as the naval forces, succeeded in all but shutting down the U-boat offensive after its short initial period of success. Canadian forces achieved these results with minimum resources despite a difficult operating environment that strongly favoured the enemy and scathing public criticism of inadequate defences that helped fuel a larger political crisis over leadership of the war effort.

Yet Canadian governments and the armed forces had for decades been sensitive to the imperatives not just to defend these territorial waters, but to be seen vigorously defending them. The gulf and river, the route to the heartland of the country, were on the shores of the province whose population most intensely questioned international military commitments, most particularly in support of the British Empire. Mackenzie King's Liberals were dependent upon political support from Quebec, and that was one reason why the security of the St. Lawrence had been a foundation stone of Liberal defence policy since the party returned to office in 1935. The story of the St. Lawrence battle is a striking example of the manner in which the government nearly reversed its military priorities starting in 1940. During the German conquest of France in the spring of that year, the Canadian government supported the military in stripping the country's home defences in order to provide all possible assistance to beleaguered Britain.

The assistance most urgently needed was naval forces. With German access to Atlantic ports in France and Norway came a revolution in naval warfare. U-boats could now operate in larger numbers and for longer periods of time across the full breadth of the Atlantic and, with benefit of modern radio communications, concentrate for effective attacks on merchant ship convoys on the high seas. The urgent necessity, if Britain was not to be starved into submission, was to provide convoys with anti-submarine escorts through the whole crossing, rather than only in coastal waters where submarines had previously focused their efforts. At Britain's request, Canada willingly committed its best destroyers and all of the sixty-four newly built corvettes to the protection of trans-atlantic convoys as they completed construction in 1941; the destroyers and corvettes were the vessels that were supposed to have been available as the main naval defence of the Gulf of St. Lawrence. When in January 1942, following the United States' entry into the war, the U-boat offensive moved into North American waters and the U.S. Navy had too few anti-submarine vessels to organize its own convoys, Canada expanded its ocean escort commitments to protect shipping through to U.S. Atlantic ports. This effort absorbed the additional corvettes built in follow-on programs and many of the Bangor minesweepers that had been intended to support the corvettes in the protection of the approaches to Canadian ports. The pressing Allied demands for ocean escorts, in 1940, 1941, and 1942, were the reason why only a shoestring defence was available for the St. Lawrence despite the years of planning and preparation.

Although the tide turned against the U-boats in the Battle of the Atlantic in May 1943, the pressure for increased Canadian naval and maritime aviation commitment in the central and eastern ocean did not ease—quite the reverse. Increased forces were needed to ensure the suppression of the still-strong U-boat force to allow more rapid transport of increased numbers of military personnel and larger stockpiles of resources to the United Kingdom to sustain Allied counteroffensives, ultimately with the invasion of occupied Europe at Normandy in 1944. Britain had already reached its maximum effort in terms of manpower and resources in 1943 and relied more heavily than ever on Canadian support. Thus Canada continued to keep only minimal forces in North American waters while continually expanding its effort on the central ocean and overseas, including the commitment of some 100 warships crewed by 10,000 personnel for the Normandy invasion, even while the RCN assumed full responsibility for convoy escort across the North Atlantic.

The story of the St. Lawrence battle was one of endurance—by Canadian and Allied military personnel, merchant seamen, the civilians who succoured the victims of war, and the German submariners who persisted against odds that soon turned against them. It is also a story of imagination and innovation. The Germans learned to exploit the unusual, difficult water conditions in the gulf and river. The Canadians countered by improving the performance of the too-few, often ill-equipped warships and aircraft, building an operational intelligence organization from next to nothing to employ ships and aircraft more effectively, and cultivating the support of the rightly alarmed local population. All the while, Canadian military and political leaders kept constantly to the fore the larger objectives of the war—which, they understood, would be won or lost far away from the St. Lawrence. The greatest significance of the St. Lawrence battle was the marked limitations on the Canadian effort, despite the political and economic importance of the region to the country, in response to urgent Allied calls for essential Canadian help in other theatres more vital to the common cause. It points to the success of the thinly stretched Canadian forces, overwhelmingly made up of citizen sailors and airmen, in suppressing the U-boats after their initial victories in 1942, and all through the 1944 offensive. It says much about the nature of the Canadian war effort in 1939–45.

NOTES

INTRODUCTION: DISCOVERING UNWRITTEN HISTORY

1 Canadian, British, and American maritime forces used the British Imperial system of measurement for distance and weights, but in the present text all measurements have been converted to the metric system.

2 This account is drawn from Brian Tennyson and Roger Sarty, *Guardian of the Gulf: Sydney, Cape Breton, and the Atlantic Wars* (Toronto: University of Toronto Press, 2000), 276–79.

3 Figures on losses from Douglas How, *Night of the Caribou* (Hantsport, NS: Lancelot Press, 1988), 107–10.

4 *The Canadian Magazine* (26 February 1972), 2–7. The second part, "The man who sank nine Allied ships had trouble sinking his own," appeared in the 4 March 1972 issue, pp. 10–13.

5 James Essex, *Victory in the St. Lawrence: Canada's Unknown War* (Erin, ON: Boston Mills Press, 1984), 9 (quoted), 157–59.

ONE: NO SURPRISE: CANADIAN DEFENCE PLANNING AND THE ST. LAWRENCE

1 The account that follows is drawn from Michael L. Hadley and Roger Sarty, *Tin-Pots and Pirate Ships: Canadian Naval Forces and German Sea Raiders 1880–1918* (Montreal and Kingston: McGill-Queen's University Press, 1991).

2 Quoted in Tennyson and Sarty, *Guardian of the Gulf*, 68.

3 Roger Sarty, *The Maritime Defence of Canada* (Toronto: Canadian Institute of Strategic Studies, 1996), 65–74.

4 The following account is drawn from ibid., 110–37.

5 Mackenzie King diary, 18 December 1936, William Lyon Mackenzie King papers, MG 26 J, Library and Archives Canada (LAC), available online at www.collectionscanada.gc.ca/databases/king/index-e.html

TWO: HOW AN UN-NAVAL COUNTRY BECAME A KEY COMBATANT IN THE BATTLE OF THE ATLANTIC

1 "J.G," 9:20 AM 13[?] May 1942, file 2 "Action," Directorate of Censorship records, RG 2 C-2, vol. 5950, LAC, courtesy of Mark Bourrie.

2 [E.C. Russell,] "Captain Eric S. Brand – Interview [on 22 February 1967]," p. 4, E.S. Brand papers, file 81/145, pt. 7, Directorate of History and Heritage (DHH).

3 Brand interview, p. 5. This is confirmed by H.A.C. Lane to Brand, 3 April 1939, Brand family papers, seen courtesy of his daughter, Victoria Robinson.

4 Brand interview, pp. 6–7.

5 The account in the following pages draws upon "Outline History of Trade Division, N.S.H.Q. Ottawa 1939–1945," March 1946, file 81/520/8280, vol. 1, 8280 B, pt. 2, DHH; Brand, "Annual Report of Director of Naval Intelligence Ottawa, for year 1939," 81/145, pt. 1, DHH.

6 Brand journal 1932–1940, 186–87, 81/145, pt. 10, DHH.

7 Tactical and Staff Duties Division (Foreign Documents Section), Naval Staff, *The U-Boat War in the Atlantic, Volume I: 1939–1941*, German Naval History Series ([London]: Admiralty, 1950), 406; S.W. Roskill, *The War at Sea 1939–1945, Volume I: The Defensive*, History of the Second World War, United Kingdom Military Series (London: Her Majesty's Stationery Office, 1954), 103–04.

8 Brand journal, 1932–40, 188, 81/145, pt. 10, DHH.

9 Derek H. Aldcroft, *From Versailles to Wall Street 1919–1929* (Berkeley: University of California Press, 1977), 30, table 20; W.K. Hancock and M.M. Gowing, *British War Economy*, History of the Second World War, United Kingdom Civil Series (London: His Majesty's Stationery Office, 1949), 241.

10 Dominion Bureau of Statistics, *The Canada Year Book 1943–44* (Ottawa: King's Printer, 1944), 458.

11 Stedman to chief of the air staff (CAS), "Report on Air Mission to Washington, D.C.," 3 September 1939, 78/478, DHH.

12 Andrew Hendrie, *The Lockheed Hudson in World War II* (Shrewsbury, UK: Air Life England, 1999), 8–12.

13 Speed and endurance figures from "Eastern Air Command Operation No. 3/40," 25 May 1940, Appendix C, file 510-1-13, Department of National Defence records, RG 24, vol. 11123, LAC; see also Douglas, *Creation of a National Air Force*, 469, 476.

14 CAS to minister, 25 August 1939, file X-47, Ian Mackenzie papers, MG 27 III B5, vol. 31, LAC.

15 Douglas, *Creation of a National Air Force*, 480.

16 A.H. Self for Director General, British Purchasing Commission, New York [signing on behalf of Canada] and C.A. Van Dusen, Vice-President, Consolidated Aircraft, 12 August 1940, HQ 1021-9-95, pt. 1, RG 24, vol. 5133, LAC; the "go-ahead" letter for fifty PBYs to be completed in the United States, and components for fifty-five more for assembly in Canada. The total contract was for $14,443,700.

17 "Participation by RCN Instructed to Work in Closest Co-operation with HM

Forces," appendix A to Chiefs of Staff Committee to minister, 17 September 1939, HQS 5199, pt. 6, RG 24, vol. 2685, LAC.

18 Gill to McNaughton, 13 September 1939, file "CMA Mission to UK," pt. 1, National Research Council records, RG 77, vol. 57, LAC.

19 Nelles to deputy minister, 16 November 1939, quoted, and same to same, 17 November 1939, NSS 1017-10-22, pt. 1, RG 24, vol. 3841, LAC.

20 Norman Ward, ed., *A Party Politician: The Memoirs of Chubby Power* (Toronto: Macmillan, 1966).

21 T. Stephen Henderson, *Angus L. Macdonald: A Provincial Liberal* (Toronto: University of Toronto Press, 2007). See also John Hawkins, *The Life and Times of Angus L.* (Windsor, NS: Lancelot Press, 1969).

22 Admiralty, Historical Section, *Defeat of the Enemy Attack on Shipping 1939–1945: A Study of Policy and Operations*, Naval Staff History (London: Admiralty, 1957), vol. 1B, table 13; see also Roskill, *War at Sea*, 1: 348–52.

23 *Defeat of the Enemy Attack on Shipping*, 1B, table 7.

24 Gerhard L. Weinberg, *A World at Arms: A Global History of World War II* (Cambridge: Cambridge University Press, 1994), 175–76, 178–82, 205, 236; Ian Kershaw, *Hitler 1936–1945: Nemesis* (London: Penguin, 2000), 307–10, 341–3; Hancock, *British War Economy*, 240–41.

THREE: U-BOATS OFFSHORE, JANUARY–APRIL 1942

1 For this and following paragraphs, Eberhard Rössler, *The U-boats: The Evolution and Technical History of German Submarines*, Harold Erenberg, trans. (reprint; Annapolis, MD: Naval Institute Press, 1989), 104–10, 336–37, 344–45.

2 Information on the careers of U-boat officers is available in Rainer Busch and Hans-Joachim Röll, *German U-Boat Commanders of World War II: A Biographical Dictionary*, Geoffrey Brooks, trans. (London: Greenhill Books, 1999). Summary operational histories of all U-boats are in Kenneth Wynn, *U-Boat Operations of the Second World War*, 2 vols. (Annapolis, MD: Naval Institute Press, 1997–8). Accounts in the present book of the careers of the commanding officers and U-boats prior to and after their missions to the St. Lawrence are based on these excellent publications.

3 The account of *U-130*'s cruise off Cape Breton and of all the other U-boats that operated in the St. Lawrence area mentioned in the present book are based on English-language translations of the logs held at the Directorate of History and Heritage. The translations were carried out in two separate projects by two translators with exceptional military experience. During the early to mid-1980s Lieutenant-Colonel (retired) David Wiens translated extracts from the logs of U-boats that were pursued by Canadian anti-submarine aircraft for the official history of the RCAF. In the 1990s, Commodore (retired) Jan Drent translated additional extracts, covering the whole period in which particular U-boats operated in Canadian waters or in the vicinity of Canadian naval forces overseas for the official history of the Royal Canadian Navy.

4   Whitehead, "Supplementary Remarks of Sinking of S/S Frisko by Interviewing Officer," n.d., NSC 1062-13-10, pt. 6, RG 24, vol. 4023, LAC.

5   George Young, *The Short Triangle: A Story of the Sea and Men Who Go Down to It in Ships* (Lunenburg, NS: Lunenburg County Press, 1975), 58.

6   W.A.B. Douglas, Roger Sarty, Michael Whitby with Robert H. Caldwell, William Johnston, William G.P. Rawling, *No Higher Purpose: The Official Operational History of the Royal Canadian Navy in the Second World War, 1939–1943, Volume II, Part 1* (St. Catharines, ON: Vanwell Publishing and the Department of National Defence, 2002), 414.

7   Admiralty records indicate he was a naval cadet for only a "few months" in 1904 and resigned "for private reasons." Minute sheet 15669/21, dated 23 March 1921, quoting an Admiralty report dated 6 March 1918, Pensions and National Insurance records (PIN) 26/22337, The National Archives (TNA), Kew, United Kingdom.

8   Admiralty, [record of service], 3 October 1924, ibid.

9   Minute sheet 15669/21, 23 March 1921, ibid.

10 M.L. Prout [unclear], medical advisor to Colonial Office, to Commander H.B. Brasier Creagh, Ministry of Pensions, 31 March 1922, ibid.

11 De Marbois to secretary, Special Grants Committee, London, 19 July 1923, ibid.

12 C.H. Little, "Early Days in Naval Intelligence, 1939–41," in *Salty Dips: Vol. 2: "... and All Our Joints Were Limber"* (Ottawa: The Ottawa Branch, Naval Officers' Associations of Canada, 1985), 111–13.

13 Catherine E. Allan, "A Minute Bletchley Park: Building a Canadian Naval Operational Intelligence Centre, 1939–1943," Michael L. Hadley, Rob Huebert, and Fred W. Crickard, *A Nation's Navy: In Quest of Canadian Naval Identity* (Montreal and Kingston: McGill-Queen's University Press, 1996), 158–68.

14 "History 1942 D/F Plotting Section – N.S.H.Q.," DHH.

15 Naval secretary, "Defence of Shipping – Gulf of St. Lawrence," 29 April 1940 and "Defence of Shipping – Gulf of St. Lawrence (Short Title – Plan GL)," 25 April 1941, NSS 8280-166/16, pt. 1, RG 24, vol. 6788, LAC.

16 Fraser McKee, *Armed Yachts of Canada* (Erin, ON: Boston Mills Press, 1983), 53, 57–59; Gilbert Norman Tucker, *The Naval Service of Canada: Its Official History, Volume II: Activities on Shore* (Ottawa: King's Printer, 1952), 182–83.

17 Ibid., 48–51; Donald E. Graves, "'Hell Boats' of the RCN: The Canadian Navy and the Motor Torpedo Boat, 1936–1941," *The Northern Mariner* II (July 1992), 31–45; Department of Munitions and Supply, *Quarterly Summary*, 1 January–31 March 1941, p. 38, copy in the Canadian War Museum's Military History Research Centre; ibid., 1 January–31 March 1942, p. 50.

18 "Daily State – H.M.C. Ships," 11 May 1942, 81/520-1650-DS, DHH.

19 Heenan to director of naval intelligence (DNI), "Steamship Service Saint Lawrence River ...," 9 April 1942, NSS 8280-166/16, pt. 1, RG 24, vol. 6788, LAC.

20 Naval staff minutes, 16 March 1942, NSS 1048-48-32, RG 24, vol. 3976, LAC; initial plans were to gather convoys in the vicinity of the mouth of the Saguenay River, about sixty-five kilometres west of Bic Island.

21 Naval staff minutes, 12 March 1942, NSHQ to Admiralty, commander-in-chief, United States Fleet (Cominch), 1409Z ["Z" was the military designation for Greenwich Mean Time] 13 March 1942, Admiralty to NSHQ, 1312A 27 March 1942 (quoted), all in ibid.

22 Richard Oliver Mayne, "Vice-Admiral George C. Jones: The Political Career of a Naval Officer," Michael Whitby, Richard H. Gimblett, and Peter Haydon, eds., *The Admirals: Canada's Senior Naval Leadership in the Twentieth Century* (Toronto: Dundurn, 2006), 126–30.

23 Minutes, Naval staff, 23 March 1942, reported in deputy secretary (staff) to director operations division "for action," 26 March 1942, NSS 1048-48-32, pt. 1, RG 24, vol. 3976, LAC.

24 H. Nelson Lay, *Memoirs of a Mariner* (Ottawa: the author, 1982).

25 Roger Sarty, *Canada and the Battle of the Atlantic* (Montreal: Éditions Art Global and the Department of National Defence, 1998), 95–96.

26 E.g., Richard O. Mayne, *Betrayed: Scandal, Politics and Canadian Naval Leadership* (Vancouver: UBC Press, 2006), 124–26.

27 This and the following paragraphs are based on secretary, Naval Board, "Defence of Shipping – Gulf of St. Lawrence – 1942 (Short title – Plan GL 2)," 1 April 1942, H1002-1-8, pt. 1, RG 24, vol. 11692, LAC.

28 Roger Sarty, "The RCAF's First Catalinas and Cansos" (unpublished paper, 1986).

29 *Globe and Mail*, "Expect U-Boats to Enter Gulf of St. Lawrence," 25 March 1942. This and the other English-language newspaper stories were consulted in the Second World War "morgue" or archive of the *Hamilton Spectator*, now held by the Canadian War Museum's Military History Research Centre and available online in a word-searchable database, "Democracy at War: Canadian Newspapers and the Second World War," www.warmuseum.ca/cwm/exhibitions/newspapers/intro_e.shtml

30 Reprinted in William Lyon Mackenzie King, *Canada and the Fight for Freedom* (Toronto: Macmillan, 1944), 46.

31 Ibid., 124.

FOUR: FIRST BLOOD IN THE GULF, MAY 1942

1 Karl von Clausewitz, *On War*, Michael Howard and Peter Paret, eds. and trans. (Princeton: Princeton University Press, 1976), 119.

2 U-boat headquarters war diary, 4 May 1942, 79/446, DHH; *U-553* log, 5 May 1942, quoted.

3 *U-553* log, 6 May 1942.

4 *U-553* log, 7 May 1942; 119 Squadron and RCAF Station Sydney operations record books (ORB), 7 May 1942, microfilm, DHH.

5 The USAAC reports are attached as Appendix A to "Weekly Intelligence Report from R.C.A.F. Station Gander," Serial No. 29, 10–16 May 1942, 181.003 (D4099), DHH.

6 McEwen to air officer commanding [AOC] Eastern Air Command [EAC], 2052 Greenwich Mean Time [GMT], 11 May 1942, 181.002 (D124), DHH.

7 Unsigned, undated marginal note, "Minutes of St. Lawrence operations Conference held in Ottawa February 22nd–24th, 1943," 79/179, DHH.

8 Naval officer in charge [NOIC] Sydney, report of proceedings for May 1942, NSS 1000-5-21, pt. 1, DHH; naval control of shipping officer (NCSO) to NOIC Sydney, "Summary of Convoy Season 1942," 2 February 1943, 48-1-1, pt. 2, RG 24, vol. 11079, LAC; Defended Port of Sydney, situation report, week ending 9 May 1942, 321.009 (D124), pt. 1, DHH.

9 NOIC Gaspé, report of proceedings for May 1942, NSS 1000-5-17, DHH.

10 La Malbaie had been commissioned into the navy, that is, accepted by the government from the builder after basic equipment trials, only on 28 April, and Granby on 2 May.

11 Commanding officer (CO) HMCS La Malbaie to Captain (D) Halifax, 14 May 1942, CO HMCS Ungava to Captain (D) Halifax, 14 May 1942, 81/520/48-2-2C, pt. 1, DHH; Burgess and Macpherson, Ships of Canada's Naval Forces (Toronto: Collins, 1981), 125, 235.

12 EAC ORB and 119 Squadron ORB, 11 May 1942, DHH.

13 Jügen Rohwer, Axis Submarine Successes of World War Two: German, Italian and Japanese Submarine Successes, 1939–1945 (Annapolis, MD: Naval Institute Press, 1983), 89.

14 "Sub Gave No Warning, Says Ship Captain," Hamilton Spectator, 16 May 1942.

15 "Two St. Lawrence Sinkings Show Canada Vulnerable, Nazi U-Boat 'Very Big One,'" Toronto Telegram, 18 May 1942.

16 "Sub Gave No Warning, Says Ship Captain," Hamilton Spectator, 16 May 1942, quoted; "Two St. Lawrence Sinkings Show Canada Vulnerable, Nazi U-Boat 'Very Big One,'" Toronto Telegram, 18 May 1942; "List of Survivors of the S.S. 'Nicoya' at Gaspé," n.d., 5-2-3, pt. 3, RG 24, vol. 11014, LAC.

17 Quotations from "Attack in St. Lawrence Last Thing Crews Expected," Hamilton Spectator, 14 May 1942; see also "Ottawa Has No Reports of Sub in St. Lawrence Taking Additional Toll," ibid.

18 "Ottawa Has No Reports of Sub in St. Lawrence Taking Additional Toll," Hamilton Spectator, 14 May 1942; Form "Wr. 1(d) Shipping Casualties" [Leto], "Entered May 30/42," Department of Transport records, RG 12, vol. 887, LAC.

19 Lacasse, "S.S. Nicoya – Torpedoed in the St. Lawrence River," 13 May 1942, NSS 8871-5502, RG 24, vol. 6893, LAC.

20 Commanding officer Atlantic coast (COAC) to address group 097A, received at NSHQ Ottawa 0421Z/11[sic 12] May 1942, ibid.

21 War diary, Headquarters, Defended Port of Gaspé, 12 May 1942, RG 24, vol. 13856, mfm T-10875, LAC.

22 NOIC Quebec to COAC et al., 1430Z/12 May 1942, NSS 8871-5502, RG 24, vol. 6893, LAC.

23 The available evidence suggests that Armit changed plans as he received more information. The item most immediate to the event (staff officer Gaspé to COAC,

1415Z [10:15 AM] 12 May 1942, NSS 8871-5502, RG 24, vol. 6898, LAC) states that the truck convoy was originally headed for Cloridorme. The Gaspé report of proceedings for 12 May, presumably written after the event, states that Armit's objective was Fox River, about fifteen kilometres closer to Gaspé than L'Anse-à-Valleau, and thirty kilometres closer than Cloridorme. That suggests Armit's objective had changed because of the bad road conditions, which is confirmed by a mid-afternoon telegraph message from the staff at Gaspé to the RCMP that Armit's plan at that time was to bring the Cloridorme survivors by boat to meet the truck convoy on the main highway near Fox River (Lacasse, "S.S. Nicoya," 13 May 1942, ibid.). It is not clear from the written records where Armit joined the fishing boat, but a reasonable guess is that the sighting report from Fame Point led him to head to L'Anse-à-Valleau, the harbour closest to Fame Point.

24 Essex, *Victory*, 77.

25 Lacasse, "S.S. Nicoya," 13 May 1942, RG 24, vol. 6893, NSS 8871-5502, LAC.

26 NOIC Gaspé to COAC, 2445Z/12 May 1942, NOIC Gaspé to COAC, 14 May 1942, NSS 8871-5502, RG 24, vol. 6893, LAC; CO HMCS *Fort Ramsay* report of proceedings for May 1942, NSS 1000-5-17, DHH.

27 81/145, pt. 15, p. 52, DHH. Brand was promoted to acting captain 1 January 1940 and to substantive captain 1 July 1941.

28 Mackenzie King diary, 11 May 1942.

29 Mackenzie King diary, 12 May 1942.

30 "Suggested Draft Statement for the Minister at Press conference – 15th January [1942]," and following correspondence to 20 May 1942, NSC 1029-6-2, pt. 4, RG 24, vol. 3881, LAC, copies provided by Tim Balzer.

31 E. McM., "Ruling. Re: Sinking, The St. Lawrence," [12–13 May 1942], 2 "Action," RG 2 C-2, vol. 5950, LAC, transcript provided by Mark Bourrie.

32 For an excellent recent account see Mark Bourrie, *The Fog of War: Censorship of Canada's Media in World War Two* (Vancouver: Douglas and McIntyre, 2011).

33 House of Commons, *Debates*, 13 May 1942, 2389–90.

34 Unsigned note, "Captain Brand called at 2 p.m.," no date, but probably 13 May 1942, 2 "Action," RG 2 C-2, vol. 5950, LAC, transcript provided by Mark Bourrie. This item suggests that Macdonald may have been compelled to make the second announcement about the loss of a second ship because the original press release on the first ship had mentioned there were only forty-one survivors. Reporters quickly discovered that there were many additional survivors, and the initial newspaper accounts on 13 May remarked that in fact over eighty survivors had been landed. Brand admitted that press inquiries about this discrepancy "had now gouged this information" from the navy about the loss of the second ship.

35 "St. Lawrence Incident. May 11th 1942. Notes on Consequences of Publicity," 81/145 pt. 5, DHH.

36 *Montreal Gazette*, 13 May 1942, 8.

37 Quoted in *Globe and Mail*, 21 May 1942, 2.

38 Orders were given in COAC to NOsIC Sydney, Gaspé, Quebec, 1836Z 13 May 1942, which states they were based on the new revision of the gulf defence plan, "Plan GL 2," NS 1048-48-2, RG 24, vol. 3976, LAC.

39 CO HMCS *Arrowhead* to Captain "D" Halifax, "Report of Proceedings SQS 1," 22 May 1941 and other correspondence, NSS 8280-ON90, microfilm, DHH; NSS 8280-ON91, ibid.; CO HMCS *Arrowhead* to Captain "D" Halifax, "Report of proceedings QS 1 and SH 2," NSS 8280-QS 1, ibid.; ns., n.d., "H.M.C.S. Medicine Hat Report of Proceedings," forwarded by NOIC Sydney to COAC, 2 June 1942, 81/520/48-2-2(c), DHH.

40 "Annual Report of Director of Trade Division, 1942," 81/145, pt. 1, DHH. Effective 1 July 1942, convoy and other shipping control functions were separated from the naval intelligence division of the naval staff to create a new Trade Division, with Brand as director. C.H. Little, promoted lieutenant-commander, became director of naval intelligence.

41 From the operational records available, it appears that there may have been no "SQ 2" or "QS 2." The records, however, are not well organized, and each time I take another plunge into the events of May 1942 I find interesting items in out-of-the-way places.

42 116 and 117 Squadron ORBs, May 1942, DHH.

43 EAC ORB, 14 May 1942, DHH; COAC to NSHQ, 1446Z 14 May 1942, NSHQ to COAC, 2230Z 14 May 1942, NSS 1048-48-32, RG 24, vol. 3976, LAC.

44 "A History of Naval Control Service at Sydney, Nova Scotia," p. 12, 81/520/1440-127, DHH.

45 Daily States, 30 May 1942, 81/520/1650-DS, DHH.

46 RCAF Station Sydney "Weekly Intelligence Report," week ending 15 May 1942, 181.003 (D43), DHH.

47 Analysis of overall air operations based on EAC ORB, May 1942, DHH; daily signal reports of air coverage, HQ EAC to Air Ministry Whitehall, 12–22 May 1942, S19-6-5, pt. 4, RG 24, vol. 5217, LAC.

48 "St. Lawrence Incident. May 11th 1942. Notes on Consequences of Publicity," 81/145 pt. 5, DHH.

FIVE: HOLDING THE HOME FRONT, JULY 1942

1 EAC to AFHQ, signal A.39, 1900/15 July 1942, DHH 181.009 (D121), a full account of air support for QS 15. A fairly full collection of EAC daily operations report signals for early July 1942 is in 181.003 (D304), DHH.

2 Unless otherwise noted, the account of *Drummondville*'s movements is drawn from CO HMCS *Drummondville* to NOIC Gaspé, "Report of Proceedings of Convoy Q.S. 15," 11 July 1942, G018-1, pt. 1, RG 24, vol. 12009, LAC.

3 *Globe and Mail*, 5 April 1944.

4 John F. White, *U-Boat Tankers 1941–45: Submarine Suppliers to Atlantic Wolf Packs* (Annapolis, MD: Naval Institute Press, 1998), 51.

5 CO HMCS *Clayoquot* to NOIC Gaspé, "Report on Q.S. S.Q. 16," 6 July 1942, NSS 8280-SQ 16, reel C-5535, LAC.

6   Forms "Particulars of Attacks on Merchant Vessels by Enemy Submarines," for *Anastasios Pateras* and *Hainaut*, 264-4-1-1, RG 24, vol. 11973, LAC; Powers, "Summary of Statements by Survivors of the Belgium SS 'HAINAUT,'" 31 July 1942, and "Summary of Statements by Survivors of the Greek SS 'ANASTASIOS PATERAS,'" 31 July 1942, NSS 1870-173, pt. 3, RG 24, vol. 8191, LAC.

7   Marc Milner, *The U-Boat Hunters: The Royal Canadian Navy and the Offensive against Germany's Submarines* (Toronto: University of Toronto Press, 1994), 114–15.

8   NSHQ, "Loss of S.S. 'Dinaric,'" 28 August 1942, NSS 8871-2276, RG 24, vol. 6891, LAC. CO HMCS *Clayoquot* to NOIC Gaspé, "Report on Q.S. S.Q. 16," 6 July 1942, reports that *Drummondville* signalled about the attack at 0138 Atlantic time, a full hour before the alert by COAC. But it is possible that *Clayoquot*'s report is in "standard," not "daylight saving" time, meaning the actual time was 0238 Atlantic Daylight Savings.

9   130 Squadron ORB, 6 July 1942, microfilm, DHH; EAC to AFHQ, signal A.39, 1800/15 July 1942, 181.009 (D121), DHH; CAS to minister of national defence for air, 18 July 1942, Little to Anderson, 18 July 1942, S19-6-5, pt. 5, RG 24, vol. 5217, LAC; Taillefer to Bezeau, 3 March 1942, 130 Squadron permanent reference file, DHH.

10   Wilkins, "Summary of Accident Investigation – No. 326," 4 August 1942, 181.003 (D3898), DHH; 130 Squadron ORB, 6–8 July 1942, microfilm, DHH.

11   Taillefer to Bezeau, 3 March 1982.

12   NSHQ, "Loss of S.S. 'Dinaric,'" 28 August 1942, NSS 8871-2276, RG 24, vol. 6891, LAC.

13   NSHQ to Commanding Officer Pacific Coast for CNS, 1607Z/7 July 1942, NSS 8280-QS 15, RG 24, reel C-5530, LAC.

14   CO HMCS *Ville de Quebec* to Captain (D) Halifax, "Report of Proceedings – A/S Sweep ... and subsequent escort of Convoy Q.S. 16," 12 July 1942, NSS 8280-QS 16, ibid.

15   Douglas, *Creation of a National Air Force*, 500.

16   Mackenzie King diary, 5 July 1942.

17   Mackenzie King diary, 5 July 1942. Mackenzie King records that he got word of *U-132*'s attack on the afternoon of 5 July, which cannot be correct, as Vogelsang struck on the night of 5–6 July. Mackenzie King notes that he dictated his diary just before lunch on 6 July and suggests he brought it up to date, but that could not be the case. His diary records that he received word of the sinkings in the "afternoon," and as that could only have been the afternoon of 6 July, it would have been after he did his dictation. He did not get a chance to dictate again until the evening of 8 July, when he noted that he covered his very busy day of 7 July. It seems likely that on 8 July he dictated the entries for 5 and 6 July as well as for the seventh. His activities on 5 and 6 July were in fact similar; he did little but work on his speech. Thus it is possible he transposed the news of *U-132* from the sixth to the fifth, which would not have been remarkable because of his hectic schedule on the seventh and eighth.

18 Conrad Black, *Duplessis* (Toronto: McClelland and Stewart, 1977), 77; J.L. Granatstein, *The Politics of Survival: The Conservative Party of Canada, 1939–1945* (Toronto: University of Toronto Press, 1967), 88.

19 Douglas, *Creation of a National Air Force*, 498, 500.

20 House of Commons, *Debates*, 13 July 1942, 4124–5.

21 House of Commons, *Debates*, 13 July 1942, 4126.

22 House of Commons, *Debates*, 16 July 1942, 4278–4290.

23 Mackenzie King diary, 16 July 1942.

24 All Mackenzie King's long-time political foes, and ardent supporters of overseas conscription: George Drew, leader of the Ontario Conservative party; Mitchell F. Hepburn, Liberal premier of Ontario; George McCullagh, publisher of the Toronto *Globe and Mail*; John Bassett, publisher of the Montreal *Gazette*.

25 Mackenzie King diary, 17 July 1942.

26 Mackenzie King diary, 18 July 1942.

27 Evident in the fact that COAC and NSHQ immediately reported developments by signal to Admiral Nelles, who was then in British Columbia and confirmed all actions taken with him (Signals between NSHQ and "COPC for CNS," 6–8 July 1942, NSS 8280-QS15, RG 24, reel C-5530, LAC). Macdonald himself commented acidly in the House on the fact that enemy action in the St. Lawrence excited so much political and media commentary in contrast to the more numerous attacks on the Atlantic coast (House of Commons, *Debates*, 13 July 1942, 4125).

28 Robert Fisher, "Caribbean Run: The Royal Canadian Navy's Oil Convoys 1942," unpublished narrative, June 1993, pp. 40, 42–43, DHH. See also his "'We'll get our own': Canada and the oil shipping crisis of 1942," *The Northern Mariner/Le marin du nord* III, no. 2 (April 1993): 33–39.

29 Entries for HMCS *Shawinigan* and HMCS *Trail*, 81/520/DS, Daily States 4–9 July 1942, DHH.

30 Tennyson and Sarty, *Guardian of the Gulf*, 266–67.

31 NSS 8280-SQ 20, RG 24, reel C-5535, LAC.

32 AOC EAC to Air Ministry, signal 0615Z/20 July 1942, 181.003 (D304), DHH.

33 CO HMCS *Charlottetown* to NOIC Gaspé, "Report of Proceedings – Convoy S.Q. 20," 23 July 1942, NSS 8280-SQ 20, reel C-5535, LAC.

34 CO, HMCS *Weyburn* to NOIC Gaspé, "Report of Proceedings, Convoy Q.S. 19," NSS 8280-QS 19, RG 24, reel C-5530, LAC.

35 Rundle to Torpedo Officer, HMCS *Cornwallis*, "Investigation of S.S. 'Frederika Lensen,'" 26 August 1942, 5-2-3A, RG 24, vol. 11015, LAC. This adds some details to Russell and Arthurs, Chief Officer, "Following is my report on the loss of the S.S. Frederika Lensen," no date, ibid.

36 Rundle to Torpedo Officer, HMCS *Cornwallis*, "Investigation of S.S. 'Frederika Lensen,'" 26 August 1942, 5-2-3A, RG 24, vol. 11015, LAC.

37 CO, HMC M/L *Q-074* to NOIC Gaspé, "Disabling of 'Frederika Lensen' in Q.S. 19," 22 July 1942, NSS 8871-3769, RG 24, vol. 6892, LAC; Executive Officer, HMCS *Fort Ramsay* to NOIC, HMCS *Fort Ramsay*, "Examination of S.S.

'Fredericka Lensen,'" 23 July 1942, 5-2-3A, RG 24, vol. 11015, LAC; see also Russell and Arthurs, "Report on the loss of the S.S. Frederika Lensen," ibid.

SIX: SQUADRON LEADER SMALL STRIKES; ADMIRAL DÖNITZ PROBES FOR SOFT SPOTS, SUMMER 1942

1   The following is based on Small's personnel file, C-1379, National Personnel Records Centre. See also Richard Goette, "Squadron Leader N.E. Small: A Study of Leadership in the RCAF's Eastern Air Command," *Canadian Military Journal*, 5, no. 1 (Spring 2004), 43–50.

2   181.009 (D4990), DHH.

3   Commander-in-chief Coastal Command to AOC EAC, 18 November 1941, Air Ministry records (AIR) 15-368/4134, TNA.

4   "Coastal Command Tactical Memorandum No. 22. Hints on Anti-U-boat Warfare," 2 January 1942, "Coastal Command Tactical Instruction No. 18. Attacks on Submarines," 15 December 1942. These were distributed by AOC EAC to distribution list, 28 February 1942, 181.009 (D1147), DHH.

5   Kingsland to air member personnel, minute number 10, 19 February 1942, S19-6-1, RG 24, vol. 5216, LAC.

6   CAS to EAC, signal A922, 4 March 1942; Pearman, "Summary of Anti-Submarine Air Effort of Eastern Air Command, Halifax, N.S. [for February 1942]," 29 March 1942, 181.009 (D1147), DHH.

7   "History 1942 D/F Plotting Section – N.S.H.Q.," p. 3, DHH.

8   "Chronological History of Operational Intelligence Centre, 1942," p. 9, NSS 1440-18, DHH.

9   Notes of interview with Air Marshal Annis by F. Hatch and J.D.F. Kealy, n.d., pp. 6–7, notes of interview with Annis by W.A.B. Douglas, 11 September 1979, "Annis, C.L.," biography file, DHH; Small to AOC EAC, "Standby Aircraft for DF Bearings," 24 December 1942, 181.002 (D68A), DHH, is Small's own explanation of the practice his unit developed earlier in the year; see also AOC EAC to Secretary, DND for Air, "Anti-Submarine Operations – Eastern Air Command," 5 August 1942, 181.009 (D1147), DHH.

10   Douglas, *Creation of a National Air Force*, 520; "EAC Anti-Submarine Report July 1942," pp. 12–14, 181.003 (D25), DHH.

11   Just twenty minutes before that contact, the aircraft again sighted *Mojave* and saw nothing amiss. If the timings of the aircraft's report are correct, *Mojave* had just begun an anti-submarine search after *U-517* fired two torpedoes into *Chatham* at 7:45 AM, but the U.S. warship made no effort to communicate with the Canadian aircraft.

12   ORB 116 Squadron, 26 August 1942, microfilm, DHH; the patrol report was distributed almost verbatim in a signal by AOC EAC 0300Z, 29 August 1942, 181.003 (D304), DHH.

13   NCSO Sydney to NOIC Sydney, 3 September 1942, enclosing the sailing telegram, NCSO Sydney to Commander Greenland Patrol, Senior Officer Present Afloat

Greenland, CTF 24, CTU 294, 8, 12 repeated Connav, Admiralty, NSHQ, COAC, FONF, Army Chief of Staff for Air Washington, three parts, 1723Z, 1725Z, 1727Z, 25 August 1942, NSS 8280-SG 6, microfilm, DHH.

14 Costello to Anderson, 29 August 1942, 181.009 (D121), DHH, explains the air coverage provided for LN 6 and SG 6 on 25–28 August 1942; the more detailed daily signals for these dates are available in 181.003 (D304), DHH.

15 "Attached [report on attacks on SG 6] compiled for the interest of Commander Task Force 24 ...," n.d., "Convoy SG-6 Record of Despatches," [convoy file for SG 6], Records of Naval Operating Forces, RG 313, Red, CTF 24, box 8702, Washington National Records Center (WNRC), Washington, DC, National Archives and Records Administration (NARA).

16 "Recapitulation of Survivors – Convoy SG-6," n.d., ibid., shows one "known dead" and gives two figures for "Missing," 12 and 14, without explanation. Twelve missing would appear to be the correct figure, as there were 549 survivors and one known dead from the total of 562 on board, but possibly there were ambiguities in the reports received when the table was compiled.

17 CTF 24 to Sydney, CB, 1927Z, 27 August 1942, "Coastal Convoys SG ... GS, June 1942–30 April 1943," "Coastal Convoys Signals," DHH.

18 "Convoy SG-6 Record of Despatches," [convoy file for SG 6], RG 313, Red, CTF 24, box 8702, WNRC, NARA; CTF 24 to CinC US Fleet via CinC US Atlantic Fleet, 28 September 1942, Confidential 1942, A14-1, folder 3, box 8814, ibid.

19 CO USCGC *Mohawk* to CinC US Atlantic Fleet, 29 August 1942, quoted; see also CO USCGC *Algonquin* to CTF 24, 31 August 1942, Confidential 1942, A14-1, folder 3, RG 313, Red, box 8814, WNRC, NARA.

20 "Recapitulation of Survivors – Convoy SG-6," n.d., [convoy file for SG 6], RG 313, Red, box 8702, WNRC, NARA shows losses as thirteen missing in *Arlyn* and four "known dead" and one missing in *Laramie*.

21 CTF 24 to COAC repeated NOIC Sydney, *Mojave*, 0413Z 3 September 1942, NSS 8280-SG 6, microfilm DHH.

22 Brainard to COAC, 14 September 1942, ibid.

23 Nelles to Brainard, 1 October 1942, ibid.

24 CTF 24 to Commander Greenland Patrol Force, 21 September 1942, [convoy file for SG 6], RG 313, Red, box 8702, WNRC; CTF 24 to CinC US Fleet via CinC US Atlantic Fleet, 28 September 1942, Confidential 1942, A14-1, folder 3, RG 313, Red, box 8814, ibid.

25 *U-517* log, 1 September 1942.

26 ORB 117 Squadron, 2 September 1942, microfilm, DHH.

27 NSHQ to *Weyburn, Clayoquot, Shawinigan, Trail,* 2125Z 2 September 1942, 89/34 reel 16, NSS 8280-LN 7, DHH.

28 CO HMCS *Trail,* "H.M.C.S. 'TRAIL' Report of Proceedings of Convoy L.N. 7," n.d., ibid.

29 CO HMCS *Shawinigan* to NSHQ, "Report of Proceedings after Attack," 9 September 1942, ibid.

30   CO HMCS *Weyburn* to NOIC Gaspé, "Report of Proceedings – Convoys SQ.32 & NL.6," 5 September 1942, 89/34, NSS 8280-SQ 32, DHH.

31   CO HMCS *Shawinigan* to NSHQ, "Report of Proceedings after Attack," 9 September 1942, NSS 8280-LN 7, microfilm, DHH; CO HMCS *Trail*, "Form for Reporting Submarine Attacks on Convoys," n.d., NSS 1062-13-19, pt. 1, RG 24, vol. 4027, LAC.

32   Captain (D) Halifax to COAC, 18 September 1942, NSS 8280-LN 7, microfilm, DHH.

33   "E.A.C. Anti-Submarine Report ... for September 1942," pp. 7–8, 181.003 (D25), DHH, quoted; see also the report for the attack in 76/278, DHH, and AOC EAC, "Operations September 3rd," 0600Z, 4 September 1942, 181.003(304), DHH.

SEVEN: CRISIS AND CLOSURE OF THE GULF, 3–9 SEPTEMBER 1942

1   CO HMCS *Hepatica,* "Report of Proceedings. S.Q.33," 4 September 1942, NSS 8280-SQ33, reel C-5535, LAC.

2   "Raccoon's Report of Attack while with S.Q. 33," 4 September 1942, ibid.

3   NSHQ to Weyburn, Trial, Hepatica, Red Deer, Kenora, et al., 1737Z/3 September 1942, NSS 8280 SQ 33, reel C-5535, LAC.

4   U-boat headquarters war diary, 4 September 1942.

5   EAC to Air Ministry et al., operations report signals for 3–5 September 1942, DHH 181.003 (D304).

6   U-boat headquarters war diary, 30 August 1942, DHH 79/446.

7   Quoted in Sarty, *Canada and the Battle of the Atlantic*, 110.

8   Geoffrey W. Smith, *Naval Talk by "Jock"* (Np.: privately published, [c1997]), "U-Boats Breach the Gulf in '42," p. 3.

9   "Navy Casualties," *Globe and Mail*, 15 September 1942; "Patrol craft Raccoon lost ...," *Hamilton Spectator*, 15 September 1942.

10   CO *Fort Ramsay* to COAC, "Report of Proceedings for month of October," 3 November 1942, NSS 1000-5-17, DHH.

11   "Minutes taken at board of inquiry on board H.M.C.S. 'Fort Ramsay' at 1000 hours, 18th September, 1942," G22-1-2, RG 24, vol. 12009, LAC.

12   *U-517* log, 6–7 September 1942.

13   The following account is based upon reports of the attack by all the escorts present attached to COAC to Cominch, "Report of Submarine Attack on Convoy QS 33," 23 November 1942, NSS 1062-13-19, pt. 1, RG 24, vol. 4027, LAC.

14   Rohwer, *Axis Submarine Successes*, 120.

15   EAC signals, 9–11 September 1942, 181.003 (D304), DHH.

16   181.003 (D1321), DHH.

17   J.9240, National Personnel Records Centre.

18   U-boat headquarters war diary, 17 September 1942.

19 Signals, 9 September 1942, 27-D-36, RG 24, vol. 11572, LAC; CO HMS *Witherington* to Captain (D) Halifax, "Report of Proceedings ... Ninth to Fourteenth September, 1942," 17 September 1942, 48-2-2, pt. 63, RG 24, vol. 11091, LAC.

20 NSHQ to Admiralty, repeated CONNAV, BAD, NMCS Washington, COAC, FONF, CTF 24, 2223Z 9 September 1942, NSS 8280-166/16, pt. 3, RG 24, vol. 6789, LAC.

21 Tucker, *Naval Service of Canada*, II, 391–93.

22 Kevin Smith, *Conflict over Convoys: Anglo-American Logistics Diplomacy in the Second World War* (Cambridge: Cambridge University Press, 1996), 58–63; High Commissioner for the UK to acting under-secretary of state for external affairs, 15 May 1941, Howe to Robertson, 24 May 1941, RG 25 G-1, vol. 1994, file 1177-39C, LAC.

23 Mitchell, "General Situation at Halifax and Saint John ... Ship Repairs, Loading Delays ...," 5 March 1941, NS 30-31-2, RG 24, vol. 5632, LAC.

24 Huband, Montreal to Shipminder, London, telegram 12523, timed 2025/7 November 1941, Ministry of Transport (MT) 59/940, TNA. Munitions and Supply also placed orders for the construction of two corvettes at Saint John and, in a much more ambitious scheme, for two large Tribal-class destroyers at Halifax, far and away the most complex warship-building project ever attempted in Canada, to provide stable employment for the trades needed for ship repair. Work on the vessels would take second priority to repair of damaged vessels. There were problems with the new building projects in the fall of 1941, however, because of delays in delivery of steel.

25 Huband to director general, Ministry of War Transport (MWT), London, 10 August 1942, ibid.

26 Secretary, Naval Board to Admiralty and Cominch, 25 July 1942, forwarding "Minutes of Ottawa Conference on Trade and Escort Problems 23–24 July, 1942," Records of the Office of the Chief of Naval Operations, RG 38, box 152, College Park, MD, NARA, copy in 89/100, pt. 8A, DHH.

27 In December 1941, King became commander-in-chief U.S. Fleet, in charge of all the U.S. Navy's forces, a title abbreviated as "Cominch." In March 1942 King had also taken on the senior administrative position, chief of naval operations, giving him authority unique in the history of the U.S. Navy, a reflection of President Roosevelt's great confidence in this hard-driving officer.

28 Fisher, "Caribbean Run," 39, 75–76, 94–95.

29 81/145, pt.15, p. 55, DHH; Samuel Eliot Morison, *The Battle of the Atlantic September 1939–May 1943*, History of the United States Navy in World War II, vol. I (Boston: Little, Brown, 1947), 260.

30 Secretary, Naval Board to COAC, et al., "Rearrangement Convoys East Coast of North America," 3 August 1942, 81/520/8280B, pt. 3, DHH.

31 Brand to director of merchant seamen, et al., 8 August 1942, ibid.

32 Huband to director general, MWT, 30 July 1942, MT 59/940, TNA.

33 Mackenzie King diary, 30 August 1942.

34   BAD Washington to Admiralty "Personal for 1st Sea Lord," 1543Z/31 August 1942, Office of the Prime Minister (PREM) 3/439/16, TNA; Churchill to King, 5 September 1942, *Documents on Canadian External Relations*. Vol. 9: *1942–1943*, John Hilliker, ed. (Ottawa: Department of External Affairs, 1980), 353.

35   Cabinet War Committee minutes, 9 September 1942; MG 26 J4, vol. 424, LAC.

36   Mackenzie King diary, 9 September 1942.

37   Mackenzie King diary, 6 September 1942; he reiterated these same points in discussion with the British high commissioner, Malcolm Macdonald, on 7 September.

EIGHT: THE CRISIS DEEPENS BUT THE BALANCE SHIFTS, 9–30 SEPTEMBER 1942

1   "Minutes taken at board of inquiry on board H.M.C.S. 'Fort Ramsay' at 1430, 12th September, 1942," G22-1-2, RG 24, vol. 12009, LAC.

2   Lade to NOIC Gaspé, "Report on sinking of H.M.C.S. 'Charlottetown,'" ibid.

3   "Minutes ... board of inquiry," ibid.

4   Moore to NOIC Gaspé, "Report on loss of H.M.C. Ship," 13 September 1942, G018-1, pt. 2, ibid.

5   Ibid.

6   Lade, "Report on sinking," G-22-1-2, ibid.

7   Moore, "Report on loss," G018-1, pt. 2, ibid.

8   "Minutes ... board of inquiry," G22-1-2, ibid.

9   Moore, "Report on loss," G018-1, pt. 2, ibid.

10   CO HMCS *Fort Ramsay* report of proceedings for September 1942, NSS 1000-5-17, DHH.

11   "'Charlottetown' Casualties," *Globe and Mail*, 19 September 1942; Fraser McKee and Robert Darlington, *The Canadian Naval Chronicle 1939–1945: The Successes and Losses of the Canadian Navy in World War II* (St. Catharines, ON: Vanwell Publishing, 1996), 78.

12   Moore, "Report on loss," G018-1, pt. 2, RG 24, vol. 12009, LAC.

13   "Findings of the board of inquiry ... to inquire into the loss of H.M.C.S. 'Charlottetown,'" G22-1-2, ibid.

14   Michael L. Hadley, *U-boats against Canada: German Submarines in Canadian Waters* (Kingston and Montreal: McGill-Queen's University Press, 1985), 126.

15   Staff anti-submarine officer, COAC, "Attack on a U-boat by H.M.C.S. 'Clayoquot' on 11th, September 1942," 21-1-14, RG 24, vol. 11, 504, LAC.

16   Operations Division, "H.M.C.S. 'Charlottetown,' 16 September 1942, [Operations Division, NSHQ] Weekly Operational Summaries," DHH.

17   On *Salisbury*'s movements prior to her entry into the gulf, see 27-D-39, RG 24, vol. 11572, LAC.

18   Arnold Hague, *Destroyers for Great Britain* (rev. ed.; Annapolis, MD: Naval Institute Press, 1990), 83.

19   CO HMCS *Arrowhead* to NOIC Gaspé, "Report of Proceedings While Senior Officer of SQ 36," 19 September 1942, NSS 8280-SQ 36, RG 24, reel C-5535, LAC; table of merchant ships in SQ 36, ibid.

20   AOC EAC to AFHQ et al., signal 0625Z/15 September 1942, 181.003 (D304), DHH.

21   The account that follows is based upon CO HMS *Salisbury* to COAC, "Report of Proceedings of S.Q. 36 and Q.S. 35," 18 September 1942, G018-1, RG 24, vol. 12009, LAC, and the logs of HMCS *Arrowhead*, vol. 7059, ibid., and HMCS *Summerside*, vol. 7905, ibid.

22   Staff A/S officer, COAC, "Analysis of Attacks by a U-boat on Convoy SQ 36 on 15th and 16th Sept. 1942," 3 November 1942, 21-1-14, RG 24, vol. 11504, LAC.

23   Rough notes, unsigned, undated on forms "Particulars of Attacks on Merchant Vessels ..." for *Inger Elisabeth* and *Saturnus,* n.d., G22-2-1, RG 24, vol. 12009, LAC; Henderson, "Summary of Statements by Survivors of SS SATURNUS ...," 6 October 1942, and "Summary of Statements by Survivors of SS INGER ELISABETH ...," 6 October 1942, 264-4-1-1, pt. 2, RG 24, vol. 11973, LAC.

24   D. Williams, master and commodore of convoy, *Llangollen*, "Master's Log," 18 September 1942, NSS 8280-SQ 36, RG 24, reel C-5535, LAC; NCSO Montreal to director of trade division, 21 September 1942 enclosing reports by SS *Cragpool*, NSS 1062-13-9, pt. 1, RG 24, vol. 4027, LAC.

25   For this and following paragraph see, in addition to *Salisbury* report of proceedings, CO HMCS *Arrowhead* to NOIC Gaspé, "Narrative of H.M.S. 'ARROWHEAD's Movements during attacks on SQ 36 ...," 19 September 1942, NSS 8280-SQ 36, reel C-5535, LAC.

26   "Particulars of Attacks on Merchant Vessels ..." forms for *Joannis* and *Essex Lance,* n.d., RG 24, vol. 11973, file 264-1-1, pt. 2, LAC; "Shipping Casualties" form for *Essex Lance,* n.d., RG 12, vol. 887, LAC; CO HMCS *Vegreville* to SOE, SQ 36, "Report of Proceedings on being detached from S.Q. 36," 26 September 1942, D022-14-1, RG 24, vol. 11558, LAC; NSS 8341-390, RG 24, vol. 6790, LAC.

27   Staff anti-submarine officer, COAC, "Analysis of Attacks ... on SQ 36," 3 November 1942, 21-1-14, RG 24, vol. 11504, LAC.

28   Staff anti-submarine officer, COAC, "Analysis of U-Boat Attack on Convoy Q.S. 33 ...," 16 November 1942, NSS 1062-13-19, pt. 1, RG 24, vol. 4027, LAC.

29   113 Squadron ORB, Chatham, N.B., detachment, 15–16 September 1942, microfilm, DHH; EAC Monthly AS Report, p. 9, 181.003 (D25), DHH.

30   CO *Q 054* to commanding officer *Fort Ramsay*, "Report of Proceedings ...," 23 September 1942, NSS 8280-QS 35, RG 24, reel C5530, LAC.

31   Costello to Deputy Air Member Air Staff (Plans), Ottawa, 17 September 1942, 181.009 (D121), DHH.

32   Ibid.

33   NOIC Sydney to COAC, "New Proposals for Gulf of St. Lawrence Convoys," 15 September 1942, COAC to NOIC Quebec et al., 1529Z/19 September 1942, NSS 8280-166/16, pt. 3, RG 24, vol. 6789, LAC.

34   Signal traffic for SQ 28, 19–20 September 1942, "SQ Convoys 7-43," 81/520/8280, DHH.

35   CO HMCS *Georgian* to COAC, 23 September 1942, NSS 8910-443/23, RG 24, vol. 6905, LAC.

36   German, Transcript of inquiry into *Georgian*'s anti-submarine attack on 21 September, n.d., p. 5, CO *Fort Ramsay* to COAC, 22 September 1942, ibid.

37   COAC to Cominch, "A/S Attack by H.M.C.S. 'Georgian,'" 26 October 1942, ibid.

38   Pilkington, "Weekly Intelligence Report R.C.A.F. 113 (BR) Detachment, Chatham, N.B., 15-9-42 ... to 24-9-42," 181.003 (D161), DHH.

39   Quote from "EAC Anti-Submarine Report September 1942," p. 11, 181.003 (D25), DHH; see also 181.003 (D1325), DHH.

40   "EAC Monthly Anti-Submarine Report September, 1942," p. 12, 181.003 (D25), DHH.

41   CO HMS *Witherington* to Captain (D) Halifax, "Report of Proceedings ... Escorting Convoy Q.S. 38 ...," 2 October 1942, CO *Salisbury* to Captain (D) Halifax, "Report of Proceedings ... Convoys SQ 38 and QS 37," 26 September 1942, 48-2-2, pt. 63, RG 24, vol. 11091, LAC.

42   Axel Niestlé, *German U-Boat Losses during World War II: Details of Destruction* (Annapolis, MD: Naval Institute Press, 1998), 123, 237, note 132.

NINE: ACHIEVEMENT AND TRAGEDY, OCTOBER–NOVEMBER 1942

1   U-boat headquarters war diary, 15–17 September 1942.

2   "Submarine Situation and Intended Operations," U-boat headquarters war diary, following entry for 30 September 1942.

3   U-boat headquarters war diary, 19 September–19 October 1942; Admiralty, Tactical and Staff Duties Division (Foreign Documents Section), Naval Staff, *U-Boat War in the Atlantic, Volume II: January 1942–May 1943*, German Naval History Series ([London]: Admiralty, 1952), 57.

4   "E.A.C. Operational Intelligence Summary No. 21," week ending 4 October 1942, S.28-5-12, pt. 1, RG 24, vol. 5272, LAC; "E.A.C. Weekly Intelligence Report," week ending 2 October 1942, 181.003 (D423), DHH.

5   RCAF Station Sydney ORB, 2 October 1942, microfilm, DHH.

6   *U-69* log, 29 September 1942.

7   CO HMCS *Red Deer* to NOIC Gaspé, "Special Gaspé–Rimouski Convoy," 4 October 1942, 48-2-2, pt. 63, RG 24, vol. 11091, LAC.

8   NCSO Quebec to NOIC Quebec, 28 September 1942, NSS 8280-QS Organization, RG 24, reel C-5530, LAC.

9   CNS to minister, deputy minister et al., "Traffic in St. Lawrence River and Gulf," 7 October 1942, ibid; secretary, Naval Board to COAC, FONF et al., "Local Shipping in St. Lawrence," 6 October 1942, 1-14-1, RG 24, vol. 11503, LAC.

10   CO, HMCS *Ganonoque* to NOIC Gaspé, "Letter of Proceedings re. Q.S. 39 ...," 7 October 1942, 48-2-2, pt. 63, RG 24, vol. 11091, LAC.

11   "Letter of Proceedings re. Q.S. 39 ...," and attached signals, and CO HMCS *Fort Ramsay* to COAC, 11 October 1942, ibid.

12 EAC weekly intelligence report, week ending 9 October 1942, 181.003 (D423), DHH.

13 Rössler, *The U-boats*, 196.

14 HMCS *Arrowhead* log, 8–9 October 1942, RG 24, vol. 7059, LAC; HMCS *Hepatica* log, 8–9 October 1942, vol. 7393, ibid.

15 Canadian Shipping Board, 91ˢᵗ Meeting, 15 October 1942, minute 2001, D-25-1-M, Canadian Shipping Board records, RG 2 B-2, vol. 15, LAC, quoted. See also 8117-46, RG 12, vol. 1425, LAC.

16 EAC weekly intelligence report, week ending 9 October 1942, p. 11, "Later information from RCAF Station, North Sydney," 181.003 (D423), DHH.

17 81/520/8000 "Vison," DHH.

18 Stebbins, "Summary of Statements by Survivors of SS WATERTON ...," 12 November 1942, NSS 1870-173, pt. 4, RG 24, vol. 8191, LAC.

19 *U-106* log, 12 October 1942.

20 *U-106* log, 12 October 1942.

21 *U-69* log, 11 October 1942.

22 *U-106* log, 12 October 1942.

23 *U-106* log, 15 October 1942.

24 *U-106* log, 22 October 1942.

25 Williams, "Report of attack on doubtful target ... at 1550Z/21/10/42 ...," 21 October 1942, NSS 8280-SQ 43, microfilm, DHH.

26 CO HMCS *Trail*, "Report of Proceedings of Convoy LN-12," 15 November 1942, NSS 8280-LN 12, RG 24, reel C-5520, LAC. No logs survive for either *Trail* or *Shawinigan* for this period. I am grateful to Doug Knight, who carried out an exhaustive search of navy and air force records for the St. Lawrence area on this date and tracked down all surviving reports of depth charge attacks.

27 "EAC Operational Intelligence Summary No. 24," week ending 25 October 1942, S28-5-12, pt. 1, RG 24, vol. 5272, LAC; 181.003 (D1327), DHH.

28 *U-106* log, 22 October 1942.

29 "E.A.C. Operational Intelligence Summary No. 25," week ending 1 November 1942, S28-5-12, pt. 1, RG 24, vol. 5272, LAC, quoted.

30 U-boat headquarters war diary, 1 January and 1 December 1942.

31 Steve Neary, *The Enemy on Our Doorstep: The German Attacks at Bell Island, Newfoundland, 1942* (St. John's: Jesperson Press, 1994), 49–113, reproduces the most important Canadian and Newfoundland documents and a good translation of *U-518*'s log for 1–2 November 1942.

32 Dean Beeby, *Cargo of Lies: The True Story of a Nazi Double Agent in Canada* (Toronto: University of Toronto Press, 1996), 102–14, 165–66. The account that follows owes much to this excellent work.

33 Earle J. Annett, "Quebec spycatcher tells his own story," *Toronto Daily Star*, 14 May 1945.

34 German to secretary, Naval Board, "Apprehension of suspect at New Carlisle, P.Q.," 7 December 1942, MS0011, RG 24, vol. 11127, LAC, quoted; Douglas, *No Higher Purpose*, 467–68.

35 Brand journal, chapter 32 (1941), p. 30, chapter 33 (1942), p. 52, 81/145, pt. 15, pp. 30, 52, DHH; "Mr. Wilfred Samuel," obituary, *The Times* (London), 15 December 1958, p. 14; signals, 10–11 November 1942, MS 0011, RG 24, vol. 11127, LAC.

36 The interrogation reports are printed in Neary, *Enemy on Our Doorstep*, 97–110.

37 *U-518* log, 10 November 1942.

38 *U-183* log, 29 October–6 November 1942, and, appended, Dönitz, "Remarks concerning the War Diary of 'U-183' for the period 19.9–23.12 1942" (quoted); U-boat headquarters war diary, 10 November 1942; Tennyson and Sarty, *Guardian of the Gulf*, 281.

TEN: THE POLITICS OF DEFENCE AND THE ULTRA TOP-SECRET WAR, NOVEMBER 1942–DECEMBER 1943

1 The best account is William R. Young, "Making the Truth Graphic: The Canadian Government's Home Front Information Structure and Programmes during World War II" (Ph.D. thesis, University of British Columbia, 1978), 39–46.

2 Clarke, "Most Secret and Urgent," 17 October 1942, D-2032, C.G. Power papers, box 70, Queen's University Archives (QUA).

3 Ketchum to Thorson, "The Committee on Morale," no date, 8-2-2, pt. 1, Wartime Information Board records, RG 36-31, vol. 12, LAC. See also Daniel J. Robinson, *The Measure of Democracy: Polling, Market Research, and Public Life, 1930–1945* (Toronto: University of Toronto Press, 1999), 94–101.

4 Irving, "Report, for the Committee on Morale, of Research on Rumors," 5 September 1942, 8-2-3, RG 36-31, vol. 12, LAC.

5 *Public Opinion Quarterly*, vol. 6, no. 4 (winter 1942): 659; on the growing links between the Canadian Institute of Public Opinion and the Committee on Morale and the Wartime Information Board in this period see Robinson, *Measure of Democracy*, 106–7.

6 Godbout to King, 21 October 1942, MG 26 J1, reel C-6806, p. 276171, LAC.

7 Mackenzie King diary, 28 October 1942.

8 Power to Godbout, 9 November 1942, D-2032, Power Papers, box 70, QUA; see also Breadner to minister, 27 October 1942 and 5 November 1942, 181.002 (D107), DHH.

9 Connolly to Sharpe, 22 October 1942, D-2032, Power Papers, box 70, QUA; Connolly to DNI, 3 November 1942, NSS 1880-237, RG 24, vol. 8195, LAC.

10 *Hamilton Spectator*, 2 November 1942.

11 Ottawa *Evening Citizen*, 24 November 1942. See NSS 1880-237, RG 24, vol. 8195, LAC, which shows that Macdonald and his advisors elected to hold the press conference rather than issue a press release, a decision that was in line

with the Wartime Information Board's emphasis on personal contact with opinion leaders.

12 *Globe and Mail* and *Hamilton Spectator*, 16 December 1942; Flying Officer Hughes' account is quoted in both.

13 *Hamilton Spectator*, 5 March 1943.

14 NSHQ Ottawa to Admiralty and Cominch, 1623Z/13 March 1943, NSS 1188-365, RG 24, vol. 8038, LAC. I am grateful to Tim Balzer for this and the following reference.

15 House of Commons, *Debates*, 17 March 1943, 1338.

16 Admiralty to NSHQ Ottawa, 1234A/19 March 1943, NSS 1188-365, RG 24, vol. 8038, LAC.

17 House of Commons, *Debates*, 10 March 1943, 1131.

18 House of Commons, *Debates*, 17 March 1943, 1344. This material had also been assembled by the naval staff in the fall of 1942 to respond to the *L'Action Catholique* articles: "Addition to the Minister's Release," [early November 1942], NSS 1880-237, RG 24, vol. 8195, LAC.

19 Chiefs of Staff Committee minutes, 4 December 1942, 193.009 (D53), DHH.

20 W.A.B. Douglas, Roger Sarty, Michael Whitby, et al., *A Blue Water Navy: The Official Operational History of the Royal Canadian Navy in the Second World War, 1943–1945, Volume II, Part 2* (St. Catharines: Vanwell Publishing and the Department of National Defence, 2007), 36.

21 Ibid., 60–2; Lawrence J. Bliquez, "John Brodie McDiarmid June 6, 1913–April 15, 2002," *Classical News from Denny Hall, University of Washington, Department of Classics* vol. 37 (November 2002), http://depts.washington.edu/clasdept/Newsletter02.html, accessed 9 February 2011. See also SRMN-038, "Functions of the 'Secret room' (F-211) of Cominch Combat Intelligence, Atlantic Section Anti-Submarine Warfare, WWII (Undated)," p. 5, Records of the National Security Agency, RG 457, NARA, which refers to Admiralty transmission of detailed daily digests of Ultra signals to Washington and Ottawa.

22 C.R. Vincent, *Canada Wings Vol. 2: Consolidated Liberator and Boeing Fortress* (Stittsville, ON: Canada's Wings, 1975), 244.

23 Admiralty, Naval Intelligence Division, "U-517, Interrogation of Crew," BR 1907 (55), 80/520, pt. 16, DHH.

24 Quoted in Douglas et al., *No Higher Purpose*, 473.

25 Schull, *Far Distant Ships*, 115–120; p. 120 quoted.

26 Admiralty to Cominch, 1828Z 29 April 1943, SRH 208, pt. 1, RG 457, NARA. This series is available online: www.uboatarchive.net/AdmiraltyMessage1943-APR-Frame.htm (accessed 3 March 2010).

27 NSHQ to CinC CNA, repeated NOsIC Sydney and Gaspé, 2258Z 29 April 1943, 181.002 (D68A), DHH.

28 The account of *U-262*'s voyage is based on Hadley, *U-Boats against Canada*, 169–175, and a translation of *U-262*'s log by Jan Drent, DHH.

29 Richard O. Mayne, "The Great Naval Battle of North Point: Myth or Reality?" *Canadian Military History* 16 (summer 2007): 4–12.

30 EAC Anti-Submarine Report, May 1943, 181.003 (D25), DHH.

31 EAC Weekly Intelligence Report, week ending 21 May 1943, 181.003 (D423), DHH.

32 EAC Anti-Submarine Report, June 1943, 181.003 (D56), DHH.

33 For example, Jack Brayley, "On the Alert: Force Ready to Defend St. Lawrence," *Globe and Mail*, 16 June 1943.

34 House of Commons, *Debates*, 8 June 1943, 3420.

35 Admiralty to Cominch, 1935Z 6 September 1943, OIC serial 639, www.uboatarchive.net/AdmiraltyMessage1943, accessed 11 October 2008.

36 Admiralty to Cominch, 1123/16 September 1943, OIC serial 652, same to same, 1359/20 September 1943, OIC serial 659, ibid.

37 Camp commandant, Bowmanville to Headquarters Military District No. 3, 1 September 1943, 113.3V1009 (D30), DHH.

38 Harald Busch, *U-Boats at War* (New York: Putnam, 1955), 98–101.

39 Camp commandant, Bowmanville to Headquarters Military District 3, 26 September 1943, 113.3V1009 (D30), DHH.

40 *Hamilton Spectator*, 13 October 1943.

41 Piers, [revised report of interview with Hal Lawrence,] 14 September 1982, pp. 166–7, DHH.

42 RG 24, vol. 7460, LAC.

43 Admiralty to Cominch, 2046Z 29 September 1943, SRH 208, pt. 2, RG 457, NARA.

44 Admiralty, Naval Intelligence Division, "'U-536' Interrogation of Survivors," CB 04051(93), January 1944, 80/582, item 54, DHH.

45 Digest of signals for October 1943, HMS *Chelsea* movement card, DHH.

46 McKee and Darlington, *Canadian Naval Chronicle*, 110–112; "'U-536' Interrogation of Survivors."

47 "War Log 'U-536' Final Report," translation by David Wiens, DHH.

48 NSS 8280-QS 68A, reel C-5531, RG 24, LAC. Knowles, "U-Boat Intelligence Summary," 12 October 1943, SRMN 037, p. 198, RG 457, NARA, reports an Ultra signal that gave *U-536* information for shipping off Halifax and St. John's, but "Otter" signal 0801Z 26 October 1943, NSS 8910-20, pt. 1, RG 24, vol. 6897, LAC allows for the possibility that the submarine might alternatively be hunting west of Gaspé. This is a correction of the account in Douglas, et al., *Blue Water Navy*, 98, which attributes the reintroduction of convoy in the gulf to the operations by *U-537* off Labrador later in October. I was the one who carried out the research and analysis for this part of the official history; the error is my fault.

49 W.A.B. Douglas, "The Nazi Weather Station in Labrador," *Canadian Geographic* 101, no. 6 (1981): 42–6.

50 Knowles, "U-Boat Intelligence Summary," 14 November 1943, SRMN 037, p. 224, RG 457, NARA.

ELEVEN: SUPPORTING THE LIBERATION OF EUROPE, APRIL 1944–MAY 1945

1 Tucker, *Naval Service of Canada*, II: 274.

2 *L'Action Catholique*, 11 February 1944, 1, 8; see also *Hamilton Spectator*, 11 February 1944.

3 Karl Dönitz, *Memoirs: Ten Years and Twenty Days*, R.H. Stevens, trans. (Annapolis, MD: Naval Institute Press, 1990), 420.

4 U-boat headquarters [to *U-1223*], sent 1339 to 2058, 23 September 1944; repeats signal earlier sent to *U-802* and *U-541*; clear text sent from "Naval Section" Bletchley Park to Admiralty Intelligence Division 8G 1755[no time zone given]/27 September 1944, ZIP/ZTPGU/31873, Ministry of Defence records (DEFE) 3/736, TNA.

5 Roger Sarty, "Ultra, Air Power, and the Second Battle of the St. Lawrence, 1944," in *To Die Gallantly: The Battle of the Atlantic*, Timothy J. Runyan and Jan M. Copes, eds. (Boulder, Colorado: Westview, 1994), 186–209, is a technical study that cites most of the relevant Ultra decrypts opened at TNA and NARA. The account in this chapter also draws on Tennyson and Sarty, *Guardian of the Gulf*, chapter 13.

6 *United States Fleet Anti-Submarine Bulletin* (September 1944), 15–21.

7 Commander-in-chief, Canadian Northwest Atlantic (CinC CNA) war diary, August 1944, part II, 30-1-1, pt. 35, RG 24, vol. 11054, LAC.

8 S.T. Richards, *Operation Sick Bay: The Story of the Sick Berth and Medical Assistant Branch of the Royal Canadian Navy 1910–1965* (West Vancouver, BC: Cantaur Publishing, 1994), 126–27 quoted; see also NSS 8280-HJF 24, microfilm, DHH.

9 *U-802* log, 13 September 1944.

10 CO HMCS *Stettler* to NOIC Gaspé, 19 September 1944, 7-13-7, RG 24, vol. 11025, LAC, quoted; see also entry for 14 September 1944 in NSS 8910-23, pt. 3, RG 24, vol. 6897, LAC.

11 Samuel Eliot Morison, *The Atlantic Battle Won, May 1943–May 1945*, History of the United States Navy in World War II, vol. X (Boston: Little, Brown, 1956), 328.

12 Smith to CO HMCS *Fort Ramsay*, 23 October 1944, 8000 "HMCS Magog," DHH.

13 "Otter" signal 0718 9 November 1944, NSS 810-20, pt. 2, RG 24, vol. 6897, LAC.

14 Wynn, *U-Boat Operations*, 2: 236; U-boat headquarters war diary, 26 November (quoted), 24 and 25 December 1944.

15 *U-1228* log, 14 November 1944.

16 U-boat headquarters war diary, 20 September 1944.

17 Entry at 0115 [GMT] 25 November 1944, NSS 8910-23, pt. 3, RG 24, vol. 6897, LAC.

18 Senior officer, EG 16, HMCS *Springhill* to NOIC Sydney, "Recovery of Bodies on 27th November, 1944," 2 December 1944, NSS 1156-331/93, RG 24, vol. 4108, LAC.

19 *Toronto Telegram*, 8 December 1944.

20 *Globe and Mail*, 8 December 1944.

21 *Hamilton Spectator*, 11 December 1944.

22 CO HMCS *Matapedia*, "Report of Proceedings Q.S. #107," 9 December 1944, and attached minute sheet, especially comment of staff officer anti-submarine, 21 December 1944, 48-2-2, pt. 64, RG 24, vol. 11091, LAC; *U-1231* log, 3–4 December 1944.

23 CO HMCS *Melville* to NOIC Sydney, "Report of Proceedings. Convoy QS 109," 16 December 1944, ibid.

24 See Roger Sarty, "The Limits of Ultra: The Schnorkel U-boat Offensive against North America, November 1944–January 1945," *Intelligence and National Security* 12 (April 1997): 44–68.

25 Simpson, "A History of Naval Control Service at Sydney, Nova Scotia," n.d., pp. 23–24, 81/520/1440-127, DHH.

26 "U-Boat Surrendering," n.d., NSC 1926-102/1, pt. 1, DHH.

27 Simpson, "A History of Naval Control Service at Sydney," p. 25, 81/520/1440-127, DHH.

28 Tucker, *Naval Service of Canada*, II: 394.

CONCLUSION

1 Niestlé, *German U-Boat Losses*, 4.

2 *Defeat of Enemy Attack on Shipping*, 1B, tables 13, 15.

3 *Defeat of Enemy Attack on Shipping*, 1B, plan 10.

4 Douglas et al., *No Higher Purpose*, 634.

5 Mayne, *Betrayed*.

6 *Hamilton Spectator*, 15 June 1951.

7 Mayne, "Jones," in *The Admirals*, 136–49; Roger Sarty, "The Ghosts of Fisher and Jellicoe: The Royal Canadian Navy and the Quebec Conferences," in David B. Woolner, ed., *The Second Quebec Conference Revisited* (New York: St Martin's, 1998), 157–65.

8 Marc Milner, "Rear Admiral Leonard Warren Murray: Canada's Most Important Operational Commander," in *The Admirals*, 119.

9 *Globe and Mail*, 27 October 1972, p. 5; PIN 26/2337, TNA, correspondence about pension in the 1960s and early 1970s.

10 David Twiston Davies, ed., *Canada from Afar: The Daily Telegraph Book of Canadian Obituaries* (Toronto: Dundurn, 1996), 13–15; www.iode.ca/file/MARGARET%20BRAND%20CHAPTER.doc (Accessed 4 August 2011).

11 Bezeau, "Brief for the Naval Board: Battle Honours for HMC Ships," 17 November 1986, file 1065-1 (DC). I am grateful to Major Paul Lansey for this reference.

12   Maritime Command Headquarters, "News Release: New Battle Honour for
     Canadian Warships," 29 September 1992, DHH 1065-1, pt. 6; National Defence
     Headquarters, "The Insignia and Lineages of the Canadian Forces Volume 2, Part
     1 – Extant Commissioned Ships," 8 January 2001 (Canadian Forces publication
     A-AD-267-000/AF-002).

13   How, *Night of the Caribou*, 143, 145–46, 152–53; "Commemoration of the
     55th Anniversary of the Battle of the Gulf of St. Lawrence – Port-aux-Basques,"
     www.veterans.gc.ca/eng/sub.cfm?sourace=feature/week99/stlawrence/nov8[1999]
     (accessed 2 August 2011); www.caperfrasers.wordpress.com/2010/11/24/mv-
     caribou-retires (accessed 2 August 2011).

BIBLIOGRAPHY

The bulk of this book is based on first-hand accounts, written by participants at the time of events. Paperwork—log entries, daily, weekly, and monthly reports, and special reports on anything out of the ordinary—was a relentless travail for Allied and German military personnel alike during the Second World War. Much of this extraordinary record has survived even if, in some cases, more by good luck than good management.

The main repository for Canadian sources, including everything from papers on high-level Alliance diplomacy to reports on specific military operations, is Library and Archives Canada in Ottawa. The Directorate of History and Heritage, National Defence Headquarters, also in Ottawa, has its own important archives that includes original air force and naval records, together with collections from British, American, and German archives gathered for the official histories program of the Department of National Defence.

The reference notes in the present book emphasize newly discovered materials and documents used to explore particular incidents in more detail than in the official histories or to reassess accounts in those histories. For fuller information on sources, see the copious references in the official histories and in other documented publications mentioned at the appropriate places in the notes.

The official histories—and the present book—owe much to collaboration with independent and university-based scholars. They, with the encouragement and assistance of the official historians, produced the first publications in the 1980s and 1990s that drew on newly opened Second World War materials in the Canadian, British, American, and German archives. These works in turn helped lay the groundwork for the official histories research program. The present book continues this decades-long and always profitable and stimulating dialogue.

ARCHIVAL SOURCES

DIRECTORATE OF HISTORY AND HERITAGE, NATIONAL DEFENCE HEADQUARTERS, OTTAWA

Army and Air Force Kardex Collection (includes the files of Eastern Air Command, Royal Canadian Air Force)
Biographical Files
Document Collection (includes the microfilm collections cited in the notes)
Naval Historian's Collection
Permanent Reference Files
Public Record Office and Related Materials

LIBRARY AND ARCHIVES CANADA, OTTAWA

Canadian Shipping Board (RG 2 B-2)
Department of External Affairs (RG 25)
Department of National Defence (RG 24)
Department of Transport (RG 12)
Directorate of Censorship (RG 2 C-2)
National Research Council of Canada (RG 77)
Wartime Information Board (RG 36-31)
Ian A. Mackenzie fonds (MG 27-IIIB5)
William Lyon Mackenzie King fonds (MG 26-J)

NATIONAL ARCHIVES AND RECORDS ADMINISTRATION, COLLEGE PARK, MD

Microfilm Copies of Records of the German Navy [U-boat logs] (RG 242.8)
National Security Agency (RG 457)
Naval Operating Forces (RG 313)
Office of the Chief of Naval Operations (RG 38)

QUEEN'S UNIVERSITY ARCHIVES, KINGSTON, ONTARIO

C.G. Power papers

THE NATIONAL ARCHIVES, KEW, UNITED KINGDOM

Air Ministry (AIR)
Ministry of Defence (DEFE)
Ministry of Transport (MT)
Prime Minister's Office (PREM)
Pensions and National Insurance (PIN)

BOOKS, ARTICLES, AND THESES

Admiralty. Historical Section. *Defeat of the Enemy Attack on Shipping 1939–1945: A Study of Policy and Operations*, Naval Staff History (London: Admiralty, 1957).

_____. Tactical and Staff Duties Division (Foreign Documents Section), Naval Staff. *The U-Boat War in the Atlantic, Volume I: 1939–1941*, German Naval History Series. [London]: Admiralty, 1950.

_____. *The U-Boat War in the Atlantic, Volume II: January 1942–May 1943*, German Naval History Series. [London]: Admiralty, 1952.

Aldcroft, Derek H. *From Versailles to Wall Street 1919–1929*. Berkeley: University of California Press, 1977.

Beeby, Dean. *Cargo of Lies: The True Story of a Nazi Double Agent in Canada*. Toronto: University of Toronto Press, 1996.

Black, Conrad. *Duplessis*. Toronto: McClelland and Stewart, 1977.

Bourrie, Mark. *The Fog of War: Censorship of Canada's Media in World War Two*. Vancouver: Douglas and McIntyre, 2011.

Busch, Harald. *U-Boats at War*. New York: Putnam, 1955.

Busch, Rainer and Hans-Joachim Röll. *German U-Boat Commanders of World War II: A Biographical Dictionary*. Geoffrey Brooks, trans. London: Greenhill Books, 1999.

Clausewitz, Karl von. *On War*. Michael Howard and Peter Paret, eds. and trans. Princeton: Princeton University Press, 1976.

Davies, David Twiston, ed. *Canada from Afar: The Daily Telegraph Book of Canadian Obituaries*. Toronto: Dundurn, 1996.

Dönitz, Karl. *Memoirs: Ten Years and Twenty Days*. R.H. Stevens, trans. Annapolis, MD: Naval Institute Press, 1990.

Douglas, W.A.B. *The Creation of a National Air Force: The Official History of the Royal Canadian Air Force, Volume II*. Toronto: University of Toronto Press in co-operation with the Department of National Defence, 1986.

_____, Roger Sarty, Michael Whitby with Robert H. Caldwell, William Johnston, William G.P. Rawling. *No Higher Purpose: The Official Operational History of the Royal Canadian Navy in the Second World War, 1939–1943, Volume II*,

Part 1. St. Catharines, ON: Vanwell Publishing and the Department of National Defence, 2002.

_____. *A Blue Water Navy: The Official Operational History of the Royal Canadian Navy in the Second World War, 1943–1945, Volume II, Part 2*. St. Catharines, ON: Vanwell Publishing and the Department of National Defence, 2007.

Essex, James. *Victory in the St. Lawrence: Canada's Unknown War*. Erin, ON: Boston Mills Press, 1984.

Fisher, Robert. "'We'll get our own': Canada and the oil shipping crisis of 1942." *The Northern Mariner/Le marin du nord* III, no. 2 (April 1993): 33–39.

Goette, Richard. "Squadron Leader N.E. Small: A Study of Leadership in the RCAF's Eastern Air Command." *Canadian Military Journal* 5, no. 1 (Spring 2004): 43–50.

Granatstein, J.L. *The Politics of Survival: The Conservative Party of Canada, 1939–1945*. Toronto: University of Toronto Press, 1967.

Graves, Donald E. "'Hell Boats' of the RCN: The Canadian Navy and the Motor Torpedo Boat, 1936–1941." *The Northern Mariner* II (July 1992): 31–45.

Hadley, Michael L. *U-boats against Canada: German Submarines in Canadian Waters*. Kingston and Montreal: McGill-Queen's University Press, 1985.

_____, Rob Huebert, and Fred W. Crickard. *A Nation's Navy: In Quest of Canadian Naval Identity*. Montreal and Kingston: McGill-Queen's University Press, 1996.

_____ and Roger Sarty. *Tin-Pots and Pirate Ships: Canadian Naval Forces and German Sea Raiders 1880–1918*. Montreal and Kingston: McGill-Queen's University Press, 1991.

Hancock, W.K. and M.M. Gowing. *British War Economy*, History of the Second World War, United Kingdom Civil Series. London: His Majesty's Stationery Office, 1949.

Hawkins, John. *The Life and Times of Angus L.* Windsor, NS: Lancelot Press, 1969.

Henderson, T. Stephen. *Angus L. Macdonald: A Provincial Liberal*. Toronto: University of Toronto Press, 2007.

Hendrie, Andrew. *The Lockheed Hudson in World War II*. Shrewsbury, UK: Air Life England, 1999.

How, Douglas. *Night of the Caribou*. Hantsport, NS: Lancelot Press, 1988.

Kershaw, Ian. *Hitler 1936–1945: Nemesis*. London: Penguin, 2000.

King, William Lyon Mackenzie. *Canada and the Fight for Freedom*. Toronto: Macmillan, 1944.

Lay, H. Nelson. *Memoirs of a Mariner*. Ottawa: the author, 1982.

Mayne, Richard O. *Betrayed: Scandal, Politics and Canadian Naval Leadership*. Vancouver: UBC Press, 2006.

_____, "The Great Naval Battle of North Point: Myth or Reality?" *Canadian Military History* 16 (Summer 2007): 4–12.

McKee, Fraser. *Armed Yachts of Canada*. Erin, ON: Boston Mills Press, 1983.

_____ and Robert Darlington. *The Canadian Naval Chronicle 1939–1945: The Successes and Losses of the Canadian Navy in World War II*. St. Catharines, ON: Vanwell Publishing, 1996.

Milner, Marc. *North Atlantic Run: The Royal Canadian Navy and the Battle of the Convoys*. Toronto: University of Toronto Press, 1985.

_____. *The U-Boat Hunters: The Royal Canadian Navy and the Offensive against Germany's Submarines*. Toronto: University of Toronto Press, 1994.

Moon, Peter. "The Second World War Battle We Lost at Home," *The Canadian Magazine* (26 February 1972), 2–7 and (4 March 1972), 10–13.

Morison, Samuel Eliot. *The Battle of the Atlantic September 1939–May 1943*, History of the United States Navy in World War II, vol. I. Boston: Little, Brown, 1947.

_____. *The Atlantic Battle Won, May 1943–May 1945*, History of the United States Navy in World War II, vol. X. Boston: Little, Brown, 1956.

Neary, Steve. *The Enemy on Our Doorstep: The German Attacks at Bell Island, Newfoundland, 1942*. St. John's: Jesperson Press, 1994.

Niestlé, Axel. *German U-Boat Losses during World War II: Details of Destruction*. Annapolis, MD: Naval Institute Press, 1998.

Richards, S.T. *Operation Sick Bay: The Story of the Sick Berth and Medical Assistant Branch of the Royal Canadian Navy 1910–1965*. West Vancouver, BC: Centaur Publishing, 1994.

Robinson, Daniel J. *The Measure of Democracy: Polling, Market Research, and Public Life, 1930–1945*. Toronto: University of Toronto Press, 1999.

Rohwer, Jürgen. *Axis Submarine Successes of World War Two: German, Italian and Japanese Submarine Successes, 1939–1945*. Annapolis, MD: Naval Institute Press, 1983.

Rössler, Eberhard. *The U-boats: The evolution and technical history of German submarines*. Harold Erenberg, trans. Annapolis, MD: Naval Institute Press, 1989.

Roskill, S.W. *The War at Sea 1939–1945, Volume I: The Defensive*, History of the Second World War, United Kingdom Military Series. London: Her Majesty's Stationery Office, 1954.

Salty Dips: Vol. 2: "... and All Our Joints Were Limber." Ottawa: The Ottawa Branch, Naval Officers' Associations of Canada, 1985.

Sarty, Roger. *Canada and the Battle of the Atlantic*. Montreal: Éditions Art Global and the Department of National Defence, 1998.

_____. "The Ghosts of Fisher and Jellicoe: The Royal Canadian Navy and the Quebec Conferences," in David B. Woolner, ed. *The Second Quebec Conference Revisited*. New York: St Martin's, 1998, 143–70.

_____. "The Limits of Ultra: The Schnorkel U-boat Offensive Against North America, November 1944–January 1945." *Intelligence and National Security* 12, no. 2 (April 1997): 44–68.

_____. *The Maritime Defence of Canada*. Toronto: Canadian Institute of Strategic Studies, 1996.

_____. "Ultra, Air Power, and the Second Battle of the St. Lawrence, 1944," in *To Die Gallantly: The Battle of the Atlantic*, Timothy J. Runyan and Jan M. Copes, eds. Boulder, Colorado: Westview, 1994, 186–209.

Schull, Joseph. *The Far Distant Ships: An Official Account of Canadian Naval Operations in the Second World War*. Ottawa: Queen's Printer, 1950.

Smith, Geoffrey W. *Naval Talk by "Jock."* n.p.: privately published, [c1997].

Smith, Kevin. *Conflict over Convoys: Anglo-American Logistics Diplomacy in the Second World War.* Cambridge: Cambridge University Press, 1996.

Tennyson, Brian and Roger Sarty. *Guardian of the Gulf: Sydney, Cape Breton, and the Atlantic Wars.* Toronto: University of Toronto Press, 2000.

Tucker, Gilbert Norman. *The Naval Service of Canada: Its Official History, Volume II: Activities on Shore.* Ottawa: King's Printer, 1952.

Vincent, C.R. *Canada Wings Vol. 2: Consolidated Liberator and Boeing Fortress.* Stittsville, ON: Canada's Wings, 1975.

Ward, Norman, ed. *A Party Politician: The Memoirs of Chubby Power.* Toronto: Macmillan, 1966.

Weinberg, Gerhard L. *A World at Arms: A Global History of World War II.* Cambridge: Cambridge University Press, 1994.

Whitby, Michael, Richard H. Gimblett, and Peter Haydon, eds. *The Admirals: Canada's Senior Naval Leadership in the Twentieth Century.* Toronto: Dundurn, 2006.

White, John F. *U-Boat Tankers 1941–45: Submarine Suppliers to Atlantic Wolf Packs.* Annapolis, MD: Naval Institute Press, 1998.

Wynn, Kenneth. *U-Boat Operations of the Second World War,* 2 vols. Annapolis, MD: Naval Institute Press, 1997–98.

Young, George. *The Short Triangle: A Story of the Sea and Men Who Go Down to It in Ships.* Lunenburg, NS: Lunenburg County Press, 1975.

Young, William R. "Making the Truth Graphic: The Canadian Government's Home Front Information Structure and Programmes during World War II." Ph.D. thesis, University of British Columbia, 1978.

ACKNOWLEDGMENTS

I did the initial research upon which this book is based for official military history projects at the Directorate of History (now the Directorate of History and Heritage) at National Defence Headquarters in Ottawa in the early 1980s. W.A.B. (Alec) Douglas, the director, designed the studies I undertook on the St. Lawrence battle. Norman Hillmer, the senior historian, supervised the day-to-day work and refined the results. Stephen Harris, Brereton Greenhous, M.V. (Vince) Bezeau, and Owen Cooke mentored the first projects on the air force side of the St. Lawrence story. David Wiens and Jan Drent translated the U-boat logs upon which my work on the official histories and the present book has heavily depended.

I was also fortunate in the staff who joined at various times in the late 1980s and 1990s to undertake the new official history of the navy. Research and analysis by Catherine Allan, Shawn Cafferky, Robert Caldwell, Robert Fisher, William Glover, Donald Graves, Bill Johnston, Richard Mayne, Gabrielle Nishiguchi, Bill Rawling, Jane Samson, and Michael Whitby is reflected all through the present book. Serge Bernier, who became director of history in 1994, and Stephen Harris took on my management duties so I could continue research in the midst of deep government cutbacks that all but stopped the naval project. In

1998, when I moved to the Canadian War Museum, J.L. Granatstein, the museum's director, made it possible to continue the naval work on a volunteer basis; he, Dean Oliver, and Rachel Poirier covered for me on critical days when deadlines loomed. Doug Knight, a volunteer researcher at the museum, took on challenging tasks for both the naval official history and then the present book. Michael Whitby, who succeeded me as head of the naval official history project, supervised and edited my continuing work and brought the history's two volumes to publication in 2002 and 2007.

Historians cannot function without archivists. Barbara Wilson, Glenn Wright, and Paul Marsden at Library and Archives Canada and Isabel Campbell and Donna Porter at the Directorate of History always went the extra distance to provide the quickest access to the fullest range of materials.

Michael Hadley, Marc Milner, and David Zimmerman, friends who published pioneering works on Canada and the Battle of the Atlantic, shared documents and ideas in what has become a thirty-year seminar. Tim Balzer, Mark Bourrie, and R.H. ("Tex") Thomas provided invaluable material from their own work, and in the United Kingdom Marcus Faulkner located important sources not available in Canada. Nathan Greenfield consulted with me on his own book on the St. Lawrence battle and has been generous in this and his other publications in promoting the work of the Canadian government's military historians.

Students and colleagues at Wilfrid Laurier University, where I now teach, have endured trial runs of chapters in this book and improved them through their questions and comments. Terry Copp, John Laband, Joyce Lorimer, and George Urbaniak have ensured that I have had the time for writing and opportunities to promote the project. Matt Symes did the work on the photographs; Michael Bechthold created the maps and diagrams. Patricia Jones, the copy editor, has saved me from errors and inconsistences and endeavoured to banish murky military and technical phraseology. Davidson Tate kindly allowed access to his father's splendid photographs taken during his Second World War naval service.

The idea for the present book came from the series editors, Robert Bothwell and Margaret MacMillan, who have shaped the results at every stage with full support from Diane Turbide, a model publisher. Their understanding was particularly important when Glenn and Joan, my parents, became terminally ill just as I was starting work on the project. I had intended to do a good part of the writing while staying with them in Cape Cod, where they had retired to escape the Canadian winters. I did write in their house, a peaceful twenty-minute walk from Hardings Beach on Nantucket Sound, but with their spiritual rather than physical presence. Certainly their spirit infuses the book. They loved history and the English language, were wonderful raconteurs—and tough editors.

Brenda, my wife, holds everything together. This is something like the fourteenth book project that has disrupted our household, but she is delightfully good humoured about the madness of writing. She is the 9-1-1 emergency response for editing, research, and computer crises, despite her own demanding public service career and management of our unruly cats, Simon, Reilly, and the late Edgar.

INDEX